IN THE
SHADOW OF RUSSIA

Eastern Europe

in the

Postwar World

NICHOLAS HALASZ

THE RONALD PRESS COMPANY � NEW YORK

Library of Congress Catalog Card Number: 59-8391
PRINTED IN THE UNITED STATES OF AMERICA

For

Mike and *Bob*

Preface

The seven states presented here, Poland, Rumania, Bulgaria, Jugoslavia, Albania, Hungary, and Czecho-Slovakia, may seem remote; yet in our generation their vicissitudes have fatefully involved America and the whole world.

When, in 1914, a Jugoslav fanatic killed the successor to the throne of the Hapsburgs, he fired the first shot in World War I. Hitler's tanks rumbled into Poland in 1939 and World War II began.

These countries are wedged between the two great powers, Germany and Russia. The Germans forced them into their orbit in two world wars. In the years between the wars their territory served as a *cordon sanitaire* isolating the Soviet Union from capitalist Europe, saving both from ideological contamination. The Russians brought them under their sway when they reversed the German tide in 1944–1945 and turned the area into a zone of transition between the two political and social systems. Moscow coined the name People's Democracy for the states in the Soviet orbit, admitting both public and private ownership and a measure of parliamentary democracy.

Apart from Czecho-Slovakia, the people's democracies dislodged no democratic regimes but merely replaced royal cliques of military and civilian bureaucrats. Actually, the Soviet-initiated republics for a time infused the nations and their governments with the untapped creative energies of the broad masses. The fervor displayed in the reconstruction of the war-ravaged countries and a genuine cultural efflorescence testified to a national rebirth. The Communist parties paraded as champions of nationalism since Stalin deemed nationalism indispensable as an incentive to the

v

collective sacrifices necessary for industrialization. Popular enthusiasm was the only investment available.

The prime mover of enthusiasm was the peoples' craving for a better life. They hailed the large-scale industrialization programs as instruments of its fulfillment. They were ready for the sacrifices the program demanded.

But tension was mounting in the field of international power relations. With Germany defeated and Western Europe exhausted, growing Russian might threatened to subdue the Continent, and America had to throw her full weight into the balance to keep Russia within bounds. The territory of the seven states now became a buffer not between Germany and Russia but between East and West. The Cold War began.

The Cold War caused Stalin to direct popular energies which had been active in building a better future for themselves and their children into channels that fed the Soviet war machine. Only totalitarian governments relying on Russian bayonets could enforce such an abuse of good will. All-pervading propaganda covered up the fraud. Since nationalism in the seven states, by representing local interests, threatened to obstruct their subjection to a colonial status, Moscow branded it a heresy. But at the same time it expected all Communists in its orbit to promote and serve Soviet nationalism.

The Jugoslav Communists refused, in 1948, to submit to such an imposition; the Polish and Hungarian Communists rebelled against it in 1956. The masses of non-Communists closed ranks behind them in a national protest against foreign domination. In the dignity of this protest there was a resurgence of the original national idea of universal brotherhood of peoples free from tyranny.

However, the sinister connotations of nationalism still linger. As its force became bound up with the drive for industrialization, nationalism transcended its bounds and sought to deprive others of the freedoms it had claimed for itself. Such a narrow nationalism has disrupted the solidarity of the seven states in the face of threats to the inde-

pendence of each. Serbian and Croatian hostility is alive
in Jugoslavia; Slovakian separatism has remained a problem to the Czechs in Czecho-Slovakia. The peace between
Rumanians and Hungarians in Transylvania may prove to
be but an enforced armistice. Communism is no safeguard
against nationalism: Jugoslav and Bulgarian Communists
have come to no agreement on Macedonia; Albanian and
Jugoslav comrades continue to disagree on the Kossovo region. The Soviet system itself may be regarded as the Russian form of industrializing nationalism with a messianic
bent.

To obtain a rounded view of these seven countries, a
vantage point has to be found neither too close to nor too
distant from the problems that beset them. One who in-
timately shared their aspirations and frustrations may be
prone to share their megalomania as well. On the other
hand, too detached a view might fail to do justice to their
distinctive achievements as each wrestles with practically
the same predicament. The present writer has had the advantage of having spent his formative years in that area and
his mature age abroad in reflection upon them. He once
took the stability of the Hapsburg empire for granted, but
lived to see its total eclipse. He found no Poland on his
school maps, but was a witness to its resurrection and subsequent subjection. He saw the principles of kinship bridging the Carpathian mountains and the obstacles of centuries-
old different traditions, yet had to take note of the violence
with which Slovaks and Croatians refused to merge into
dominant nations with their own kin.

However, there were also hopeful signs. In 1956, the
Hungarian rebels revealed their deep-felt desire for neutrality on the model of Austria, a little country with no ambition to dominate anyone. The fact that Hungarian nationalism, once dreaded and hated by all peoples under its sway,
has divested itself from such an ambition, is grounds for
confidence that the small Eastern peoples may still share
in brotherly freedom.

On the material level, there was the significance of industrialization for the solving of problems of overpopulation in agricultural lands, and also the effect of armaments on this process. No one could miss the important changes in the economic, social, and intellectual fields as the seven states are gradually transformed into highly industrialized countries.

This book is the result of observations such as these and lifelong reading and writing on the problems of the area. It is to be hoped that it will help bring into focus for Western readers the many problems and aspirations of the peoples of Eastern Europe.

The author is indebted to Mrs. Jane Dawson-Jackson and Mr. Robert Halasz for their conscientious and resourceful editing of the manuscript. He is grateful to the Harvard University Press for permission to reprint the quotation from Suzanne K. Langer's *Philosophy in a New Key*.

Nicholas Halasz

New York
   January, 1959

Contents

Men fight passionately against being forced to do lip service because the enactment of a rite is always, in some measure, assent to its meaning; so that the very expression of an alien mythology incompatible with one's own vision of "fact" or "truth," works to the corruption of that vision.

Suzanne K. Langer
Philosophy in a New Key

Part I

THE SEVEN STATES

CHAPTER ONE

Poland

When the conference at Yalta opened on February 4, 1945, final victory was beginning to dawn on the global horizon of World War II. Soviet armies were surging toward all the enemy capital cities they had failed to capture in the previous year. The great offensive of the Western Allies moved forward relentlessly although momentarily bogged down in parrying the Nazi counterattack in the Ardennes. The Allied timetable was upset, but the very fierceness of the counterattack which delayed it spent the last forces of the Germans.

Neither was there hope left for the Axis powers in the Pacific, though military experts estimated that a struggle of two or more years might be required to defeat Japan. The last secret report to President Roosevelt intimated that the first atomic bomb would not be ready until the following August, so it was to assure Stalin's entering the war in the Pacific and to fix the time of Russian intervention, its extent and price, that he undertook the long, dangerous voyage to the Crimea. In Manchuria, intact and practically self-sufficient, Nipponese armies threatened to carry on the war even after the Japanese islands had been captured. Only the Soviet army could destroy them without an immensely complicated and dangerous assault from the sea.

As concern for the war against Japan moved into the foreground, the center of gravity in the Grand Alliance shifted from Britain toward the Soviet Union. In Malta, where Roosevelt had landed from a warship, Churchill was disturbed when he observed how ostentatiously the Americans avoided having too many meetings between the two Western allies before they joined Stalin. The British contribution in the Pacific theater could not be substantial, and was not desired by the United States to be so, because the military considered it destructive to the morale of American soldiers to see the flag of a colonial power flying behind their fighting lines. Here was the great chance for America to gain the sympathies of colonial peoples as the leader, by birthright, in the struggle for liberation from colonialism. Roosevelt was confident that his people would support such a genuinely American foreign policy and back his offer to the other great anti-colonial power for cooperation in its execution.

But the President also had far broader cooperation in mind. In the unprecedented political and social earthquake caused by war, empires, new and old, were crumbling. The first tremor was to sweep away the German and Japanese empires, and the second, in turn, might shatter the British, Dutch, and French. Such upheavals might throw the world into a century-long turmoil of wars, revolutions, and a tidal wave of mass migrations unless the two remaining world powers, America and Russia, could channel the liberated energies into peaceful development.

Roosevelt had intimated this to the Soviet Foreign Minister, Molotov, when the sour-faced Russian visited Washington in 1942 to complain of the absence of a second front in the West to relieve Soviet armies from Nazi pressure. Roosevelt, at that time, had emphasized his concern for the backward areas in the postwar period and his plan to put them under international trusteeship, including explicitly British and Dutch possessions in the Pacific. The Russians thus at an early date took cognizance of the fact that the Americans might shift postwar cooperation, at least in the Pacific, from Britain to the Soviet Union.

Reading the President's far from concealed thoughts, Churchill became morose, especially when Roosevelt secluded himself with Stalin to discuss war and peace in the Pacific.

But Churchill was sure that the other main subject on the agenda would bring the Americans back to realities—which to him meant the paramount importance of Europe and the pitfalls of cooperating with Russia in that area. The Polish question would serve as a warning. It had bedevilled allied relations ever since Russia had been driven into war in 1941 by Nazi aggression. Poland had a government-in-exile with headquarters in London which viewed the Soviet not as an ally against a common enemy but as enemy number two. The hostility went so far that the Soviet Union in 1943 broke diplomatic relations with the Polish London government. Meanwhile, the Russian offensive enveloped Poland and, just before the Yalta conference, the Soviets recognized a pro-Soviet Polish group as the provisional government. This was a dangerous development with the West recognizing one government and the Soviet Union the other. Their hostility threatened to be a windfall for the Nazis, whose last hope remained in splitting the Allies. This danger made it imperative for the Big Three to reach some agreement and enforce it on the Poles.

The discussions on Poland consumed almost every day of the week-long conference. The participants had stumbled on a question of principle which divided East and West. Stalin insisted that Russia had the right to have a Polish government friendly to her, emphasizing the fact that twice Poland had been a corridor for enemy attacks. Neither Roosevelt nor Churchill questioned his position. But the Western leaders wanted to replace the Stalin-picked provisional government with a broader one including persons and parties whom the Russians suspected of being inimical to the Soviets. The West also wanted a guarantee that this government would hold free elections, hoping that eventually one supported by the majority of the population would take power.

Stalin made no secret of his conviction that a free election would return no pro-Soviet majority in Poland. The Western statesmen had even fewer illusions on this point. But then the Russians faced the crucial question of whether

Roosevelt and Churchill actually wanted a Polish government friendly to Russia. If all they needed was face saving
as, in fact, they had both implied, Stalin would be helpful.
Churchill kept reminding him that Britain had declared war
to defend the independence of Poland so that this was a
point of honor for Britain at the conference table as well.
Stalin remarked that for the Soviets it was not only a matter
of honor but of security. For his part, Roosevelt hinted that
the importance of the Polish vote in America might stir
opposition in Congress to his concessions.

Stalin was willing to sign high-flown declarations as window-dressing for his Western partners, but with the firm
understanding that they covered hard facts of power politics.
He expected the help of the British war leader since only a
few months before, in October, 1944, they had struck an
agreement on spheres of influence in the Balkans at Churchill's proposal. Stalin had kept the bargain when the British
had used troops to force a government on the Greeks. He
made no objections and saw that the Soviet press kept silent
about the affair although the American and even the British
public protested in an uproar.

During their meeting Roosevelt showed how uninhib-
itedly he could dispose of huge territories such as Manchuria, Tibet, or Outer Mongolia, assigning the latter two to
China, disregarding the principles of the Atlantic Charter
and those announced at Teheran whenever he thought that
vital interests of the United States were involved. Stalin
thus trusted that Roosevelt had a real understanding of
Russia's intense concern about having a friendly government for her neighbor.

But the help which Churchill was expected to supply on
the basis of their agreement and the mutual understanding
with Roosevelt appeared to be getting lost in endless debates on semantics. The words, though of great consequence, threatened to blur the line between façade and fact,
principle and reasons of state. The West wanted a new
government for Poland, but the Russians would only admit
new members to the old government of their own creation.

Foreign ministers of the Big Three were to implement the agreement. The Soviets wanted to restrict their jurisdiction to consultation on the persons to be considered for additional posts in the cabinet. The West would give them power actively to assist in reforming the government, supervising the elections, and reporting on them.

Stalin fought most stubbornly on this point. He was concerned lest the West empower its foreign ministers to choose and support candidates unfriendly to Russia who would take exception if the elections did not conform to those in the West. The Soviet Union was entitled to a friendly government in Poland, but free elections, in the Western sense, would not return such a government. If Western insistence on the words "free elections" was intended only to soothe the public, Stalin would accept their insertion into the resolution. But somewhere it must be made clear that a friendly government had priority over one issued from genuinely free elections.

Stalin carried his point when both requirements found a place in the document.

There was nothing new in the Allies accepting ambiguity in order to veil controversy on principles or on their interpretation, nor in their tacit understanding on the use of words that had different meanings for all. This procedure had started at the very beginning of the alliance against Nazi Germany, which had been branded not only as an aggressor but also as a tyrannical and totalitarian state. The West accepted the Soviet system as a democracy of a peculiar type. Moscow also, without blinking, began to speak of the "front of democracies," including the Soviet Union, against Fascists and Nazis. After decades of abuse and ridicule, the word "democracy" seemed to have become respectable to the Russians.

This expediency in considering Russia a democracy was the platform on which East and West cooperated ideologically during the war. On that basis the Western powers were able to hail Soviet adherence to such declarations of

democratic principles as those expressed in the statement
issued in 1943 at the Teheran conference:

> We shall seek the cooperation and active participation of all na-
> tions, large and small, whose peoples in heart and mind are dedicated,
> as are our own peoples, to the elimination of tyranny and slavery,
> oppression and intolerance. We will welcome them, as they may
> choose to come into a world family of Democratic Nations.

The controversy of principles threatened to be revived
over the Polish question. It had not been unexpected. Indeed, Russian distrust of the West had not vanished even
in the heyday of war-time collaboration. But collaboration
had worked, and could continue to work even after the war.
To smooth the way, Stalin dissolved the Comintern in 1943,
which indicated that he intended to follow the interests of
the Soviet state and dispense with the assistance of international Communism. This was only a gesture, since he did
not actually break with his parties abroad; yet it might have
been a first step toward a break. At least it acknowledged
that ideological differences had hindered cooperation and
could do the same in the future. Anxiety over the Polish
discussions grew from the suspicion that this time the West
was sharpening with ideology the edge of a real or imagined
controversy.

Russia needed postwar cooperation with America. The
loss in human lives, means of production, and housing in the
Soviet Union could produce unbearable strains on the population, and a new, gigantic effort would have to be imposed
on it unless a large American long-term loan lightened the
burden. Friendly relations were also needed with America
for security against Germany. Stalin had strong reasons for
being apprehensive of German military power. Twice in
his own lifetime Germany had attacked Russia, and almost
the entire world had had to join in the fight to defeat her
when she was only inches from victory. A Poland that
could not associate with Germany would also be a part of
Russia's security. Hence the vital importance of the Polish
question. Stalin fought to the end to restrict the role of
the foreign ministers to consultation on the reconstruction

of the Polish provisional government which he had chosen, because this government would ultimately determine the meaning and extent of "free and unfettered elections."

The conference appeared to have allayed his suspicions of the West. Consequently, he assumed that his partners were ready to proceed on the basis of the fallacy which served as the platform of cooperation. In this case, the extent to which the provisional government was to be representative, as well as the freedom of elections, might safely be limited.

This assumption moved Stalin to adhere to the Declaration on Liberated Europe as proposed by Roosevelt. If it proved wrong, the Soviet dictator was still determined to have friendly governments in the Russian zone, in spite of the Declaration's statement that:

> The establishment of order in Europe and the rebuilding of national economic life must be achieved by processes which will enable the liberated peoples to destroy the last vestiges of Nazism and Fascism and to create democratic institutions of their own choice. This is a principle of the Atlantic Charter—the right of all peoples to choose the form of government under which they will live—the restoration of sovereign rights and self-government to those peoples who have been forcibly deprived of them by the aggressor nations.

The Yalta conference also reached an agreement on the Polish-Russian frontier. This was the main bone of contention between the Soviets and the Polish government-in-exile as well as the bulk of the Polish underground and public, but it presented no particular difficulties to the great powers. The border ran roughly along the Curzon line, so called because Lord Curzon had proposed it as the Polish-Russian boundary after World War I. Then as now, the British and American foreign offices held it as conforming to the ethnic divide. Moreover, the Soviet army already occupied the land east of the line. It had changed hands at a dazzling rate in the last quarter of the century. Before World War I it belonged to Russia; in 1921, Poland's Marshal Pilsudski wrested it from the Bolsheviks; in 1939, the Soviets occupied it on the basis of the ill-fated Molotov-Ribbentrop agreement; in 1941, the Nazis overran the territory; and in 1944–45, the Soviet army had recovered it again.

Then, on the last day of the conference, the Soviet representatives appeared to be more reserved than before, and shortly afterward Edward R. Stettinius, the American foreign secretary, as well as Anthony Eden, his British colleague, wondered whether Soviet foreign policy had not abruptly changed. They suspected that the Politburo had objected to Stalin's conciliatory attitude toward the West.

Eden apparently failed to link two episodes, one in which he had a part and one to which he was a witness. In 1943, he told President Roosevelt of an impression he had gained in talking with Stalin, that the Soviet leader had two plans for the postwar years: one contingent on Anglo-American cooperation with the Soviet Union and the other in case America became disinterested in Europe. At the Yalta conference, Stalin suddenly asked Roosevelt how long he thought America would be willing to keep occupation forces in Germany after the war. Those who heard the question and the President's reply appeared to have missed the significance of both. Roosevelt said, "I can get the people and Congress to cooperate fully for peace, but not to keep an army in Europe for a long time. Two years would be the limit." This meant for Stalin that two years hence he would face British power policies alone on the Continent.

If Roosevelt, so conscious of the magnitude of postwar problems and of the necessity of cooperation with the Soviet Union in solving them, could not guarantee that America would have military forces on the Continent long enough to keep Germany disarmed and prevent her from becoming an aggressor again, how could Stalin stake all on cooperation?

The Poles were one of the Slav peoples who advanced into central Europe from the east during the seventh century A.D. They settled between the Vistula and the Elbe rivers while other Slav tribes moved down into Pannonia, Thrace, and the Adriatic. The territory which the Poles occupied was part of the great plain extending from the Ural Mountains to the Atlantic Ocean, with no interfering natural barriers. This geographical position determined Polish history by putting them in constant danger of exposure to aggression from east and west, from the Russian and Germanic worlds. On the other hand, when these neighbors were weak, this fact proved to be a temptation for the Poles.

In one of the most momentous battles in history, at Tannenberg in 1410, the Poles stopped the relentless and aggressive advance of the Germanized Prussians, who were pushing them east from their habitat and cutting them off from the Baltic Sea. This victory was accomplished by an alliance with the Lithuanians, an alliance which later developed into a union. Feeling secure from the west now, they yielded to the temptation of expanding to the east, where Russia, in the wake of Mongolian rule, was having her Time of Troubles. The Polish-Lithuanians stretched their rule over the Ukraine down to the Black Sea and held Kiev, the main highway between the Baltic and Black seas. In 1610, a Polish king occupied the Kremlin. To defend their gains, the Poles fought Tatars, Cossacks, the Swedes, and the Ottoman Turks. Indeed, it was a Polish king who stopped the latter at the gates of Vienna in 1683. In the sixteenth and seventeenth centuries Poland was the greatest power in Europe.

Poland was a Western country, having embraced Roman Christianity in the tenth century while the other Slav peoples further east were receiving their baptism from Byzantium. The main cultural currents of the West penetrated into Poland; the University of Cracow, established in the fourteenth century, vied in reputation with the best institutions of learning in the West. The Gothic, renaissance, and baroque periods of art left lasting monuments of Poland's stake in the European experience of humanism, Reformation, and counter-Reformation.

But ambitious expansion overtaxed Poland's powers. When, at the turn of the seventeenth century, Russia recovered, an exhausted Poland found herself wedged between two growing powers, Germanic Prussia and the Russia of Peter the Great.

Coupled with the expansion of these two powers was an internal weakness which degraded Poland into becoming a power vacuum. This was fatal for Poland, whose geography and history had destined her to be a buffer state. Poland's weakness grew out of the fact that in past times the vast country had been unprotected from her strong and ambitious neighbors. This enhanced the importance of the local lords and arms-bearing landowners who resided on the spot. These lords supplied the king with soldiers for large-scale campaigns and fought border wars themselves. For these services, the nobility exacted a high price in privileges. They won the right to elect the king. The right of succession rested on the election, even though the nobility accepted hereditary monarchy. Each election was a new opportunity for them to strengthen their privileges, and each change of dynasty meant a new charter extending their rights.

After the sixteenth century, when the Polish-Lithuanian Jagiello line died out, the elections became genuine, and open, preferably, to foreign ruling houses. To assure their complete freedom from the influence of the extant ruler, no candidacy was allowed before his death. Hence, each royal demise opened a period of anarchy, an interregnum in which competition raged for the votes of the nobles. A candidate first bribed the nobility as a whole by a promise of extending its privileges, then approached individuals and groups in an attempt to gain a majority. Occasionally the elections turned into armed fights between partisans of one candidate or the other, and more and more frequently Poland's neighbors seized the opportunity offered by chaos to enforce their own candidate, thereby turning the country into a satellite of their own orbit.

To top everything, the nobles acquired a right that later made anarchy a permanent threat. Each and every one of their members had the right to veto laws passed by the Sejm (the national assembly). In numbers the nobles consti- tuted only about 10 per cent of the population. Supposedly they all had the same rights before the law, but in terms of power the difference ran on a sliding scale from owners of entire provinces to men who had only a small piece of land, with, of course, the privilege to sell out. Local potentates kept a host of noblemen about their castles, gave them func- tions and offices, or simply kept them as steady guests, for they represented power in terms of votes in the Sejm.

The privilege of veto, called the *liberum veto*, became a complete institutional fetter, and yet the Poles called it "liberty." Moreover, the powerful magnates had the right to ally themselves with others, by arms if necessary, to pre- vent the passage of laws which they considered "injurious." And this right was called "confederation."

These excesses of "liberties," at the end of the eighteenth century, caused the downfall of Poland. She became a power vacuum that her strong neighbors, jealous of each other, could not tolerate. If they did not want to go to war to fill the vacuum, it was necessary that they make a deal to divide her among themselves. This is how the first parti- tion of Poland, in 1772, came to pass.

The embittered Poles then tried to play one partitioning power against the other. Against the two massive empires, Russia and Austria, they allied themselves with Prussia. Meanwhile, the French Revolution had so impressed the nobility that in 1791 they voted a new constitution which abolished the sources of Polish frustration. It cancelled the *liberum veto*, opened state offices to non-titled townspeople, and established a place in the constitution for the peasantry. But the reactionary magnates, the great landowners, set up a "confederation" and appealed to the tsar for help against this "tyrannical" new constitution, maintaining a wish to restore Polish liberty. Catherine the Great, though involved in wars, grabbed her chance. She managed to dispatch troops to Poland. Prussia was committed to support Poland against Russian attack, but she defected, preferring a new Polish partition to war with Russia. So, in 1793, Poland lost half the territory left to her after the first partition. In 1794, the military successes of the French Revolution inspired her to a revolt against the tsar, but the expected revolutionary support against tyranny failed to materialize, and the insurrection resulted in the third partition in 1795.

While Poland ceased to exist as a physical body, she became an international problem through repeated revolts, conspiracies at home, and the activities of her emigrés abroad. After each revolt misfired more and more of the patriotic intelligentsia fled. In poetry, dreams, and intrigues they kept alive a free, independent Poland, while the people back home tried to adjust themselves to three widely different political and social systems: those of Russia, Germanic Prussia, and Austria. And there were times when they almost lost sight of each other.

During the century and a half of her partition a process of amalgamation started. Serfdom was abolished, the privileges of nobility began to vanish, and poor nobles entered professions. In Prussia the Poles suffered under a policy of ruthless denationalization, but since this policy centered on the Polish language it fused Poles in all walks of life. Also, the higher standard of living in Prussian Germany lifted peasants' sons into the lower middle class and made the peasants in general susceptible to national consciousness.

In Russia, conditions became favorable for the creation of industries in the Polish province, which opened an opportunity for the surplus peasant population in the factories. The industrial workers, therefore, became a new factor in Polish national life. Led by the intelligentsia, chiefly of noble origin, they tied Polish national liberation to the revolutionary movements in Russia. Socialism became the inspiration of a renascence in which all Poles might become members of the nation.

Only in Austria was there stagnation instead of social evolution. The Austrian regime favored the Polish aristocracy and protected its power, but at the same time it was lenient to Polish nationalism, granting considerable self-government to the Poles in Galicia. It closed its eyes to movements which concentrated on liberation of the Russian-held Polish lands since they served as a shield against Russian-spread pan-Slavism.

When World War I erupted, some kind of Poland was bound to rise from the defeat either of Russia, or of Germany and Austria. The question was on whose defeat to stake her future. Joseph Pilsudski decided to bet on the defeat of Russia. He was a Polish Socialist of Lithuanian noble origin who believed that the collapse of Tsarist Russia resulting from a Russian revolution was the most positive hope for liberty for Poland. Pilsudski organized the Polish youth in Austria at the approach of war. He also established a military school, in which he was joined by a circle of friends who later became known as the "Colonels" and formed his future staff, both military and political.

Who could foresee that not only Russia would fall in the holocaust of war, but her enemies, Prussian Germany and Austria as well? And all three held parts of Poland! It was a miracle surpassing all hopes. The Polish eagle spread its wings again and began to soar.

Poland could now be free since the powers threatening her existence lay prostrate: Germany defeated, Russia in the turmoil of revolution, and even the Austrian Empire disintegrated. What kind of Poland was to be reconstructed? The peace conference in Paris accepted an eastern border proposed by Lord Curzon, which delineated the territory within which the majority of the population was Polish. Beyond this line, Ukrainians and White Russians formed the bulk of inhabitants. However, Pilsudski, who from the beginning of the new Poland had acted as head of state, commander-in-chief, and prime minister, was haunted by Polish greatness and the mission it entailed. His country now had the opportunity, indeed the duty, to organize the peoples on the vast plain down to the Black Sea into a great confederation dominated by the Poles in whose higher culture the ruling strata of other nationals should fuse. He opposed the nationalists who denied self-determination to any extent to all non-Poles.

Pilsudski did not heed the warnings of Poland's friends in the West, but attacked Bolshevik Russia in 1919, and was defeated. He appealed to the Western powers for help, but instead of help he received orders to retire behind the Curzon line. The Bolsheviks in turn became ambitious in victory. They pursued the Poles into Poland itself and demanded that they form a Soviet republic. Then at the gates of Warsaw, the Poles defeated the Red Army. In the treaty of Riga, in 1921, Pilsudski received vast territories inhabited by Ukrainians and White Russians. Yet it took two more years for the Western powers to accept the accomplishment that placed millions of these people under Polish rule. But by then they had abandoned hope that a non-Communist Ukraine could rise from the civil wars in Russia.

Polish armies performed another *fait accompli,* wresting from Lithuania her capital city of Vilna, allegedly as a national gift to Pilsudski, since his family had originated there. Tiny Lithuania, once senior partner in Poland's greatness, responded to the blow by cutting rails, roads, and telegraph lines, blocking all communications so completely that not a single person or vehicle crossed the frontier between the two neighbors for more than a decade.

In the west, Poland received from Germany former Polish lands, a corridor cutting through Prussia to the harbor of Danzig on the Baltic Sea, and a part of Silesia; and from Austria, Galicia and part of Teschen.

Reborn Poland was a large country of 150,052 square miles, with almost 27 million inhabitants, but the greater part of the land was devastated by war—fields laid waste, livestock slaughtered, factories dismantled, communications disrupted, and the threat of famine hanging over it like a dark mist. Nevertheless the government began as a democracy. A constituent assembly, elected by universal ballot, convened early in 1919 and truly reflected the incoherent state of a people united after more than a century of separation. Although the assembly broke into thirteen parties, the peasants had the strongest representation, and the broad lines of nationalist, peasant, and socialist groups could easily be distinguished. The latter two formed the first coalition, the constitution mirroring the same fear of a strong executive as its French model. The fervor of the assembly in stripping the powers of the president recalled the deadly "freedom" of the past. Land reform was adopted which limited individual holdings to 150–250 acres, except in the east where a higher limit of nearly 1,000 acres was allowed.

Land and the folk living on it became the gravest problem of the republic. It had to support 70 per cent of the population. More than two million families lived on 15 per cent while 19,000 owners held 43 per cent of the total agricultural area, and the contrast between the way of life of the big landowners and the peasantry was appalling. In the castles all the luxury of the ancient regime survived. The family flag fluttered over the towers, old guns adorned the lawns. Some estates had a nursery, a sawmill, a forestry school, and a factory for canning fruits, while the castle would boast several dining rooms, theaters, concert halls, golf courses, enormous stables, and large numbers of coaches. A twentieth-century visitor felt as if he were living far back in the past.

Not far from this grandeur squatted the miserable village huts, enveloped in utter darkness as soon as the sun had set, for although Poland had rich oil wells, the peasants could not afford petroleum for light. Several households would contribute toward buying one box of matches, then keep a log burning in the stove in order to save them. Water in which the staple potato was boiled was carefully preserved for another day to save salt. On his dwarfholding the peasant produced only enough to keep his family alive, and bought or sold almost nothing.

Land distribution seemed to hold the magic cure for all the peasant's trouble, but actually it offered no solution for the problem as a whole. The land was overcrowded and the population was increasing by 400,000 a year. There was simply not enough land. Even so, the distribution which had been declared in principle was never fully accomplished. The state had not the financial means to compensate an owner relinquishing part of his estate nor the money to lend a new landowner for equipment, fertilizers, and better seed with which to raise productivity. Any increase of productivity, however, required education as well, and a large part of the people was illiterate—a quarter of them remaining so even after two decades of independence, with more than three million children of school age having no educational facilities.

Large-scale emigration would have been the only real remedy, but America closed her doors to this outlet, and other countries overseas also limited the influx from eastern Europe. Industrialization remained the only means of absorbing the surplus. But foreign investments went only into specific industries such as mining and oil, and these on a limited scale. It was up to the state to finance other new industries, but its income was among the lowest in Europe since the bulk of the population, the peasantry, had no part in the monetary economy. Foreign loans were intended and used for the stabilization of currency, and the financial policy favored a balanced budget, not government spending. However, achievements such as the building of a great new harbor, Gdynia, on the Baltic, to challenge the old German "free city" of Danzig, showed the Poles' patriotic enthusiasm for the spectacular and the symbolic—if not for the practical.

The wealth of raw materials, especially coal and oil, proved to be the greatest assets of the country in foreign commerce apart from the hard work to which the majority of the people were accustomed. Unfortunately, the problems were immense and the means of grappling with them inadequate.

Moreover, danger signals against the development of a peaceful economy soon appeared on both the eastern and western horizons. At the end of World War I, France had accepted Poland as a substitute for Russia in her system of military alliances aimed at keeping German power in check. She appeared later to have taken a sober look at the military potentials of Poland, for in 1925 France, England, and Germany entered into an agreement at Locarno which guaranteed frontiers and security in the west but disregarded Germany's eastern borders. A year later, Poland's two neighbors moved closer to each other with a Soviet-German treaty.

Meanwhile, there was a shift of strength in the Sejm. The Peasant Party switched from the left toward the nationalists, occupying a center position between right and left. The better-off peasants had common interests with the owners of big estates with regard to prices, labor policies, and taxation, while the dwarfholders sided with the workers in the cities, even though by instinct, tradition, and religion they were conservative and distrustful of anything coming from the towns. The peasant leadership abandoned its radicalism, preserving the old slogans while it switched with the well-to-do toward respectability. The party leader, Wincenty Witos, a colorful and shrewd politician, carried the party to the right, a move directed against Pilsudski's course which had guided the country since her rebirth.

Pilsudski ceased to consider himself a socialist after Poland had been liberated, but he consistently held the Right to be a greater danger to the state than the Left, since the Rightist parties prevented a strong executive from being established in the Constitution, thus inviting a return of the fatal anarchy of eighteenth-century Poland. Authoritarian by nature and haunted by history, Pilsudski's main concern was for a strong government, and next to that a strong army. But his haughtiness estranged many friends and brought about perplexing situations. He appeared to be coveting the highest offices, but refused to accept them when offered. He did not shy away from applying force to turn a government out of office, yet he insisted it be made legal by taking votes of public confidence; then, when he did not win them by imposing pluralities, he stepped down and ruled by proxy.

In 1926 Witos, as prime minister, appointed a general hostile to Pilsudski as minister of war. Pilsudski called out the troops faithful to him, and after bloody clashes with soldiers obedient to the government, forced Witos out of office. He installed a friend of his as president, himself retaining leadership of the army as its inspector general and minister of war. The Socialists supported his putsch to prevent the Right from governing, but broke with Pilsudski when he showed himself to be establishing an authoritarian regime.

What divided Pilsudski and his group from the nationalists, who represented tradition and wealth, was not his socialist leanings, which faded with the reconstruction of Poland, but the concept that the army and the bureaucracy were above class, group, or party. It was Pilsudski who stopped the land reform because he thought large estates would be better able to supply the army with food in case of war than the small holdings; it was only as a byproduct that land distribution was suspended, turning the big landowners toward his regime. Nevertheless, more than 8 million acres were allocated to dwarfholders and landless peasants in 1928.

Pilsudski's idea of a large confederation of Slavs between Germany and Russia was reflected in his attitude toward minority groups within Poland—especially the strongest one, the Ukrainians. It outraged the nationalists when the left-wing coalition in the Sejm elected a president with the help of Ukrainian and Jewish votes. Yet the regime did not improve Polish relations with the Ukrainian minority. The fact that the land reform act allowed Polish landlords in the east, where the non-Polish peasantry lived, to retain far more land than elsewhere was injurious enough, but the government also gave priority to peasants of Polish stock over the local Ukrainians. Such favoritism remained a per-

manent feature of policy and caused hostility, particularly
when propaganda from Germany emboldened the Ukrainians to avail themselves of the League of Nations' minority
control machinery and file protests and complaints. An intelligent Polish policy could have made good use of the fact
that only the poorest peasants and a fringe of the intelligentsia among the Ukrainians and White Russians in Poland
had any wish to join their kin in the Soviet republic; but the
danger to the unity and strength of the state from any self-
government by non-Poles, though perhaps exaggerated, prevailed over all attempts at broadmindedness.

The Ukrainian and White Russian minority amounted to
over 6 million out of about 35 million of the total inhabitants,
even on the basis of the not-too-reliable national census of
1938, but the Germans, though numbering less than 800,000,
constituted no lesser problem. Economically and intellec-
tually on a much higher level than the Poles, they represented, with the Reich behind them, a foreign rather than
a national policy headache.

The three million Jews, however, became both a social
and a political problem. In the new Poland, population
pressure and general education speeded the evolution toward a genuine middle class of craftsmen, merchants, and
professionals. The propertyless descendants of the nobility
and the sons of peasants entered such unfamiliar occupa-
tions as the Jews had been following for centuries. Instead
of fulfilling a function in the economy and society as they
had been doing since the fourteenth century, the Jews now
stood in the way of a natural development in their adopted
country. They continued to live the jealously segregated
life of strangers and the Gentile population considered them
as such.

The Pilsudski regime assailed their position in several
ways. In connection with armament, the state had expanded its ownership in industry; and in time of economic
crisis it intervened to restrict commerce and private business activities in general. These policies worked to the detriment of the Jews only because they were active in this field.

But as state intervention increased, the government used its
influence to eliminate Jews from business and replace them
with Poles. Orders, subsidies, and licenses favored Poles;
and when Jewish enterprises could not be by-passed, the
government brought pressure to bear on them to employ
Poles in every capacity from management down to such positions as were still compatible with Polish dignity. The
number of Jewish students in higher education and their
admittance to the bar were also restricted. But society was
not satisfied with a planned displacement of the Jews. It
organized a boycott to strangle their businesses, while the
growth of credit and sales cooperatives among the peasants
pushed Jewish shopkeepers and middlemen out of the villages. Only wholesale emigration could have alleviated the
situation. The government launched trial balloons for a
trusteeship from the League of Nations, hoping to settle the
Jews in a colony of their own.

As a stroke of irony to the Poles, who insisted that overpopulation lay at the bottom of their economic problems,
Hitler brought the solution to them wholesale. He deci-
mated the Gentile population, Poles and Ukrainians alike,
and exterminated almost three million Jews.

But before Hitler rose to power Poland had already become the target of German nationalism. The German government kept complaining of the maltreatment of the Germans by the Poles in the "free city" of Danzig which the
peace treaties had reserved for Poland as an outlet to the
sea, and in the territory called the "corridor" that split Prussia. German foreign policy made public the fact that Germany did not accept these territorial arrangements as final.
The origins of Ukrainian unrest also could be traced to Germany.

Pilsudski trusted only force and the readiness to fight to
keep his western neighbors from imposing a revision of the
territorial provisions. He concentrated on building up the
army and national self-sufficiency in case of war. This policy involved government investments in industries manufacturing supplies for the military, and expenditures for

strategic roads. It suffered a grave setback when the world
economic slump reached the nation. Poland was particularly affected by the collapse of the prices of her raw materials and agricultural products, her main sources of foreign
currency. Unemployment in the towns and utter poverty
in the villages plagued the country. In 1935, when the
world-wide crisis had passed its peak, working families in
the towns earned less than $2.50 weekly, and yet they fared
better than the peasants. The death rate from tuberculosis
and infant mortality was among the highest in Europe.

When Hitler rode into power on the crest of the crisis,
the Pilsudski regime resolved on an independent policy toward Nazi Germany, entering in 1934 into a nonaggression
pact with the sinister dictator. Pilsudski and the "Colonels,"
particularly Joseph Beck, his foreign minister, liked to explain why they expected Hitler to deviate from the traditional German nationalistic line which held that Germany
could not tolerate an independent Poland. Hitler, they
philosophized, was an Austrian who did not share the Prussian hatred of everything Polish; besides, as a realist, he
must know that a strong, neutral Poland, which refused to
associate with efforts to block the Fuehrer's ambitions,
strengthened his position. Outsiders suspected a prospective
coalition of authoritarian regimes, but actually Pilsudski's
stand issued from a cool estimate of the international situation that might have been as correct as anyone else's. He
did not expect the West to go to war to preserve the status
quo in the east. Hitler would expand in the direction of the
least resistance, first Austria and then southeastern Europe,
following the classic road of the German *Drang* to Asia
Minor. Poland must be too strong to tempt Hitler, but
otherwise aloof. Pilsudski ruled out a Nazi-Communist alliance. In case of a Russo-German conflict, he would be
friendly to Germany but remain neutral.

In 1935, the regime pushed through an authoritarian constitution in a rigged Sejm, a concoction of sham parliamentarianism and corporation state behind which power rested

on the military and the bureaucracy. Pilsudski died shortly afterward.

Outwardly, Polish society did not show a substantial shift in its stratification. The new ruling class—the watered-down nobility, and the newly risen commoners in state offices, the army, and the professions—displayed and even exaggerated the old social attitudes: clan spirit, superficial amiability, and real arrogance. The chasm between them and the people working with their hands remained deep and wide, while the peasant continued to be socially untouchable.

Toward the late 1930's, the economic situation improved. The rearmament of the European countries set industrial activity in fresh motion. The regime succeeded in enlarging the export trade to the west and overseas, and government spending began to pump money into the parched areas of the economy. Progress was attained in many fields. But then the international situation became tense and the public, aware of the danger of a single false step, wondered about the tight-rope-walking of Polish foreign policy. The ostentatious visits of the number-two Nazi, Hermann Goering, to hunting parties in the Polish forests puzzled Foreign Offices abroad, especially in the Soviet Union, and disquieted those at home who were faithful to Western ideas and distrustful of the Germans. Nationalist radicals formed terror groups to press for a more violent course of anti-Semitism, but the majority of the people trusted the government in at least one respect: its concern for the defense of the country.

Events seemed to prove that Foreign Minister Beck was right in holding to Marshal Pilsudski's inheritance. The Germans, in 1936, reoccupied the Rhineland in open defiance of the peace treaty, provoking no effective action by either France or England. How then could Poland rely on the military support of the West when France lacked the determination to protect herself from a German break through her security system? So Poland proceeded on her independent course. In March, 1938, the Germans overran Austria, after a disturbing prelude in which a pro-Fascist govern-

ment and the support of Mussolini proved to be no obstacle
to Hitler. Poland wanted no part in collective security,
foreseeing that it would not work and would only draw
Hitler's hostility. But she strengthened her army, and the
public in growing anxiety made great sacrifices for it.

The lightning soon struck nearer home. The prime ministers of France and England made a pilgrimage to Munich
to approve of and assist in the dismemberment of Czecho-
slovakia. Her fate made plain how foolish it was to trust in
a military alliance with the West. On one point government and people concurred: Czechoslovakia was not ready
to fight, but Poland was. The public felt uneasy nonetheless when Colonel Beck made Poland a party to the crime
by collecting a morsel of the Cieszyn (Teschen) region from
among Hitler's spoils. The Polish left wing resented it,
especially the Socialists, but they had no influence. The
Socialists also distrusted the Soviet Union, which ought to
have been a pillar of collective action against the Nazis run
amuck. The Communists had been outlawed all during the
Pilsudski era. Their number amounted to about 20,000 in
the prisons and as many again at large. As an organ of the
Soviets on foreign and unfriendly soil, the Party had appeal
only to a fringe of the industrial workers, to the poor Ukrainian peasants, and to part of the Jewish intelligentsia. Even
so, the Comintern found it permeated with nationalism and
Trotskyism, and in 1938 ordered it dissolved. It was not
until 1942 that Poland again had a Communist Party.

Hitler's march into Prague in the spring of 1939 and his
splitting of Czechoslovakia into two protectorates should
have shattered the regime's illusions, but then the unexpected, the unbelievable happened. Chamberlain, the arch-
appeaser of Hitler, offered a guarantee against aggression.
Poland received on a silver plate what Czechoslovakia, who
had built her security on the West, was denied. Colonel
Beck was not in a hurry even in that triumphal moment.
He refused a British guarantee of the joint security of Poland and Rumania in the same pact, although Rumania was
the only country on Polish borders still friendly to her.

Beck's reluctance was a hint to Hitler to direct his next
move toward Rumania, in which case Poland would still
refrain from obstructing his drive.

The public shared the government's trust in the strength
of the army and the weakness of at least one of her big
neighbors, Soviet Russia. Wishful thinking also lulled the
West into disregarding the facts. Poland had been spending half of her income on the army, but the amount was
modest. She possessed no war industry capable of equipping a modern army, while supplies from abroad came
sparsely if at all. Yet Viscount Halifax, the British Foreign
Secretary, told the United States Ambassador as late as
March 24, 1939, that Poland was of more value to the democratic cause than Russia because the Russian air force was
very weak, old, and short ranged; her army poor; and her
industrial backing frightful. The most that could be expected from Russia, he insisted, would be some ammunition to Poland in the event of trouble.

Real danger would thus threaten Poland only if both
Germany and Russia were powerful, and this only on the
condition that they formed an alliance against Poland. This,
the government and the public deemed unthinkable. They
were thunderstruck when, on August 24, 1939, the Hitler-
Stalin agreement was announced, and rumor had it that the
pact contained a secret protocol which covered a new partition of Poland.

On September 1, Hitler's panzer divisions crossed the
Polish border, while the Luftwaffe controlled the air above
them unhampered. Proud Polish cavalry put up a defiant
show of brave men and horses against heavy armor and
bombers. The war was decided on the first day, and ended
completely in two weeks. On September 17 Stalin declared
that Poland had ceased to exist. This, he stated, imposed
a duty on the Soviet government to protect the Ukrainians
and White Russians of former Poland so that they might
live and work in peace.

The Soviet army occupied the zone designated by the
secret protocol. It corresponded roughly to the territory

delineated by Lord Curzon as belonging ethnically to the
Ukraine and White Russia, and the Soviet incorporated it
into these two of her constituent republics.

The Nazis made no secret of their intentions with regard
to Poland. The Gauleiter of the district of Poznan, which
had again changed from Polish to German rule, stated:

> In ten years there will be not a single plot of land that is not
> German . . . If God exists, it is He who has chosen Adolf Hitler to
> drive this vermin (the Poles) hence.

Another Gauleiter declared:

> It will be our highest and most honorable task to do whatsoever
> lies in our power so that in a few years everything which is in any
> way reminiscent of Poland shall have disappeared.

In central Poland, the Nazis reserved a territory for the
Poles, called the General Government, which they intended
to make into a reservoir of labor for the Reich. They ordered that raw materials needed by the Reich be removed
to Germany and only such enterprises left as would suffice
for the bare subsistence of the population. Only primary
and vocational schools were allowed to be open. The Polish
intelligentsia was to be frozen in the bud.

Young Poles fled from the Nazis through Rumania—as
many of them as could reach that narrow gate still opening
into the free world. Generals and high officials spearheaded
the exodus, for somehow they had the fastest legs and
wheels. The president of the republic, sick and tired, but
anxious for strict legality, appointed his successor and
stayed away from politics while the stream of refugees proceeded to France and eventually to England. Leaders as
well as the rank and file felt strongly that authoritarian Poland had failed when it could not even raise a modern army,
and the consensus among them was that Poland had to be
rebuilt on the broad basis of the common people. The new
president gave expression to this feeling by appointing General Wladyslav Sikorski to head the government in exile.

To the Poles at home the Nazis left no hope for a decent
future. Resistance to the wanton destruction of the nation

was instantaneous, being activated by former soldiers who could not escape. It split into loose organizations based on party lines, with nationalist, peasant, and socialist groups, the Pilsudski supporters being discredited. They got in touch with the government abroad, subsequently building up regular communications through radio and messengers. The exiled government appointed a representative to the underground committee, who was raised to the rank of a vice-premier and commander-in-chief of the troops known as the Home Army. But some fighting groups still remained aloof, distrusting the government in exile.

The leaders of the home movement arrived at the fantastic idea of keeping the state alive underground, as if to disprove the contention that Poland no longer existed. Government offices and even Parliament, composed of parties which had opposed the authoritarian regime, began to function. There was an army, a court, and even schools in which to educate Polish youth. The underground also possessed a regularly issued newspaper and an ammunition factory. There was a complete shadow state, with an army ready to rise at a word to fight the Nazis from the rear whenever the West should launch its great offensive. Meanwhile, sabotage was performed systematically and with great efficiency, as was seen from the increasing brutality of Nazi retaliation. The British, whom the government in exile kept informed on the activities of the underground, took the news with a grain of salt as only another evidence of Polish exaggeration. But the fiction was the ingenious protest of men left without a flicker of hope for an organized existence. By it they hoped to preserve at least the semblance of a functioning state.

The situation changed abruptly when Hitler attacked Russia. The people of Poland still considered Russia as a second enemy. Now they qualified her diplomatically and in deference to the British as "the ally of our allies." The government in exile took up diplomatic relations with the Soviet Union and came to an agreement that an army was to be organized from Poles who remained or had found refuge in the Russian-occupied territories of former Poland. The commander was to be appointed by the government in London, but he was to be subordinate to the Red Army. Under tremendous pressure by Churchill, the Soviets repudiated the Ribbentrop-Molotov agreement, but in a statement so ambiguous that it lacked all validity. The fact that the Supreme Soviet had incorporated into the Union the territories acquired by Russia on the basis of the agreement remained uncontested by the statement. Stalin left no doubt as to the validity of this legal act. He insisted on it even when the Germans advanced toward Moscow and Leningrad.

The Poles could now only hope that the miracle of 1918 would repeat itself. This miracle would consist of a German defeat of the Soviet Union, and, in turn, a defeat of the Nazis by the Western Allies. Like the West, the Poles believed in Germany's victory over the Soviets. The Polish general, whom the London government had commissioned to recruit an army in Soviet territory, held this view so strongly that even after the war he attributed German failure to Hitler's amateur strategy against the advice of his general staff. Sure of Russia's defeat, the general was anxious to avoid having Polish units join the Soviet army, at that time hard pressed at Stalingrad. He succeeded in getting Stalin's consent to the movement of his troops to Persia for training and equipping, and eventually to their joining the Allies.

The Poles wanted a second front from the West as much as did Stalin—but for vastly different reasons. Their hope was that the West would exploit the situation while the Germans were heavily engaged on the Russian front, and invade Europe before the Russians could do so. The underground army was geared for action.

After the tide turned at Stalingrad, fear of Russia and anti-Soviet feeling gained strength in London. In Poland itself, the mood was not uniform. The Home Army followed the London government's lead, but parties on the left and right had their own views and forces, intermittently cooperating with the Home Army or working on their own. Most important among them was a pro-Soviet guerilla force made up of Communists, who had organized a new Polish Party after the German attack on Russia, and the left wing of the Socialists. At the same time, the Russians set up a Polish division led by Polish generals who had not joined the exodus of the armies to Persia. This nucleus of the pro-Soviet Polish army was to fight by the side of the Russians. As the Russian counteroffensive gained momentum it became a source of great anxiety to the Allies as to what was going to happen when the Soviet forces reached the borders of prewar Poland. Would they meet the bulk of Polish underground as enemies in addition to the Germans, or could they suspend their controversy until the common enemy had been defeated? The foreboding was welcomed by the Nazis as an opportunity to drive a wedge between the Allies. It was their hope that the Polish conflict might be the issue upon which the "unnatural alliance" of the democratic West and Communist Russia would founder.

Goebbels, in the spring of 1943, finally hit on an issue that held the kernel of a grave conflict. The German propaganda chief unveiled the gruesome story of the Katyn Forest. Unfortunately for him, he had cooked up too many lies in the past to allow the world to believe him. The horrors the Nazis had perpetrated were becoming so revolting that when the Soviets replied that Goebbels was ascribing to them atrocities which the Nazis themselves had committed, the Western public held that at best both versions were possible and, disgusted, left the story at that.

The fact was that in the Katyn Forest, near Smolensk, mass graves were uncovered by the Germans in which more than four thousand Polish officers, all shot in the back of the head, had been buried. The Polish general who had organized the army in Russia had had a list of the officers known to have been interned in camps near the place and had made inquiries, but had not been able to get any information on their fate. After the Goebbels disclosure, the London government requested the International Red

Cross to investigate—a step which Stalin suspected had been taken in conspiracy with the enemy since Goebbels made the same request to the Red Cross the very same day. This gave Stalin the pretext of breaking diplomatic relations with the London government. On March 1, 1943, he set up a Committee of Polish Patriots, the nucleus of a pro-Soviet government.

Responsibility for the massacre has never been satis-factorily placed. However, the Russian prosecutor at the Nuremburg trial of war criminals failed to insist that the court pass judgment on the case when it turned out that evidence from other than Russian sources would be ex-amined. An inside story appears to be plausible: A Polish official, long before Goebbels blew open the story, asked Stalin about the officers. Stalin lifted the receiver of his telephone and made a call—probably to Beria. After listen-ing a moment, he put down the instrument and said not a word.

A Russian officer is said to have been told that the murder of the men was due to a misunderstanding. A Red Army officer had telephoned Stalin for instructions as to what to do about the camps. The dictator gave the laconic reply: "Liquidate." The commander believed that his chief re-ferred to the inmates instead of to the camps. If he ever had doubts he did not dare have them dissipated. But he wanted nothing to do with such a horrible matter, and passed the job over to the NKVD.

If true, the story throws a flood of light on the atmosphere around the dictator in the Kremlin.

Meanwhile, the Russians advanced into prewar Poland. The awkward situation of the Soviets recognizing one Polish government and the West another was likely to arise and cause serious consequences. At the Teheran conference, at the end of 1943, Churchill and Stalin agreed that the future Polish-Russian border would be the Curzon line, but that Poland would be compensated for the territorial loss by the German lands of East Prussia and Silesia to the Oder and Neisse rivers. Roosevelt neither protested nor

approved, true to his principle of not engaging in decisions
on frontier arrangements before the peace conference. The
London Polish government accepted the compensation but
rejected making the sacrifice for which Poland would be
compensated. There were other serious setbacks at the
time. Prime Minister General Sikorski, that rare type of
realistic Pole, was the victim of an airplane accident, and
the commander of the underground army was captured by
the Germans.

Churchill brought pressure, sometimes violent, to bear
on the new Premier of the London government, Stanislaw
Mikolajczyk, to accept Stalin's conditions for resuming diplomatic relations—first of all the recognition by the Poles of
the Curzon line. But Mikolajczyk had far less prestige than
his predecessor. At home, Polish underground units east
of the Curzon line cooperated with Russian troops. At the
end of such operations, however, the Russians demanded
that they either join the Soviet-commanded units or disband. Those who chose to disband were arrested or shot.

When the Red Army reached the line which Moscow
considered the future border, Stalin presented a Polish authority to take over the administration of reconquered
Polish lands. A committee, The National Committee of
Liberation, also called the Lublin Committee, was headed
by a left-wing Socialist lawyer. It would function as a government, and a supreme national council of delegates from
local councils would take the place of a legislative assembly.
Members were hand-picked, partly from Polish refugees in
Russia, and partly from pro-Soviet or opportunist elements
in Poland. The Soviet army called upon the Polish people
to support the Committee for the sake of brotherly cooperation in the future.

The hour of decision had struck for the London government, and particularly for the Home Army command.
At the end of July 1944, the Germans retreated over the
Vistula, hard pressed by the Russians who were approaching
the outskirts of Warsaw. The Germans gave the impression
of giving up the city, feverishly evacuating hospitals and

dismantling factories. But what appeared to be panic did not last long. Almost immediately, fresh Nazi troops marched in and began to fortify the town, and the commander issued orders that all people between the ages of 17 and 65 were to gather at designated points to participate in works for the defense of Warsaw. The Polish underground command advised the population not to obey the order. Instead, it ordered the Home Army to take up positions for a general uprising. But it was to have no contact with the Russians, for the uprising had a dual purpose. The' idea was to attack the Germans from the rear while they were fighting the Soviets, but at the same time to seize the city before Soviet troops could take possession and hand authority over to the Russian-sponsored committee.

Broadcasts of this committee kept calling on the people of Warsaw to rise as the Russians would soon enter. On August 1st, the commander of the Home Army issued the order to revolt. It took possession of the city except for its suburb on the other side of the Vistula. Half of the city remained in Polish hands during all of August. But the Russians suddenly halted their offensive. Whether they changed their plans because of heavy German reinforcements, or in order to frustrate the Home Army's scheme, is not certain. Perhaps their military plan was first to strike two bridgeheads over the Vistula south of the city, which they actually did, and to storm Warsaw afterwards. The facts are that fresh German panzer divisions repulsed a Soviet attack near Warsaw, while no Soviet fighter plane appeared over the city after the uprising began. Russian big guns stopped firing as 40,000 men of the underground were hurled into battle, but the latter were lost when the assumption that the Red Army offensive would proceed did not materialize. Though they remained entrenched in important sections, the Poles failed to wrest the critical strategic positions from the Nazis. Their equipment stood in no proportion to the formidable task they faced. The London government frantically urged the Allies to help, and they in turn forwarded the request to Stalin who alone could

give effective support to the insurrection. Stalin first denied that there was any uprising, later branded it as a foolish
and irresponsible action, and refused to have anything to
do with it.

As a frightful example to prevent uprisings in other
towns, Hitler ordered his S.S. men to destroy Warsaw and
its population, leaving the insurgents no alternative but to
fight to the finish. The British dispatched planes by night
from bases in Italy and England, manned mostly by Polish
crews, to parachute down supplies. But these usually fell
on German-held sections, and the loss of planes was serious.
Once a wing of American aircraft appeared in broad day-
light over Warsaw and at least lifted the morale of the
people.

The uprising lasted more than two months, with the insurgents slowly losing ground until they communicated
with each other only through the sewers. Toward the end,
however, the situation changed. The Germans recognized
the anti-Soviet aspect of the insurrection and planned to
capitalize on it. They suddenly accepted the status of
prisoners-of-war for those who were captured or surrendered. The Russians also changed their minds and
began to send supplies, probably to keep the men from giving up. It was too late. The 15,000 survivors of the Home
Army surrendered to the Germans on October 2. Losses,
especially among the civilian population, were stupendous,
and Warsaw itself was almost a total loss. A year before,
the Warsaw ghetto had been obliterated as the remainder
of the 400,000 Jews isolated there in 1940 went down in a
hopeless fight.

It is worth noting that Polish forces fighting with the
Red Army attempted to cross the river Vistula to join the
insurgents. They failed, suffering terrible hardships, and
their commander has not been heard of since.

While the Warsaw uprising raged full blast, the Premier
of the London government tried to negotiate an agreement
with Stalin. Stalin remained adamant with respect to the
frontiers, and Premier Mikolajczyk had no power to yield.

In December 1944, the Lublin Committee publicly announced that it had been transformed into a provisional government. On January 5, 1945, Stalin formally recognized it as such, in order to place an accomplished fact before the Yalta conference. Only after the Yalta conference, when reports from the homeland revealed that resignation and realism were getting the upper hand, was Mikolajczyk ready to break with the diehards in the government in exile. He and other members of his Peasant Party resigned their offices and put their trust in the committee of foreign ministers from the Big Three which had been assigned to assist in the reorganization of the Soviet-sponsored government into one of national unity.

The price of the Yalta agreement was ambiguity at all points where East and West had not actually come to agreement. To satisfy the Russians, the provisional government was to be the one (Stalin backed) active in Poland, reorganized on a broader democratic basis; but it also had to be a new government as the West insisted.

When the ministers began their discussions on the new set-up, the controversial interpretations revealed that the original disagreement had only been camouflaged in the text. Molotov would accept only propositions for additional members to the functioning government. This government would have the right to select from the names listed by the British and American ambassadors, and Molotov refused to allow other individuals and political groups to be consulted. The implementation of the agreement stumbled on this issue.

In reality, with every day following the Yalta conference the offensive on the Western front demonstrated a more irresistible sweep toward victory, and postwar considerations moved increasingly into the foreground in the minds of the Allied leaders. Churchill especially showed mounting signs of alarm over Russian penetration into central Europe. In his correspondence on the stalemate in the implementation of the Yalta agreement, he made it clear that the Polish issue had a broad significance. "Far more than Poland was involved," he wrote to Roosevelt. "This was the test case between us and the Russians of the meaning of such words as democracy, sovereignty, representative government, and free and unfettered elections. . . . Surely we must not be maneuvered into becoming parties to imposing on Poland—and how much more on Eastern Europe—the Russian version of democracy."

On the other hand, Stalin in a letter to Churchill wanted to reduce the issue to reasons of state. He reminded the British Prime Minister that the British had used naked force in installing a Greek government to their liking, and emphasized his understanding of the full significance of Greece (or Belgium) to the security of Great Britain. He did not know, Stalin wrote, whether a truly representative government had been set up in Greece, since the Soviet Union was not consulted and claimed no right of interference. Poland had the same importance for the security of Russia as Greece had for Britain.

The difficulties in coordinating the efforts of the Big Three to form a representative government in Poland had a depressing effect on the San Francisco conference of the United Nations. Both the government in exile in London and the one in Warsaw claimed the right to be invited. The dismal way out of the impasse seemed to be to rule that neither would be invited unless a government of national unity was formed.

Meanwhile, the Soviet Union achieved another *fait accompli* to insure that any future government should be friendly to her. In April 1945, Stalin and the head of the Warsaw government signed a Treaty of Friendship, Mutual Assistance, and Post War Collaboration. The salient point was that it obliged both parties not to sign a peace treaty with Germany that encroached on the territorial integrity or the security of either nation. This guaranteed Poland's new frontiers with Germany, in regard to which there was still no final agreement of the Big Three.

The San Francisco conference opened on April 25, 1945, without Poland's being represented—the nation which had been the victim of Hitler's aggression that had avalanched into a world war.

Roosevelt had died on April 12, 1945, and as a last attempt to resolve the situation, the new President, Harry Truman, sent Harry Hopkins on a mission to the Kremlin. Hopkins, a friend of the deceased President, was familiar with Roosevelt's feelings about Russia and collaboration with her after the war, and although gravely ill at the time, he undertook the journey. He told Stalin that the Russian attitude in the Polish case was about to alienate the section of the United States that had been for cooperation with Russia both in and after the war. He also emphasized that the issue was bigger than Poland, which served only as a symbol of the possibility or impossibility of collaboration. First Churchill and now Hopkins had raised Poland explicitly as a test case, a fact of which Stalin was well aware. The warning, from the man who had done most in order that Lend-Lease supplies should reach Russia rapidly and abundantly, made a strong impression on Stalin.

Hopkins sought some reassuring statement from Stalin to the effect that the countries in the Soviet orbit would not be Sovietized. The dictator indicated that they would follow the pattern of Western democracies, adding, however, that limitations would be necessary both during and after the war.

The question of future cooperation loomed large behind these long and patient discussions. Stalin had been given to understand that he could not expect American financial help for the reconstruction of his war-ravaged country to be extended with such abundance as during wartime. In January, 1945, he had opened the question of postwar credit, estimating that Russia would need about six billion dollars. His approach had been rebuffed by the Americans, who stated that so large a sum was not available. With a new President in office, the entire problem of collaboration might come up for revision at a time when common peacetime interests would have to take the place of common enemies.

Stalin and Hopkins reached agreement essentially on the basis of the Russian interpretation of the Yalta settlement. The committee of the three foreign ministers was to invite twelve Poles to consult on the formation of the provisional government. There were to be three from London (but not from the London government), five representative personalities from Poland, and four from the Warsaw government.

At the end of June, the invited Polish politicians came to an understanding with the Warsaw group on a reorganization of the Warsaw government, which was to be complemented with representatives of four parties: the Peasant, Socialist, Christian Labor, and Democratic. The Peasant Party carried by far the most weight, and the West succeeded in overcoming Moscow's opposition to its leader, Stanislaw Mikolajczyk, who had first, however, to make a declaration of his acceptance of the Yalta agreement with respect to Poland's eastern frontier.

The successful bridging of the gap between East and West over the Polish question dissipated the initial gloom that had hung over the San Francisco conference. It caused relief and joy in Poland. But the right-wing underground groups did not give up, especially since they already had nothing to lose. Their leaders had already been lured away by an invitation from alleged emissaries of Marshal Zhukov for consultation with him, but instead of the Marshal's headquarters, they found themselves in the Lubianka prison in Moscow. In a spectacular trial most of them were convicted of sabotage and guerilla warfare against the Soviet army. The court took cognizance of the disquiet the trial stirred in the West, and the sentence was lenient. A letter from the commander of the Home Army was read in the court in order to incriminate him. In it he had summed up the future prospects of Poland and evaluated the world situation, discarding any optimistic view of East-West relationships. His words threw light on the desperate state of mind of the historic classes in Poland, and also on the commander's perspicacity:

Until Japan is defeated, we cannot expect any improvement in our political situation. The Western world will try to obtain Russia's help in the struggle for the Far East, and will be inclined to make further concessions for this. Later they will see how much Soviet greed and power will become a menace . . . The Anglo-Saxons will have to mobilize all their forces in Europe to enable them to halt the Soviets. We shall probably even see some Germans there who will be under Anglo-Saxon command . . .

As soon as the Government of National Unity was established, it allayed fears of Communism by stating that the democratic constitution of 1921 would serve as a basis for the new regime, which intended to rely on all classes; only such a government could direct and inspire the reconstruction of the morally and materially disrupted country. The presence in the cabinet of Mikolajczyk vouched for this program. The public considered him the trustee of the West in testing whether the government would live up to the principles for which it claimed to stand. No party insisted more loudly than the Workers (Communist) Party on freedom, democracy, and a genuine Polish way of establishing them. To deny its class character the Party threw its doors open wide to people in all walks of life. But doubts still persisted.

The government program trimmed landed estates over 120 acres in the east and 240 in western Poland, and in a significant gesture exempted the estates of the Catholic Church from distribution. The long overdue reform had been realized at last, apportioning land to 387,000 families in lots from 2.4 to 12 acres each. In another move to relieve overpopulation, the government encouraged migration to the west to settle the territories vacated by the Germans. No wholesale socialization of industry was contemplated. Only German-owned factories came under state ownership; enterprises employing over fifty workers, and all those connected with transportation and banking, came under government supervision. Former owners were in-

vited to stay as directors. Commerce remained wholly unrestricted, and crafts were free.

But even if it had commanded the trust and wholehearted
cooperation of the people, the task the government faced
was formidable. As soon as the territory was liberated, the
one million men whom the Germans had herded into the
general government got on the move toward their former
homes. The population of Warsaw, which had dispersed
after the uprising, was returning, even though the city appeared so hopelessly devastated that the government first
hesitated as to whether or not to make Cracow, the king's
ancient residence, the capital city. But burning with patriotic zeal, the people of Warsaw insisted on rebuilding the
monuments of the past, holding high the symbols of the
continuity of their nation. The government fanned this
zeal for which there was no substitute in facing the tremendous work ahead.

Planned and voluntary migrations crisscrossed the country. One and a half million Poles were repatriated from
the territories ceded to Russia. About two million poured
back from Germany, on whatever vehicle they could get
hold of—mostly on their own two legs—from the army,
forced labor, concentration and prisoner-of-war camps. Another wave of migration swept Lithuanians, White Russians,
and Ukrainians from Poland into the Russian-held parts of
the former Poland. About half a million of them refused
to move into the Soviet Union; and when the Polish insisted
that they join their kinsmen beyond the border, many burnt
their houses, slaughtered cattle, banded together, and
turned into desperate, armed gangs. Polish peasants, re-
vengeful and hungry for the Ukrainians' land, were assisted
by local police in leading punitive expeditions against them.
More than two hundred thousand right-wing guerillas also
roamed about endangering life and property. They
swooped down on villages and towns, driven by bitter
hatred of Russians and Communists or simply by hunger.
It was only after the general amnesty in September, 1945,
that the desperadoes surrendered.

Fortunately, new land in the west, more civilized than any part of Poland, lay waiting for the uprooted millions. Poland lost to the Russians valuable forests, oil, natural gas, and potassium salts, but otherwise poor and marshy land; while she received from Germany huge coal deposits, zinc, lead ore, and large refining industries as well as a three-hundred-mile coastline on the Baltic Sea, with such great harbors as Danzig and Stettin. The new acquisition increased the country's industrial capacity by 94 per cent; coal production by 81 per cent; railroad network by 88 per cent; and electric energy by 85 per cent. In area Poland lost in the east 68,667 square miles, while in the west she gained 38,974 square miles.

As to the inhabitants, most of the Germans left voluntarily, but in 1946 there still remained two million of them to be repatriated. Three million Poles settled in their wake in 1947.

Although the Poles had taken actual possession of the land, legal title to it was still missing. This became a subject of the Potsdam conference in the summer of 1945. Stalin tried to get President Truman and Prime Minister Churchill to agree to the line of the Oder and Western Neisse rivers as Poland's western border, but they both refused to make a commitment before the peace conference with Germany. However, Stalin did succeed in getting their consent to handing over the administration of the disputed territory to the Poles. By that the three great powers sanctioned the accomplished fact. They also agreed on the transfer of the German population from the area. The Soviet Union alone guaranteed the western frontier of Poland, thereby gaining hold of such power as no Polish regime could disregard, whether Communist or not. But the last word had not been said. The Soviets might verbally oppose the return to Germany of the new Polish territory and let the West override its vote, or they might make clear that they would oppose it by force. So, insecurity could not entirely vanish from Poland, although Polish determination to fight—alone if need be—mitigated it. On the other hand, hope of recovering the lost land kept hovering over the Germans. Until the chips were down Russia held the trump card.

But the Polish Communists held a trump in the new territories. The prime minister was only a Socialist "fellow traveler," but the vice-premier was Wladislaw Gomulka, the Communist leader who had charge of the administration of "recovered" territory. The settlers there, according to his thinking, should become pro-Russian since the Soviet alone kept the Germans from retaking the land on which they had built a new life. The administrator who directed the settlements had a huge stock of patronage in store: poor or richly cultivated lands, war-torn or intact regions, fine buildings or shabby cottages. It was up to him to assign them to the many who expected a land of promise.

The Communists also retained other undisputed positions of power in the coalition cabinet. Apart from the Presidency, held by Boleslaw Bierut, a former printer who had been twice jailed by the prewar regime and was a trustee of Moscow, they had direct supervision over the police, the army, trade, shipping, and food. Moreover, they put the Party's brain trust in inconspicuous places, exerting power from behind the scenes, probably because some of the most influential were Jewish intellectuals such as Jakub Berman and Hilary Minc, the architect of the first Three-Year Economic Plan in 1946.

But the Party needed more than power. It must have popular support if for no other reason than to muster strength at the elections the government had promised to hold within a year—free and unfettered elections in exchange for recognition by the West.

The peasants mistrusted the Communists under any form or name. The country at large, although forced to acknowledge that the government, and specifically the Communists, had worked harder and more efficiently than any previous Polish government, considered them tools of Russia and as such hostile. A British journalist writing of his visit in Poland in 1946 stated that "Polish Communists give the impression of being Poles first and foremost, Communists only next, and pro-Russian last, sometimes not at all."

Only one group of Communists, headed by Gomulka, was trusted. They had fought in the underground and organized the local national councils practically under the noses of the German Gestapo. These councils had delegated to the first governing committee authority from the people. The public considered these men as Poles first and Communists afterward, in contrast to the Muscovites who marched into Poland behind the Red Army, and the Jews. A trickle of only about thirty thousand survived of the three million Jews, but anti-Semitism persisted and even spread to people who had not before been affected by it. This was perhaps because the public largely identified Moscow's henchmen with Jews; or perhaps the immense suffering the Germans and Russians had inflicted on the Poles on the pretense of liberating their kinsmen, the foreign national groups in Poland, had made them more suspicious of strangers than ever.

The government displayed great reverence for Polish traditions. Communists ostentatiously participated in the Corpus Christi processions. It also demonstrated its Polish patriotism when it successfully resisted Russian encroachment on Poland's economic independence in the agreement concerning reparations from Germany. It refused the Russian claim of a controlling interest in industries acquired by the Poles on former German territories. In this instance the Russians bowed before the show of Polish independence, as they were no less anxious than the Polish Communists that the government increase its popularity in the country. The agreement turned out satisfactorily for the Poles. They were to receive 15 per cent of the reparations due the Soviets from Eastern Germany and 30 per cent of those delivered to the Soviets from the occupied parts of Western Germany. However, they were to repay to Russia with Polish goods one half of the West German reparations.

Coal especially was high on the list. It was a most precious item in the postwar years. The price set on this commodity clearly showed the economic and financial pattern of Soviet empire building. The price of $1.25 per ton, which Russia was charged, was hardly more than 10 per cent of what Sweden was offering in August, 1945 at the time the agreement was signed.

The Communists had great trouble with the industrial workers, although socialism was a deep tradition in the ranks. This was most embarrassing, for they had intended to rely on their support. After the liberation, workers' councils spontaneously took over the management of factories, opposing government direction and ownership. Factory elections for the councils turned against the favorites of the Communists and government Socialists. The organized workers stood for the old Socialist leaders who had returned from concentration camps, instead of those who had been travelling along with the Communists in Russian-sponsored committees and governments.

Frantic efforts were made by the Communists first to neutralize, then to eliminate the influence of democratic Socialist leaders on the workers and their unions. The gray Socialist leader, Zygmunt Zulawski, attempted to make an agreement with government Socialists but was rebuffed. He then decided to found a new party, but he was made to understand that no new party would be allowed to organize. Weighty arguments eventually persuaded the genuine Socialist leaders to join the government. Their help was needed in order that a government friendly to Russia be returned by the elections, for if the results aroused mistrust in the Soviet Union it might be the end of Poland. Also, it was possible that reactionaries might win a majority and undermine the great social reforms which alone could regenerate the country.

Seemingly more dangerous than the Socialists was Mikolajczyk's Peasant Party, but actually it presented a lesser threat because it could more easily be placed in a light hostile to the democratic order and so eliminated.

Mikolajczyk felt strong and safe, knowing that the masses of the peasantry stood behind him. He was willing to have his party merge with the peasant faction in the government, but rejected the conditions which were put on cooperation. The government wanted all coalition parties to go into the elections on the same list while the proportions of the seats each party was to receive would be agreed upon beforehand. Mikolajczyk demanded 75 per cent of the representatives elected on the coalition list. This was a preposterous demand unless he intended to run the next government alone. But Mikolajczyk could not realize such extravagant plans so long as Russian troops were in the country. He may have laid down such an unacceptable condition because he did not want to run on a government list, or it is possible that he trusted too much that the West would put teeth into their insistence on free elections and hoped to head a government that issued from such elections. He was, of course, aware of the source of his popularity, which was expanding beyond the confines of the peasantry. The old conservatives and pro-Pilsudski parties, not allowed candidates, flocked to his banner, and he did not decline the support of even the die-hards of the underground, so bent was he upon getting an overwhelming vote.

The government, thinking it had found a way of evading the obligation to hold elections within a year from the Potsdam conference, decided to hold a plebiscite instead. The questions selected were such as to make it impossible for the majority to answer in the negative. "Yes" or "No" was expected on the following: "Do you want the abolition of the Senate? Land reform? Nationalization of the large enterprises? The western frontiers of Poland as actually administered by Poland on the basis of the Potsdam agreement?"

However, Mikolajczyk was no less ingenious. He discovered how to show the extent of popular support for himself even within the restricted framework of the plebiscite. He advised the voters to answer the first question with "No." His supporters must have known that he and his

party had always advocated the abolition of the undemo-
cratic Senate. Consequently Mikolajczyk trusted that they
would grasp the fact that his suggestion to vote against his
own old demands served only as an opportunity for the
public to demonstrate its disapproval of the government.

The plebiscite took place on June 30, 1946. Its true results probably confirmed the broad support of the people
for Mikolajczyk. However, when it was made public it
failed to show this. In any case the West refused to accept
the plebiscite as a substitute for elections.

The times were gone when Soviet-Polish relations could
be settled on the strength of a local war, as in 1921. Secret
agreement between Poland's two powerful neighbors could
no longer regulate them, as in 1939. Nor could they be
examined now from the point of view of the continental and
European balance of power. Since Japan's "Greater East-
Asian Coprosperity Sphere" was to disappear, the huge
area of the Pacific and Far East entered into consideration
whenever Soviet-American understanding was needed on
any issue. America had laid great stress on the war in the
Pacific being pre-eminently her own war. This gave her
the main responsibility for the problems that were expected
to arise from the chaos which the collapse of colonialism
and Japanese conquest would leave behind, and which
would engulf lands in all oceans and many seas.

A strong, pro-Soviet government in Poland had become
the immediate concern of Stalin as East-West relations
rapidly deteriorated. This process can be dated from the
dropping of the first atomic bomb on Hiroshima on August
6, 1945. President Truman had been informed of the success of an experimental detonation on July 16, 1945, while
he was at the conference in Potsdam. He intimated to
Churchill the content of the message and eventually communicated it to Stalin. The Soviet dictator showed no surprise. He may have known of the progress of atomic re-

search in America from less official sources. But the fact
that the bomb was dropped after the Japanese had asked
Stalin to intervene for peace with America made it appear
that the epoch-making show of the new weapon might not
have been staged for Japan alone. It revealed to the world
America's freshly won power superiority. A few days more
and Japan would have sued for peace, giving no opportunity
for the demonstration which may have been made more for
the benefit of Stalin's attention than anyone else's.

No one could spell out the power situation with more
clarity and authority than the heads of the two remaining
great nations that emerged from the vast no-man's-land
into which most of the earth had been thrown, each greater
than ever before in global influence and ambition. When
the blinding light shot up from Hiroshima and the huge
mushroom cloud formed over the city's ruins, Stalin explained to the Soviet people his declaration of war on Japan:

Henceforth Sakhalin and the Kurile Islands will serve as a defense
base against Japanese aggression. . . . From now on, we may consider our country safe from the threat of German invasion on the
west, and from Japanese invasion from the east.

And later he added: "Our motherland has been transformed
from a backward country into a world power."

President Truman, at the other end of the victorious war
front, stated:

America has emerged from the war as the most powerful nation in
the world . . . A society of self-governing men is more powerful,
more enduring, more creative than any other kind of society, however disciplined and however centralized.

In the field of world power relationships a perilous polarization took place after the first atomic bomb. In 1946,
however, a tenuous balance kept the peace. The sole possession of the atomic weapon put America in the position
of being able to destroy Moscow, the center of political
power and one of the most important industrial and transportation hubs in the Soviet Union. At the same time, the
makers of foreign and military policies knew that at the first
sign of atomic attack the Soviet army would invade the Con-

tinent. In order to defeat it, America would have to destroy West Germany, France, Belgium, and Scandinavia.

In this situation cooperation between the two powers should have been imperative so as to insure sheer survival, and yet to put all stakes on it was suicidal. While the Americans, in October, 1946, invited the Russians to discuss the Lend-Lease settlement, Stalin declared to the *Manchester Guardian* that he still wanted an American loan with no strings to it. The American answer was that such a loan must be part of a general economic settlement. Collaboration was still not ruled out, but both powers began working hard to strengthen their positions so as to tip the scales in their favor.

In the final phase of operations against Japan, the U.S. military made it plain that it considered the Pacific theater an American affair, and gave even face-saving credit to the British and other allies reluctantly. After the Japanese surrendered on August 10, 1945, President Truman briskly served notice that the United States was free from war-time ties and would now make a foreign policy of her own. On August 21, he announced the end of Lend-Lease without previous negotiations with Britain and Russia. Even supplies already in process of delivery were supposed to be renegotiated on the basis of being paid for. The blow hit Britain catastrophically and Russia painfully—more by its significance than by immediate effect, the more so because Stalin had applied in the same month to the Foreign Economic Administration for a sharply reduced loan of a billion dollars and had received no acknowledgment of the request. True, the agency was dissolved soon after the application arrived and its records were transferred to the State Department, but neither the agency nor later the State Department appeared to be eager to come to a decision on it. Not until February, 1946, when negotiations on the settlement of Lend-Lease debts began, was it uncovered. The State Department wanted to treat the question of the loan within the framework of the foreign economic policy of Soviet Russia, as it did with respect to Great Britain.

The Department succeeded in bringing pressure to bear on Britain to promise the loosening of imperial preferences that had hampered the flow of American goods to the British Empire. Obviously, the intention was to induce Russia, which had tied the Eastern European countries to itself by preferential treaties, to do the same. But Stalin refused to accept loans with strings attached, and the United States saw no reason why the Soviets should merit more consideration than Britain.

Both Britain and Russia believed that America would have to associate with either one or the other—depending on what line she decided to follow in her postwar foreign policy—and both tried to bring her to their side. Stalin cautioned America on allying herself with Britain. On April 4, 1946, he told an American newspaperman that it appeared to him as if the United States had definitely aligned herself with Great Britain against the Soviet Union. For home consumption in Russia a propaganda campaign was set in motion to tear down sympathy with former Western allies. Molotov stated that one could not be a real Soviet citizen unless he rid himself of the "obsequious worship of the West, of capitalist culture." The Communist Party underwent a postwar purge of those suspected of leaning toward the West, and great military leaders vanished from the columns of newspapers and from public view. The Party began reasserting its power and control in the old way. The announcement of the new Three-Year Plan served as an opportunity to deprecate the capitalist system as containing in itself the elements of general crisis and war.

At the same time, Churchill, now out of office, took it on himself to wake the American statesmen and public to a realization of the dangers of a Russian and Communist expansion to the West. He went so far as to appeal directly to the American public to face the danger in all its frightfulness. On March 5, 1946, at Fulton, Missouri, President Truman stood by while the British war leader sounded the tocsin.

Both Stalin and Churchill underestimated America's potentialities as a world power. Just as few people would
have believed before the war that America's productive
capacity would be of such fantastic proportions as to supply
her own war needs, furnish the allies with equipment and
food, and at the same time produce plenty for home use,
so time was now needed before the new American ambition
to go it alone in world affairs could unfold, be understood,
and acted upon. Actually, her postwar foreign policy
turned with more caution but no less determination against
the British Empire than against the Soviet Union. It was
not motivated by hostility or a feeling of inferiority where
the British were concerned, but by the fact that in almost all
parts of the world an independent American foreign policy
bumped against British vested interests. In the Pacific, a
military alliance with Australia and New Zealand was of the
first order, but the tie of the two dominions with Britain
would have involved such colonial positions as Hong Kong
and Malaya. America's support of Britain would have
paralyzed America's efforts at leadership of the colonial
peoples. Even on the American continent, Canada would
be no part of the Pan-American Union on account of her
British ties, nor, for this reason, did the United States wish
her there. In the Middle East Britain also stood in the way
of an American policy. Churchill's anti-Soviet campaign
therefore had a rather mixed reception. Uncertainty and
hesitation characterized the attitude of both America and
Russia as the wartime alliance began to disintegrate.

In view of this international situation, Stalin summoned
the Polish Communist and Socialist leaders to the Kremlin.
He resolved to thin the face-saving devices into transpar-
ency rather than to tolerate an anti-Soviet majority in the
election. First of all, the Socialists who were dissatisfied
with their positions in the government had to be prevented
from joining Mikolajczyk and his Peasant Party—a possibility that Mikolajczyk himself had discarded when the Socialists made overtures for this purpose. He may have lost
his diplomacy as it became more and more evident that his

party would not be allowed to assume a legal position corresponding with his strength—or he may have had exaggerated information as to the deterioration of relations between Russia and the West and thought a showdown to be in the offing.

The public read significance into Mikolajczyk's intransigence as a true reflection of East-West relations. In Stalin's presence, the Polish Communists and Socialists negotiated an agreement on a stronger representation of the Socialists in the government and on the independent future status of their party. The agreement aimed at a common Communist-Socialist front against Mikolajczyk's party, which decided to run independently in the elections. The date for balloting was set for January, 1947. It was too late.

The government had missed its chance to receive support when it failed to hold elections in 1945. At that time the vast majority of the population was permeated with the desire to break with the past and to accept the friendship of Russia. The Russian-supported coalition government had showed much unexpected understanding for Polish idiosyncrasies, and had courted national feelings, anxious to gain the sympathies of wide social groups outside the industrial workers. And the response had been favorable. The Communists may have felt that they needed more time in which to entrench themselves in the hearts of the public through moderation, through showing their efficiency in tackling the huge tasks of reconstruction and resettlement. But time used up sympathy, and as the Communists tried, through infiltration and camouflage, to bend the institutions to their purposes, the public became suspicious of their sincerity and concerned over its freedom. The people resented partisanship in the distribution of UNRRA aid, which amounted to almost half a billion dollars and made the difference between starvation and muddling through the difficulties of a new beginning. The economic policies of the government hurt many interests, and favoritism in the distribution of newly attached lands caused bitterness.

Open dissatisfaction was also caused by the cooling off of the East-West alliance. People started to wonder whether their resignation to Russian dominance and Communist rule had not been precipitate, and hope began to germinate that Russia would have to yield to the West and loosen her hold on the country.

The Stalin-forged Communist-Socialist party replaced the Socialist Prime Minister, who appeared to the public to be a respectfully but cleverly handled instrument of the Communists, with another Socialist, Joseph Cyrankiewicz, known to the public from the days of the underground. Cyrankiewicz had returned from the concentration camp in Auschwitz. He came from an upper-middle-class family, had great charm, intelligence, and political acumen. He took a stand for a common front against reaction right after his return.

The reinforced government set to work systematically to destroy Mikolajczyk and his party before the elections. The election lists of his party were disqualified in those electoral districts where he had the strongest following. Police raided Peasant Party centers and arrested its prominent members. Others were brought to trial to prove that the party had connections with the right wing and the anti-Russian underground, and its press received a sharply reduced allocation of paper during the election campaign. An incident came in handy to brand Mikolajczyk's well-known connections with the Americans—a crime bordering on treason. James F. Byrnes, United States Secretary of State, made a speech in Stuttgart in which he emphasized the fact that the Polish borders toward Germany had not been finally settled. He might have promoted German sympathy for America by making this statement, but he dealt a serious blow to Mikolajczyk. On the question of western borders no difference of opinion existed in Poland. Right and Left, Communist and anti-Communist considered them unalterable and the territory enclosed as rightful compensation for the lost provinces, for the brutal devastation by the Germans of Polish life, property, and

national and cultural treasures. The Poles also protested—
and history supports them—that the reconquered territory
had once been their ancestral abode before the Germanic
"Drang" pushed their forefathers to the east. Byrnes'
speech put Mikolajczyk's favor with the Americans in a
disreputable light before the Polish public.

Organized violence marred the Peasant Party's meetings
and drove Mikolajczyk to lodge a protest with the governments of the Big Three who had guaranteed free elections
under the provisional government. The American government dispatched a note to the two other partners in the
Yalta agreement, warning that if the Polish elections were
not free and unfettered, as its information on the campaign
foreboded, the Polish government would violate an international obligation. The note invited the other two governments to join the United States in its warning to the
Poles. Stalin, in his reply, strongly defended the Polish
government. He charged that the information referred to
by the Americans originated in bandit underground circles.
The Polish government, he wrote, was entitled to take
measures against bandits, even if some of them belonged to
Mikolajczyk's party. The Soviet dictator thus made clear
to the Polish public that no matter how the West protested,
the elections would stand as the government maneuvered
them. The result was a foregone conclusion. The government "Democratic Bloc" received 80.1 per cent of the votes
—Mikolajczyk's party polled 10.3 per cent.

At the first session of the Sejm, the Socialist leader,
Zygmunt Zulawski, rose to protest against the elections.
They could not be called elections, he said, but organized
violence on the electors and on their consciences. The
Communist answer to his protest revealed the abyss between democratic socialism and Communism. It stated:
"History is being made by great social movements which
have the courage to destroy obstacles if the interest of the
nation and of progress demand it. Politically, we had no
right to lose the elections."

CHAPTER TWO

Rumania

On October 9, 1944, Churchill arrived in Moscow for an urgent "meeting of minds" with Stalin.

British troops had landed in Greece to insure order in the wake of the retreating Nazis. Two resistance groups ruled the country, each administering the parts under its sway—most of the left wing being led by Communists. The British brought the two groups under the same roof in a "government of national unity," gave it authority, and prevented Left and Right from clashing in civil war. But the leftist resistance and the right-wing guerilla forces accepted temporary unity only in order to take part in the control of the distribution of emergency supplies the British were unloading for the famine-threatened population. Both groups watched jealously that this aid should not favor the rival territory.

Greece was the Balkan country at war whose rugged shores reached into the Eastern Mediterranean, a zone of vital interest for Britain. The impoverished country seethed with hatred of the king and the dictatorship he cloaked under royal authority. The people held him responsible for the hardships of foreign occupation and war, and the great majority supported the left-wing resistance. If left alone, the Greeks would have set up a pro-Communist government, but Churchill was not inclined to tolerate a Soviet outpost which would place British Middle East interests in jeopardy. Stalin alone, he thought, was able to impose

moderation on the Greek left wing. But the intervention of
the Soviet dictator had to be part of a more comprehensive
delineation of interests between the Allies. The Soviet
army at that time was linked with Jugoslav forces, liberating all Jugoslavia, and other powerful Russian divisions
were crossing the frontiers of Hungary. In the north,
Soviet troops had reached the Baltic coast. Yet the Western
Allies still fought at the Siegfried line.

The fear which Churchill had conveyed to the House of
Commons two years before now became his immediate concern: "It would be a measureless disaster if Russian barbarism were to overlay the culture and independence of the
ancient states of Europe." Greece, preserving the strains of
a glorious past, was certainly an ancient state, and was
certainly in great danger. Churchill realized he was asking
a large favor of the Soviet dictator, but he was ready to pay
the price.

He found the Russian in a businesslike mood. This encouraged him to make a straight offer. The merchandise
was "predominance," and concerned five Eastern European
countries. He wrote it down on a slip of paper. Russia's
90 per cent influence in Rumania was to offset Britain's 90
per cent in Greece. Stalin's free hand in Bulgaria was to
be limited by a 25 per cent presence of the West. In Jugoslavia and Hungary, East and West would share and share
alike.

Churchill passed the slip across the table. Stalin checked
the items with a blue pencil, then pushed it back. It lay half
way between the two statesmen, and a long silence followed. Both understood that the matter was too delicate
to give it even a minimum of publicity and that facts, not
written words, would confirm its validity.

Churchill offered to burn the paper but Stalin insisted
that he keep it. An unexpected thing made the Britisher
uneasy. Stalin did not haggle, and the Prime Minister
wondered whether he had not oversold. He also began to
have remorseful qualms for the "rather cynical" way in

which they seemed to have disposed of "issues so fateful to millions of people."

A few months before, in May, he had initiated a similar agreement and tried to get American consent to it, but the State Department had protested against spheres of interest in any guise. President Roosevelt would have condoned Churchill's proposal only as a matter of military expediency and valid only for a trial period of three months. "We must be careful," the President wrote, "to make it clear that we are not establishing any postwar spheres of influence." Stalin would not proceed in the negotiations under such restrictions.

Now Churchill made no reservations and Stalin put no questions. Churchill sent a cable to the President, hinted at the agreement, and promised a report. He failed to send it. But he wrote a report to the British War Cabinet, a remarkably insincere one, qualifying the agreement as a guide that expressed the "interest and sentiment" of the two governments, in no way committing the United States. He also wrote Stalin a long letter in which he tried to put the agreement in the light of a temporary measure to guide military operations, a replica, as it were, of the understanding he had proposed in the spring. However, he did not mail the letter.

But Churchill felt that he was in the right although others lacked the insight to appreciate his motives. A couple of years later, when America risked war rather than tolerate the Communists' taking over Greece, he had his satisfaction.

The prime minister made prompt use of the agreement. He had the British army prevent the popular front and its Communist-led forces from seizing power in Greece. Indignation welled up in Britain and in the United States at his flagrant breach of the Atlantic Charter. But he noted that Stalin "adhered strictly and faithfully" to the agreement. While British troops fought in the streets of Athens "not a word of reproach came from *Pravda* and *Izvestia*."

Events in Rumania would show how far Stalin was able to turn the agreement to his own advantage.

The ruins of two bridges over the lower Danube still testify to the one-time presence and power of the Romans in what is now Rumania. Over those bridges marched the Roman legions of Emperor Trajan in the second century A.D., to defeat the Dacians, who formed a kingdom in the territory now called Transylvania (beyond the forest), north and west of the Carpathians. The Dacians may have been a branch of the Indo-European Thracians, the oldest known inhabitants of the Eastern Balkan region and beyond.

Emperor Trajan settled his legions in Transylvania and ended the centuries-old harassment of the Roman Empire's frontier on the Danube. After more than a century and a half, the Emperor Aurelian withdrew the outposts of the empire before barbarian invasions.

The Dacians, Romanized by the legions, may have stayed behind in Transylvania and become the ancestors of the Rumanians. Through slow migrations, Slav tribes moved into the lowlands and hilly pastures south of the Carpathians and mingled with the natives. They adopted Eastern Christianity and the Slav liturgy from the Bulgars, one of the Slavic peoples who, in the ninth century, ruled over most of the Balkans.

Many Rumanians probably fled into the Carpathians from the dark waves of migration from Central Asia. Huns, Avars, Bulgars, Magyars, Cumanians, Petchenegs followed each other until, in the thirteenth century, the Mongolians were the last. Thereafter, the Rumanians may have descended the slopes and populated the two provinces of Wallachia, south of the Carpathians, and Moldavia, east of the mountains.

But a new Asiatic conqueror, the Ottoman Turks, entered Europe in the fourteenth century and remained for a long, long time a menace to the entire Christian world. Within two centuries, they had occupied the Balkans, captured Byzantium, and defeated the Hungarians.

The two Rumanian principalities were saved from occupation by offering tribute to the Sultan. But they fell into the devious web of the Byzantine Greeks who first took hold of the administration of Christian churches in the Balkans, then all commerce, and eventually the nonmilitary government of the Turkish Empire. The Sultan was the sole source of power, which he exercised through his Christian slaves. Since no Muslim could be a slave, the Sultan needed Christians to man the offices. A Greek patriarch, invested with spiritual authority over all Christians, set up headquarters in the Phanar district of Constantinople. He paid the Sultan for the investiture, but took care to be richly compensated by offering the bishoprics for sale. Monasteries mushroomed in the occupied lands and capitalized on their connections with the patriarch in Constantinople, the latter in turn profiting from his influence with the Greek administrators in the Sultan's court. Greek merchants farmed out the taxes, paying heavily for the commission, but getting a free hand to set the rates and make the collections. They cared nothing for justice but accepted bribes the fast and easy way.

This system ate into the two Rumanian provinces even though they did not come under Turkish military rule. Each had its prince elected by the big landowners, called "boyars," but the elections had to be approved by the Sultan. To win approval, the elected man had to bribe the Greek dragoman. To increase the source of money, the term of office was shortened from life to various receding periods. The princes levied the expense of being elected, plus their own due, on the boyars, and ultimately the bribes and dues fell on the serfs. The serfs also paid a head-tax to the Sultan for freedom to pray for salvation in the next world. This all-permeating corruption was not to vanish with foreign domination. When Rumania later became independent it imbedded itself in the system of administration. The citizen paid a fee to the official for each and every action. The rate of the bribe was known, accepted by the public and tolerated by the authorities.

The situation further deteriorated in the eighteenth century when Russia and Austria began to roll back Turkish power. The Sultan, fearing that the Rumanian princes would eventually conspire with his enemies, decided to play safe. His Greek advisers knew what to suggest. The Sultan should abolish the election of native princes and appoint reliable Greeks to the high offices instead. The Greek princes, coming from the Phanar district of Constantinople, were known as Phanariots. Greek became the language of the Rumanian princely courts, replacing the Slavic of church liturgy. Rich Greeks of the princely suite intermarried with boyars, and these Grecized boyars became the ruling class in the two Rumanian provinces.

Tsarist Russia put an end to the Phanariot rule in 1829. She compelled the Sultan to restore the right of the boyars to elect a prince for life. In a single century Moldavia alone had seen forty-one princes on her throne. After the accession of Peter the Great, Russia launched ever new campaigns against the Turks to wrest the Balkans from their grip, to capture Constantinople, and resurrect it as the capital of Eastern Christianity, the tsar to become the successor to Roman emperors.

Fortunately for Rumania, the European powers combined to restrain Russian ambitions. While the tsar was turning the provinces into a thoroughfare for his campaigns, and Russian commanders ruled them as vassals, the French and the British defeated him in the Crimean War, and the Peace of Paris in 1856 declared that the concert of all European powers was to exercise a protectorate over Moldavia and Wallachia. It ordered elections, the results of which caused general consternation. Both Wallachian and Moldavian boyars elected one and the same person, Alexander Ion Cuza, as prince. By this act, the two provinces fused into a single country, called Rumania. The West bestowed an increasing measure of independence on Rumania, rescuing her from falling prey to Russian imperialism.

In 1866, this prince abdicated. Rumanian statesmen decided to ask the mentor of their country, Napoleon III, to recommend some member of foreign royalty in order to begin a hereditary monarchy. He suggested a German,

Charles of Hohenzollern-Sigmaringen, who noted in his diary after a survey of the land and its people: "Rumania has links with three great powers—that of race with France, of religion with Russia, of family with Prussia, but the latter concerns the prince only."

The former Prussian officer devoted himself to organizing and equipping an army, and in 1873 joined with Russia in war against the Turks, being given command over Russian troops as well. The war ended in the Treaty of San Stefano and the complete independence of Rumania. Three years later, as Carol I, he was crowned her king.

Carol tied the country's fate to Germany, but not because of family sympathies. Fear of Russia overrode all considerations so that his approaching Germany for a military alliance against Russia found approval with his strongly pro-French prime minister. But the Germans advised the king that he first negotiate with Austria, their ally, who was more directly involved in Balkan affairs than the Reich. If an alliance with Germany would antagonize the francophile upper class and intelligentsia, a military pact with Austria would insult all articulate opinion in Rumania. Austria had given the Hungarians a free hand to magyarize the Rumanian population in the Hungarian province of Transylvania by trickery and force, and this policy was followed with excited revulsion by the public in Rumania. Poets on both sides of the Carpathians dreamed of the unity of all Rumanians, but unity would have presupposed dismemberment of the Hapsburg Empire which was seen to be neither feasible nor desirable at that time. Nevertheless, they would not go so far as to approve an alliance with a country hostile to national ambitions.

In 1883, the king concluded the alliance with Austria and Germany. But he dared not make the obnoxious treaty public, and except for a select few, he kept it secret even from his cabinet. The sole copy was retained in his possession, hidden in the private safe of his summer residence in the Carpathians. The treaty was the best kept secret of the era.

World War I broke out in 1914, but Rumania failed to honor her word in the secret alliance. The public was strong for the Western powers but jittery about their Russian ally. Victory would enhance Russia's ambitions in the Balkans, and the road led through Rumania. Rumania remained neutral. However, the country was too rich in oil and food for Germany not to channel them into her war effort and for the Allies not to do everything possible to deny the Germans access to these resources. Hence, Rumania's chances for remaining neutral lessened to the vanishing point as the war dragged on. Secret offers poured in to the king and his advisers from both camps. But the West had an irresistible asset in promising the whole of Transylvania from the Hapsburg Empire, which was to be dismembered. In 1916, Russia forced Rumania by an ultimatum to enter the war against Germany and Austria, and soon afterward the Germans occupied almost the entire country including the capital, Bucharest. In 1918, Rumania concluded a peace treaty with Germany, but by then Russia, in the throes of revolution, had ceased to present a military threat. Rumania received Bessarabia from Russian possession and alertly waited for the collapse of the Central Powers to re-enter the war on the side of the West and be present at the distribution of spoils.

The wildest dreams of the Rumanians came true. The peace treaties doubled her territory to 118,000 square miles with a population in 1919 of 15,500,000. To the "old kingdom" was added Transylvania; the plains of Crisana between Transylvania and the reduced Hungary; the wooded Maramures that connected the now Greater Rumania with her future ally, Czechoslovakia; the eastern part of the Banat in the south of former Hungary, one of the most fertile lands in Europe and with considerable manufacturing around the old city of Timisoara; Northern Dobrudja and Bessarabia with their great ports; and the Black Sea harbor of Constanza.

Greater Rumania now possessed huge fertile plains, hilly grazing lands, oil wells producing five to eight million tons

yearly, immense forests in the Carpathians, one of the
largest deposits in the world of methane gas (in Transylvania), gigantic water-power resources, and a dazzling
variety of races.

Rumanian national consciousness dawned in the eighteenth century, and strangely enough, not in the old provinces but in Transylvania, which was divided from them by
the Carpathians. The Magyars conquered the land in the
eleventh century. Their kings granted the privilege of
nobility to a Hungarian tribe called "Szeklers" who were
entrusted with frontier guard duties, and the privilege of
self-government to German colonists called "Saxons" who
tilled the soil, founded towns reminiscent of their ancient
homes, and formed a prosperous enclave preserving the
German language, traditions, and customs.

The books of law did not even take notice of the presence of Rumanians, although they probably kept increasing
to the extent of outnumbering the Magyars, Saxons, and
Szeklers. "There is no race," a French geographer wrote,
"that would be able to spread as vehemently as the Rumanians. All power of a conquering army cannot match
the accomplishment of a little colony of Rumanians in national conquest by slowly but surely Rumanizing the environment." Perhaps they were numerous, but they were
serfs who had no status or nationality. When the Turks defeated the Magyars in 1526 at Mohacs and occupied the
great Hungarian plain, they did not bother to conquer the
mountain-enclosed Transylvania. It became an independent principality, keeping a tenuous balance between the
Sultan and the Hapsburgs, playing a skillful game of foreign
policy under Gabriel Bethlen in that European civil strife
known as the Thirty Years' War. Transylvania had a
tumultuous time in the century and a half of her independence, but she never failed to be an active agent in European
history.

Her social and political systems were peculiar. A terrible peasant uprising almost swept away feudalism and privileges in 1437. When the Magyar landlords finally prevailed they entered into a union of mutual assistance with the privileged Saxons and Szeklers. The union of "three nations" tied them "against the Turks and peasants, against despot and social disorder in fidelity to the kings of Hungary."

Transylvania was first in the world to declare religious freedom for the Hungarians who were Calvinists and Unitarians; the Szeklers who remained true to the Catholic church; and the Saxons who turned Lutheran at the Reformation. The Rumanians and their Greek Orthodox religion received no recognition. Their priests remained in serfdom as did they themselves.

When the Hapsburgs reconquered Hungary from the Turks in the seventeenth century they did not reunite Transylvania with Hungary but ruled it as a province of the crown. On the advice of the Jesuits, they offered the Rumanians recognition of their church, and its clergy freedom from serfdom, if the church would accept the Pope as its head. The clergy would be allowed to preserve their beards and marry as before, the language of the liturgy would remain Greek so that the flock should see no change at all, yet they would become free at least in the spiritual field. The clergy accepted, and with it the majority of Rumanians became "Uniates" in 1698.

This first breeze of freedom wafted in some unforeseen cultural developments. A newly founded Uniate seminary sent its best students to Rome. Sightseeing in the Eternal City, the young Rumanians stopped at Trajan's Column, erected in commemoration of the emperor's victory over the Dacians. On its spiraling bas-reliefs, they saw the Dacian dignitaries and common men and recognized their ancestors. Despised back home for their nationality, they realized that they were descended from an ancient people who had been ennobled by intermingling with Roman conquerors. In touch with the Italians and studying Latin, they discovered proofs of their affinity in the Rumanian language, which remained Latin underneath the Slav and Asian surface and the Cyrillic alphabet. Their find started a fever of re-Latinization in spirit and letters at home and led to the cult of a romantically distorted past in literature and historiography.

National consciousness slowly percolated from Transylvania through the passes of the Carpathians into the two Turkish vassal Rumanian states, but it received real impetus only when Austrian pressure on the Turks opened the vista toward the West. The Rumanians now looked to the French for inspiration and help—the greatest "Latin brother." The sons of boyars went to Paris to study, returned with broad liberal ideas, and found their country in dismal backwardness in comparison. French political ideas permeated the young people, and French displaced Greek in society, becoming the second, and often the first, language in the boyar families.

The revolution of 1848 in Paris evoked instant response in Bucharest. Liberal youth declared for a Rumanian republic, but they neither trusted the peasants nor were they trusted by them. Russian and Turkish armies quickly put out the flame.

However, the Rumanians beyond the Carpathians in Transylvania, in a powerful popular and national uprising, turned against the fire of revolution which had inflamed the youth in Hungary in March, 1848. The Hungarians had imposed on the Diet a liberal constitution abolishing serfdom and privileges at a single stroke. It also declared the union of Hungary with Transylvania. At the first shock of revolution flaring up in Vienna, Prague, and Budapest the Emperor yielded to the Hungarians, but after the risings subsided elsewhere he went back on his concessions and decided to quell the Hungarian revolt by force of arms. He appealed to his Rumanian subjects to turn against the Magyars and promised them full freedom as a nation. The Rumanians gave more credence to the Emperor's word than to the liberal legislation of the Hungarian revolutionary assembly and joined the imperial armies against it.

Nor did the Emperor keep his word after defeating the Hungarians with the humiliating assistance of the Russian Tsar. In 1867, he came to an agreement with the Hungarians and delivered the Rumanians to a frenzy of Magyarization. From kindergarten up the state-supported schools became instruments for turning Rumanian children Magyar. The use of their native language was restricted to the parochial schools, but even these came under Magyar attack. At the beginning of the present century only four secondary schools were left for three million Rumanians.

The law restricted the ballot to those having a certain amount of property. Most Rumanians being poor peasants, they did not have the right of franchise. The few who did were frightened away from supporting the Rumanian National Party, since the ballot was not secret. At one time only seven deputies represented in Parliament all the non-Magyar nationals, the majority of the population. Though but a handful, the Rumanian deputies dared a storm of contempt and derision to protest against Magyarization. Juliu Maniu, attorney for the Uniate church, was the leader of the protest, though it appeared to be lost in a desert of hopelessness.

Meanwhile, the Kingdom of Rumania established the institutions of modern statehood; the constitution of 1866 provided for a Parliament. Actually, a royal clique ruled autocratically excluding the immense majority of the population from the right of having its say in the government. The constitution remained a dead letter by tradition. But the country experienced its first development of modern industries and railroad communications, and the Conservative Party had to yield to the Liberals. These were recruited from the sons of the boyars who followed the course of French intellectual and political life with emotional intensity. Graduates of French universities, whose fathers had carried home the torch of liberty, equality, and fraternity, now observed how a plutocracy developed in France from the rise of the middle class to power and property. They applied their French experiences to Rumania, entered politics as Liberals, and steered legislation to help an influential and enterprising group to accumulate capital. Prohibitive tariffs, direct subsidies, tax exemptions, and compulsory participation of Rumanians in foreign business ventures made the government an instrument of practically risk-free private monopolies held by a very small upper-middle class of lesser boyars who founded and controlled banks and financed industrial enterprises. Several generations of the Bratianu family led Rumania with only short interruptions through her adolescence and growth. In very close cooperation with Queen Mary, a lady of majestic beauty and brilliant intelligence, they identified the expansion and strength of Greater Rumania with that of a powerful group around the royal court.

Liberal ideas of political reform originated with Western influence. However, impulses for the reform of the social order as it affected the fate of the downtrodden peasantry came always from the East. A Russian military commander of the provinces was the first to make the relations between landlord and serf subject to public law. The new law tied the serf legally to the estate at a time when the Black Sea had opened for grain export and the boyars needed labor to draw the maximum benefit from their sudden ingress into the world market. Though the law favored the landlords, it at least laid down the duties of the serf, protecting him from the arbitrary treatment of his master.

In 1861, the Tsar with a stroke of the pen abolished serfdom in all the Russias. Three years later, Alexander Cuza, the first ruler of both Wallachia and Moldavia, emancipated the serfs and abolished feudal dues. He also secularized the lands of the monasteries, which had acquired one fifth of all land in the Phanariot era. But the law gave too little land to the peasants, and at too high a price.

The revolution in Russia in 1905 made the peasants in neighboring Moldavia restless. The accumulated hatred blew up in 1907, first against the Jews, then mounting to engulf the boyars. Castles were burned in various parts of the country. Peasants armed with scythes, pitchforks, and knives roamed the big estates and converged for a march on the capital city. An army of 120,000 men was mobilized to stop them. Its big guns swooped down on the nests of the rebels, shelled the villages, and killed more than ten thousand peasants.

When, in 1917, a new revolution shook Russia, fear that its flame would spread to Rumania took hold of the royal Rumanian court. They were still haunted by memories of the peasant revolt of ten years before. Now the last act of World War I would begin in which Rumania would rise high or fall low. All depended on whether the peasants' sons in the barracks and in the field would obey their superiors or turn their weapons against them. The king personally rushed to their quarters to make sure of their support, and he solemnly promised "land will be given you" as they boarded the trains for the last decisive phase of the war.

The land reform was incorporated into law the next year, providing for the expropriation of lands over 250 acres to be distributed among the peasants in individual holdings of about 12 acres. This was the most extensive land reform in Europe. Much depended, however, on the way in which the government put the program into effect. The first elections in Greater Rumania returned two parties which might have governed in behalf of the peasantry: the Peasant Party in the Old Kingdom and Juliu Maniu's National Party in Transylvania. But the king and his advisers had different ideas about the future administration. The king by-passed the majority and appointed a general as Prime Minister with the task of ordering new elections and rigging them. In 1922, Bratianu's old Liberal Party came to wield power for the financial oligarchy, and the professionals and bureaucrats who revolved around it.

The government put the land reform into effect, but land distribution alone was no remedy for the plight of the peasant. He needed cheap credit in order to buy equipment, fertilizers, and seed so as to raise productivity. Only in such a case would he be able to pay compensation to his former landlords. A financial policy was needed to organize investment in agriculture, and to promote cooperatives. Above all, the peasants, in exactly the same condition as those in Poland, were to a great extent illiterate and had to be educated in the use of fertilizers and the production of crops other than corn and wheat.

Even if the land sufficed to sustain a family, equal inheritance broke it up in a couple of generations. Industrialization alone could absorb the overpopulation—the inevitable consequence of fragmentation of the land through divisions by inheritance. To attain maximum benefit from reforms in a peasant country like Rumania, the government should have been most seriously concerned with the welfare of the peasant; but in the hands of a government that served entrenched oligarchies even large-scale land reform and industrialization worked out to his detriment.

The law itself left a loophole in favor of the big landowners. It delayed expropriation to the actual time of distribution. As a consequence, 16 per cent of the privately owned estates were still over 250 acres each when World War II started, and 58 per cent of the peasant holdings still remained under 8 acres each—far under the subsistence level.

Inland capital shunned agriculture, and banks preferred giving credit to business. Interest rates on loans to peasants ran from 9 to 30 per cent. Cooperatives became a business branch of the government parties, instruments of vote getting and even of tax collecting.

The "Liberal" governments opposed foreign investments in industry except when the capital needed was so large that domestic groups could not supply it, as in the case of the petroleum and lumber industries. There the clique at least shared in the profits by extorting money for licenses, subsidies, and tax exemptions in exchange for their good offices with the government. However, these industries worked for export, the merchandise like the profit mostly going abroad. Other industries grew under the shield of insurmountable tariff walls which insured a high profit at low production cost. The resulting high prices meant that per-capita income was lower between the years of 1925 and 1934 than in 1914—indeed, one of the lowest in Europe.

In 1927, a landslide swept into power the two popular parties, the Transylvanian National Party and the Peasant Party of the Old Kingdom. The two had merged a year before for the main task of breaking down the financial oligarchy. From this fusion an instance of the bankruptcy of the peasant parties in Eastern Europe came to light. The Rumanian Peasant Party hungered for land and was hostile to capitalism. But the distribution of the land as it materialized left many old problems and created new ones. The fact that it did not have the expected miraculous effect disheartened the peasants. On the other hand, the peasant policy of the Transylvanian Nationalist Party was part of its program to wipe out the superior economic position of the Magyars. The amalgamation of the two parties produced a policy of economic liberalism with no specific stress on the interests of the peasantry. They fostered foreign loans and investments by foreign capital, lowered tariffs on consumer goods, and generally tried to reform the situation through economic liberalism. The policy was inadequate in itself; and in addition it ran against the world economic crisis which halted the free flow of credits and encouraged autocracy.

A dynastic crisis also hindered the government in promoting democratic financial and economic legislation. Prince Carol, the successor to the throne, had fallen in love with Magda Lupescu, a Jewish girl, and in 1925 had given up the right of succession in favor of his adolescent son, Mihai, leaving his wife and country for the woman he loved. When the king died in 1927, a council of regents took over the royal functions, but Juliu Maniu, leader of the National Peasants, was by-passed when it came to advising the court on the composition of the regency. As Prime Minister,

Maniu had difficulties with one of the regents who opposed
and tried to frustrate his reform program. Maniu got in
touch with Carol abroad and negotiated with him on his
return home and his ascent to the throne. It was understood that he would come alone, leaving his sweetheart behind. He did so, took over the royal power from the regents, and succeeded his son by relegating the boy to the
position of his successor. When Magda Lupescu also returned to join the king, Maniu resented it as a breach of the
royal word of honor and resigned. But the king's love affair
may have been a mere pretext for Maniu to part with power.
He had grown in moral stature by his dignified and stubborn protest against the Magyars in the Hungarian Parliament but could not shift to constructive leadership in
Greater Rumania although the public looked to him to regenerate the country morally and politically.

Carol's resumption of his throne coincided with the world
economic crisis which hit Rumania as an agricultural country particularly hard. Through traditionally rigged elections, Carol resorted to the expediencies of other East European countries to stave off the catastrophic effects. He supported grain prices and eventually converted agrarian debts
so as to assure the peasants of at least a bare survival. As
soon as the crisis had subsided, in 1934, Carol's financial
policy turned to industrialization. Hitler's rise to power
signaled the threat of war for countries like Rumania which
opposed any change in political geography and power relations as they had been created by the peace treaties after
World War I. The result was increased armament and a
state-financed boom which took away investment capital
from agriculture while it did not substantially absorb the
overpopulation of the land. Moreover, wages remained
scandalously low so that the prosperity of heavy industry
brought no relief to the peasant nor a rise in the general
standard of living.

In international affairs, Rumania's Foreign Minister,
Nicolae Titulescu, was a leading and eloquent partisan of
the French military alliance system, promoter of collective

security against aggression, and supporter of sanctions against Italy in the Abyssinian war. He would have stood fast on the violated peace treaty when Hitler marched into the Rhineland, had France and Britain not so fatefully defected. Carol understood the full meaning of this. He replaced Titulescu and began to explore ways in which he might gain favor with Hitler and at the same time safeguard his own power by keeping the country politically independent of Germany. This pattern of royal dictatorship appeared in most East European and Balkan countries. It installed domestic fascism to save the throne and the skeleton of independence of the state from a clear-cut pro-Nazi totalitarianism. The system involved opening the country to German economic penetration. Germany bought agricultural and industrial raw materials, food, oil, and lumber, and paid with finished goods. This created some prosperity, and as the requirements of the Nazi remilitarization grew, the Germans sold equipment to further productivity of the land, directing production to the growing of industrial crops, especially soybeans.

However, Carol's intended dictatorship ran into the strong opposition of Maniu's National Peasant Party and the much more dangerous resistance of genuine fascism. Indeed, Maniu, exponent of parliamentary democracy, went so far in hostility as to conclude a pact in 1937 with the increasingly popular Fascists not to oppose each other at the elections.

Rumanian fascism originated in Moldavia from an anti-Semitic political movement in the last century. Moldavia had been invaded by Polish and Russian Jews to the extent that there were 118,000 in the province in which fifty years earlier only 2,000 families had been counted. The Jews became middlemen between landlord and peasant, bought cheap, sold dear, lent money at high interest rates, and kept the inns which sucked away the little money the peasant earned. Shortly after World War I, a fascinating young man, Cornelius Zelea Codreanu, founded the "Legion of Archangel Michael" and its militant vanguard known as the

Iron Guard. It loathed capitalism, socialism, communism, democracy, everything alien, and more than all, the Jews who represented all. The movement had immediate appeal for the students who hated the prospect of competing with Jews in the professions, and it drew public attention when its members murdered the chief of police, who dared to restrict their atrocities, in Iassy, the capital of Moldavia. The public trembled when the court acquitted the murderers.

The Iron Guard perpetrated a morbid death cult, a creed of self-sacrifice. "What is the final aim of a nation?" Codreanu asked. "Life? If so, then it makes no difference what means life uses to perpetuate itself. All means are good, even the most evil. The ultimate aim is not life but resurrection to life in the name of Jesus Christ. The last moment of resurrection of the dead is the noblest aim to which a nation can rise." Simple people read into this gibberish the solution for their woes. The peasant had become free of bondage only to fall into a more intricate one— that of indebtedness. Commercialism had caught him in its web and seemed to benefit everyone but him and his like who produced the food that kept all alive. The financial oligarchs lived beyond his scope, but he saw the middlemen, aliens, and Jews turning all things into money.

The peasants' frustration was aggravated by nationalistic irritation over the fact that the country was not secure from alien groups commanding the support of foreign powers. The Hungarians had succeeded in enrolling the good will of the Latin dictator, Mussolini, behind their schemes and aimed at the disintegration of Rumania. The Communists worked to undermine the country while Russia stood on the border, never recognizing the incorporation by Rumania of the province of Bessarabia. Hatred of the aliens and of the Communists attracted frantic nationalists in the middle class to the racist Iron Guard. The Iron Guard made spectacular advances in popularity, and when the government decided to outlaw it the Guardists killed the Prime Minister. The court again acquitted the criminals, and the movement polled a huge vote at the elections of 1937.

"We took over the doctrines of the middle-class revolution of 1789 in France without having a middle class. For this birth-failing of our political life we are now suffering," was Carol's credo when, after deviously undermining one political group after another, he abolished the parties and established his personal dictatorship with a government of "national unity" in 1938. He may have received Hitler's encouragement, since the German was most interested in exploiting Rumania's resources for his expanding military might, best served by calm work in that rich country. Knowing this, Carol had the leaders of the Iron Guard arrested and Codreanu with thirteen other Guardists murdered in prison.

The king personally skimmed the profits from the new prosperity while Austria and Czechoslovakia went down to the policy of appeasement. But all his ruthless opportunism foundered when in 1940 Stalin, relying on the secret protocol of the Ribbentrop-Molotov agreement, demanded that Carol immediately yield to Russia Bessarabia, which Russia had possessed from 1812 to 1917, and also Northern Bukovina, which she had never held but which was inhabited mostly by Ukrainians, Germans, and Jews. Carol had to comply. This blow would not have toppled him from the throne had not Bulgaria followed the Russian demands by its claim to Southern Dobrudja, the land between the delta of the Danube and the Black Sea, which Bulgaria had lost to Rumania in 1913, and, worst of all, had not Hungary presented her claim to Transylvania. A Nazi-Fascist arbitration awarded the northern part of Transylvania to Hungary and left the southern part with Rumania. Carol could not survive this national catastrophe. He boarded an armored train loaded with valuables and left Rumania on September 6, 1940 to his young son. Fifty per cent of her adult population were still illiterate, and Rumania had the highest infant mortality rate in Europe.

Twenty-five years is too short a time in the life of a state to draw a balance of its successes and failures. Events of world-wide scope such as the economic crisis, German Nazism, and Russian Bolshevism, would have thrown the best built nation off its axis. But Greater Rumania failed in instances of her own making.

She annexed Bessarabia when Russia, who never recognized Rumania's acquisition, was in the turmoil of revolutions. As a result, the Rumanian governments never attempted to gain the loyalty of its Russian and Ukrainian population. They kept the province under military rule in a permanent state of emergency, settled it with Rumanian and German colonists instead of giving land to the native peasants. They crushed more than a hundred revolts during the interwar years and killed thirty thousand Bessarabians. At great financial sacrifice they fortified the region against a Soviet attack, then eventually yielded it to the Soviets without firing a shot.

The peace treaties had enriched Balkanic Rumania with such lands as Transylvania and the Banat, whose past was embodied in the mainstream of European history, while Rumania had stagnated under the insidious rule of the mercenaries of an oriental despotism. Yet the system of the Old Kingdom insisted on spreading over all Greater Rumania. A centralist bureaucracy bred corruption, the inheritance of the Phanariots, in the new provinces instead of having their higher political morality transfused into the circulation of the whole body of the state.

The government did little to help the alien national groups, comprising one third of the total population, to adjust to their new situation in Greater Rumania. The peace conference handled the peoples of Eastern Europe cavalierly by entrusting a country like Old Rumania to govern large alien groups, some of them vastly above the level of the Rumanians in cultural development and political experience. Rumanian nationalism was prompt in retaliating against the million and a half Magyars in their country for grievances they had suffered in the past because of high-handed policies in Old Hungary. They not only denied the Magyars self-government but also participation in the administration, banned their language from offices and public schools, and discriminated against them in the whole field of public life. One third of these Magyars lived in the towns as members of a middle class of professionals, craftsmen, and skilled workers. They had a centuries-old tradition of participation in government and political affairs. Though far removed from the centers of Hungarian culture, they were nevertheless devoted to its institutions and language. Rumanian efforts to dispossess and degrade them into second-class citizenship did not make them more ready to accept their situation. The million and a half Magyars also constituted a problem of foreign policy because of the stubborn claim of Hungary for revision of the territorial decisions of the peace treaties.

The German minority received exceptionally good treatment in deference to their higher cultural and economic standards. Moreover, the Saxons of Transylvania had lived separate from the German world for seven hundred years, the Schwabians of the Banat and the Germans of Bukovina for two hundred. No one would have anticipated that Hitler would carve them out of their adopted environment by making them citizens of the Reich and enrolling them in the German army.

Anti-Semitism was an inveterate tradition in Rumania. When the Congress of Berlin, in 1878, recognized the independence of Rumania, it attached a rider to the recognition imposing on her the extension of citizenship to Jewish inhabitants. The government resisted and the Rumanians resented the interference. Finally, however, when they came around to admitting the Jews as citizens, they did it on an individual basis—judging the case of each Jew on its own merits. Only after 1918 were they accepted unqualifiedly as citizens. Even then no Jew was employed in civil service, and they were restricted in higher learning as well.

Behind the façade of a Western-type constitution, Rumania remained a backward country. The rise of the masses to a permanent factor of importance in government was dependent on raising the productivity of the land and on industrialization. Foreign loans, scarce as they came, tended to serve the interests and security of the creditors; foreign investment went into colonial exploitation of raw materials not integrated into the framework of domestic economy, or else into armament. Foreign aid in capital and "know how" to turn potential into actual wealth was outside the scope of the interwar era.

The young king followed his father by making General Ion Antonescu head of the government, in which all the great parties were represented with the addition of the Iron Guard. But titular appointments did not appease the Guard, which seethed with lust for vengeance and power. German troops arrived in the country to insure undisturbed toil in Rumania, and the Guard broke out in violent actions to assume power and have the Germans face the accomplished fact. It killed about sixty imprisoned politicians who were responsible for measures of repression against the Guard, and perpetrated bloody pogroms against the Jews. The future course of Rumanian policies now rested entirely on Hitler. At the end of 1940 he made preparations for the conquest of the Balkans. He wanted not only submission but also order in Rumania to protect the oil wells. Consequently, General Antonescu received the green light to suppress the Guard. When, in January 1941, it staged an uprising accompanied with bestial murders of Jews in the capital city itself, Antonescu called out the army to crush it. Even so he needed the military assistance of the Germans and three days of bloody fighting to accomplish it. The Guard's roots were deep and widespread in the population.

The same year, Antonescu joined the Nazi armies in attacking Russia. The Rumanians quickly reconquered Bessarabia and Bukovina, murdered about 200,000 Jews, and dumped many more on the occupied Ukrainian lands. Up to this stage, participation in Hitler's war generated satisfaction and even enthusiasm in the country. Many began to wonder, however, when the Fuehrer encouraged the Rumanians toward conquest in the Ukraine and let them carve out of it a new province called Transnistria, where their soldiers did not lag behind the Nazis in ugly killing and looting. But when Hitler drew the Rumanian divisions into the battle for Stalingrad and news of grave losses became known, the public could only console itself with the vague hope that the contribution of powerful help to Hitler's victory would lead him to reverse the award of 1940 and return all of Transylvania to Rumania.

But the Russians turned Stalingrad into the starting point of their victory. Deeply disturbed, the opposition to Antonescu put out feelers in neutral capitals to explore the chances of a separate peace with the Western Allies. Their propositions revealed how much people in the Nazi camp misjudged the relation between the West and the Russians during the war. The Rumanians wanted the West to dispatch troops to Rumania to prevent the Soviet from retaking Bessarabia and Bukovina, and they were incredulous when the report came from abroad that the Allies would enter into no peace negotiations without the Russians. All the same, such revelations coming from the Nazi satellites gave fresh food to Stalin's suspicions regarding the true intent of his allies.

In March 1944, the Soviet army smashed into Bessarabia. Now a Rumanian emissary, Prince Barbu Stirbey, with the foreknowledge of the "Conducator" Antonescu, departed to Cairo and got in touch with the Allied ambassadors. They advised him to call on the Soviet envoy. There Prince Stirbey received the conditions of an armistice. Bessarabia and Bukovina were to be returned to Russia, but otherwise the Soviet offered to guarantee Rumania's territorial integrity, which implied the return of northern Transylvania to Rumania. Rumania was to pay reparations for the damages caused by her armies in the Ukraine. The Soviets would not interfere with the social order in Rumania. She would be allowed to join the Soviet army in the fight against the Nazis and the Hungarians, to which end she was to declare war on Germany.

Prince Stirbey returned home, but his friends hesitated, still believing that the Allies would land in the Balkans and save them from the Russians. Meanwhile, the Soviet army was penetrating deeper into the country, and in July, Juliu Maniu, leader of the Transylvanian National Party, sent a former diplomat to resume contact with the West. However, young King Mihai resolved to take the initiative in a bold step. On August 23, 1944, he invited Marshal Antonescu and Foreign Minister Mihai Antonescu (not related) to an audience. The dictator had been used to handling the royal youngster with fatherly condescension, but now the king called him to order when he struck the old tune. Bluntly the king told him that he stood face to face with his sovereign, and stated that an armistice must be requested without delay in order to save Rumania from the Russians.

The Conducator suspected a trap in the king's sudden maturity. He did not protest, but asked for time to inform the Germans so that they might disentangle themselves from Rumania. He made a deep impression on the king, insisting that the honor of an officer toward a former ally would not allow him to desert the Germans without a word of warning. But the king was determined to make the best of an unpleasant situation. He gave a prearranged signal to his advisers, who rushed in and arrested the two Antonescus.

The king then read a proclamation over the radio announcing that he accepted the conditions of the armistice and ordered a cease fire on the Russian front. He made public the appointment of a new cabinet headed by General Constantin Sanatescu and including several high officers of the army and the leaders of the opposition Liberal, National Peasant, Socialist and Communist parties, the latter represented by Lucretiu Patrascanu, a lawyer and intellectual of high culture who was considered to be a Rumanian before being a Communist. He became minister of justice.

On the news of Rumanian defection, German planes raided Bucharest, which furnished the king with a pretext for declaring war on Germany. His cabinet made immediate arrangements to switch fifteen divisions from fighting the Russians to fighting with them against their former allies—Germans and Hungarians. By participating in the invasion of Transylvania, King Mihai hoped to assure that province for Rumania, and the same hope fired the soldiers who fought bravely in this last part of the hostilities and suffered 160,000 casualties.

Significantly, the armistice was signed in Moscow, and by Marshal Malinowski alone on behalf of the Allied High Command.

It appeared that the Russians were not sure then—before the Stalin-Churchill percentage agreement—that they could lay hold on Rumania. Their army seized ships, tugs, barges, half the railroad stock, and about 50,000 tons of pipe and drilling equipment, showing that they preferred booty to advantages they might gain later by leaving the equipment to be used by the Rumanians under their direction.

As far as power was concerned, the Russians unmistakably showed where it lay. According to the armistice, an Allied Control Commission was to be the official instrument to supervise the fulfillment of its conditions. However, after the Stalin-Churchill deal, a Russian commander acted alone on behalf of the Commission as the Western Allies had done in Greece and Italy.

But the Russians surprised everyone by the moderation of the social and political programs they instituted. They made public the fact that Rumania, though dominated by the Soviet Union, would not be Sovietized. The Russians had the means of convincing the population that they had to accommodate themselves to Soviet military domination, but otherwise they would be left to themselves. All the Russians wanted was a change in the coalition government so that men they trusted would hold positions of power in the state. However, Russian interference ran up against general mistrust and hostility. In Rumania, the Soviets had no prospect of banking on such sympathies as they enjoyed among most Slavic peoples. The Rumanians were Latinized Thracians, imbued with fear of the Russians who had been roaming on their soil for centuries. Nor had Communism any attraction for them, since this Party was considered merely a Russian outpost. At no time did membership rise to more than two thousand, and these were recruited almost entirely from alien national groups.

But there was enough dissatisfaction rife in the country against the oligarchy-managed regime, the Fascists, and the war criminals who still crowded the highest offices. The Communists had only to stay behind the scenes and pull wires while democratic groups and opportunists acted on the stage. Communist leadership was back from Moscow and from the prisons. As an exception to the rule, Moscow's trustee was a woman, Ana Pauker, a former teacher from a Moldavian Jewish family who married an engineer and had three children. She organized a Rumanian division from prisoners of war in Russia and returned with them in the company of Vasile Luca, another militant Communist, a Szekler, his original name being Lukacs. A former officer of the Rumanian army, Emil Bodnaras, a Ukrainian, was a ruthless organization man, while Gheorghiu-Dej, a railway worker, emerged from prison. He and Teohari Georgescu were the only ethnic Rumanians on the Party's general staff.

These men sponsored the formation of a National Democratic Front consisting of the Ploughman's Party of Petru Groza, a Transylvanian leftist peasant leader, of dissidents from the historical parties, and of Socialists and Communists. The Front demanded immediate distribution of all estates over 125 acres, and of all lands belonging to war criminals; elimination of war criminals from all positions; and fulfillment of the conditions of the armistice. They succeeded in penetrating the factories and organizing the workers for demonstrations against the government and police. Meanwhile, the army was engaged in grave battles under the command of the Soviet forces in Hungary.

The king and the parties opposing the leftist front resisted the pressure, trusting that the conference of the Allies would give the West the right and power to limit Soviet interference with Rumanian internal policy. They had no knowledge of the Stalin-Churchill agreement which directly affected Rumania.

After a clash between army troops and pro-government demonstrators in the streets of Bucharest, in February 1945, Deputy Prime Minister Andrei Vyshinsky arrived in the Rumanian capital and called on the king. Vyshinsky had the fearful reputation of having been the prosecutor who had heaped malice and contempt on the apostles of the revolution before he drove them to the gallows at the Moscow trials in the 1930's. He showed polite restraint at the first meeting, telling the king that the Soviet army was entitled to have behind its fighting line in Rumania a government it could trust to keep order.

But the next day he called again and inquired about the king's decision. When the king answered that he was engaged in consultations, Vyshinsky changed his tone and stated that Petru Groza of the Ploughmen was the only premier acceptable to Moscow. To lend weight to his words he pounded the table and gave the king an ultimatum of two hours and five minutes in which to make up his mind, then departed, slamming the door behind him. King Mihai immediately sent for Groza. Groza was a handsome, ingratiating, and ambitious man; his party had never grown out of local proportions, but it inclined toward the policy Russia intended to lay down in Rumania—the conciliation of Rumanians and Hungarians. Groza had the list of his cabinet members already prepared. It contained personalities from the Liberal, Peasant, Socialist, and Communist parties. As to the number of posts, Communist representation was modest, but it included the key Ministry of Interior which controlled the police and also the Ministry of Justice and Public Works.

The bluntness of Vyshinsky's intervention was calculated. It took place right after the Yalta conference which, viewed by outsiders, resulted in the "Declaration on Liberated Europe" stressing "the rights of all peoples to choose the form of government under which they will live." The Russians

wanted to demonstrate the fact that the Declaration had not
superseded the Stalin-Churchill agreement which had given
them 90 per cent "say" in Rumanian affairs. But the Americans held the opposite view. They reminded Vyshinsky of
Roosevelt's reservations to the effect that the deal covered
only military policies and not the political affairs of the
liberated countries. The British joined the Americans, but
their good faith was open to question. In fact, the conference left the question open to ambiguous interpretation
since that appeared to be the only way to save publicizing
a disagreement between the Allies while the war was still
on.

The Groza government started with precious assets. It
took over the administration of the whole of Transylvania
from the Soviet army which had withheld it from previous
Rumanian governments. When the Russians had cleared
the territory of Nazi and Hungarian troops, Rumanian nationalists had swooped down on the domestic Magyars making them the target of their wrath over past and present
adversities. Thereupon the Soviet army conferred on local
joint Rumanian-Hungarian Liberation Committees the management of civilian affairs. They worked with remarkable
smoothness. Many liked to believe that this move might
serve as a rehearsal for an autonomous Transylvania. But
the revival of the past had not the same attraction for both
nationalities. To the Hungarians once-independent Transylvania represented a glorious episode when a fragment of
their race had saved the continuity of the whole nation then
submerged in disaster; but to the Rumanians it recalled the
time when both their nation and their religion had been
outlawed.

The Groza regime began immediately to expropriate
blocks of land of over 125 acres and all lands belonging to
war criminals, and gave the green light to the local authorities to set about distributing them. No restrictions were put
on trade or commerce or private property except that of
Germans and war criminals. The four freedoms remained
about as free as they ever had been in Rumania.

Yet the government had not been recognized even by the Russians. Everything seemed to be temporary.

The public looked forward to the Potsdam conference in the last two weeks of July, 1945. It was evident that the continent was being more sharply divided by the day into Russian and Anglo-American orbits. The West did not want the Russians to share in control over Italy and the Ruhr within western Germany, yet insisted on participating in control over the countries which had fallen into the Soviet orbit. Stalin, on the other hand, rejected Western interference, pointing out the fact that he had left a free hand to the West in Italy, western Germany, and Japan.

The West argued that the lands under its control had set up governments of their own choice in the spirit of the Yalta declaration, and that all they wanted of the Soviet orbit was for it to live up to the same requirement.

The Russians also referred to the Yalta decision that conceded them the right to governments in the liberated countries friendly to the Soviet. They wanted no more than that, as proven by the fact that they allowed coalition governments to rule in the Russian sphere with democratic, not even socialist programs. Stalin passed over the fact, however, that he was actually interfering in the West through Communist parties which, although the Comintern had been dissolved, remained pledged to Moscow. Yet the insistence of the West that the line dividing East from West was in reality the borderline of the free and the unfree world, while Stalin wanted it accepted by both sides only as the limit of power orbits, put the Soviets for the first time on the defensive in the ideological controversy. The controversy had existed since the Russian Revolution in 1917, but Communist ideology had kept on the offensive all the time. It had drowned out timid attempts to defend democracy, while to utter a good word for capitalism would have exposed the speaker to ridicule. The Nazis had wrested the offensive from the Communists only to wedge the democrats between two opponents.

During the war, Stalin accepted democracy as the common platform on which Russia and the West stood in their
fight against Nazism and Fascism. He also accepted it as
the principle which the liberated countries would have to
follow. But now, in spite of his earlier mental reservations,
he could no longer deny responsibility for failing to keep to
its standards—he could only deny the fact that he was failing to do so.

Stalin hastened to recognize Groza right after the Potsdam conference. The next day, after Soviet recognition,
the American and British military missions lodged protests
with the king against the government as unacceptable to
the West. This was the event King Mihai had waited and
prayed for. Now he could act, backed by the Western
powers. He requested Groza to resign. Groza consulted
the Soviet representative and as a result declared that only
the Allied Control Commission, not its individual members,
had the right to interfere. He refused to resign.

The king and his advisers thought that at this point he
should let things develop into a showdown. He would
have to risk his kingdom, but actually ran no unusual risk,
since, should the Russians prevail over the West, the kingdom was done for anyway. Mihai left the palace for his
summer residence and declined to sign any document the
validity of which depended constitutionally upon his signature.

A most peculiar situation arose, unprecedented in modern
history. The Groza government proceeded undisturbed as
if the royal prerogatives were of no consequence. In a way
it humiliated the king, but it also exposed Groza as deriving
power and the title to power exclusively from the Soviet
army of occupation.

On Mihai's birthday, November 8, 1945, a mass demonstration in favor of the king was organized in front of the
royal palace. The Communists rushed truckloads of workers for a counter demonstration. The two camps clashed
and blood was shed.

The Council of Foreign Ministers of the Big Three powers took up discussion of the deadlock in Moscow in December, 1945. Obviously, the West wanted a peace treaty with Italy, and in general, to terminate the state of war with all countries in Europe. Unless they were ready for an open break with the Soviets, the West had to accept a subterfuge to blur the contradiction inherited from Yalta. They still professed to support a Rumanian government friendly to Russia and acknowledged that free elections could not return such a government; yet they did not give up the demand for free elections. But now they found a face-saving mechanism tacitly agreed upon with the Russians. The Russians would reduce their requirements as to the set-up of the Groza government, which would then be recognized by America and Britain. One representative each from the Liberal and the National Peasant parties would be added to the cabinet, and the ambassadors of the three powers would check the selected members not only to see that they were representative but also to insure that they would work loyally with the government. The agreement applied only until elections could be held.

Upon having reassured the ambassadors on these two points, Groza was to declare that he intended to hold free elections in which all democratic and anti-fascist parties would be allowed to put up candidates. After this, the Western powers would accord recognition to the Groza government. Groza complied and was recognized. The king resumed his royal functions.

The election campaign began. The Communists succeeded in gaining the approval of a majority of the Social Democrats for a common list, at the cost of their right wing leaving the party. Then they did their best to restrict the means by which the opposition could be in contact with voters. The Western Allies sent protest after protest over Groza's breach of the promise on free elections. On November, 1946, the elections took place.

The results showed how little freedom was left to the voters in expressing their preferences. The parties supporting the government received 348 seats in the 414-member one-chamber parliament; the Communists won 73.

An individual who counted the ballots revealed to the author that he had participated in falsifying the results. He had been told that, regrettable as it was, the country's vital interests required the presentation to the Soviets of a government acceptable to it. Yet the Communists still only dared to claim 73 seats.

The West lodged a last protest for the record.

The armistice had imposed on Rumania the payment to Russia of reparations in the amount of $300 million in goods, the value of the dollar calculated on the basis of world prices in 1938 which actually meant double the stipulated sum. It must be noted, however, that the loot taken by the Rumanian army in the Ukraine amounted to as much if not more.

As early as 1945, the Soviets concluded several treaties with Rumania which indicated the pattern of Soviet empire building. They created joint Soviet-Rumanian (Sovrom) companies for the exploitation of petroleum. The two countries were to share and share alike, but the Russian shares consisted of German assets which included not only German stocks but also French, Belgian, and Dutch investments which the Germans had acquired by force during the Nazi occupation. The company, named Sovrompetrol, thereupon received back the equipment which the Soviet army had seized before the armistice. This was followed by a joint transport company which was intended to embrace shipping and harbor installations, and a Sovrombank to finance and administer the joint undertakings. Obviously, the Soviets laid down the institutions for exploiting Rumania's most important resources in a colonial style, since the other "contracting party" was merely her straw man.

In 1945–46, such transactions did not include private property. The word "socialization" was missing from the Communist vocabulary. In this connection, the opinion of the great industrialists in Rumania on the prospects of the country in the Soviet orbit might be of real interest to recall. Max Ausnit, general manager of the vast Reshitza Steel and Brass Works, director of the French-owned munitions plant near Bucharest, agent-general for Vickers-Armstrong, and partner of Malaxa, the locomotive king, stated to this author that he believed Rumania's inclusion in the Russian economic sphere would turn out to her advantage. The Germans had treated Rumania as an economic colony by importing her raw materials in exchange for finished goods, thus hampering her industrial development. With the Russians the role would be reversed. Russia would ship raw materials to Rumanian factories which would produce finished goods. New industries would be created in Rumania and the existing ones expanded in order to undertake production for the vast Russian market. This would bring about a higher standard of living and would also exploit the reserves of raw materials lying idle. He said he was sure that Russia's presence as an economic factor in southeastern Europe would stimulate economic development there, and above all, industrialism.

The prospect that the countries in the Russian orbit might economically colonize the more backward Soviet Union was in many people's minds, but more took a pessimistic view on the awkward situation wherein a powerful country, though short of articulated industry, politically colonized economically more developed lands. They held that the Soviets could not afford to tolerate such a humiliating position as having a lower standard of living than her dependencies. Consequently she would bring down these countries at least to her own level by ruthless exploitation and looting.

While the new regime left intact, for the time being, private property in industry and commerce, it immediately resorted to land distribution. Privately owned land was limited to 125 acres. Among 800 thousand beneficiaries, 2½ million acres were distributed. The average plot received was about 5 acres, but dwarf landowners also were included among the receivers to complement their lots.

Still, the holdings thus created appeared so small as to be uneconomical, and many suspected that the land reform aimed at just that. It would help to convince the peasant that he should enter a collective farm rather than toil on a strip that did not return enough for a living.

Still, the land reform gained some popularity for the Groza government among its beneficiaries. Moreover, the Soviets gave the government another asset which, in theory, was bound to enhance its prestige not with a section but with the entire ethnic Rumanian population. It had promised in 1944, when Rumania was ready to desert the Nazis and join the Soviet army, to restore to her Transylvania or a "greater part of it." When, in 1946, the matter came up in the peace negotiations, only James F. Byrnes, United States Secretary of State, proposed some frontier revision in favor of Hungary, while Russia stood for the restoration of Rumania's border toward Hungary as it had been in 1920. The Russians may have come to the conclusion in the meantime that Rumania was a more important satellite than Hungary. But they may have left a strong Magyar minority within Rumania as a threat to Rumania that the whole province might at any time be returned to the Hungarians.

Upon hearing the decision of the peace conference, Premier Groza rushed to Nagyvarad, a largely Hungarian-speaking town near the border. He appealed to the Hungarians and stated that there could be no triumph of one of their peoples over the other. They were fated to live peacefully side by side no matter to which of them Transylvania belonged. He promised them full national equality and hinted that the two countries should enter a union to end national rivalry forever. Whether or not Groza acted on Russian suggestions was not known. The Prime Minister of Hungary, reading the Groza speech, knew of no Soviet encouragement for such a federation. Actually, Stalin had broached this idea at his meeting with Churchill in October, 1944. This was the more remarkable in that the union of the two countries would have widened the gap between Northern and Southern Slavs, and this ran counter to the

Pan-Slav propaganda which the Soviets still harped upon in 1946.

But the Rumanian public rejected Russian overlordship as well as the government it sponsored so firmly that it showed no jubilation, nor even satisfaction at the great news on Transylvania. The still numerous non-Communist papers simply registered the event. No spontaneous demonstrations were held in Bucharest, and the government did not "arrange" demonstrations so as to be tactful and spare Hungarian feelings.

But in Transylvania itself the so-called Maniu guards, members of the Rumanian National Party of Juliu Maniu, had prepared themselves for a pogrom against the Hungarian population in case the peace conference gave even a piece of Transylvania to Hungary. Now, even though this had not occurred, they insulted and beat Hungarians in the streets.

CHAPTER THREE

Bulgaria

Crossing the Danube on a ferryboat from Rumania one enters a poor country and meets a crude but diligent, healthy, and thrifty people. Whether they work on their tiny pieces of land or in offices in the towns they are cut from the same cloth—peasants and peasants' sons. Luxury has no place in their lives. Indeed, it would offend common decency in this homogeneous simple setting which has little to offer those who strive to get rich and show that they enjoy it.

There is no demarcation between classes, and social mannerisms are absent. But a keen sense of power divides the people who have it from those who passionately covet it. It is as though all the ambition and emotion of this seemingly phlegmatic and taciturn people had been loosed in the quest for the exercise of power. All otherwise restrained violence explodes in the field of politics, and murder is a short cut often resorted to for its efficacy. Perhaps it is the equalitarian character of the land which generates furious hatreds and jealousies, for the "outs" appear no better than the "ins."

The great powers saddled this peasant democracy with a German prince, shrewd and cynical, who considered political power his private asset and enjoyed risking it in the big game with the great. As a consequence, Bulgaria became a chronic loser.

Power rested with the king and his circle of favorite officers, lawyer politicians, and some industrialists and merchants of standing. Appallingly ruthless themselves, they expected the same treatment from their opponents and did all they could to keep them from being able to retaliate.

When the Soviet army crossed the Danube, the cold hostility and fear with which they had been greeted in Rumania was left behind, and they were met by wildly jubilant crowds of Bulgarians. The peasants brought food; their wives and daughters offered flowers. In the towns a forest of red flags floated over tumultuously happy masses as old and young thronged to cheer the army's approach. Here for the first time since he had quit his native soil, the Russian soldier met spontaneous friendliness. Elsewhere, even those in sympathy with Bolshevism harbored fear of the Russians as strangers to their world, as having customs, emotions, and reactions disquietingly different from what they could safely expect of the people they knew. Eastern central Europe, despite its baffling variety of races and tongues and mutual hostility, was still the same world, with more or less the same traditions and past. But the Russians, with their horizons stretching to the Japanese Sea and Central Asia, were utter strangers—all the more frightful for their power.

For the Bulgarians, however, they represented the big protector who had liberated them from five centuries of Turkish occupation and given their country room to realize their boldest national ambitions. Other great powers had curtailed that never forgotten accomplishment, and the Bulgarians repeatedly ran into trouble with their neighbors in their tenacious attempts to reconquer what they had once possessed. But whether the Tsar or the Soviets backed their ambitions, they trusted Russia to stand by them if she could.

Yet, in both world wars Bulgaria had fought in the camp opposing Russia. In World War II, her king, Boris, the perfect prototype of an undertaker with his long nose, gloomy face, and shrewd narrow eyes, had joined the Axis in 1941 when Hitler was forced to rescue Fascist Italy's armies from a humiliating defeat by the Greeks. The road to Greece led through Bulgaria and Jugoslavia. Boris let the Nazi army

pass through and had Bulgarian troops march into Jugoslavia and Greek Macedonia, which had been lost in 1913.

He declared war on Britain and America, but not even
Hitler expected him to do the same on Russia. The country was rather prosperous during the war. The Germans
did not occupy it, and national ambitions were satisfied
with holding the territories they had lost and now reclaimed,
even if Hitler refused to allow their formal annexation. But
they would certainly have revolted against even a nominal
war on Russia.

In 1943, the critical year for Hitler's world conquest, the
Fuehrer summoned Boris to his headquarters. Nothing
leaked out from their conversation, and on his return the
king suddenly died. Rumor had it that this time Hitler had
insisted on the Bulgarian army's joining his own against
Russia but that Boris had remained adamant in refusing.
Suspicion that he had been poisoned could not be confirmed.

Whether Boris had joined the Axis through pro-German
sympathies, being a German prince, or because he believed
that the Germans would win the war, he followed in the
footsteps of his father, the big-nosed, cynical Ferdinand.
Together they landed Bulgaria on the losing side in two
great wars. The regency which ruled on behalf of young
Simeon, son of the deceased king, might have been as pro-
Russian as any Bulgarian, but they definitely feared and
hated the Bolsheviks.

When King Mihai of Rumania suddenly deserted the
Nazis, on August 23, the Bulgarian regents and the pro-Nazi
clique around them were seized by panic. They called in
conservative politicians who had not supported the war and
commissioned them to form a government to include members of the so-called Fatherland Front.

This Front combined the parties which had actively opposed the war as early as 1942. Its prime movers, the Communists, had joined then with the leftist Agrarians, both
representing powerful revolutionary forces which, in the

past, had weakened one another by their competition to gain favor with the masses, not relenting even when faced by destruction. The Social Democrats had also joined the Front, relying on the not too numerous industrial workers and craftsmen for support. When the so-called Zveno group joined, the Front certainly became representative of the overwhelming majority of the population. The Zveno comprised officers and intelligentsia, friendly to Jugoslavia and the Soviet Union.

The Fatherland Front refused, however, to take part in the government as the "tolerated" opposition. The government sent emissaries to Cairo to negotiate an armistice with the British and Americans, but the envoys of these two powers stalled the business since the Soviet army alone was directly involved in eventual military operations in Bulgaria. In the meantime, on September 5, 1944, the Soviet Union declared war on Bulgaria. This made a terrible impression on the population. Somehow they had trusted that Russia would appreciate the fact that Bulgaria had not gone to war against her and had tolerated her ambassador with a large staff which was unrestricted during the war. Not even the regents had objected to allowing the Soviet army passage through Bulgaria. This was a portent for the nation as to what the Soviets expected from defeated enemies. The government hastened to rectify past mistakes. It broke with the Axis powers a few hours after the Soviet declaration of war, declared war on them, and requested an armistice with Russia. The public was unanimous in believing that the Fatherland Front alone could save the country from Russian hostility. It went wild with relief and triumph when, on September 9, the Front seized power. Partisans descended from their hideouts in the mountains, where they had been harassing only Bulgarian troops. Never too numerous or popular, these partisans were mostly young Communist students. They now organized cells everywhere while the Agrarians, confident of the support of the majority in an 80 per cent peasant country, neglected to do so.

Public enthusiasm cooled when the Soviet troops, obviously under orders, did not reciprocate in fraternizing. The young Communists, freshly baked, little disciplined and indoctrinated, felt rebuffed when word came to discard the red flags since this was no revolution but the rising to power of all patriotic elements as a consequence of Soviet victory. But nothing could be nor was attempted to prevent the improvised People's Court from passing judgment on Nazis and collaborators and summarily executing them. It is difficult to assess the number of victims. The official figures showed that three ex-regents, twenty-two former members of the cabinets, sixty-eight members of Parliament, many high officers—altogether 2,138 persons—were sentenced to death, and about 7,000 were sent to prison with terms up to twenty years. There was no appeal.

The armistice terms renewed the sense of frustration which had afflicted the Bulgarians since they had emerged from Turkish rule. It imposed upon them the condition that they evacuate the Jugoslav and Greek territories occupied by their troops. People deemed it peculiar that the great Allies had made no better provision than the restoration of the state of affairs as it had been before the war (although these had largely made the war possible): national states burdened with minorities, arbitrary frontiers, and so on. It appeared especially significant that Communists were wrangling among themselves about national frontiers. Tito not only insisted that the Bulgarians evacuate Macedonia, which had been incorporated into Jugoslavia, but also claimed a part of that province which had belonged to Bulgaria before the war. Meanwhile, the Bulgarian armies went on fighting the Germans in Jugoslavia, liberated the southern part, and cut the main German communication lines.

The Bulgarian armistice was signed in Moscow, but this time not by the Russians alone. The Western Allies also concurred. The Stalin-Churchill agreement allowed the West a 25 per cent "say" in Bulgaria, 15 per cent more than in Rumania. Hard as it was to measure Russian concessions to the West in percentages during further developments, these undeniably were made.

The government lived up to general expectations. Strong anti-Fascist and pro-Russian parties had risen to power at each democratic turn in Bulgarian politics, for they had deep roots. The Communists, Peasants, and Zveno received equal representation. A pro-Russian (yet anything but democratic) Zveno filled the post of minister of war. Social Democrats and Independents also held posts in the cabinet. However, although they held only the same number of portfolios as the Peasants, the Communists kept the all-important Ministries of the Interior and Justice for themselves. They captured the strongholds of power, ruling over the police and the courts, while the army fought under Soviet command.

The government made preparations for prompt elections. The Agrarians, though a part of the Fatherland Front, resolved to fight for their share of real power, confident that they commanded the allegiance of the bulk of electors. In one respect, opposition to the Communists had brighter prospects in Bulgaria than in any Soviet occupied country, for the Soviets could not support the Communists on the pretext that the other parties were not truly friendly to Russia.

Indeed, Nikola Petkov, leader of the Agrarian Party in the Fatherland Front's agrarian section from its inception in 1941, proposed an alliance with the Communists to end the animosity between peasants and townspeople which had caused the bloody suppression of both by a right-wing dictatorship. Petkov also advocated that Bulgaria submit to Soviet foreign policy. He now refused, however, a Communist proposal to set up a common list of all Fatherland Front parties with the proportion of seats in Parliament prearranged between them.

Thereupon, the Communists picked an Agrarian straw man as head of a splinter group which was to be included on the common list as the Agrarian Party. They staged the same farce with the Socialist Party, and these splinters displaced the genuine parties in the government. But Bulgarian leaders rarely went down without putting up a fierce fight. Petkov lodged a protest with British and American members of the Control Commission, and the representatives agreed to apply to Bulgaria, as they had to Rumania, the machinery for molding a set-up that, on the surface at least, satisfied the requirements of the West for a representative government. To this effect, they resolved to have the government postpone the elections shortly after the Potsdam conference. The elections had been set for August 26, but at the last minute the postponement was made public, causing the general belief that either the West had prevailed over the Russians or that all three powers had dealt a blow to the prestige of the Bulgarian Communists.

Meanwhile, Mark Ethridge, a special United States envoy on an official fact-finding mission, visited Bulgaria. Interviews with him lifted the morale of the Agrarians and Socialists. The government permitted them to put up candidates on opposition tickets, but they terrorized the voters to such an extent that the opposition decided to abstain. At the elections the government list polled 86 per cent of the votes.

A government issued from such elections had, of course, no hope of being recognized by the West; yet recognition was essential for the signing of peace treaties, which was to the interest of all Allies as well as Bulgaria.

The Moscow conference in December, 1945, resorted to the machinery set in motion in Rumania. The Bulgarian government was to be reinforced by adding to it leaders of the parties heretofore excluded. The measure carried the usual qualification that the additional members should be truly representative and work loyally with the government. Unfortunately, face saving did not run smoothly in Bulgaria. Petkov and Kosta Lulchev, the leader of the Social Democrats, demanded a real share in the power. Due to the following they commanded in the country they claimed for their party the two ministries which the Communists had reserved for themselves (Interior and Justice), no matter what parties held the rest of the high offices.

The negotiations did not progress, even when Deputy Prime Minister Andrei Vyshinsky paid a visit to Sofia in January, 1946. While he pounded the desk of the Rumanian king and got what he wanted, he could not persuade the Bulgarian leaders to yield. Vyshinsky, knowing whom he faced, banged and bounced and squarely told the two leaders that it would be the Russians and no one else who would ultimately judge whether or not the recommendation of the Moscow conference was heeded. But the business was left unfinished.

In the meantime, that gray eminence of Bulgarian Communists, Georgi Dimitrov, returned from Moscow and was elected President of the Central Committee. Dimitrov had risen to world fame in 1933 when, as a defendant in the Reichstag fire case, he had defied the formidable Marshal Goering, the probable instigator of the fire. The indomitable courage he had demonstrated and the cold logic with which he disproved the accusation mobilized world opinion to save him from the wrath of the Nazis. Acquitted, he left for Moscow, became Secretary General of the Plenary Committee of the Comintern and a Soviet citizen. He guided the Bulgarian Communists by remote control until November, 1945, when he took over. Dimitrov came from a family of martyrs of the revolutionary movement, and had been persecuted and imprisoned, but he stood diametrically opposed to Petkov, who had much the same background. In this political duel, Dimitrov held physical power while the good wishes of the majority of the country and of the representatives of the West went to his opponent. Circumstances being what they were, such support proved to be inadequate.

On the other hand, the Communists for a time handled with kid gloves the authoritarian Zveno who had fought

against the pro-German, anti-Slav policies of the royal dictatorship. But with the war over, the Communists now
purged the officer corps under the guise of restricting the
army and thus had no further need for the Zveno. The
leader, General Damian Velchev, received the post of Minister to Switzerland where he later died.

In September, 1946, the government held a plebiscite on
the question of whether or not the monarchy should be retained. It was not necessary to interfere with the plebiscite
nor to falsify its ballot. The country hated the German
dynasty which had kept involving it in unpopular wars,
ending unfailingly in disaster. The government paid $20,-
000,000 compensation for the property of the royal family.
Young Simeon thus received a fair deal and joined his grand-
father, the former King of Italy, Victor Emmanuel, in exile.

Since the government was not willing to meet the conditions of the Agrarians and Social Democrats, they went into
the elections of October 27, 1946, on opposition tickets.
The West insisted on the Allied Control Commission's imposing compliance with the demands of the Moscow conference by admitting opposition candidates and insuring a
free campaign.

American and British notes protested against the way in
which the campaign was conducted, and hinted that they
might not recognize the government formed on the basis of
such an election. The opposition was free to put up its lists
and publish newspapers and pamphlets, but many candidates and supporters were jailed while the campaign was
on. On the eve of the elections Dimitrov warned that to
vote for the opposition was equivalent to treason, and with
this warning ringing in their ears, many voters hesitated before entering the polling booth. Even so, 22 per cent voted
for the oppositional Agrarians and Social Democrats. They
received 101 seats, while the government parties took 364
places in the Constituent Assembly.

Ilya Ehrenburg, the Soviet propagandist, on a visit to
Bulgaria at that time, mused over the undaunted Petkov,

and his sinister words boded ill for the man. Ehrenburg wrote:

Strange is the fate of this man: he is blinded by vanity. He is only a card in the game, but he thinks he is a player. Some months will pass, the play will come to an end, the cards will be shuffled again and nobody will remember Nikola Petkov.

Less than a year later Dimitrov—as Nikola Petkov kept challenging him in the Assembly, unconcerned with the consequences of his bold and eloquent stand for freedom— had him arrested and tried on trumped-up charges. Petkov protested from the dock that the Communists had intimidated, arrested, and beaten the supporters of the Agrarian Party, thrown many into concentration camps, and killed many, asking at the same time that he and his party be allowed to cooperate with the Communist Party. He said further:

The Prime Minister said that the opposition was the mouthpiece of international reaction—Britain and America. The Prime Minister gave no proof for these allegations . . . Tell us the truth, Mr. Dimitrov. Back your charges with facts. Our parliamentary immunity, our liberty, our fate, our very heads are at your disposal and anyhow within your power . . .

These were Petkov's last words in court:

I declare that I am not afraid whatever fate awaits me nor am I perturbed by shouts of "traitor," for both my father and my brother were murdered in the streets of Sofia, denounced as traitors, only to be recognized as national heroes by the Bulgarians afterward.

He was condemned to death and hanged.

Twice in the Middle Ages the ancestors of the Bulgarians had united most of the Balkans under their rule. The Bulgars, warrior horsemen, had followed the Huns in the migration of peoples from central Asia. They founded an empire on the Volga but the expanding Kazars pushed them further to the west. They then crossed the Danube, proceeded south, and subjugated the Slavs who lived in a tribal society.

Submerged by the more numerous Slavs, they adopted their language so that their present speech bears no trace of the ancient Bulgar. Nothing but the name has survived from their inheritance.

The old Bulgars continually attacked Byzantium but could not capture it. Tsar Boris "of the Bulgars and Serbs," did not become Roman Emperor, but when he adopted Christianity in the ninth century the Byzantine Patriarch recognized the independence of the Bulgarian church and its Slavonic liturgy.

For a century the Bulgars sank into subjection to Byzantium, but from a revolt there arose a new Bulgar dynasty, the Asens of Trnovo, who made the southwestern part of the Balkans one of the great centers of contemporary civilization. In the fourteenth century a short-lived Serbian empire engulfed it, but this was the last of the Christian attempts to embrace the peoples of the peninsula into one empire before the Ottoman Turks conquered it for Mohammedanism.

The Turks laid waste the countryside, burned towns, killed men, women, and children. People fled into the mountains, leaving the plains for Muslim landlords and peasants. Some Bulgarian nobles converted to Mohammedanism, as did those peasants who belonged to the heretic Bogomil sects, and these retained their land. The converted peasants were freed from serfdom while the Christians became serfs of the Turkish office holders who received the lands of Christian nobles. The Bogomil sect originated in Bulgaria, became the state religion of Macedonia and Bosnia, spread over the Alps to the northern Italians, and eventually reached Provence where it unfolded into the great heresy of the Albigenses. The essence of Bogomilian belief was that Satan, the first son of God, created the visible world. This explained the presence of evil. To renounce the world was their only means of salvation.

All Christians paid a head-tax and a tithe from their crops to the landlord, but the harshest levy was that on boys between the ages of ten and twelve, who were recruited for the Sultan's janissaries. Many a peasant felt only passing sorrow at this, however, for his sons had a chance of making a career in the service of the Sultan, while those who remained at home had no hope for a better life.

Moreover, the church denied the Bulgarians true consolation. A Greek Phanariot patriarch took the place of the Bulgarian. He appointed Greek parish priests, substituted the Greek for the Slavonic liturgy, and had all Slavonic holy books destroyed. In the very few schools, Greek was the language of education and slowly the people lost their consciousness of being Bulgarian. The Christian world lost track of them.

American Protestant missionaries rediscovered the Bulgarians in the eighteenth century. They found that the peasants spoke a Slav dialect but called themselves Greek. No literate people were found in the villages except for the Greek shopkeepers. The mountains teemed with outlaws and bandits, but some villages enjoyed the privilege of freedom from taxes in return for military service.

National revival began through the struggle for emancipation of the church. When the Greeks themselves revolted against Turkish rule the Sultan ceased to support their church domination in the Balkans, and in 1872 he established a Bulgarian exarchate, thereby restoring the Bulgarian national church.

In 1876, a horrible event brought the attention of the world to Bulgaria's existence. The Bulgarians revolted against the Turks who suppressed the uprising with their usual ruthlessness, killing fifteen thousand men, women, and children, and destroying fifty-eight villages as well as many monasteries. The English liberal, Gladstone, wrote a pamphlet on the massacre, which created broad interest in the Bulgarians. A year later Russia launched a war on the Turks, and the victorious Tsar, in 1878, dictated the terms of the peace treaty of San Stefano, which gave birth to modern Bulgaria.

As an autonomous province within the Turkish empire, Bulgaria had included Macedonia, though the rich harbor city of Salonika remained with Turkey. Its borders followed the Rhodope Mountains and reached the Black Sea near the port of Burgas.

However, the great powers, especially England and Austria, became alarmed at having a strong Russian satellite in the vicinity of the Dardanelles, and at the Congress of Berlin they forced Russia to agree that Bulgaria be substantially reduced in territory. The land between the Balkan and the Rhodope Mountains was made a separate province and called Eastern Rumelia. Russian troops occupied Bulgaria proper while the assembly elected the first prince. This body wished the prince to develop some measure of independence, but at the same time required him to be acceptable to the Tsar. The choice fell on the Hessian prince, Alexander of Battenberg, of whom a contemporary wrote:

. . . a favorite nephew of the Tsar, related to the English ruling house, a German prince, the son of an Austrian general, closely connected with Russia by virtue of his participation in the campaign of 1877-78 and yet not a Russian. The choice gave the impression of pleasing Disraeli, a compliment to Bismarck, a favor to Austria, and at the same time it seemed to place a willing tool in the hands of Russia.

At first the prince ruled with the help of Russian generals, but later, emboldened, he seized Eastern Rumelia without the consent of the Tsar. The Tsar promptly shipped him out of the country, but not before he had signed his abdication.

Germany had a large stock of princes for export. The assembly elected another one, Ferdinand of Saxe-Coburg-Gotha, which pleased the anti-Russian powers, the Sultan, Austria, and England. But Ferdinand was a shrewd man who knew that he could not long be in disfavor with the Tsar and still keep his throne. Slowly he gained the Tsar's confidence, and to reinforce the situation he had his son baptized in an Orthodox church.

But then that dormant volcano, the Macedonian question, erupted and threw the Balkans into a turmoil. (It re-

mains a bone of contention even now between three countries and their Communist parties.) The Congress of Berlin had left Macedonia with Turkey, cancelling the Tsar's
donation of the province to Bulgaria. But, unfortunately,
it was claimed not only by the Bulgarians but also by the
Serbs, Greeks, and Albanians.

The name of Macedonia is well known because of her
kings Philip and Alexander the Great who united Greece
in the fourth century B.C. The Romans conquered it in the
second century B.C. and, except when it was included in the
Bulgar and Serb empires, it remained with the Eastern
Roman Empire. The Turks took it over and held it for
five hundred years. Long ago the Slavs had migrated
there and become the majority of its inhabitants. These
Slavs considered themselves Bulgarians, but Serbs, Vlachs,
and Greeks also lived there. Macedonia, although a very
poor country, was coveted by all Balkan peoples for a good
reason. The road from central Europe to the only important harbor on the Aegean Sea, Salonika, led through it.

When the Congress of Berlin returned the country to
the Turks, Macedonians fled to Bulgaria in great numbers.
They formed IMRO (Internal Macedonian Revolutionary
Organization), a terrorist movement which was closely
linked to the Bulgarian government. It aimed at the autonomy of Macedonia in principle, but for all practical
purposes IMRO wanted to wrest parts of that province
from Serbia and Greece, unite them with the portion left
to Bulgaria, and incorporate the whole into Bulgaria. The
raids and bombings of IMRO made headlines in the world
press for over half a century. Though few people understood what the unrest was all about in that Balkan nest, it
kept the world on the brink of war.

In 1912, the Balkans surprised the world by demonstrat-
ing the fact that they had outgrown the tutelage of the
great powers. Bulgarians, Serbs, Greeks, and Montenegrins agreed on a common war against Turkey to liberate
Macedonia. The participants reached an agreement as to
the share of each of the territories to be liberated, and in

the summer they struck. The Turks were beaten, but then the great powers interfered and quickly destroyed the Balkan league. They ordered the Serbs off the Adriatic coast. Austria and Italy wanted to deny Serbia an outlet to the sea. The Serbs had to comply, but their agreed share having been cut, they asked the Bulgarians to revise the agreement. When the latter showed reluctance to release any of her share, Greeks and Serbs agreed on a new division. The Rumanians, who had not participated in the war, also put in claims. Threatened from all sides, the Bulgarians decided to strike first and in 1913 started the Second Balkan War. Greeks, Serbs, and Montenegrins, as well as the Turks and Rumanians, rushed in and, in a month, defeated the Bulgarians. The new distribution of spoils left Bulgaria bare of all territorial gains. In place of the Balkan League the Balkan states were in practice allied against Bulgaria to keep their shares.

In the meantime, Austria annexed Bosnia and Herzegovina; and when a Bosnian student shot Archduke Francis Ferdinand of Austria, World War I burst into flame.

Bulgaria stayed out of the holocaust for a while. Germany and Austria had far more to offer than the West, the latter being obligated to the Serbs. She could regain what she considered Bulgarian territory only at the expense of countries allied to the West. Moreover, to the German Prince Ferdinand of Bulgaria, it looked very much as if Germany was going to win. So Bulgaria, in 1915, entered on the German side and seized Macedonia.

As the war dragged on it became more and more unpopular. The Russian revolution finally undermined the morale of the army. Bulgaria collapsed first among the countries fighting on the German side, losing even the little foothold left her on the Aegean Sea.

At the end of the war, about seven million people, predominantly Bulgarians, populated Bulgaria, which extended over 42,796 square miles between the Danube and the Black Sea on the north and east, and Jugoslavia, Greece, and Turkey on the west and south. She was a land of peasants, who cultivated every inch of arable land by an old cooperative tradition. These sober people lived on goats' milk cheese, sour milk and vegetables, and they were noted for longevity. Seventy-year-old men still worked hardily all day long in the fields, and to have a hundred birthdays was no rarity. They drank neither coffee nor tea, beverages which were a habit in other Balkan countries.

After the war, in general dissatisfaction with the pro-German policy of the royal clique and politicians of the townspeople, the peasants brought about a legal revolution by electing Stambulisky's genuine Agrarian Party to an absolute majority. It could have swept away the king and his staff, as the other strong popular movement—that of the left-wing Socialists and later the Communists—advocated, but Stambulisky had a broader program in mind. He intended to reform the entire administrative system of the state so that it would actually serve the interests of the peasants. He shared the intense animosity of the peasants toward the sophisticated town people who lived on what the landfolk produced and manipulated prices and taxes in a manner which deprived the peasant of the fruits of his labor. Alexander Stambulisky as Prime Minister had a land reform law passed by Parliament which clearly mirrored this antagonism. No big estates existed in the country, and the reform expropriated tracts of over 75 acres. Yet the townspeople could retain only 25 acres if married and 10 if single. He introduced compulsory elementary education in order to wipe out illiteracy and revised the tax law so that it became progressive. Since the peace treaty had restricted the Bulgarian army, Stambulisky legislated for a year of labor service for public works, an institution which has not gone out of fashion since.

The military clique, high bureaucrats, and the few industrialists and merchants, frightened and disgusted, could do nothing against the formidable popular force active in the Stambulisky government until the peasant leader attempted a bold change in foreign policy. He tried to make peace with the Jugoslavs as a first step toward a South Slav federation. Such a policy involved wiping out the IMRO which relentlessly terrorized Serbian Macedonia and prodded the foreign policy of Bulgaria toward recovering the Bulgarian territories from Jugoslavia, Greece, and Rumania. At this point, Stambulisky went counter to the popular current, as the country was smarting over the loss of these territories. His new orientation offended not only the IMRO terrorists but also the large Macedonian refugee colony in Bulgaria and their sympathizers in the army. IMRO did not wait long. Stambulisky was shot in the street in 1923. A coup followed that put the old gang back in power and began a hunt for the peasant politicians. The Communists let the Stambulisky party go down without help, but seeing a most aggressive reaction seizing the government, they staged an uprising after the morale of the peasants had already been broken. The uprising was smashed by the police, and the Communist Party outlawed.

While terror raged, thousands of Agrarians and Communists were killed. Agrarian leaders who fled in time went to the West, and the Communist chieftains Georgi Dimitrov and Vasil Kolarov reached Moscow. The hunted Communists also resorted to violence. In 1925, they attempted to kill Boris in the Sofia Cathedral. A time bomb exploded during a full service and 125 worshipers perished, but Boris was not among them.

Meanwhile, the Comintern deemed Macedonia to be the ideal nucleus of an all-Balkan revolution. For this purpose it advised the Communist parties of the involved countries to ally themselves with the Macedonian IMRO and go to work. The Comintern and Stalin himself supported an independent Macedonia, which was the Bulgarian claim, but the Jugoslav and Greek Communists balked since such a policy would have ruined their popularity even with their own rank and file. A Communist-IMRO joint front was negotiated abroad, but those who were to sign the agreement were shot by one group of IMRO and those who opposed it by another.

IMRO raids concentrated on Jugoslav Macedonia. The royal clique there had wiped the name of Macedonia off the map, incorporating it into South Serbia, while Greece settled so many refugees in Greek Macedonia that they overwhelmed the Slav minority. Fascist Italy financed IMRO to harass Jugoslavia, and Bulgarian politics became immersed in IMRO machinations.

In 1927, the Communists reappeared behind the front of a "Workers' Party," and the left-wing Agrarians, although subdued appreciably, had also lifted their voices by 1933. The depression reached Bulgaria and made the political chaos even worse. War with Jugoslavia constantly threatened. In 1934, a group of young officers led by Damian Velchev, commander of the Military Academy, seized power. This group, the Zvenos, had close connections with pro-Russian intellectuals and were determined to reverse foreign policy radically, to dissolve and disarm IMRO, and to seek friendship with Jugoslavia. King Boris bowed to the *fait accompli* but only in order to wait for an appropriate time for revenge. A year later the opportunity presented itself in a disagreement between members of the group. Boris and his favorite generals got the upper hand. Damian Velchev was court-martialed and sentenced to death, but the sentence was commuted to life imprisonment. The Zvenos had cut down the Macedonian terrorists so that Boris inherited better relations with Jugoslavia. Boris now instituted his own personal dictatorship while the Agrarians and Communists formed a "constitutional bloc" aiming at the restoration of parliamentarianism. This produced a sympathetic echo throughout the country, but all the while, Nazi Germany was drawing Bulgaria nearer to herself by ever deeper economic penetration.

Finally there came a year when king and country were reconciled. This happened in 1939, when Hitler and Stalin surprised the world with their pact. Boris was now able to remain pro-Nazi and pro-German and still be friendly to the Soviet Union, and the people were allowed to demonstrate their pro-Russian feelings. But they parted company again when Boris joined the Axis. A year before, under Hitler's pressure, Rumania had returned Dobrudja, and now Hitler let Bulgarian armies occupy Macedonia. Although he withheld his last word on the future of the tormented province, the Bulgarians lost no time in eradicating Serb influence. Bulgarian took the place of the Serbian language in schools and offices, and even a King Boris University was inaugurated. Bulgarian priests seized the parishes, but it was difficult to say whether the Macedonians were happier under the Bulgarians or in Jugoslavia. Tito's partisans were welcomed there, but whether because they were Communists or Jugoslavs was not clear. In 1944, Bulgarian soldiers kept deserting to join Tito. It appears that Stalin switched to Jugoslavia's side in the Macedonian question under the condition that it become an autonomous republic within the future Jugoslav federation. As Tito interpreted it the new republic would include Bulgarian and Greek Macedonia as well, but many things were shrouded in the mist of the future—Bulgarian-Jugoslav federation plans, first supported then disavowed by Stalin, Greek civil war, Tito's break with Stalin, and Khrushchev's reconciliation with Tito. Meanwhile, Macedonia still remains split among three countries.

When the Fatherland Front took over the government, Bulgaria was, in many respects, in a more favorable position than others liberated by the Russians. She had suffered no war damage, nor did she have to pay reparations to the Soviet Union. Only to Greece and Jugoslavia was she indebted for $75 million, though Jugoslavia renounced $25 million of her share. The number of Soviet troops the country had to provide for was far smaller than in Rumania and Hungary. Bulgaria alone in all the Soviet orbit went through no period of inflation.

Nevertheless, she had basically the same problems to

solve. She was overcrowded, but there was no land to distribute to satisfy the landless. Nor was there much prospect for large-scale industrialization to absorb the population, since the country lacked industrial raw materials. Coal mines could produce enough to meet domestic needs, and there was a small output from iron ore, lead, chrome, and manganese deposits which might have been more intensively exploited. Existing light industries, mostly the processing of tobacco, cotton and fruit, employed only about 100 thousand people—less than were employed in various handicrafts.

Much could have been accomplished through raising productivity of the land, electrification, and irrigation; but on the other hand, though the method of cultivation was primitive, the Bulgarian peasants had made progress in cooperation. Credit and farming cooperatives began functioning in the second half of the last century, and the government founded an Agricultural Bank to support the peasants with cheap credit. The Fatherland Front government planned, in 1945, to extend farming cooperatives to village units. Members would retain ownership of their land with the right to withdraw from the pool. They would receive not only labor dividends from the profits but also capital dividends from land and equipment they had contributed —a deviation from the Soviet kolkhoz type of arrangement. The pool would pay taxes in money instead of in produce, thereby avoiding being exposed to exploitation by government price manipulations.

But the peasants received with mistrust even the obviously useful interventions of the government. During the first two years, no matter how much it insisted that it stood for private ownership, the peasants suspected that the Communists would take the land from them.

CHAPTER FOUR

Jugoslavia

On October 20, 1944, Tito's Partisan troops and the Soviet army under the command of Marshal Tolbukhin captured Belgrade, the capital of Jugoslavia. The Russians threw bridges over the Sava and Danube rivers, at whose confluence Belgrade had historically stood guard over the gate opening on the Balkans to the south and central Europe to the north. The Soviet army pursued the Germans who were retreating toward Hungary, while the Partisans fought to clear Jugoslavia of the enemy.

In the spring of 1945, Jugoslavia was reconstituted. It had fallen apart in 1941, mainly along the lines tracing the borders of seven lands united in 1918 but never really fused. The fact that Jugoslavia as a unit was reborn in pain and blood proved belatedly that the growth of its component parts into one state body was organically justified. World War II had given rise to a national revolution in the country. It began in 1941 with an almost total destruction of the makeshift unification of peoples and lands, and it ended in a real community.

Prior to this development, Jugoslavia appeared to be the classic example of the fatal consequences of President Wilson's message calling on all peoples to determine their fates for themselves. His first message accomplished its purpose. Like Joshua's trumpet call at the walls of Jericho, it caused the Hapsburg empire to come tumbling down. It was his second message, interpreting the first to the effect that each people was entitled to live in its own state, that set in motion a process of fragmentation in Eastern Europe which was to culminate in anarchy and despotism. The call came too late for the idea of a common origin and language to create a national state. The idea of nationalism had worked in the West where it had first permeated the middle classes. There the middle classes had made the state or made it over in their own image; and when the people became educated and lifted into this middle class the character of the nation had already been determined. But by the time the East Europeans could act upon the call, national consciousness had already penetrated into the deep layers of the common people. They had learned to venerate their particular traditions, culture, and languages while there was no middle class with such overwhelming prestige as to impress its traits on them all. Traditions and common historical experiences proved, in such cases, to be a stronger force for division than a community of origin and language was for fusion. No sooner did the new national states begin to function than powerful movements for national autonomy within sprouted from Slovakia in the Czechoslovak Republic and from Croatia in Jugoslavia. The claim for the right to national individuality within the "national" state sprang from the cult of tradition, tinged with Catholicism, as a protest against dissolution into an abstract, rational, lay form of nation.

In the case of Jugoslavia, the movement of the Croats for self-government started almost at the moment when the state was formed. Its specific vigor originated in the fact that the Croats had had their own state, although dependent on stronger ones, for more than a thousand years. More than any other centrifugal force, this movement became the instrument of the German Nazis and Italian Fascists to unleash passions, hatred, and revenge among national groups in order to destroy the state. Yet Jugoslavia emerged from the bloody fratricidal war as a unit, as a federal union of

South Slav peoples and not as a national state—true to the first inspiration of Wilson's message. This was the result of a national revolution, initiated by a Croat leader and his Serbian peasant followers, driven by the desire for long overdue social vindication on the part of the peasantry of all nationalities, and organized by professional revolutionaries.

The Croats had been settled by the Byzantine Emperor Heraclius in Illyria, in the territories bounded by the rivers Sava, Drin, and Morava and the Adriatic Sea. In the ninth century they already formed a vassal state of the Pope, developing into a kingdom in the next century. The king's power rested on the support of the tribal nobility. When King Zvonimir attempted to make himself independent by relying on the high clergy and the privileged coastal towns, he was slain at the assembly of the nobles. They offered the throne to the king of Hungary after he had solemnly confirmed their privileges. From then on, for nine hundred years (until 1918), Croatia was a land under the Hungarian crown.

At times the person of the king was the only tie between the two countries, but during most of their history they lived in organic political, military, and economic cooperation. A turning point in their relations took place when the Ottoman Turks, in 1526, defeated the Hungarians and occupied their fertile lowlands for a century and a half. A weakened Hungary and a small Croatia both lost their independence to the Hapsburgs. They might have parted company altogether but for an incident. At the end of the eighteenth century, two Austrian rulers, Maria Theresa and her son Joseph II, initiated an enlightened policy toward the serfs which drove the Croat nobles into a common defense of their privileges with the stronger Hungarian nobility. The Croat nobles had no second thoughts about sacrificing self-government to their interests and empowered the Hungarian assembly of the estates to look after their affairs. They further stated: "The rights and privileges granted by the ruler to Hungarian and Croat nobility are common goods of both countries. It thus behooves them that the Hungarian assembly, in which the Croats are also represented, should decide upon them."

The loss of autonomy had painful consequences when, in the beginning of the nineteenth century, nationalism infected the Hungarian nobility. Up to that time, the language of conversation and of discourse had been Latin in Hungary as well as in Croatia, the native language being in both cases left to the serfs. The Hungarians suddenly decided to substitute their own tongue for Latin, not only in their own land but in Croatia as well. With the impact of nationalism the Hungaro-Croatian community became increasingly unnatural, unrealistic, and unbearable for the weaker partner in spite of its very long standing. The Croats fought desperately to ward off Hungarian encroachment on their precarious self-government, and even sided with the Hapsburg emperor when, in 1848, the Hungarians revolted to safeguard their own independence. But in World War I it became clear to the Croats that they could expect no self-government within the Hapsburg empire. In 1918, the Croatian Diet declared its union with Hungary dissolved, the Hapsburg dynasty deposed, and the rights of the Diet transferred to the National Council of the Slovenes, Croats, and Serbs. And so was born South Slav, or Jugo-Slav, unity.

Yet the drama of unification had a short prelude. Napoleon had wrested Dalmatia from Venice, the Slovene territories from Austria, and Croatian provinces from Hungary, and unified them into one country which he called Illyria. He needed these lands to reinforce the continental blockade on Britain and conferred on them the blessings of the French Revolution. He replaced the Latin and German languages with the native Slavic in the administration, declared all people equal before the law, the serfs to be owners of the land they tilled, and tithes to the church abolished. These benefits fell on the deaf ears of a stupefied peasantry while provoking the savage hostility of the nobles. Napoleon's four-year rule left behind excellent roads and a bewildering memory. His sketch of a future Jugoslav country caused poets to envision it as a coming reality instead of a passing dream. No one but the professional dreamer, the poet, actually believed that the call of common descent and language could cause Dalmatians along the Adriatic coast, Slovenes in the Austrian Alps, Croats in union with the Hungarians, Bosnians still under Muslim overlordship, and Montenegrins independent in their inaccessible mountain abodes, to join the Serbs—a sturdy peasant people of whom Procopius, the historian of the Emperor Justinian, had already noted: "This people was never subject to a single man but has lived since ancient times in democracy."

Dalmatia, located on the long coastline of the eastern Adriatic, also joined the new state of Jugoslavia. Ancient and medieval history had left monuments of great prosperity there from the time when the Adriatic ports were the hub of east-west trade. The Hungarian kings exercised suzerainty over the land until one of them, in financial straits, sold it to Venice for 100,000 ducats in the fifteenth century. Venice left an indelible mark on the architecture of most Dalmatian towns, and also on the mountains behind them which she laid bare of forests in order to use the timber for shipbuilding. Napoleon ended Venetian rule when he remade the map of these parts.

Behind Dalmatia, another South-Slav inhabited province, Bosnia-Herzegovina, had its own history. When the Turks overran it in the fifteenth century, they gave the province a privileged status as a result of a peculiar turn of events. The feudal lords in Bosnia and many of their serfs converted to Mohammedanism, with the consequence that the lords preserved their estates and privileges and the converted serfs became free peasants exempt of the head-tax that all Christians had to pay to the Sultan. Feudalism lasted there through all the four hundred years of Turkish rule and well beyond it. In 1878, the Congress of Berlin authorized Austria to occupy the land though nominally it remained under Turkish suzerainty. The Austrians introduced an administration which was modern except that they did not touch the feudal system, for they intended to rely on the support of the landlords.

In 1908, Austria formally annexed Bosnia to the monarchy, causing distress and bitterness in neighboring Serbia. The bullet of a Serbian extremist killed the successor to the Austrian throne in 1914 and led to World War I.

The westernmost branch of the South Slavs, called Slovenes, had formed no self-governing community in a thousand years. They inhabited the Austrian Alps in Styria and Carinthia, and also the Istrian shores of the Adriatic, including the outskirts of Trieste, living in close intercourse with Germans and Italians. German influence captured the Slovene aristocracy with its bright prospects for advancement in the civil service and in the professions. But the Slovenes remained a homogeneous community organized around the Catholic church. They learned advanced methods of agriculture and industrial exploitation of their forests, fruit farms, and dairy products. Cooperative movements had an early start among them as protection against the strong impact of their German environment.

Moving east from the Slovenes, Dalmatians, and Croats, one leaves the Catholic Slavs, exposed as they have always been to German and Italian influence. In Bosnia-Herzegovina the Slav Mohammedans present a frustrating buffer between Catholic Croato-Slovenes and Orthodox Serbians. But Serbia proper was and is the basis of any Jugoslav community.

Serbia rose from the southernmost part of present-day Jugoslavia, and as early as the thirteenth century grew into a splendid center of medieval civilization. This was not a bubble that burst and vanished without a trace, for it left great monuments, churches, and monasteries shaped with the strength of Byzantine art though without its frozen rigidity. As in the Byzantine Empire, church and state were born simultaneously and presented two faces of one power. In the fourteenth century, under Stephen Dushan, Serbia rose to the height of power, conquering Macedonia, Al-

bania, Thessaly, and Bulgaria. Dushan proclaimed himself
Emperor of Serbs, Bulgars, and Albanians, and had set out
to seize Constantinople itself and become Roman Emperor,
when suddenly he died. He was a great prince as well as
military leader. His code of laws can be compared to the
Magna Carta.

Shortly after his death the Ottoman Turks intruded into
his empire, and Prince Lazar, at the head of Serbian and
other Christian armies, engaged them in one of the great
battles of history at Kossovo in 1389. Both Prince Lazar
and the Sultan lost their lives, but the Turks prevailed and
subjugated Serbia. For more than four centuries, the
Serbian church remained the only institutional force in the
nation.

In the seventeenth century the Hapsburgs launched the
Christian counteroffensive to force the Turks out of Central
Europe and subsequently out of the Balkans. But a century
later, Tsarist Russia began imposing herself on the Turks
in the role of protector of the Sultan's Christian subjects.
Austrian-Russian rivalry over Serbia and the Balkans in
general made the road to liberation hazardous.

At the beginning of the nineteenth century the Serbs revolted against Turkish rule. Two families supplied leadership, one relying on the Russians, the other on the Austrians.
After the Serbs succeeded in gaining self-government, the
two factions intermittently ruled the country as hereditary
princes, murdering or forcing each other out of the country.

Under the Obrenovich dynasty Serbia became a dependency, economic and political, of the Hapsburg empire.
When Austria occupied Bosnia-Herzegovina in 1878, it
blocked Serbia from the sea, leaving her commerce to Austria's mercy. After many revolts, Serbian officers killed the
Obrenovich king and queen, and Peter Karageorge assumed
the throne and reversed the subservience to Austria by a
pro-Russian orientation. Austria retorted with the so-called
"pig war," closing the frontiers to pigs and other Serbian
articles of export. But the king and the shrewd Pashich,
leader of the pro-Russian party, refused to submit, found

an outlet to foreign markets through Salonika, and bought arms in the West with the money. The defiance of little Serbia drove Austria into moves of exasperation which in several instances brought the world to the verge of war before it actually broke out.

In two Balkan wars, prior to World War I, Serbia expanded in the south at the expense of the Turks in 1912, and of the Bulgarians the following year. By annexing most of Macedonia she frustrated Balkan unity and reaped a harvest of plots, assassinations, and enmity in the heart of the Balkans in her struggle with Bulgaria, Albania, and Greece.

Another Serbian land, Montenegro, was still outside the Serbian nation. The Turks had never entirely succeeded in smoking the natives out of their mountain abode above the eastern Adriatic. The tallest people in Europe, dark haired, and with fierce black eyes, they lived in an ancient tribal society. Most of the monetary income of this tiny principality flowed in from Russia. Since Peter the Great, the tsars had supported their most faithful Orthodox Montenegrins by a yearly stipend. Their peasant prince was a favorite subject of Viennese operettas, but he was an astute observer of international political intrigue and did not hesitate, while standing unfailingly for the Tsar, to accept plums from any state which had a finger in the Balkan pie.

Serbian colonies existed in autonomous Croatia-Slavonia and in the south of Hungary, in the Bachka, Baranja, and the western Banat. At first, refugees from the Turks settled there, but later, when the Hapsburgs had reconquered the Hungarian plains and pushed the Turks back, they established a military frontier in southern Hungary and settled Serbians there as free peasants except for the lifelong duty of being frontier guards subject to the emperor. The Hapsburgs also invited settlers from abroad—Germans, Slovaks, Rumanians, and even French from Lotharingia—to the depopulated area and especially to the Banat, one of the most fertile lands in Europe.

These Serbs of central Europe profited by the proximity of peoples of higher cultural standards and also from currents of Western ideas, and their colonies developed into the foci of cultural and political renaissance for the South Slavs.

Serbia itself, emerging from four centuries of Turkish rule, was a country of free, crude, straightforward, mostly illiterate peasants imbued with a ferocious will for independence. Feudalism was abolished there in the twilight of semi-independence between 1815 and 1833, the peasant becoming owner of the land he tilled without having to pay compensation to the Turkish feudal lords. Serbia became a peasant democracy with no big landowners or privileged class. Yet its political development lagged. As in other Balkan lands, politics became the profession of a circle of the intelligentsia. Just one generation removed from the peasantry, this group rose to power with the help of a peasant program but changed its outlook once inside the power bracket. At best the over-all interest of the state replaced the requirements of the masses, which were considered incorporated in the dynasty; the high officers, bureaucrats, and self-styled statesmen revolved around the court. They liked to speak in the name of the peasantry, true to the cynical phrase they coined that one can legislate against the peasantry but not without it. Instead of a true democratic government, an autocracy of the king and his favorites was instituted, superficially changing its aspects through upheavals and murders. This ruling caste attended to its own interest in the firm conviction that what was good for it would turn out to be beneficial for the rest, but it stood also for the military and political aggrandizement of the state. The Serbian ruling clique eyed Macedonia, Bosnia-Herzegovina, and Montenegro, but shied away from the Jugoslavian idea as conceived by the South Slavs in the Hapsburg monarchy. It wanted no large numbers of Germanized and Italianized Catholic Slavs with their sophisticated cultural and political traditions and ambitions.

However, Jugoslavia fell into their laps inevitably with the collapse of the Hapsburg empire. Croatia, Slovenia, and Dalmatia could not stand alone in the face of Italy's covetous eye on the coastlands of the eastern Adriatic. Little Austria would not have them, and Croatia had had enough of partnership with Hungary. So the reluctant Serb clique could not avoid accepting Jugoslavia, but it did so with the mental reservation that it was to be but an extension of Serbia.

There was no objection from other Slav groups against Serbia serving as the base for Jugoslavia, since it was the most populous state, comprising more than one third of the population, and also represented the Orthodox Slavs who numbered more than half the inhabitants of the new Jugoslavia. Moreover, the Catholic Slavs had fought on the opposite side in World War I, against Serbia and the West, except toward the end when the prisoners of war joined the Serbian armies. The addition of South-Slav lands rewarded Serbia's epic valor on the Allied front. The Serbs had been unbending in the first distress of defeat, though forced out of their land by the superior forces of the Germans and Austrians, and they had resumed the fight until final victory.

Jugoslavia faced an enormous problem in welding into a unit a population shaped in such widely differing fashions by geographical position, cultural environment, historic traditions and economic progress. It required a gigantic effort to bridge the distance in degrees of civilization. The single fact that in South Serbia about 80 per cent of the population over ten years of age was illiterate, while in Slovenia the figure was only 6 per cent, indicated the magnitude of the problem of creating a community of any sort of conformity.

Economically, the country as a whole was backward, with about 80 per cent of its people engaged in agriculture. But while the Serbs and Montenegrins were independent smallholders, the peasants in Bosnia and Dalmatia lived practically in serfdom, burdened with feudal dues against the use of their little plots of land. In Croatia-Slavonia and in the formerly Hungarian Voivodina, large estates dominated the dwarfholder who did part-time work on the estate as well as on his strip in order to make ends meet.

Land hunger drove the peasants, without waiting for the law, to seize the land during the years of upheaval at the end of the war. The land reform by and large legalized the seizures and the liquidation of the feudal survivals which actually had taken place when the peasants stopped paying feudal dues.

Through the law more than half a million families received about two million acres. The unit varied according to regions and the category of the applicant. War volunteers received more than simple local residents; Slav settlers near the border also enjoyed special favors.

The repopulating of war-torn South Serbia contributed to the solution of the general problem, which was growing with the high birthrate, but little happened otherwise to raise the productivity of this fertile region. Out of every thousand peasants, only 438 were tilling the fields with iron ploughs as late as 1940—almost twenty years after Jugoslavia had been constituted. In Bosnia, however, the abolition of feudalism produced immediate results in increasing production and in the variety of produce.

On the other hand, the highly modernized agriculture and the processing industry in the Voivodina suffered a setback as a consequence of the breaking up of the large estates which, incidentally, belonged mostly to foreigners—Austrians and Hungarians. But the region still remained the largest source of income from agricultural export.

About half the farmers participated in cooperatives for buying equipment and seed and for selling their produce, but a long time was needed for education, investment, and industrialization in order to solve the basic problem of raising the standard of living. There was also need for a government dedicated to the pursuit of such solutions. Jugoslavia had none of these requirements.

She did have a great wealth of industrial raw materials, especially nonferrous ores and metals, copper, antimony, and bauxite; but foreign, mostly French and British, enterprises exploited them. Germany gave a fresh impetus to light industry when she began to penetrate and organize the Balkan market for her rearmament. She helped Jugoslavia weather the depression by buying agricultural produce at prices above those of the open market, and she rapidly replaced other buyers of Jugoslavian export commodities, traditionally sold to Austria, Italy, Germany, and, to a lesser extent, other Western countries. Since Jugoslavia participated in the sanctions against Italy when she embarked on the conquest of Abyssinia, Germany displaced the Italian trade. She then annexed Austria and subsequently occupied Jugoslavia's important client and friendly investor, Czechoslovakia, so that Jugoslavia was at Germany's mercy economically years before she became so politically.

Politically, Jugoslavia had an ominous start. As soon as the new country was legally instituted, the royal camarilla set the goal of transforming Jugoslavia into a greater Serbia. This course ran contrary to the expectations of all groups other than the Serbs in Serbia itself, since even the Serbs in Croatia hoped that a great measure of self-government would be granted to each constituent province. A Serb leader in Croatia wrote:

Not only the Croats and the Slovenes, but, let us frankly admit, even the Serbs outside the borders of the old kingdom of Serbia refuse to suffer the hegemony of Serbia . . . There is no power on earth capable of breaking the Croatian idea. It is easier to imagine the Velebit mountains crumbling down and into the sea, or the rivers Sava and Drava running dry, than the Croats renouncing their aspirations to a free and unimpeded development of their individuality and the necessary guarantee to safeguard it.

The Croatian Peasant Party represented the claim of self-government. It was originated in a sheer peasant protest against the system of big landed estates predominant in Croatia and owned, moreover, by foreign lords and Magyarized or Germanized Croats. The high property requirement for the right to vote when Croatia had lived in union with Hungary had given no room for the party to unfold its strength. But in 1919, at the first elections in Jugoslavia, the party captured almost all Croatian districts.

Stephen Radich, the uncontested leader of the Croatian peasantry, realized that the sweeping success of his party was due to its uncompromising nationalist stand. He took into account the religious feelings of his followers and noted that resistance to Serb hegemony would of necessity take on a Catholic character. However, he did not subordinate the movement to church politics. On the contrary, he often voiced the resentment of the Croat public over the support that the high clergy had given to Austrian and Hungarian policies. Radich hoped to reverse the pan-Serbian course of the kingdom by the intervention of the great Western powers responsible for Jugoslavia as a creature of the peace treaties. His party therefore boycotted the Constituent Assembly and the Parliament in Belgrade. The centralist constitution fared poorly even in the rump Assembly which passed it by a simple majority and then only after some groups of deputies had been bribed by the government.

The elections demonstrated, in fact, that two antagonistic and competing sectionalisms faced one another and not an all-national front opposing separatism. The only all-national party that issued from the elections was the Communist, which finished fourth and was soon outlawed and driven underground. The other parties restricted their appeal to regional groups. The fact that the Communists alone represented an all-national program would have gone unnoticed had not Radich given it some significance. He first visited the Western capitals for support for his federalistic claim. Receiving no encouragement, he went to Moscow, but what he heard and saw there was even less

enticing. As a result, he gave up the boycott of the P
ment. By this resolution Radich accepted the platfo
the state, making it possible for other groups to suppoιι ⅲ
claim for autonomy without exposing themselves to the accusation of treason. Actually, the party gained strength in
Parliament through the support of groups that had no separatist traditions but wanted more self-government and less
Serbian centralism.

Serbs entrenched themselves in high positions in the administration and other national institutions. The army had
165 general officers, and all but two were of Serb nationality.
Ninety per cent of the officers corps consisted of Serbians.
The proportion was similar in all important positions. It is
not simple to show the true proportion of Serbs and Croats
in the state since both claim, for instance, that the Bosnian
Muslims are Serbs or Croats respectively. Also, to measure
the strength of both groups one must keep in mind the fact
that the Serbs in Croatia mostly supported the Croat claim
for autonomy. The Slovenes and Dalmatians opposed the
Serb-centered regime along with the Croats, but they did
not claim autonomy for themselves.

In 1931, in a total Jugoslav area of 154,000 square miles,
3,095,000 Serbs lived in Serbia proper and 2,789,000 Serbs
in other provinces of Jugoslavia, as against 2,100,000 Croats
in Croatia proper and 1,990,000 Croats in other provinces.

Hatred for Radich and the Croatian Peasant Party grew
among the Serbian die-hards and resulted, in 1928, in his
murder, together with two deputies of his party, by a Serb
member at an open session of Parliament. The effect of this
political murder was that the Croat Peasant Party resumed
the boycott of Parliament and this time the party of the
Serbs in Croatia joined in the move. King Alexander then
dismissed the Parliament, suspended the constitution and
assumed a dictatorship.

Jugoslavia was a member of the Little Entente along with
Czechoslovakia and Rumania, but was more involved in its
anti-revisionist aspect directed against Hungary than in its
role as part of a French military alliance system for keeping

Germany within its treaty-designated bounds. Jugoslavia had no directly conflicting interests with Germany, but Italian designs for making the Adriatic Sea an Italian lake kept their relations tense and many times on the verge of open conflict. Those who saw a Serbian infantry unit marching had the strong feeling that these fierce warriors would more than stand fast against three times as many Italian soldiers. But later events demonstrated that the Jugoslav army, in spite of the relatively great expenditures for its fitness, was poorly equipped. To strengthen his country's position towards Italy, King Alexander visited the King of Bulgaria who refused to join the Little Entente, since Bulgaria would not renounce Macedonia which had been wrested from her by Serbia in 1913 in the second Balkan War.

For the same purpose, Alexander also planned to visit France. But the calm imposed by his dictatorship indicated only its efficiency in suppressing the opposition while dissatisfaction mounted and spread. Hardly had he disembarked in Marseilles when a terrorist shot him and the French Minister for Foreign Affairs who had come to greet him. The murderer belonged to the Croat Fascist organization called "Ustasha" which had a terrorist training ground in Hungary financed by Mussolini.

Peter II, successor to the throne, was a minor and a regency took over the royal functions. Actually, Prince Paul, one of the regents, exercised control. Meanwhile, Jugoslavia became increasingly dependent on Germany economically, and at first the political effects appeared rather beneficial as a counterbalance to the Italian dictator's persistent ambitions. But after Hitler's annexation of Austria and his subsequent destruction of Jugoslavia's closest friend, Czechoslovakia, Belgrade became concerned over internal tensions. The case of Czechoslovakia ominously demonstrated how Slovak separatism had helped Hitler in dismembering the country. To avoid tempting his application of the same method to Jugoslavia, the Belgrade government accorded autonomy to Croatia in 1939.

The move caused consternation among officers, bureaucrats, and influential sections among the Serbian public. However, fast moving events began to involve Jugoslavia in the war. The regent tried to appease Hitler by declaring the country neutral and speaking out against the British guaranty to the Balkan countries in case of aggression. Hitler might have been satisfied for a time with the economic and political domination of Jugoslavia had not Mussolini taken the military initiative by attacking Greece. Instead of a swift and victorious conquest, the Italians were beaten by the valiant Greeks in the fall of 1940. Hitler was busy preparing for the great adventure of war on Russia, but it was risky to start it while his Balkan economic hinterland might go to pieces under the impact of an ultimate failure by Mussolini in Greece. He quickly enrolled one central European and Balkan country after another in the Axis pact, encircling Jugoslavia, while his troops marched into Bulgaria as a first step toward the rescue of Mussolini in Greece—and also toward invading Serbia.

In March, 1941, Hitler summoned Prince Paul to Berchtesgaden and demanded that Jugoslavia join the Axis. The prince went home, called the Crown Council, and submitted the request for a decision. The Council found no alternative to capitulation. The pact proposed by Hitler, known as the Vienna Protocol, did not require Jugoslav participation in the war. It even guaranteed that no Axis troops would be transported through Jugoslavia, and also that the territorial integrity of the country would be assured.

But there was strong feeling among the Serbian public against submitting to the Axis. Although the fall of France and of Poland left no hope for any chance of successful resistance, bitter resentment against Prince Paul and the government turned into violent anger. Two days after the signature of the pact, young officers headed by General Dushan Simovich went into action. They seized power, dismissed the regency, exiled Prince Paul, and proclaimed King Peter of age.

The *coup d'état* electrified Serbia, but the public may have misunderstood its significance. Although rumor persisted that the defeatist attitude of the Croat members of the Crown Council had been influential in the decision to submit to Hitler's demands, the Serbian public considered the coup as an outbreak of Serbian protest against the Council's subservience and ultimate submission, and did not connect it with the opposition in the army and bureaucracy to the federalization of Jugoslavia. The presence of Dr. Machek, leader of the Croat autonomist Peasant Party, dispelled any suspicion that the moving force of the putsch had been the hope to halt or reverse the trend of federalization. Actually, the conspiracy against Prince Paul may have been of an earlier date, with action reserved for an appropriate moment.

On the other hand, the new government showed no signs of hardening toward Hitler. It hastened to reassure the German Fuehrer that it stood for all agreements signed by its predecessor, specifically for the one obliging Jugoslavia to join the Axis. The government instructed its representatives abroad to the effect that "the principal care is to pursue a policy of good and friendly relations with Germany and Italy and that it will energetically resist being drawn into the present conflict. With a view to preserving all vital national interests of Jugoslavia, the royal government will take a particular interest in the manner of application of the Vienna protocol."

Whatever the actual motives behind the coup, the public was relieved to see its protests resulting in action. It had seen two examples illustrating two divergent attitudes taken by friendly countries who lay in Hitler's path. Czechoslovakia and Poland both had gone down, the first without a fight, the second in fire and blood. The Serbian public was satisfied that the young men at its helm had chosen to fight. It was confident anyway that in the end the West would prevail over the Germans.

But Hitler could take no risks and time was pressing.

On April 6, 1941, his Stukas bombed Belgrade to shreds, although it had been declared an open city. German, Italian, Hungarian, and Bulgarian troops invaded Jugoslavia, and less than two weeks later, the Jugoslav army surrendered.

In Jugoslavia Hitler and Mussolini found a proving ground on which to show how a multinational country could be so disrupted as to make any healing process almost hopeless. The two dictators dismembered Jugoslavia. Hitler attached the greater part of Slovenia to Austria and left the coastal lands and Montenegro to Mussolini. He allowed Bulgaria to occupy Serbian Macedonia, Albania to annex the Kossovo region in South Serbia, Hungary the Bachka and Baranja. Croatia was made an "independent state," enlarged with Bosnia-Herzegovina and its Mohammedan and Serbian population. He left Serbia as it had been in 1912, to be governed by a Serbian government of a kind. The Banat was turned over to its German minority to run.

Hitler approached Machek as the logical choice to run an independent Croatia, but he refused to head a puppet government. It was then that Ante Pavelich, leader of the Croat terrorist Ustasha organization, long on Mussolini's payroll and responsible for the murder of King Alexander, took over as "Poglavnik" (Fuehrer). Pavelich offered the ancient crown of Croatia to the Italian dynasty, and the king assigned it to one of his cousins who showed, however, no haste in ascending the throne.

In Serbia, Hitler found quite respectable people to assume responsibility for a government restricted to internal administration. A general, Milan Nedich, formerly Minister of War, accepted what he considered to be the role played by Petain in France, although with clearly less chance of any shred of independence from Hitler than the French marshal was anxious to preserve. While the Croat

Fuehrer declared war on the Allies and became a full-fledged partner of the Axis powers, Serbia was considered by the Axis an enemy country.

A colonel on the General Staff, Drazha Mihailovich, refused to surrender when the order came. Instead, he issued an appeal to the people for resistance to the invaders. He took up the organization of guerilla forces named after the Chetniks, who had had a great tradition of underground warfare during the Turkish occupation. Mihailovich believed in the ultimate victory of the Allies and wanted to build up army cadres to be mobilized for a final assault when the Allies should land. He also wished to have a nucleus harassing the invaders to prove that Jugoslavia had never stopped fighting on the side of the Allies.

The defeated army dissolved. Several groups engaged in sabotage, for which the Germans retaliated savagely. For each German a hundred Serbs had to die; for a destroyed convoy a whole village was burnt to the ground. Many Serbian soldiers went into the woods and joined guerilla forces commanded by army officers who paid allegiance to Mihailovich but had little contact with him. All occupying armies applied bloody terror to their zones in order to consolidate their hold in the face of a hostile population that kept its arms in hiding and burned with the lust to kill their oppressors. The Hungarians, who had concluded a treaty of eternal friendship with Jugoslavia just before the invasion, murdered more than ten thousand Serbs and Jews in the Bachka. The Albanians were not far behind in atrocities. The Bulgarians alone behaved decently, but they garrisoned Macedonia, a province friendly to them.

The raids of extermination launched by the Croat Ustasha overshadowed the horrors perpetrated by the occupation armies. They set out to kill all Serbs in Croatia and Bosnia-Herzegovina and incited the population to participate in a campaign to seize the land and homes of the Serbians. The movement took on a medieval aspect when priests, especially Franciscan monks, turned it into a crusade to make the Orthodox Serbs convert to Catholicism or perish. The Catholic clergy approved of the crusade, bishops gave their blessing to the Ustasha, and even Archbishop Stepinac helped to make the Poglavnik and his gang respectable by appearing publicly at his side on platforms. The Ustasha showed brotherly tolerance toward the Muslims in Bosnia, who massacred the Serbs as Serbs and not as heretics. Reports to the effect that the crusade had victims amounting to a million may have been exaggerated, but their numbers were staggering. The hunted Serbs fled into Serbia or the mountains. With revenge in their hearts, they wanted to fight and kill and they flocked to the guerillas who did just that regardless of the consequences. But these guerillas, calling themselves Partisans, were led by Tito, not by Mihailovich.

Tito's real name was Josip Broz. A Croat and a locksmith by profession, he became a prisoner of war in Russia during World War I, took part in the revolution, and on returning home became a professional revolutionary. In 1937, as Secretary General of the Communist Party, he proved to be an outstanding organizer and a true Stalinist, while the Party in the underground went through several purges of Trotskyites and anarchists. After the surrender of the Jugoslav army to Hitler, Tito left Zagreb, in Croatia, for Belgrade and began to organize a movement of national liberation. The Germans were invading Russia and withdrew much of their army from Serbia, leaving thin forces in the western parts of the country. Tito set up headquarters in Uzhice, a rugged region of that land, which had a small ammunition factory in operational order. As commander of the Partisans he got in touch with Mihailovich to negotiate cooperation with the Chetniks. The two guerilla leaders met three times in September and October of 1941. They agreed not to fight each other, but Mihailovich had received authority from London, where King Peter and Prime Minister Simovich had established a government-in-exile, to be the commander of the home front, and he would not negotiate with Tito on an equal footing. Moreover, Mihailovich was a staunch anti-Communist and one

of the bulk of Serbian officers who did not want to restore
Jugoslavia with its separatist Croats and Slovenes. Tito
was a Croat and a Communist—a double reason why he
would not cooperate for long with the Chetniks. Even
their working agreement foundered on Tito's organization
of local councils in the Uzhice region. Mihailovich wanted
no part in these since he claimed to represent the established authority, and the councils were a revolutionary institution. While the Partisans preached and practiced relentless fighting against the Germans, Mihailovich was
anxious to preserve his forces and to give no pretext to the
Germans for decimating the population.

The Germans were tipped off in the meantime on the
dissension between Partisans and Chetniks and launched
an offensive on the Uzhice "republic" in which Tito also ran
the civilian administration. Mihailovich, instead of helping
the Partisans, moved his Chetniks out of the area. The
Hitler-sponsored Prime Minister, General Nedich, got in
touch with Mihailovich and attempted to reach an agreement on cooperation against the Partisans. It came to
nothing though negotiations were resumed from time to
time.

The Partisans made a last-minute escape from the German ring, and from that moment they and the Chetniks
became more and more bitter enemies as the merciless
guerilla war proceeded.

The youth, even girls, flocked to the Partisans, not only
eager to fight but longing for a new Jugoslavia in which
fraternity instead of fratricide would prevail, the people
itself wield power, the country's natural treasures serve
their welfare, and the principles of fraternity and cooperation be embodied in the institutions. At first, mostly Serbs
heeded the call, but soon the other national groups followed. Orthodox priests joined the Partisans, also Franciscan monks and Communist students, but the vast majority were peasants.

Meanwhile the Jugoslav government-in-exile appointed

Mihailovich its Minister of War and, in the absence of on-the-spot information, succeeded in magnifying his accomplishments in harassing the enemy, even attributing to him the successes of the Partisans.

The country had little respect for the politicians who had fled the country, and Tito and his Partisans had none. In 1942, when he again succeeded in establishing his hold more or less safely, this time in Bosnia, Tito called a congress of delegates from several Serb, Croat, and Slovene parties to the town of Bihach. This congress elected an Anti-Fascist National Council which laid down a program of national equality, stressing that any social changes would have to originate from the free will of the people.

Tito and his Partisans received recognition by the Allies in 1943. Mihailovich's Chetniks had openly cooperated with the enemy troops against them in Bosnia, and Allied officers had arrived in their camp and bore witness to the actual situation. Their reports reversed the policy of the Allies with respect to Mihailovich and discredited the Jugoslav government-in-exile which from then on began a series of reappraisals in order to avoid the reproach that it represented pan-Serbian and reactionary circles. In November, Sir Henry Maitland Wilson, Commander of the Mediterranian area, warned the Jugoslav guerillas who were helping the Germans, and a few weeks later the British government officially announced that the British were giving more help to Tito's Partisans than to Mihailovich's Chetniks "for the simple reason that the resistance of the Partisan forces to the Germans is very much greater." The United States promptly declared that it was supplying the Partisans with military help.

In September, Tito convened another congress of the Council of National Liberation which adopted the resolution that Jugoslavia was a federation of six equal units: Serbia, Croatia, Slovenia, Macedonia, Montenegro, and Bosnia-Herzegovina. It also denied the government-in-exile the right to represent Jugoslavia and forbade the king

to return. In the meantime, one of Mihailovich's lieutenants
massacred Croats and Muslims in South Serbia. For the
Chetniks the war had definitely turned into a civil war, all
enemies of the Partisans becoming their allies.

In December, 1943, at Teheran, the Western Allies decided to supply Tito with arms. It was Churchill who
pressed the issue and promoted Tito's case resolutely,
though Tito and his staff bore the Soviet star on their caps.
But Churchill clung stubbornly to his plan to invade the
Balkans from Italy, in which case he would rely heavily
on the help of the fighting Partisan army. The Russians
opposed the plan as no substitute for the Allied invasion
of the continent through France. The Balkan front would
draw away manpower and supplies from the main forces
and blunt the overwhelming effect of the major offensive.
The Americans refused to consider the plan, but Churchill's
insistence was not without influence on Roosevelt who, at
the Teheran Conference, mentioned it as a possibility.

Although he could not overcome the combined American-
Soviet opposition to his pet plan, Churchill brought strong
pressure to bear on King Peter and the government-in-exile
to drop Mihailovich and form a government acceptable to
Tito for cooperation. As a result of a series of government
crises, for the first time in the country's history a Croat
was appointed to head a new Jugoslav government consisting of moderate and democratic members. Stalin, on his
part, managed to soften Tito into agreeing to a "representative" government. This came about as a result of negotiations between Tito and Dr. Ivan Shubashich, the new
Prime Minister of the London government and former
Regent of Croatia. The agreement gave authority to Tito's
Parliament and its National Committee of Liberation to
administer the country temporarily, provided for a new
government composed of progressive and democratic elements, and left the question of the monarchy to the country
to resolve after liberation.

Tito's relations with Stalin, however, took a much rougher
course than those with Churchill. As early as 1942, Stalin

made a point of the fact that Tito had overstepped the line.
He wrote:

Do not consider your struggle only from your national point of view,
but from the international point of view—from the point of view of
the English-Soviet-American coalition.

Yet Tito's deviation had started even earlier. He and his
Communist lieutenants were, before they realized it, caught
in a national revolution which carried them to its leadership.
When they had first organized the Partisan movement as a
common front of people from all walks of life for liberation
from foreign invaders and their domestic helpers, they had
concealed their plan to maneuver it into the Communist
Party camp. But fraternity formed in the face of death
and torture before death tolerated no hypocrisy. The Party
men felt guilty of a betrayal of their non-Party comrades,
and this resulted in their determination that fraternity
should survive the war and the party line—even the Party
itself. Before Tito and his Communist staff realized it,
the popular front became genuine—the fighting front of a
national revolution.

Tito may have thought that his social revolution was national only on the surface, and he was right to the extent
that nationalism and social reform both played their part.
Beyond liberation, other common aims fed the enthusiasm
and demanded the devotion and sacrifice of the fighting
peasants, students and workers, boys and girls. They fought
for a more decent life for themselves and for others, for
more honesty and more appreciation of the common people,
their strivings, and their work. Above all, they fought for
a new Jugoslavia—a community of South Slav peoples living
according to their traditions, respecting their brethren's
ways as well as their own. It was seen that only fundamental changes would mold the several provinces and
peoples of Jugoslavia into a nation. In the two decades of
Jugoslavian life, the regime had never tolerated any true
representation of the people. Concealed and open dictatorship and sheer terror had kept the people mute, poor,
ignorant, and mistrusting each other. In blood and flame,

these simple people fought to make things different in the future. They wanted, in short, a more humane world. Such a spirit has always driven people to the barricades in all national revolutions.

A short review of Soviet-Jugoslav relations will help to show how the Jugoslav national revolution ran counter to proletarian internationalism, which meant the primacy of the interests of the Soviet Union, as determined by Stalin, over local national interests.

On April 5, 1941, Moscow had announced the conclusion of a Soviet-Jugoslav treaty of friendship and nonaggression. It restated Soviet interests in the Balkans which Hitler's latest moves had disregarded. The day after the announcement, Hitler invaded Jugoslavia. Impressed by the lightning success of the Nazis, the Soviets withdrew recognition from Jugoslavia three weeks after her surrender, and to give further evidence of their desire for cooperation with the Nazis, the Russians expelled the Jugoslav Minister to Moscow.

As soon as the resistance started, Moscow lauded Mihailovich's accomplishments, saying nothing of Tito's Partisans, although Tito kept Moscow regularly informed on his actions. In 1942, Moscow complained that the Partisans were recruited only from Communists and their sympathizers and warned that the British and the government-in-exile might suspect that Tito was bent on Sovietizing Jugoslavia. In the same year, Stalin offered supplies to Mihailovich through the government-in-exile, which refused to accept them, and meanwhile denied supplies to Tito in spite of constant requests—referring to technical difficulties. In April, 1942, on Tito's complaint that Mihailovich was collaborating with the enemy, Stalin advised that it would be better for Tito to appeal to the government-in-exile and ask that it give support to all fighting forces. In the fall of 1942, when Tito called a convention of the Council of National Liberation, Stalin took exception to Tito's plan of setting up a provisional government. The next year when Tito actually formed the provisional government and the Council spoke out against the king's return to Jugoslavia,

Stalin made known his dissatisfaction. Only after the Teheran conference had decided to support Tito instead of Mihailovich, did Stalin finally decide to send a military mission to Tito's headquarters. The British and Americans had kept missions there since 1942. Yet Stalin had not missed congratulating King Peter on the New Year of 1944.

At the time when Partisan and Soviet forces captured Belgrade (in October, 1944), a Jugoslav group was present in the Kremlin while Stalin and Churchill agreed to share influence on a fifty-fifty basis in Jugoslavia. The Jugoslavs had no inkling that Stalin might strike a deal on their future without consulting or even informing them.

Tito himself had been in Moscow shortly before and met Stalin for the first time. They agreed that the Soviet armies would, after the liberation of Belgrade, proceed to Hungary and leave it to the Partisans to clear Jugoslavia of the enemy. In this instance, Stalin still suggested that Peter be reinstated as king, but Tito refused.

Tito returned home and his Partisans took over the entire country by the spring of 1945. For him and his Communist staff the heroic phase of the revolution was over. The sober work ahead for them now was to shape the liberated country into the preconceived Soviet institutional mold. But Tito had resolved to make substantial departures from the Soviet pattern laid down for the so-called peoples' democracies. In the latter, the Communist Party was to act as a distinct entity in coalition with many other parties, as the most dynamic agent of a policy which, in 1945–46, professed a democratic program acceptable to the West. In the Jugoslav system, the Party remained anonymous, with no public shape or function. It was diffused in the larger unit of Partisanship, extending even further into a People's Front that incorporated and transmitted the spirit of the Partisans. But the policies of which the Front became the carrier were almost provocatively shaped on the Soviet model.

The provisional government contained genuine representatives of non-Communist democratic parties and a regency which symbolized royal powers. But when it came

to the election which was to lay down the foundations of the
new regime, Tito prevented the parties outside the People's
Front from putting up candidates. The representatives of
these traditional and democratic parties were compelled to
resign their posts in the government. The elections on November 11, 1945, had no candidates for the opposition. The
Assembly issuing from these elections abolished the monarchy and adopted a federal constitution, taking that of
the Soviet Union for its model. The country was to consist
of six republics standing for the historical lands that had
composed Jugoslavia. Within the Serbian republic an
autonomous province gave the Hungarians in the Voivodina
(about half a million souls) cultural autonomy.

The Soviet idea underlying this system of federalism was
to reduce nationalism to its cultural aspect, but to encourage its development within that restricted field. Political education of the multinational masses for unity, according to the Communist doctrine, would run more
effectively along the grooves of accustomed forms of thinking. The Party in Russia illustrated this, directed as it was
from one center and imposing a unity of political philosophy
through diverse national cultures as its most receptive
medium.

While the new institutions of government were borrowed
from the Soviet Union and the country was yet to be made
to grow into this framework, the regime left room for liberated energies to develop in social activity, to carry the
spirit of dedication and sacrifice of the Partisan fraternity
into the area of rebuilding the nation.

Indeed, in the first years of the new Jugoslavia this spirit
of dedication to nation-building was the unifying principle
rather than Communist doctrine. It mobilized energy for
a staggering task. The National Front of Women, for example, was caring for more than half a million orphans on
a volunteer basis. Three million women worked in the
organization, several hundred thousand of them full time,
registering and photographing all orphans and exhibiting
them to families willing to adopt children. From Bosnia,

where entire regions had been burned over, derelict children were moved into Croatia which had been relatively spared from war damage. Local organizations kept close check to see whether the adopting families were treating the children properly, whether they were being taught hygiene, cooking, and home nursing.

Many visitors from abroad bore witness to the astounding devotion of the youth all over Jugoslavia to the actual rebuilding of the country. Twenty per cent of Jugoslavia's buildings had been more or less ruined, leaving more than three million people without shelter. One third of all fruit trees and vineyards were ravaged, and 50 per cent of the livestock destroyed. Industry and mines had suffered crippling damage, communications were left in a paralyzed state with more than half of the rolling stock knocked out of use, and two thirds of the railroad bridges blown up. And the enthusiasm of youth had to make up for the missing 10 per cent of the inhabitants killed during the four years' fight—for the average age of the dead was twenty-two.

The dynamism of social activity filled people with a sense of purpose in life and of individual importance. The feeling also reached to the people on the periphery, such as the Hungarians living in the Voivodina. The author visited them at the end of 1945, and, coming from Hungary, the impression was amazing. He left the second largest town in Hungary, near the Jugoslav border, lying stagnant in the dejection of physical and moral defeat, and expected to find the Hungarians in Jugoslavia in a much worse state, since he remembered that the Hungarian army had killed about ten thousand Serbs and Jews in the Voivodina. But in Hungarian-inhabited Bacstopolya, Hungarian flags bearing the Soviet star fluttered from the houses. On a Sunday afternoon not one but two amateur theaters performed plays in Hungarian to overflowing audiences. The same feverish activity obtained, especially among the young and the women, as in the Slav regions. In Novi Sad, the capital city of the Voivodina, Serb and Hungarian teams worked side by side in the City Hall, in the offices of social organizations, and in the fields. Serb and Hungarian newspapers were set, composed, and printed in the same plant; new Hungarian schools were opened and a Hungarian teachers' college was being established.

But the public spirit and voluntary work notwithstanding, the country would have been on the verge of starvation without the magnificent help of UNRRA which restored the prewar number of motor vehicles in less than a year, brought in locomotives, freight cars, tractors, even horses and mules, and set up schools to teach machine operations and repair. It also opened medical stations where people learned simple first aid and home treatment. UNRRA spent more than $400 million on the rehabilitation of Jugoslavia's economy, on food, agricultural implements, and livestock.

Not all parts reacted to the new regime with the same degree of approval. In Serbia, much loyalty remained to the king and the pan-Serbian system. Members of the former civil service, of the officer corps, of the middle-sized landholders and the middle class, feared Communism and distrusted the Tito setup, before and after its inception. In Croatia, which was left almost intact by the war, the intellectuals lagged behind those in Serbia in warming up to the new order in surprising contrast, by and large, to the Croat peasantry; while in Slovenia, the Germanization of the urban elements antagonized the intellectuals so that they jumped into the forefront of the supporters of the new Jugoslavia. The corrupting influence of domestic fascism in Croatia, as in Petain's France, stood in contrast to the violent resistance and the generous union of classes in areas where foreign despotism had been imposed.

The initial economic decrees of the government, although unexpectedly restrained, showed a tendency that prepared people in the middle class and in the free professions for the worst. The currency reform gave a foretaste of what was to come. It discriminated against the propertied people by exchanging the old currency at a rate of two old dinars for one new one for small depositors, while larger depositors had to pay out seven to ten old dinars according to a set scale. Thus, with one stroke of the pen, the regime destroyed the savings of the well-to-do.

The government began to operate so-called national shops to which they gave priority in commodities directly from the factories and UNRRA warehouses. This rang the death knell for the small shopkeeper. In industry, the regime held back nationalization. It did confiscate the property of Germans and collaborators without indemnity, including plants and mines of considerable importance to which the Germans had acquired title during their economic penetration and occupation.

Confiscation of the property of the German minority in the Voivodina and Croatia made available about 2 million acres, mostly first-class land with excellent housing and agricultural implements, to former Partisans and colonists moved from the poorest sections of the country to replace the Germans who had left with the Nazis or who were expelled. Not one of these Jugoslav Germans, called Schwabians, was left in these parts. Their stables were there, and their domestic animals, and their houses complete with furniture. Family photographs still hung on the walls and their brooms stood in the corners, when the tall, black-haired Montenegrins moved in. The menfolk from the mountains at first went on hunting, or smoking and drinking black coffee, as they held that work was unworthy of a man's dignity and must be left to the women. The plains were unfamiliar and strange to them. They had electricity but had not learned how to use it. For a time, when night came, they preferred to sit in the dark as of old. They moved carefully on the wooden floors, for they had been accustomed to sharing their earthen-floored huts with the domestic animals. Food also gave them trouble. They had never before eaten bread, their staple food being a sort of maize pie. But the Montenegrins, Macedonians, and South Serbs rapidly learned to work the radio and other instruments of civilization, as they had the iron plough. It was

different in villages where the cultured Slovene peasants
were settled. They needed only a Catholic church and
Slovenian teachers in order to feel at home.

Meanwhile, Tito took up old Jugoslav territorial ambitions with great energy and determination. How much of
his expansionism was meant to strengthen the position of
the Soviet orbit and how much served Jugoslav interests
alone remained to be seen. The extent of Soviet support
for some of his rash actions is no true evidence of a Soviet-
Tito pact. The Soviets may have passively accepted Tito's
vanguard role and forward thrusts, ready to deny responsibility for them when they threatened to lead to serious
complications with the West.

One of Tito's claims was an internal Communist affair.
He intended to complement his Macedonian republic with
the part Bulgaria had been left after the Balkan War of
1913, but the Bulgarian Communists refused to release it
until Jugoslavia and Bulgaria had joined in a South Slav
union. The West vetoed the union since a powerful Slav
state would dominate Greece, turning it Communist also.
Stalin, at first, approved. Bulgaria, however, wanted it to
be the union of the two states (Bulgaria and Jugoslavia),
while Tito wanted to give Bulgaria the same status as the
six constituent republics had held within Jugoslavia. The
Communists of the two countries endeavored to settle the
issue with different degrees of sincerity in different periods.
They submitted it to Stalin who, in 1946, allegedly decided
for Tito. And at that the matter rested for a while.

Greece, however, also held part of Macedonia, and so
many Greeks had settled there that its Slav character had
vanished. At the same time the Greek nationalists, whom
the elections of 1946 had returned to a majority while the
Left had boycotted the elections, claimed parts of Jugoslavia, Macedonia, and Albania. The Balkan Soviet bloc
considered this claim a threat of aggression, with its source
in a British maneuver to provoke war in the Balkans. They
maintained that the British hoped that a Greek attack might
incite a revolt in the pro-Soviet countries, or that the war

would justify military intervention by the West. This suspicion might have moved the Soviets to support the Greek Communists who, in 1946, reopened the civil war.

Direct conflict with the West issued from Tito's renewal of an old Jugoslav ambition to acquire Istria and its great harbor, Trieste. With a maritime turnover of three and a half million tons, Trieste was an important harbor on the Adriatic, but never a natural port. The Hapsburg empire had had a chain of waterways whereby the territories which now comprise Austria, Czechoslovakia, Rumania, Hungary, and a part of Jugoslavia and Poland, were connected to the North Sea port of Hamburg by the Elbe, and to the Black Sea by the Danube. But both rivers emptied into lands outside the Hapsburg realm. So the Hapsburg regime cut tunnels through the mighty Alps to get access, by road and rail, to the Adriatic. It invested huge sums in making the harbor of Trieste a center of foreign commerce, and granted tariff subsidies for freight taking the Alpine route to Trieste instead of the shorter cuts to foreign harbors. After 1918, Trieste was joined to Italy, and its harbor turnover declined by more than a million tons in spite of the efforts of the Fascist government to keep it alive. Trieste could prosper only as the artificial outlet of a compact Central European hinterland.

Churchill was dead set against Trieste becoming a great inland harbor of the Soviet orbit. He had Allied troops occupy the city in 1945. Tito resented the fact that the heroic part which the Jugoslav Partisan army had played in the war on the side of the Allies had been so quickly forgotten, and that Jugoslavia was placed on the same footing with Italy, which, as a Fascist aggressor, had done so much damage to life and property. He felt particularly offended by the Great Powers excluding his country from their deliberations on Trieste—although he did not know that it was at these discussions that Churchill reminded Stalin of the delicate percentage agreement which gave Britain 50 per cent influence in Jugoslavia. Churchill complained that he had actually been left with a precarious 10 per cent influ-

ence. But Stalin remarked that he had no influence at all,
since Tito alone exercised the 90 per cent. Tito voiced his
protest against the Great Powers' deciding Jugoslavia's interests without her participation in a speech in Ljubljana in
May, 1945:

> We demand that everyone should be the master in his house. We
> do not want to pay other people's bills. We do not want to be used
> as a bribe in international bargaining. We do not want to get in-
> volved in a policy of spheres of influence.

The protest did not distinguish between the Soviet Union
and the West, although Stalin supported the Jugoslav claim
on Trieste. But as East and West remained adamant, discussions dragged on. The issue caused friction and animosity between the Jugoslav troops occupying one zone of
the city and the Allied troops guarding the other. Jugoslavia's case began to slip, as the West grew concerned over
Italy's turning left at the approaching elections as well as
over Tito's increasing aggressiveness. Eventually, the Russians came to the conclusion that they would have to accept
a compromise in the Trieste question and that they had
better do so while it would help the chances of the Italian
Communists. In July, 1946, they accepted a solution which
created a free territory of Trieste with most of the surrounding territory going to Jugoslavia.

But Tito refused to yield. Twice he visited Moscow and
Stalin told him that Russia would not go to war with the
West for the sake of Trieste. Finally, in 1947, Tito signed
the peace treaty with Italy, but what the treaty said on
Trieste was not to be the last word on the subject. The
Security Council of the United Nations was to appoint a
governor for Trieste, but East and West mutually vetoed all
candidates proposed by each other, and the region remained
under military occupation until the baffling change in Soviet-
Tito relations.

CHAPTER FIVE

Albania

The state of Albania was born from a great power agreement in 1913, but the race of the Albanians, the Squipetars, is ancient. The figure of the Squipetar, which means "Son of the Eagle," has been known through the recorded ages.

Skanderbeg, the Albanian national hero, organized the Balkan Christians in the fifteenth century to stop the invasion of the Ottoman Turks who eventually conquered the Balkans. Albania was submerged in the Ottoman empire for four hundred years. Most of the Squipetars embraced Mohammedanism, and many had spectacular careers in the Turkish army and administration. Four rose to be grand viziers; one of them, Mehmet Ali, became governor and later ruling prince of Egypt.

Not all Squipetars turned Muslim, however. Among the mountaineers in the north, many retained their Roman Catholic religion, while in the south, in the vicinity of Greece, part of the peasants stuck to the Orthodox church, although this involved their remaining serfs on the lands of Muslim Albanians. Yet fanaticism had no place among the Squipetars. Members of the same family often belonged to different religions. A baby baptized one day might be circumcised the next as a Mussulman. What divided them was the Shkumbi River. North of it lived the Ghegs in tribal society, Muslims and Roman Catholics; south of the river the Tosks—Muslim landlords and free peasants, Orthodox Christian serfs. Both groups speak more or less the same language, which is not spoken by other than the Albanians.

Only 10 per cent of the land is arable, but that is very fertile, with level plains and river valleys. The mountains range from 5,000 to 8,000 feet. The inhabitants are a proud people, but very poor even by Balkan standards, and they are largely illiterate.

There was no time to delineate the frontiers of Albania before World War I broke out. Wilson saved the independence of the state from the Italians, Jugoslavs, and Greeks at the peace conference.

Albanians who returned from America after the war played an important part in the political life of the country. Fan S. Noli, a Harvard graduate and Orthodox bishop, advocated land reform that would make the Orthodox peasants in the south free landholders. But the landowners found allies among the Ghegs in the mountains, and also a leader who deserted the bishop and switched to the landowners' front. This was Ahmet Zog, who organized a revolt and marched on Tirana, the capital city. The advocates of reform, among them the bishop, fled abroad.

Zog became king and opened the country to Italy for economic penetration. Other nations who had the means disclosed no interest in investing in the rugged land, but they may have been mistaken since the Italians struck oil in Albania. The Italians monopolized the exploitation of oil and shipping; lent money at high interest for harbor installations at Durazzo on the Adriatic; and built roads. The Italian grip on the country loosened when Mussolini became involved in the war on Ethiopia and in the Spanish Civil War. But in 1939, Mussolini decided to invade Greece and occupied Albania as a bridgehead. King Zog fled with his wife, a Hungarian countess, and also with the state treasury.

Young people in the south who had gone to universities abroad, mostly in Paris, returned as Communists and started to organize resistance to the Italians. However, they were few and faction-ridden. The Communist leadership was

overly intellectual and had no experience in organizing.
The workers in the oil wells, mines, cement and tobacco
factories had much stronger ties to tribes and churches than
to political groupings, the more so because King Zog had
wiped out political parties. Still, among the peasants in
the south and in the fertile valleys of the middle of the
country, who lived practically in serfdom, the slogan of land
distribution found a vivid echo. Communist emissaries
from Jugoslavia succeeded in organizing them into a party
in 1941, and the Party launched a Liberation Movement
that included nationalist groups. The landowners in the
south felt directly threatened by the Communist-inspired
movement and initiated an anti-Communist resistance group
which those nationalists who distrusted the Jugoslavs also
joined. They wanted to cooperate with the West against
Italians and Germans. In 1943, British officers parachuted
into Albania with the task of uniting all resisting groups
against the Axis troops. Each of the two resistance camps
tried to administer as large territories as they could. The
Communist-led movement spread in the south, the nationalists in the north. When the Allies knocked Italy out of the
war, and her army in Albania was dissolved, the resistants
acquired stocks of ammunition, and a large group of Italians
were ready to fight on their side.

Soon the opportunity opened for them to fight; indeed,
a bigger one than they were equipped to live up to. The
Germans parachuted in troops who captured the harbors
and soon followed up with several divisions. They drove
the guerillas into the mountains and set up a government
of respectable Albanians, leaving them free to govern.
There was no animosity against the Germans, who had
never wronged the Albanians; the Squipetars saw only their
impressive military efficiency. The conservatives collabo-
rated readily, and guerilla activities ceased entirely. But
each guerilla group used the time to organize the people
in their region for their own political aims. Partisans, led
by Communist-schooled youth, now worked at cross purposes with the other guerilla groups. The British mission

made strenuous efforts to have all fighting groups join in the struggle against the Germans, but the Partisans set out only to destroy their potential rivals.

In May, 1944, the Partisans formed a provisional government headed by Enver Hoxha, a former teacher in the French-language high school and a staunch follower of Moscow. The Minister of the Interior, however, was a trustee of the Jugoslavs, Koci Xoxe, the sole worker on a staff of intellectuals.

When it was evident that the Germans intended to leave the country, the Albanians prepared to cooperate with the British officers in attacking them. A general uprising in the north might have thrown that section into the hands of joint anti-Communist forces and thus split the country with the threat of civil war. But meanwhile the Teheran conference assigned Albania to the zone of Russian military operations. As a consequence, British military headquarters ignored the advice of their mission on the spot and stopped supplying the pro-Western anti-Communist forces with whom the Communists refused to cooperate, ordering their officers in Albania to keep out of the civil war unfolding in the country. This was a straw in the wind for Albanians in all walks of life, and the camp of the Partisans began to swell while those of the other groups disintegrated. Many people fled to Italy, and many were executed by the Partisans as traitors and collaborators, including those who had worked with the British.

Now events followed developments in Jugoslavia. A Democratic Front paraded with non-Communist chiefs, guerilla leaders, and priests. The government confiscated all blocks of land of over fifty acres (altogether about one third of the arable land), and distributed it among sixty thousand landless families.

In the spring of 1945, military and later UNRRA assistance supplied food and other relief. American and British observers came to survey the situation. After they made their reports the three principal allied powers recognized the government. The State Department asked for guarantees on the basis of the Yalta agreement that free elections would be held and foreign correspondents allowed to move about freely.

Two boxes faced the voters at the elections which took place on December 2, 1945. One was for votes for the government list, the other for the protest votes. But no list of parties or individuals challenging the government was admitted. The official count disclosed that 93 per cent had cast their votes for the government list. The Albanians are a fearless people, but they are not eager to get into trouble.

The Jugoslavs now took the place of the Italians in the economic development of this backward country. In one form or another foreign capital and know-how was needed to tap the natural resources for the benefit of a better and longer life. This had hardly been Mussolini's purpose, but his investments served it nonetheless. The main attraction of the country for Italy and Jugoslavia was the Strait of Otranto between Albania and Italy through which the Adriatic Sea widens into the Mediterranean—a strategically important position. It was strategic and political interests that motivated both rivals, and not the returns from their investments, when they extended protection to Albania. The Jugoslavs applied the Soviet technique of joint Jugoslav-Albanian companies in banking, oil, mining, and electricity. They opened up new oil wells and copper and chrome mines, and built the first standard-gauge railroad in Albania. The Jugoslav youth coming to work in the country brought along some of that prime enthusiasm that filled their own land in the early postwar years, displaying joy and energy in building a new life. It appears that Tito's economic partnership was more enlightened than Stalin's and was more concerned with the long-range goal of lifting his satellite from primitive poverty and ignorance.

It took two years for Koci Xoxe, Tito's confidant, to purge the nationalists and people of Western leanings from Party leadership, that is, those who did not accept the role of blind obeisance to orders from Moscow via Belgrade. At the same time, Xoxe intended to isolate Enver Hoxha, who appeared to be trying to build direct ties to Moscow. The internal rivalry in Albania thus antedated the open break between Stalin and his most successful disciple, Tito.

In general, the Jugoslavs did not impress the proud Squipetars and could not be popular since they had kept the precious Albanian populated territories which they had conquered in 1913 and showed no inclination to release them. But they were welcome against the aggressive designs of the other neighbor, Greece.

The nationalists in Greece, who had succeeded with the help of the British in entrenching themselves in power, claimed the southern end of Albania, which they called Northern Epirus. The Orthodox Christians living there, the Squipetars included, had been under Greek ecclesiastical influence. The Greeks mobilized all the requisites for a Nazi-type aggression. They complained that the Albanians had treated the Greek minority atrociously, and staged frontier incidents and mass demonstrations at home. They presented the situation as unbearable and asked the Allies' for intervention.

The Jugoslavs and the Russians suspected that the British had pulled wires behind the Greeks and that the West in general would have liked to wrest the Balkans, especially the shores of the Adriatic, Albania and Dalmatia, from the Communist orbit. This could be engineered, so Tito read the thoughts of the Greeks, through civil war in the Balkans.

Albania became the outpost of Tito's and Bulgaria's efforts to frustrate these alleged designs. Tito harnessed Albania into open hostility against the British. The Albanians, in fact, prohibited British warships from plying the Strait of Otranto. Shore guns opened fire on British cruisers. In 1946 floating mines damaged two British destroyers, killing thirty-eight men and wounding forty-five.

By the end of 1946, the country had become a satellite of Jugoslavia, isolated from the West. She had no diplomatic relations with Britain or the United States.

Thus Albania, a country of about 10,000 square miles, had hardly emerged from stagnation under Turkish rule before falling into the crosscurrents of conflicting interests. No opportunity was left for her to try to adjust to the modern world in her own way. Albania has about 1,300,000 inhabitants, but half as many again live in territories kept by Jugoslavia and Greece (Italy and the United States also have sizable Albanian communities). Geography and illiteracy have isolated them into three groups: those who live on the coast, the proud mountaineers in the north, and the tillers of the plains in the south and along the torrential rivers; but they are all still the same old race of Albanians.

CHAPTER SIX

Hungary

The government of Hungary took part in Hitler's war reluctantly, but the people fought it to the end as if it were theirs as well.

On October 15, 1944, Regent Horthy made an announcement over the radio which stunned the nation and electrified the dissenters. The Regent stated that he had served notice on the German Ambassador of his intention to conclude a preliminary armistice with the "former enemies" and to cease hostilities.

A writer described the reaction of the people on the streets of Budapest:

I rush along the boulevard expecting to see exalted masses celebrating their liberty . . . for it is a day to celebrate, that of armistice, of peace. "Hurrah for separate peace" I shout into the faces of those I meet, but they are infuriated and gnashing their teeth rather than being in the intoxication of enthusiasm. A few shout with me, with an expression of doubt on their faces . . . And this mood predominates, there being very few who dare celebrate openly . . . the great majority, the "real" Budapest, is uncertain and mistrustful.

A reporter recorded the reaction of the people in the industrial town of Pecs in Transdanubia. They listened mutely to the Regent's proclamation. It was followed by the Russian General Malinowski's appeal to the Hungarian soldiers to surrender. Afterwards the British Broadcasting Corporation cut in, advising the soldiers to join Tito's Partisans just over the border. But the bewilderment was soon over. General Vörös, the Minister of War, stated there was no armistice, the war was to go on. "They breathed again," the reporter commented.

The officers on the front received the transcript of the Regent's proclamation. It had no influence on them.

German tanks rolled through the boulevards in Budapest, in order to show their force and readiness to take over the country if it faltered. "The clustering crowds watched the soldiers almost indifferently, some even waved, and not a single man struck in the face one of those who waved and cheered," was the comment of a dissenter present.

A guard composed of the most reliable soldiers surrounded the castle where the Regent resided. He, his family, and a few intimate friends expected the Nazis to come and arrest them at any time. They did, and the great majority of the guard deserted their posts, while a few offered resistance but were quickly overcome. The Germans broke into the Castle and forced the Regent to approve the appointment of the Fuehrer of the Arrow Cross, Hungary's Nazi movement, as Prime Minister. Following this, the Germans escorted the Regent to Germany, to a distinguished place of internment.

The Hungarian Nazis took over, and the scum of the earth flooded the land. They perpetrated wholesale murder and robbery, and the army, with the notable exception of a couple of generals, obeyed the orders of the new government and fought Hitler's war to the bitter end.

The end for Hungary, however, arrived when the Soviet troops dashed through the passes of the Carpathian Mountains and invaded the Hungarian lowlands from the east and the north.

A mass flight took to the rails and roads before the invasion. The whole civil service, from the provincial governors down to the lowest clerk, followed the retreating German and Hungarian armies. The Arrow Cross intended to evacuate the country, people, cattle, and everything movable, promising that they would return the next spring when the Nazi counterattack would turn the tables. Many believed in the promise, holding that the Germans were invincible.

Others trusted that the Western powers would not allow the Soviets to occupy Hungary alone. Most of the people were simply terror-stricken, remembering the relentless Nazi propaganda during the war, to the effect that the Soviets, should they invade Central Europe, would transport the Hungarian people as a whole into Siberia, probably into Central Asia whence their ancestors had come in the great migration of peoples a thousand years ago.

The Russians had good reason, so the propaganda went, to clear the Carpathian basin of Hungarians, since this Finno-Ugrian race, mixed with Turkish blood, had driven a wedge between Northern and Southern Slavs when they conquered their present abode. Cleansed of Hungarians, an unbroken Slav empire would reach from the Adriatic Sea and the proximity of Berlin to the Sea of Japan in the Far East.

Since the second half of the nineteenth century, Russian-inspired pan-Slavism was felt by the Hungarians as a threat to their very existence as a nation. Also, they held a grudge against the Russians for breaking through the Carpathian passes and invading Hungary in 1849, to help the Hapsburg Emperor defeat a Hungarian insurrection for independence. The Tsar's armies returned home after defeating the insurgents and re-establishing the old order, but left behind memories of rape and loot and the intrusion of unfathomable strangers.

The Hungarian middle class had more specific reasons to fear that the Russians would deport them to Siberia. Since the short-lived Communist dictatorship in 1919 and the White Terror afterwards, the middle class considered itself—and the Hungarian nation as well—as the standard-bearers of anti-Communism. This feeling made them a logical spare part of the Rome-Berlin Axis and led them into the war, enthusiastic over its anti-Communist aspect, while their government tried to keep out of it, having a better understanding of its real impact.

Towns and villages east of the river Theiss fell to the advancing Russian armies, stripped of the civil service and local authorities. The countryside looked as if an earthquake had hit it. Rails and bridges were blown up, villages razed, cattle driven away, horses taken by one or the other army, able-bodied men either in German or Russian camps or armies, women raped or in hiding. But more than physical damage, it appeared to the peasants and the little people who stuck to their homes and land that the old order which had ruled them from time immemorial lay in ruins. Everything reminiscent of the traditional institutions or representative of the old order had become obsolete in the presence of the Russians and the Red Army.

But there was no anarchy among the ruins. Left to their own resources, the simple Hungarian people, passive instrument of the past order, suddenly discovered themselves. It was no accident that the race had established a state in unfriendly and unfamiliar surroundings and had held it for a thousand years. Awakened from centuries of torpidity, the common people seized the initiative and acted with skill, enjoying the exercise. Local committees sprouted, taking care of the needs of the day, requisitioning troops, sending delegates to discuss matters of public order with the military authorities, and so on. Realizing that the main thing was to establish law, messengers from one village to the next rode on horseback to seek information and advice. Representatives from neighboring villages deliberated to formulate common policies as to selling and buying in the towns and convoying the cargo through military zones. They organized barter and mutual aid until a national council set up in each county seat could help them. Left without a government, the people spontaneously built a democratic order.

The Soviet commanders got in touch with the new local authorities and urged the peasants to convene and distribute farms over 140 acres, and all lands owned by landlords possessing more than 1,400 acres. They made the peasants understand that they did not have to wait for legal title but could distribute it just by using sticks and strings. In this informal way 370,000 landless peasants and 214,000 dwarf-holders received a piece of land.

Eastern Hungary was in Russian hands by the fall of 1944, but Budapest, the capital, and the country west of it was under Nazi control for several more months. At the suggestion of the Russians, the local national committees elected representatives to a provisional national assembly which established itself in Debrecen, "the Calvinist Rome." At its first session in December, 1944, the assembly elected a Provisional National Government consisting of the representatives of the parties which had not participated in the pro-Nazi governments, namely the Small Landholders, Social Democrats, Communists, National Peasants, and Independents. General Miklos, who had gone over to the Russians with his troops, headed the government.

This government signed the armistice, the main provisions of which brought sad, but not unexpected news to the nation. Under the terms they had to restore territory gained from Jugoslavia, Czechoslovakia, and Rumania, awarded to them by the Axis for their help in the war. They also had to pay $300 million in war reparations of which 70 million went to Jugoslavia and 30 million to Czechoslovakia. The assembly adopted a land reform law which fixed the individual share of distributed land at an average of seven to eight acres.

The Soviet army surrounded Budapest in December and besieged it until February, 1945, when it fell. The city was a shambles. All seven bridges across the Danube, once the pride of the city, lay collapsed in the water. The skeleton of the Royal Castle looked down on the smoke and rubble of what had once been the capital of Hungary.

Three generations of ambitious and optimistic Hungarians had dreamed it into existence, the sumptuous, over-pretentious capital of a country of peasants and landlords. The splendor was fallacious but always charming. The laws of the 1848 revolution awoke the slumbering creative impulses of the middle class, people mostly of German and Jewish origins, who set to work remodeling the feudal country and its rustic towns. They built modern Pest for business, and for pleasure the villas on the hills of Buda. The castle and the old palaces of the aristocracy, the ministries and the forts, surveyed the busy city-folk with the superb indifference of grand seigneurs. At first sight it appeared that rebuilding the ruined city was beyond hope; the devastation was second only to that of Warsaw.

Old Hungary was done for, but the Soviet Union and its empire builders, the Communists, were given a unique opportunity. They brought forth, almost imposing it on the country, the solution to the problem which had eaten at the country's core, keeping a distorted system in power so that the basic questions would remain unsolved. About 20 per cent of all arable land was owned by 324 families, each holding more than 41,000 acres, as compared with four fifths of the agricultural population who owned property of less than 20 acres down to no land at all. Landlords to the number of 1,232 owned an average of 4,000 acres each while two thirds of the agricultural population owned no land or less than 5 acres. Suffocating under the huge estates, the peasants fled overseas from starvation and hopelessness. But after 1918 no mass emigration was possible. Two revolutions and a long, sterile counter-revolutionary regime brought forth no remedy or change for the better. A sense of futility drove millions of landless peasants to mass hysteria, sectarianism, and a submerged state of helpless renunciation.

The Soviet army itself was instrumental in giving land to the landless. Common sense dictated that the Soviets do this to instil a feeling of good will towards them by the beneficiaries. Later other sections of the population realized the tremendous contribution of this act to the return to health of the entire nation.

In the wake of the Soviet army, a small disciplined corps of Hungarians arrived. They were Communist émigrés from persecution in Hungary, trained in Moscow. Their leader was a short, stocky man in his fifties, Matthias Rakosi. He was making the trip from Moscow to Hungary for the third time. In 1918, he returned from a prisoner-of-war camp in Russia, and was active in setting up a proletarian dictatorship in Hungary. In 1924, Rakosi returned illegally and organized a Communist underground. The police arrested him and he spent more than a decade in prison. Due to his involuntary absence during this time, he managed to survive the purges in Moscow. Now he returned for the third time and became "proconsul" of Hungary. He sent sentinels of the empire-building Communists ahead to make contacts with the domestic resistance groups. These were composed of militant Communists, socialists driven underground by the Nazis, and Hungarian nationalists who hated German domination.

Their leader was Laszlo Rajk, a slim forceful young man, and a professional revolutionary hardened by a life-long battle against the middle and upper classes. Though his lower-middle-class family had been in favor with the extreme right, he was expelled from the University of Budapest in 1933 for Communist activities. This ended his chances for a professorial career and turned him into a permanent rebel. During the Spanish Civil War he joined the Loyalists and was wounded three times. Afterwards, he fled to France and was interned there. When the Nazi troops came, the French delivered him to the Germans, and they put him in a concentration camp. Later they delivered him to Hungary, to be jailed there. When he was released, Rajk went underground to organize the resistance and contact the Russians.

When these two leaders joined forces in Hungary, they presented Moscow with two alternatives. At a time when the need for mass support of Communism in Hungary was more important than conformity to Moscow's administrative pattern, Rajk had a chance to become Number One, thus displacing Rakosi.

Rajk's roots were deeply imbedded in Hungary, while Rakosi had lived abroad too long to feel the pulse of the people. He even became a Soviet citizen. Moreover, Rakosi was a Jew—a handicap in a country which had been fed on anti-Semitism for twenty-five years.

Neither had any reservations in following Moscow's directives. But Rajk looked forward to destroying the middle class and its influence, while Rakosi never permitted his personal feelings to affect him. The two were not antagonists. They were tools, one being intermittently better fitted than the other to carry out certain designs of Communist policy. Their careers ran neck and neck until 1949, when Rakosi sent his colleague to the gallows. They had looked forward to the opportunity of their lives, which was to be the great opportunity for their principles as well.

The reason why the bulk of the Hungarian people supported the German Nazis, and believed in a German victory even while they themselves despaired of it, follows from their history.

Harold Nicolson, the English political writer, once wrote of the Hungarians that this race of Mongolian origin had been incapable of adjusting to the European community a thousand years ago and ever since had remained a source of trouble to the neighboring peoples. This remarkable simplification is true to the extent that the Magyars (as the Hungarians call themselves) are an alien enclave amidst Germanic, Slavic, and Latin peoples.

The Magyars, a Finno-Ugrian race with a considerable Turkish influx, invaded the lowlands along the Danube and Theiss rivers in the ninth century A.D., migrating from Central Asia. Their first king, Stephen, married a Bavarian princess, but he remained independent from the Holy Roman Emperor. Stephen received a royal crown from the Pope and made the Magyars accept Western Christianity, settle down, and cultivate the land.

Since then Hungary has been one of the makers of Continental history. It reached the Adriatic Sea in the twelfth century by incorporating Croatia, and by the next century had expanded north and east to the Carpathian Mountains which formed a semicircle around the lowlands. Natural barriers thus defended the realm, open only to the West. And the West alone influenced its institutions and development—feudalism, the Renaissance, Protestantism, the Enlightenment, and the French Revolution all had their influence on Hungary. After the first national dynasty died out, the Angevin, Luxemburg, and Jagiello dynasties tied Hungary to the West, including Bohemia and Poland, until in the sixteenth century it became part of the Hapsburg empire, with the Hapsburgs occupying the Hungarian throne. The Hungarian kingdom lasted for more than nine hundred years, until 1918, comprising more or less the same territory except for one-and-a-half centuries when the Ottoman Turks occupied part of the country.

But the invasion of the Turks was a turning point in Hungarian history. As a result of the battle of Mohacs in 1526, the Turks won the plain of Hungary, populated by the descendants of the original Magyar race, but they did not subdue the mountainous border regions, populated by Slavs and Germans. The Germans had been invited into the country by the Hungarian kings to serve as craftsmen and frontier guards. When the plain was later reconquered, it was derelict and depopulated.

The battle of Mohacs had a fateful significance also because the king perished in the battle and left no descendants. The nobility elected a national king, but a minority voted for Ferdinand, the Hapsburg duke, who would not acknowledge defeat. Thus Hungary had two rival kings for a time.

When the national king allied himself with the Turks, the Pope, who strongly supported the Hapsburgs, excommunicated him. It is true that this king had made common cause with the enemy of Christianity, but he might have saved Hungary from Turkish rule. Thereupon the nobility, with almost the entire Hungarian people, turned Protestant. They adopted Calvinism, rejecting Lutheranism as German-inspired. In the year 1600 there were only three hundred Catholic priests in all Hungary, and the number of faithful was insignificant. Calvinism was called *the* Magyar religion and was considered so as long as Hapsburg rule lasted. In the nineteenth century, when the large majority of the Hungarians were again Catholics, the political leaders remained traditionally Protestant. In agreement with the emperor, two portfolios were reserved for Catholics, the Ministry of Education and the office of King's Privy. In 1845, the Hungarian Academy was said to be a Calvinist institution to which Lutherans gained admittance by mercy, Catholics by grace. Calvinism in Hungary originated in and remained as a political protest against the Catholic Hapsburgs.

After defeating the Turks, the Hapsburgs prevailed and resolved to erase Hungary as a state and nation. The lowlands were donated to German and foreign aristocrats; and Serbs, Slovaks, Germans, and even French from Lotharingia were given the most fertile land in the south, as freemen subject only to the king, and as frontier guards. At the same time, a return to the Catholic faith gave noble families their only hope to regain title to their lands, formerly in Turkish hands.

But the Magyars repeatedly rose against the Hapsburgs, who were bent on taking state, land, and religion from them. A civil war lasted for decades in which the Magyars fought for their independence, religion, and the constitutional rights of the nobility. This civil war ravaged the country more extensively than Turkish rule had done, as it encompassed the entire state. What saved the Hungarians from complete extinction was the treasure of their past achievements. The crown of Hungary possessed historical and legal title to Croatia and Dalmatia. In order to retain these lands, the Hapsburgs had to keep up the Hungarian kingdom. On the other hand, the emperor's own favorites, on whom he bestowed lands and titles to the detriment of Hungarian nobility, discovered that Hungarian constitutional laws laid down precious privileges which the kings were bound to respect. Thus, two inimical forces contributed to save the legal existence of Hungary when it swayed on the brink of an abyss.

And so great was the force of assimilation that the alien landowners became Magyars; and the peasants, except for the imperial colonists, although of the most varied nationality and speech, became indistinguishable from the old inhabitants of the plain a century after the Turks had left it a desert.

Transylvania, the mountain-enclosed eastern part of Hungary, contributed vastly to preserving the Hungarian race and speech. The Turks did not occupy it, and it became an independent principality which kept a tenuous balance between the sultan and the Hapsburg emperor, retaining its separate status even in the Hapsburg empire until 1848, when it joined Hungary. A Magyar prince ruled the province during its time of independence while three nationalities lived in self-government: the Magyars, German colonists called Saxons, and the Szeklers, a Hungarian tribe which had settled as freemen in the frontier region during the time of the early Hungarian kings. A fourth nationality, perhaps the most numerous, the Rumanians, had no rights and their Greek Orthodox religion was not recognized.

Thus, the struggle for independence and the struggle for the rights of the nobility ran parallel and were united during the period when the Hapsburgs reconquered Hungary from the Turks. This fusion persisted in the minds of the people, privileged and common alike, and survived even after the connection became obsolete and unnatural. This strange anachronism became a source of trouble not only to the neighboring peoples, as Harold Nicolson stated, but first of all to the Hungarian people themselves.

Though remarkably regenerated, the Hungarians never regained the power they had wielded before the Turkish conquest and civil wars. Desperate efforts by the Magyar nobility, and later by the Magyar ethnic nation, to rule all the peoples in Hungary were the main feature of Hungarian history up to 1944.

The nobility, after becoming heterogeneous because of the Hapsburgs, elected Latin as the official language for state business, schools, and conversation. Latin became the symbol of unity of the privileged class, eliminating the vernacular tongues which would have divided them. A paradoxical development under the reign of the only enlightened Hapsburg emperor, Joseph II, at the end of the eighteenth century, would have wiped out, by imperial fiat, serfdom and privileges as well as the language of the privileged. Joseph II ordered that the most developed vernacular, German, be substituted for Latin in government offices and schools all over the empire. The nobility resisted this attack on its privileges but was afraid the emperor might gain the support of the serfs against them. Therefore, they stressed their resistance to the emperor's desire to impose the German language on the Magyar people. Thus, although the nobles spoke Latin themselves, they succeeded in mobilizing the Magyar serfs on their side, with the result that Joseph withdrew all his enlightened measures before he died. The coupling of the struggle for national independence and the privileged status of the nobility thus turned the peasants against their own freedom, perhaps because they instinctively felt that they belonged to a race forlorn among Slavs and Germans and threatened with extinction by the hazards of history.

But when the nobility discovered they could effectively resist the encroachment of imperial power on their privileges by associating themselves with the Magyar commoners on the basis of their common language, they laid the foundations of a modern nation. From the beginning of the nineteenth century the nobility built their resistance to the Hapsburgs on this nationalistic basis. Since the Hapsburgs threatened to appeal to the commoners against the privileged class, the nobility found new strength in defending not only their privileges but the rights of the Hungarian language and culture. The Magyar nation was now conceived of as comprising all people, no matter what their ethnic origin, who adhered to the idea that this broadly interpreted Magyar community should run the state and rule dissenting national groups. The nobility pushed bills through the Diet which replaced Latin with Hungarian as the official language, even in autonomous Croatia.

When Joseph II imposed the German language on the Magyars he aroused Hungarian nationalism. When the Magyars in turn resolved to impose their language on the non-Magyar majority of the country, this called to life a number of non-Magyar nationalisms in protest and self-defense.

Great Hungarian statesmen warned against this synthetic construction of a nation. One of them, Nicholas Wesselenyi, stated in the Diet:

There are several paths by which a nation can be saved from the dangers which threaten us [from other nationalities]. The first is force, but this age is finished, when, for instance, the Slavs are extirpated by fire and sword in the German provinces. The second is assimilation, and this requires a strong culture, enormous resources, and special powers of attraction, and these we lack. There remains only the third road, to unite in spirit with the other nationalities, to make alliance with them as sisters and share all things with them.

But another nobleman and formidable orator of Slovak origin, Louis Kossuth, believed in the "strong culture, enormous resources, and special attractions" of the Hungarians. Kossuth did not even consider the use of force obsolete, and he carried the day.

In 1848, the Hungarian Diet, under the impact of the Paris revolution, passed laws which in a single stroke wiped out the old order. They spelled out equality before the law, freedom of the press and of religion, and union with Transylvania. The Emperor signed the bills, frightened by the revolutions which had flared up in several provinces of the realm. When the revolutions collapsed, however, the Emperor repudiated his signature and called upon the non-Magyar nationalities for support against the Hungarians. The Hungarians reacted to the breach of the imperial word by taking up arms to defend the country, but the non-Mag-

yar nationalities gave more credence to the Emperor's promises than to the laws of the Hungarian Diet. The laws gave
them freedom from serfdom, but the Emperor promised in
addition to guarantee their rights as nations. Thus, the non-
Magyar nationalities joined the imperial armies in fighting
the Hungarian rebels.

The war stirred immense enthusiasm among the free
peoples of the West and among peoples oppressed by the
Holy Alliance in Central Europe. A small nation had taken
up arms against one of the greatest powers of the age, the
center of the Holy Alliance which had conspired against
liberty and progress everywhere. The revolutionary Hungarians astounded the world by defeating the imperial army
as well as the guerilla forces of the other nationalities. But
the Emperor called upon his partner, the Russian Tsar, for
help. Russian armies, for the first time, crossed the Carpathian passes and saved the Hapsburg Emperor from final
defeat. The Hungarians, having received no help other
than admiration, surrendered.

Hungary was losing her identity as a state and nation
under the absolute rule of the Emperor which followed the
defeat. But the Hapsburgs suffered foreign setbacks, compelling them to strengthen what territory they still possessed. In 1867, the Emperor made a compromise agreement with the Hungarians through which they gained self-
government in their internal affairs. Thus, the Emperor
broke his promise to the non-Magyar nationalities in their
turn and delivered them to the Hungarians.

In the next and last period of Greater Hungary, the policy of substituting rule of the Magyar element for rule of the
nobility almost succeeded. The victory of the Hungarians
over the Emperor, as sealed by the famous Compromise,
enhanced a prestige which the Magyar state had accumulated through the turmoil of a millennium. The Hungarians
showed remarkable skill in re-establishing their rule but
adjusting it to the changed times. The former ruling class
lost their privileges but kept their power as the leaders of

the ruling nation, representing the "Hungarian idea," which meant that the Magyar element had the right to give its character to the state and its institutions.

Greater Hungary from 1867 to 1918 managed to uphold an anachronistic but ingenious social system behind a front of modern constitutional laws. The laws concerning freedom of worship, marriage and divorce, and the practice of industry and commerce, were far more liberal than those in neighboring countries. But they did not deal with the landed estates, relations between lord and peasants, or the administration of justice on the land.

The families who owned the huge estates occupied the top of a social hierarchy and controlled the power of the state. The small landholders held the franchise, but elections were not secret, and the votes were keenly watched. The dwarfholders and the landless peasants had no rights at all. They eked out a miserable livelihood from sharecropping. Working conditions were set by the landlords and any complaint brought the originator to jail. In an agricultural country matters concerning the land fell into the jurisdiction of a special administration. The counties possessed governing bodies independent of the national administration, and these consisted, by tacit consent, exclusively of members of the nobility. These bodies had formidable armed forces at their disposal, the gendarmes, dreaded and feared by the peasants although recruited from their ranks. County administrations retained the ancient privilege of refusing to execute the laws if they felt they ran counter to the constitution. And these bodies stood entirely at the disposal of the lords of the big landed estates.

A safety valve preventing revolution was the emigration to America of hundreds of thousands of downtrodden, landless peasants, who fled Hungary to seek a better living in the New World. The government began to limit their flight only when it caused a scarcity of labor which might have resulted in a rise in the pitifully low wages they received.

On the other hand, freedom reigned in industry, craft, and commerce. The laws left the door open for the enterprising spirit of the Jews, who were to supplement the income of the government, just as regressive tax laws protected the big landlords from substantial taxation. A modern administration, appointed by the government, took care of matters of labor and welfare. Workers were allowed to form unions, even to organize a Socialist Party, but they had no right to vote in the elections. The members of this national administration came, to a large extent, from the non-Magyar groups who had accepted the "Magyar idea," altered their foreign names to Magyar ones, and changed their manners to emulate the aristocratic ways of the ruling caste.

The Jews and Hungarian Germans marketed the products of the big estates, expanded commerce, built up modern industries. They created the capital city of Budapest, a cheap imitation of Vienna, tinged with an oriental air, but enjoying a magnificent setting on the Danube with the Buda Hills on its right bank.

The Jews were given another important role, that of spreading "the Hungarian idea" among the non-Magyars. Liberally granted licenses, they ran the village inns, spoke Hungarian, and educated their children to be professional men and full-fledged Hungarians. They showed how adoption of the Magyar idea could enable one to get ahead.

The apparent success of Magyarization attracted the non-Magyar intelligentsia, but when the government applied more and more violent measures to accelerate the process, resistance began to mount. The Hapsburg empire broke up because it was incapable of transforming itself into a supranational realm in which each nationality could freely develop its own traditional pattern. Hungary's violent denationalization policy and growing power in the empire frustrated such a transformation.

In such a state of dissolution, the Hapsburg empire precipitated the outbreak of World War I and broke up in 1918.

The non-Magyar nationalities broke with Hungary. The Slovaks and Ruthenians joined the Czechs in the new state of Czechoslovakia; the Serbs and Croats went into the new state of Jugoslavia; the Rumanians united with their kins-men beyond the Carpathians, forming a Greater Rumania. Hungary was reduced from over 200 thousand to 58 thousand square miles, its population from eighteen to nine million. All the new or enlarged states also held considerable Magyar minorities.

In Hungary, defeat sparked a revolution. Count Michael Karolyi, one of the wealthiest aristocrats, recognized the link between the anachronistic social system of the country and the ties binding Hungary to German imperialism. Shortly before the war he advocated an alliance with the West. Karolyi set an example to his fellow aristocrats which they did not care to follow by offering his huge landed estates to the peasants. An urban intelligentsia and a few members of the Parliamentary opposition, who stood for democratization of the country, formed Karolyi's inner circle. Their program embraced principles that might well have saved the country had they been applied before the war.

Karolyi became head of the government in 1918, but the new regime was overwhelmed by the despair engendered by the mutilation of the country. The national catastrophe drove the people into a short-lived Communist dictatorship when the Red Army approached the eastern slopes of the Carpathians. This army appeared to give them their only chance of frustrating the decision of the West to put an end to Greater Hungary. In a period of three months, the Communist dictatorship managed to wage war against the Czechs and the Rumanians, with the result that the latter invaded the country and paved the way for a counter-revolution.

The leader of the counter-revolution, Admiral Nicholas Horthy, became the head of reduced Hungary, which, to repeat the well-worn but characteristic description, was now a kingdom without a king ruled by an admiral without a navy. It was left with a huge army of civil service employees, since Budapest had been the center of a great state, and moreover 350 thousand former civil service men had fled from the territories which had broken away. An inflated class of bureaucrats and professionals had to live on the meager resources of the reduced country, kept in poverty by the vicious social hierarchy.

In spite of the dismemberment of the country, two revolutions, and a counter-revolution, the system survived. The lords lost most of their estates, which now lay in the detached territories, but this made them cling even more resolutely to the lands they still owned within Hungary. Their influence remained paramount but was acted out by proxy. The lesser nobility, higher bureaucrats, and army officers ran the political and administrative offices, establishing themselves as a ruling class, but remembering that their power rested on the interests of the big landowners. The latter also had changed with the times, entering into a fruitful business partnership with Jewish financiers and captains of industry. The influence of the aristocrats was used to adjust tariffs so as to insure higher profits, while wages were kept low as well as production.

The huge middle class of bureaucrats and pensioners drew very poor salaries, but as compensation they were allowed to change their plebeian names for those of the nobility. Rank and title were attached to each category of work, and an epidemic of titles infected the whole country.

The children of these titled bureaucrats wanted to free themselves from suffocating genteel poverty and embark on freer professional careers, but here the Jews were firmly entrenched. More and more of the Gentile middle class abandoned their contempt for commerce. Anxious for a better living, they ventured into business but had a hard time competing with Jews who had practiced trade for generations.

Thus, the Jews in shrunken Hungary lost their *raison d'être* in the eyes of the state and of Gentile society. Moreover, the Jews played a conspicuous part in the leadership of the Communist dictatorship in 1919, a fact which activated latent anti-Semitic feelings. The nation was now homogeneous, and had no need of synthetic Magyars. Their presence in literature and art also aroused resentment. For generations the Jews had brought a background of urbanism and Western culture into those spheres. The world in turn took cognizance of Hungarian accomplishments in the arts, through playwrights, movie producers, and musical virtuosos of Jewish extraction. Now a Gentile generation went through the same process and became aware of foreign culture, but to their dismay found their Western experiences anticipated by Jewish poets, writers, and artists, and with a slight but peculiar accent which irritated them. Anti-Semitism infiltrated everywhere. Only the upper class, who shared the profits of Jewish enterprises without any curiosity as to how or why, still felt that there were some decent Jews, and incidentally, they happened to be rich.

The industrial workers were allowed to keep their unions, but any forceful agitation for higher wages landed their leaders in jail for suspicion of Communism. The Social Democrats were represented in the sham Parliament on the strength of an agreement with the government that they would abstain from organizing the workers on the land. For the land remained taboo. The yearly earnings of a landless peasant amounted to $120, and their numbers grew when America shut the door on immigration. There was no land distribution worth mentioning. Three million people lived on a half-starvation level.

Instead of reforms, one single remedy was offered for all evil and misery, the revision of the peace treaties which had given away two-thirds of old Hungary. The treaties themselves left room for revision and gave impetus to Hungarian hopes. Revision became the daily prayer in schools, revisionist slogans filled the walls and street cars and kept the states around Hungary jittery. These states made an alliance, the so-called Little Entente, against the revisionism which became an obsession with the public in Hungary. Responsible politicians soon lost hope of its realization and played revisionism down in diplomacy, but they dared not do so in public. And though dangerous in the field of foreign policy, revisionism was convenient since thorough-

going land reform, freedom, and democracy found no place
in the public mind, beset as it was with belief in the miraculous cure-all—restoration of old Hungary, or most of it.

Restoration was interpreted outside Hungary as an attempt to reconstruct the Hapsburg monarchy in which Hungary had played an increasingly ominous role. This could
have been realized only through the complete destruction
of at least two states of the Little Entente, Czechoslovakia
and Jugoslavia. When the last Hapsburg emperor in exile
also adopted this logical interpretation of Hungarian revisionism and suddenly landed in Hungary ready to take
over, the Little Entente mobilized, ready to go to war in
order to prevent an attempt to reconstitute the empire.

But except for a very small group of Catholic aristocrats
and members of the high clergy who stood for complete
restoration of empire and dynasty, the revisionists did not
include the Hapsburgs in their plans for a resurrected old
Hungary. Moreover, the small nobility and bureaucrats
had no intention of yielding their position as the ruling class
to the aristocrats surrounding the royal court. Regent
Horthy himself, although he had been made an admiral by
the Emperor at a youthful age, learned to like his residence
in the royal castle. He also enjoyed the ceremonies, more
pompous than the emperors had ever been burdened with,
because they gave decorum to his dull personage and high
office. He and his ministers were glad that they could
excuse their lack of enthusiasm for the Emperor by referring
to the threat of war with the Little Entente which was prepared to resist any Hapsburg accession to the throne. The
Regent even had guns mounted when the Emperor and his
aristocratic bodyguard approached the capital.

Revisionism deteriorated into an operetta setting when
an English newspaper lord fell prey to the charms of the
Hungarian ruling circle. Lord Rothermere discovered that
the peacemakers had given millions of Hungarians to new
states on haphazard principles, ignoring national self-determination. He put his newspapers at the service of revisionism. The enthralled Hungarian public mistook noise

for real influence on British foreign policy and exalted the noble lord to such an extent that he began to consider whether or not to acquire the ancient crown of St. Stephen for his son.

Apart from this strange interlude, revisionism retained its sinister forms. This became evident when Mussolini embarked on a program of changing the status quo in Europe and Africa, launching his campaign in the name of the have-not nations. The Duce eyed the Dalmatian coast of the Adriatic, denied to Italy by the peace conference, but he also wanted such French territories as Nice and Corsica and colonies in Africa. He bolstered Hungary and Austria, entering into a pact with them and strengthening their spines in the face of the Little Entente. Hungarian revisionism at last acquired a powerful backer.

Illusion took a still greater stride toward reality when the improbable ambitions of an Austrian paperhanger took hold of the German people. With the advent of Hitler, revisionism entered the field of *Realpolitik*.

The world economic crisis gravely affected Hungary as a still predominantly agricultural country. It brought a young officer of German origin into power, imbued with fascism. In Hungary's tight class system the Fascist orientation of Prime Minister Julius Gombos meant an overture to the people on the bottom of the social pyramid, even though in reality it was only an overture for broader support for the aspirations of the ruling classes.

At that time, the ambitions of the Italian Duce and the German Fuehrer clashed over Austria, and the Hungarian Prime Minister deserves the dubious credit for clearing the path between Rome and Berlin and also for coining the phrase Rome-Berlin Axis, the axis about which Hungarian policy revolved from then on.

Through the narrow opening offered by the Fascist gestures of Premier Gombos a disturbing new current entered the stagnant waters of Hungarian social life. This stirring force issued from the Hungarian youth that was growing up in Czechoslovakia. These young men were now being brought up at school in a democratic spirit that estranged them from the frozen social conservatism of their domestic surroundings. Their parents were dreaming of the golden times of Magyar squirearchy. The schools taught them to think of those days as of a shameful oppression of the peasant and non-Magyar population. The prospects of this Hungarian youth were dim. While their fathers expected certain positions to be open to them by virtue of birth, the youth had to work hard for even second-rate positions, being outsiders. Cut adrift, their sympathies were with the peasants of Hungarian stock, poor and bewildered like themselves. Among them they found a purpose, and from them they expected support. First of all, they were eager to learn about them, their lives, troubles, and aspirations. They launched systematic sociographical studies resulting in startling, though often saddening, discoveries. The initiative of the Hungarians from Czechoslovakia infiltrated into Hungary itself where it gave rise to a great spiritual revolution.

Young writers, mostly of peasant origin, dispersed about the land exploring the villages and eventually publishing their discoveries in books which awakened the public from its idyllic daydreams to frightening realities. They rang the tocsin to warn the people that underneath the façade of historical Hungary the foundations of the race were rotting away. Three million landless were excluded by the immovable system of big landed estates from any hope of rising to a decent existence.

Fortunately for the ruling classes, international events rolled toward a general reversal of the European order as it had been established by the peace treaties. Hitler marched into the Rhineland, and France failed to move, although demilitarization of that zone had been considered as the pivot of her security. The ruling class found an alternative to distributing the land, and the alternative had the advantage of running parallel to the Nazi stream. They could sacrifice the Jews, dispossess them, and eliminate them from lucrative and honorable positions to satisfy the clamor for change and the greed for spoils. But they did so reluctantly. It was feared that any kind of innovation might upset the system. Moreover, the Jews had an important function in the old order, and the rich Jews, titled or not, were intermingled with the ruling class by marriage or partnership. Also, liberals among the older noblemen abhorred the thought of breaking with the principle of equality before the law through institutionalized anti-Semitism.

But the public, fascinated with the possibilities opened ever wider by Hitler, brought mounting pressure to bear on the conservatives.

In 1938, a bill removing the Jews from full-fledged citizenship, the so-called first Jewish law, came up in Parliament for deliberation. It resulted in the strangest discussion on the Jews ever revealed in public. In a way it was more outrageous to decency than the Nuremberg laws, although far less radical or cruel. The Nazis at least had a powerful argument for the laws, holding the Jews to be the source of all evil. But in the Hungarian Parliament, those who supported the bill did so with apologies and justified their stand for it on the grounds of expediency.

The scene stood in peculiar contrast with another one on the Jewish question, held in the Hungarian Parliament a century earlier. At that time a cultured aristocrat of high principles submitted the bill emancipating the Jews. The noble statesman admitted that the Jews were wicked, usurers, and cheaters, but he reminded his hearers that this was so because the law had excluded them from honorable crafts, tilling the land, and serving the state.

In the debate on the Jewish law a hundred years later, all speakers paid tribute to the Jews, emphasizing their contributions to the economy and to culture in the past. They approved of the curtailment of their civil rights only because genuine Magyars needed the positions the Jews held on the strength of being the first comers.

In fact, anti-Semitism and nazism pushed the land problem into the background as if its solution was entailed in eliminating the Jews. The public, down to the mass of

landless peasants, believed that this was so. Even the intellectuals who had discovered the peasants hesitated. Some
of them would have allied themselves with the devil to help
the cause of the peasants, which the Hungarian Nazis at
least implied they would do. Others considered nazism as
a plague, but irresistible, and wanted the country to get it
over with and then take up the basic social problems. Still
others expected the collapse of the class system only from a
Communist revolution.

But the ruling class showed remarkable reluctance to tie
their fate too closely to Hitler's. They refused to join Hitler
in destroying Czechoslovakia; though once the destruction
of the Republic was accomplished, they could not resist the
opportunity of claiming the Hungarian-inhabited borderland of Slovakia and accepting it from Hitler's hand. From
this point on they were in Hitler's power. In 1940, they
submitted their application for Transylvania to Hitler and
received a large section of it from him. And in 1941, they
participated in the campaign which overran Jugoslavia, and
seized the Bachka, which had belonged to the old Hungary.
Once they had gained back these territories, they had to
keep them—and that depended on Hitler's good will. To
deserve it, Hungary had to follow Hitler's army, even when
it led them into the huge trap of the vast Russian plains.

At the end, though the ruling class no longer believed
in Hitler's final victory and tried to extricate themselves
from his fate, the Hungarian public saw no alternative for
the nation. Some sort of Germany was bound to survive
any defeat, but for the small, lonely Magyar nation it was
different. Hungary had prevented two groups of Slavs from
uniting in the course of history, and they believed that a
victorious Russia would destroy this obstacle for good. The
simple people of Hungary were ready to fight and die for
German victory, even when the upper classes feared the
independence of the country would be endangered by it,
and even when the German Nazis themselves ceased to believe in victory.

Characteristic of the first year of reconstruction, 1945, was a prodigious upsurge of creative energy, driven by an obsessive longing by the inhabitants of the shambles of what had been Budapest to restore the old setting of their lives. But life itself was to be different. The long terror of the siege, the effects of daily facing instant and violent death, had unveiled courage and cowardice in the most unexpected quarters. People avidly wanted a new life and at the same time felt that change was imperative. Nothing suggested the presence of forces that were compelling them to rethink and reorganize their way of life as much as the sight of Soviet troops in the streets. Everywhere one saw the huge red posters on the buildings housing Red soldiers, with long white-lettered inscriptions which almost no one was able to read. Once the Russians were established in Central Europe life could never be the same.

But there was another basic change, more conspicuous in the countryside than in the capital city, which implied that the social structure of the nation, once so immutable that it seemed like the skeleton of the nation itself, had definitely collapsed. The change was the distribution of the big estates. Whether it solved the problems of the peasantry or boosted the country's economic development was unimportant; its social and political implications were paramount. Hungary at last might develop into a democratic country of peasants and a middle class bare of aristocratic pretensions. The royal castle and the palaces of the magnates in Buda might never be rebuilt, but fresh green lawns and playgrounds for children would replace the memories of the past.

Nothing symbolized the state of devastation in Hungary more than the fact that not a single bridge of consequence had been left intact. The zeal of the population centered on rebuilding them as symbols of their determination to live. The people of Budapest started building a new bridge over the Danube, working day and night—the first new bridge in Europe after the war. The condition of the workers was appalling, as their salaries were swallowed up by inflation. Inflation began to spiral since the state had no income while it had to pay salaries and also to furnish the occupation troops with currency.

No one denied that it was the Communists who stirred the mood for work and reconstruction and that they alone organized it. The Muscovites learned how to do so in Russia, while the other parties of the coalition had never been given the chance in Hungary of acquiring skill in administration. At best they had been a tolerated opposition, not admitted into the workings of the government.

Having no stocks of food or articles of bare necessity, the government did not introduce rationing, but rather let private initiative take care of supplies. The guns were still thundering over Buda when Pest started buying and selling. Salesmen folded blankets on the sidewalk or simply stood between rows of ruined houses offering old hats, wheels from bicycles, shoes, cigarettes, and food. Hidden and looted goods came to the market. The peasants did not have to come into town. City folks carried clothing and pieces of furniture to the villages in exchange for food. The country became a huge black market trading the few miserable commodities available, while the government's first task was to get industry rolling for the Russians, on account of the reparation deliveries.

Some people surmised that it was the insistence of the Russians on instant deliveries which fired the ardor of Hungarian Communists in organizing reconstruction. Even so, the Communists were conspicuous for their modesty. Their Party held only two portfolios in the provisional government at Debrecen and did not exploit the fact that the distribution of the land was due to the initiative of the Soviet army. On the contrary, they allowed the Peasant Party of the former peasant intellectuals to go into the country and execute the distribution of land. The Communists' generosity may have been calculated to weaken the more conservative Smallholders Party by helping this new radical group ingratiate itself with the small peasants. Communists visited the villages and suggested the reconstruction of the

local national councils so that they conformed to the party
structure of the government, but they acted as trustees for
all coalition parties and acted fairly. Unfortunately, interference from outside put an end to the growth of those
spontaneous organs of self-government and paved the way
for the return of a centrally directed bureaucracy.

In April, 1945, the government moved to Budapest and
resolved to hold general elections in the fall. The Social
Democrats and Communists had a previous understanding
not to oppose each other at the elections and generally to
cooperate. The Social Democrats had a traditional hold on
the unionized workers of the capital and its suburbs. Also,
about 130 thousand Jews had survived and were expected
to show their gratitude to the Soviet army for being liberated by voting Communist. Moreover, the rabble of small
Nazis would hardly find a more suitable party than the
Communists, who, having been outlawed for the last twenty
years, had very few organized followers and would appreciate anyone's support. For all these reasons, both leftist
parties concurred in the opinion that it might be intelligent
to hold municipal elections in Budapest first to give the lead
to the more doubtful and politically less sophisticated countryside. The mood in Budapest encouraged them to follow
this proposal. The public had acknowledged the merits
of the Communists in the organization and reconstruction
of the country and had appreciated their moderation.

In October the municipal elections took place, in complete freedom and without any interference. The result
baffled victor and vanquished, public opinion at home as
well as abroad. The Smallholders Party, the only nonleftist
party allowed to participate in the elections, polled 51 per
cent of the vote.

Probably the Hungarian Nazis had made deeper inroads
among the industrial workers than the Socialists had anticipated, and a not inconsiderable part of the workers
joined the middle class in a protest vote against the Russians for the rape and loot they had perpetrated when they
invaded the country. The Smallholders refused a Russian

proposition to agree on a proportional distribution of seats before the general elections, although no less a man made the offer than Marshal Klementy Voroshilov, commander of the Soviet forces. But the parties did agree to rule in coalition no matter what the results of the general election. Indeed, the Smallholders had little choice, being afraid to antagonize the Communists, and therefore the Russians. The national elections took place in November and the Smallholders received 60 per cent of the vote.

Those in the West who wanted to believe in the possibility of cooperation with the Russians rejoiced. Here, in a country occupied by more than half a million Soviet troops, free elections were held and returned a majority for a middle-class party, although the party's friendliness to the Soviets was not above suspicion. The country enjoyed making its stand public. The Smallholders were anxious to keep the agreement and share responsibility with the Communists. The share in the portfolios presented no difficulties, but the Communists' claim to the Ministry of Interior did. This ministry supervised the police, who were then just organizing and for all practical purposes held the power in the state as far as the occupation authority left any power for the state to command. The Smallholders resisted the claim, but the Communists had an effective threat to get what they wanted; they would leave the government if their demand was turned down.

America hastened to recognize the government and the British followed suit, gratified by the freedom of the elections and even more by the results. Foreign visitors noted the refreshing atmosphere of freedom, the lively political debates, the manifold opinions expressed through a host of daily newspapers. Those who had an interest in Hungary's future as a democratic country recorded the political activity of the countryside, where not long ago city folks outside of the tolerated parties found themselves escorted to the railroad station if they tried to get in touch with the peasants. The minister who now supervised the land reform, a peasant and an outstanding writer, had been beaten

before the war by suspicious gendarmes when they found
that he had ordered books from Budapest and was reading
them. A new institution pointed to the prospects of cultural expansion for the peasantry. Talented peasants' sons
were selected and brought to the capital to study at the
University and were given free and decent room and board.
They demonstrated a tremendous thirst for knowledge and
orientation. All political groups spoke to them at forums
which revealed how much intelligence had been lost to
the country during the long, long period when the peasant's
place was in the stable.

The Parliament proclaimed Hungary a republic for the
third time, twice as a result of revolution and now of a
foreign invasion. A simple, dignified Calvinist pastor,
Zoltan Tildy, was elected President, and he appointed another Smallholder, Ferenc Nagy, to be Prime Minister.
The Communist Minister of the Interior was Imre Nagy, a
man of peasant origin who had turned Communist when a
prisoner of war in Russia during World War I. He was
deeply concerned with the fate of the Hungarian peasantry
and often professed heterodox opinions. But as he did not
aspire to leadership and bowed to Party decisions he did
not fall victim to the Party purges. He was the same Imre
Nagy who played such a fateful part in the Hungarian revolution of 1956.

Several more or less authoritative sources explain why
the Russians promoted or at least tolerated a Western-type
democracy in Hungary during the first two years after
liberation. The Churchill-Stalin agreement on spheres of
influence left as much say to the West in Hungarian and
Jugoslav affairs as to the Soviets (Stalin tried hard to have
Tito accept Western suggestions but not always successfully). This alone might account for the different treatment
of Hungary by the Soviets from that of Rumania and Bulgaria. The reason why Stalin was satisfied with less influence in Hungary than in Rumania and Bulgaria lay in the
strategic position of the latter countries. Hungary and
Jugoslavia were no immediate neighbors of the Soviet

Union, except for the short section of the northeast Carpathians where Russia became adjacent to Hungary as a consequence of her incorporation of the tiny Czechoslovak province of Subcarpathian Russia, renamed Transcarpathian Ukraine.

Matthias Rakosi, the Communist dictator of Hungary, who in 1945 had the modest title of Vice-Premier but as much power as he held advisable to exercise, revealed a more sophisticated explanation. Reporting to the Party Executive in May, 1945, Rakosi related confidentially that cooperation between the Great Powers was the most significant result of World War II. Cooperation was no empty word or propaganda, but a real possibility because Russia and America had no conflicting interests, Rakosi said. Indeed they both had an interest in curtailing the British empire insofar as its survival might involve conflicts between the two most important powers. The Soviets intended to promote cooperation with progressive American capitalism, and for this purpose Moscow had suspended its revolutionary aims. The Communists in Hungary had to hold back the application of a Communist program for the same reason. Someone asked Rakosi how long the period of compromise would last. The Communist leader replied that estimates ran from five to fifteen years. Nobody inquired into the meaning of the time interval. It may have corresponded to the length of time it was estimated that the Soviets would need for the reconstruction of war-torn Russia or for the manufacture of the atom bomb.

But Rakosi offered another explanation in 1952. He said that the Communist Party in 1945–46 was not able to win the majority of the working people over to the proletarian dictatorship. A decisive majority was, however, indispensable; without it not even the intervention of the Soviet army would suffice. Moreover, at that time the Party had hardly any organization through which to rule.

For the simple Party members the explanation always stressed that the development of socialism in the East European countries took a path different from that of the Soviet

Union because these countries enjoyed security by the presence of the Red Army and the support of the Soviet Union, while the Soviets had had to fight counter-revolutions and foreign interventionist armies alone.

American-Soviet cooperation worked in one instance at least to the great benefit of Hungary. It stopped the biggest inflation the world has experienced. The government gave free reign to the maddening inflation, convinced that only the combination of three measures could effectively cope with it. Without any one of them, intervention would only undermine the confidence of the public in future measures which could really be effective.

First the peasants, especially the new landowners, were expected to cultivate the soil, raise crops, and deliver them. The shortage of food and lack of rationing kept prices high in terms of barter, or in dollars, which became the basis of calculation. The government had good reason to hope that the peasants would grow as much as they could and bring the crops to the market if they could get industrial articles in exchange.

The other conditions depended on foreign powers. If the Russians consented to defer reparation deliveries and to reduce their occupation forces, commodities would be released to cover the needs of the peasantry. Finally, the American government could make a decisive contribution to the stabilization of currency by restoring to Hungary the $32 million worth of gold, belonging to the Hungarian National Bank, which the Nazis had carried away with them when they withdrew from Hungary. The Hungarian government would use it for buying goods abroad to stock up the stores for the day when the stabilized currency would begin to circulate.

A ministerial delegation visited Moscow and received the green light to visit Washington also. All three factors cooperated to insure the success of the financial operation, so that by August 1, 1946, the inflation came to a close—with a single dollar worth 4,600,000 quadrillion pengos. By then the streets of Budapest were strewn with paper money not worth bending down to pick up. Wages and successive bank deposits were now paid in a new currency, the forint. Money became scarce and the prices in the shop windows were high, but the population was relieved of the chore of rushing about to get rid of money which melted into nothing in no time.

In another instance, however, cooperation between Americans and Russians worked to the detriment of Hungary. The Americans failed to protest the Russian-approved Slovakian plan to transfer that little country's 600 thousand Hungarians to Hungary. The Slovaks pointed out that the Potsdam conference had authorized seven million Czechs to expel three million Germans; they argued that the two million Slovaks also had a right to get rid of their Hungarian minority. The elections in Hungary had placed the Magyars in a bad light in Stalin's eyes, and the fall of their stock in the East was not compensated by a corresponding rise in the West. The Slovaks had no case with respect to the Hungarian minority. Having boasted that they were Hitler's most faithful ally, they could scarcely claim the right to punish the Hungarians for their alleged pro-Nazi leanings. In fact, the Hungarians in "independent" Slovakia had not even joined the Slovak Fascists. Their member of Parliament, Count John Esterhazy, was the only one who voted against the Jewish laws. Moreover, in 1940, when the Slovak government forbade the Protestant Czech Brethren to hold services and confiscated their church money, the Magyar Calvinist church in Bratislava offered facilities for the Czechs to gather there clandestinely and hold services in their own language.

The Slovaks deprived all Hungarians of their citizenship by law and declared all their possessions confiscated. They were mostly peasants of one of the most ancient stocks of the Magyar race, living in those parts for more than eight centuries. It was a dismal sight to witness the catastrophe which befell these innocent people because of nothing but their nationality. The schools were closed in their villages; the children became street arabs. An overseer was appointed for each Magyar peasant as he worked, and he was forced to feed an extra mouth. In other villages, police swooped down on the peasants at night, herded them together, and transported them to faraway Sudetenland. Hitler's crimes were resumed before the approving eyes of Stalin while the West looked the other way.

This unexpected act of barbarism, occurring while Eduard Benes still occupied the presidential castle in Prague, inevitably provoked a nationalist reaction in Hungary. The Hungarian government was anxious not to awaken the spirit of revisionism which had done so much harm in the past, but it could obtain no concessions from the Slovaks. An agreement was made to exchange the Magyars in Slovakia with Slovaks in Hungary. The government gave the Slovaks all necessary facilities to convince Hungarian Slovaks to leave, but though Czechoslovakia was far better off than war-ravaged, inflation-ridden Hungary, only about eighty thousand Slovaks heeded the call.

The misery of the Hungarians in Slovakia, and the government's weakness in not making a case of it before world opinion, strengthened the opposition to the government. At the same time, the Russians insisted that Hungary expel its German population, called Schwabians. Many of them were excellent fruit growers inhabiting villages around Buda and in the Transdanubian counties, where they lived in clean, model settlements, carrying on a high grade of agriculture. During the war, the Schwabians, considered German nationals by the Nazis, had been recruited into German regiments. Many Schwabian youths had been active in the S.S., but these had left when the Nazis withdrew. In contrast to Czechoslovakia, strong protests arose in Hungary against expelling innocent people on the basis of collective responsibility. Two parties were especially affected since many of their voters had been Schwabians, the Smallholders and the Socialists. The Socialist daily newspaper warned its readers that if mass transfer of population in Hungary and Slovakia actually took place, the other Danubian countries might use the same methods to expel their Hungarian minorities. The Jews also protested against the principle of collective responsibility, on the basis of which the Jews had so often been persecuted. Only the National Peasant Party was led by racist "realism" to support the transfer, to make room for landless Hungarian peasants and smallholders.

The protests and the debate, which did much honor to the Hungarians, were cut short by the Communist daily, *Szabad Nep* (Free People), which warned that the transfer of the Germans had been decided on by all great powers and must be executed. Nevertheless, the government did not show unnecessary haste, and it made every possible exception for those who said that they had embraced German nationality under compulsion or had given signs of preference for Hungary.

The persecution of Hungarians in Slovakia had repercussions on the nationalist elements in the Smallholders Party. One of their speakers proposed that if the Slovaks did not want the Magyar minority they should return them together with the soil they and their ancestors had been tilling. There was nothing wrong or reactionary in this proposal, but in Hungary it smacked of revisionism and the old Horthy regime. This outburst of nationalism gave the Communists a good pretext to bring pressure on Ferenc Nagy, the Prime Minister, to clean his party of jingo elements. Nagy himself was aware of the danger they represented to a substantially democratic party such as the Smallholders, but the right-wing voters had no more congenial party to vote for. The Communists had to mobilize the Russians to make Nagy yield and expel twenty-two nationalists from the party. They later formed a party of their own.

In fact, it was a blow to the Hungarian Communist Party that it was unable to reach a humane solution of this problem with its comrades in Czechoslovakia. It was Stalin and the Czechoslovak Communists who had created this problem by agreeing that Czechoslovakia would become a pure Slav state.

Nationalism also made inroads into the Communist Party. In view of the nationalism provoked by the Communists in Czechoslovakia, some leading Hungarian Communists, anxious for the Party to get a firmer foothold in the country, advocated a more nationalistic orientation, or at least a less transparently Russian policy for the Party. They tried to persuade the Politburo, and the Russian Ambassador to Hungary, to lean more on domestic comrades and less on the Muscovites. There was a hint in the propositions, too, for less use of the Jewish intellectuals prevalent in the Moscow staff, as a practical measure due to the fact that anti-Semitism was still rampant in the country.

Georgi Pushkin, the Soviet Ambassador, was receptive to these arguments. Yet it was perhaps not for this reason, but because the Soviets decided that the Hungarian Communists should get tough with the opposition, that the fanatical young Laszlo Rajk took over from Imre Nagy the most important government position as Minister of the Interior. Rakosi still remained the only direct channel to Moscow, however.

Behind moves within and between the parties loomed the peace conference. The non-Communists expected to gain freedom from the legal interference of the Allied Control Commission, which in practice was equivalent to Russian intervention, Western protests notwithstanding. The ultra-optimists also believed that Soviet occupation would end at that time. On the other hand, the Communists trusted that once official Allied control was over they would be free to engineer the country toward complete submission to Soviet direction.

As far as economic penetration was concerned, the Soviets made huge steps. At first, the Soviet army dismantled factories and drove away cattle and horses as war booty. As a next step, they insisted on industry producing goods to be delivered to Russia as reparations. Russia furnished raw materials at exorbitant rates and received finished goods at far below the market price and at times less than cost in the factory. Then the Soviets assumed ownership of the most important industrial enterprises on the strength of the armistice which transferred German assets to them. The Germans had gained ownership of a considerable part of Hungarian industry and banking.

Moreover, the Hungarians had to pay to the Russians what they had owed to Germany, while the much higher amount the Germans had owed them was cancelled. The Russians, finally, entered into partnership with Hungary with respect to the exploitation of bauxite, air traffic, and shipping on the Danube. In the joint-stock companies, the Russians contributed German assets as their share, and also the equipment which they had first dismantled and then returned. The Russians learned a great deal from Nazi economic penetration and applied this knowledge without sentimental inhibitions, following a policy of naked imperialism even though they were dealing with a Communist or friendly state. They had an advantage in that commercial treaties were kept under strict secrecy.

Those who expected anything good from the peace conference were thoroughly disappointed. The treaty required Hungary to negotiate with Czechoslovakia but did not make the Slovaks responsible for respecting the human and civil rights of their Magyar inhabitants. It also failed to return some part of Transylvania to Hungary, although the armistice agreement with Rumania had suggested that this be left open to consideration. Indeed, Moscow had promised Rumania in the interval that her entire prewar territory would be restored, though she had earlier implied to Hungary that the Magyar-populated frontier region of Transylvania (the name used for all territories Rumania had obtained after World War I from old Hungary) might join Hungary.

At the peace conference, however, only the American delegation advised taking the question under consideration. By this step they unveiled and put an end to Soviet duplicity, since the Soviet delegation then opposed any change of the territorial status of Rumania as far as Hungary was concerned. But the Americans did not press the discussion further, thereby leaving Russia with a powerful weapon against the Rumanians and a bone of contention to hold up between the two interested nations. Russia would always be in a position to threaten a recalcitrant Rumania that it would transfer the administration of Transylvania to the large Hungarian minority, or even give part of it to Hungary itself.

In general the indifference of the West to the problems of the Eastern states left a strong impression on the interested parties, since it revealed that the West had abandoned them. The history of these states in the between-wars period brought to light their inadequacy in the face of economic penetration or aggression by a great power. It had also put into question their general viability and the threat to general peace posed by their nationalist movements. A federation replacing the defunct Hapsburg empire was considered spontaneously by both Russia and the West after the countries between Russia and Germany had been conquered one by one by Hitler.

Russia played with the idea of several federations: two federations of Slav peoples, Czechs and Poles to the north, Yugoslavs and Bulgarians to the south; and a federation of the non-Slav peoples, the Hungarians and Rumanians, in the middle. But any such combination posed the threat of a revival of a *cordon sanitaire* with its edge against Russia. The ideal situation for Russia was to have each state face Soviet power alone.

The West unmistakably showed its displeasure when the Czechs and Poles in exile concluded a pact of federation, for this would ruin their plans for a revival of the former Hapsburg empire in one form or another. Later, when it became clear that the Danubian and part of the Balkan zone would fall into the Soviet orbit, the West also objected to a federation of Jugoslavia and Bulgaria as a threat to Greece. Finally they dropped all federation plans, indeed any constructive idea of organizing the small peoples between the two giants. The negotiations in Paris demonstrated to what extent the fate of small countries was treated from the point of view of the Great Powers, with little or no interest in their own aspirations. This was in depressing contrast with the active considerations the American delegation had made manifest at the peace conference after World War I for the political self-expression of these peoples.

In almost all respects, the peace treaty with Hungary reaffirmed the conditions of the armistice. Those who hoped that the Soviets would actually have to evacuate Hungary after the signing of the treaty did not reckon with Austria, whose fate remained pending. As long as this country stood under four-power occupation the Russians were allowed to keep garrisons in Hungary and Rumania to insure the supply and security of their military forces there.

Meanwhile, the Communists in Hungary began to destroy the foundations of resistance to the new order. The Social Democrats and National Peasants supported action against movements and groupings which opposed democratic institutions. Premier Nagy brought to light an ambivalent attitude. He was aware of the barrier the rightist elements in his party represented to true cooperation with the parties of the left. At the same time, if he allowed them to be crushed it would curtail the strength of the party and with it the forces against Communism.

But then Laszlo Rajk, the Communist head of the Ministry of the Interior, went into action. Two serious incidents occurred in which young snipers connected with the Catholic youth organization and the Smallholders Party shot Russian officers and soldiers. The commander of the Soviet occupation forces demanded that the government take effective action to dissolve the Catholic youth organization, prevent Cardinal Mindszenty from attacking the Soviet army and Hungarian democracy, and revoke immunity from arrest for two members of Parliament of the Smallholders Party involved in the shooting. The government bowed to these demands except for the suspending of immunity for the two deputies.

Here for the first time Cardinal Mindszenty became the target of attack by the Communists and the Soviets. Yet, at this time, exception to the Cardinal's political activities was taken by all democratic elements. The Catholic church had lost formidable power through the land reform. It had owned one-seventeenth of the country's total arable land, about 1¼ million acres. But 130 acres were reassigned to each parish in the land reform, and many of them turned out to be better off than they were before.

Mindszenty had been in office only a year, but he already considered himself first of all as Primate of Esztergom, where his predecessors had traditionally crowned the kings and invested them with royal power. Mindszenty contested the validity of the republic since in his eyes it lacked legality. He also publicly attacked the land reform and emphasized that the church had performed charity from the income of the landed estates it owned and had upheld institutions serving the spiritual and other interests of the majority of the people. It must be emphasized that the bulk of the nation stood for the republic as well as the land reform. Mindszenty thus weakened his own position and made it impossible for his followers to back him when he later attacked more violent Communist measures. His obsolete stand for the restoration of old Hungary and the system of landed estates would have compromised his backers.

In December, 1946, Laszlo Rajk produced a case which dealt a terrific blow to the Smallholders Party. He discovered a rightist organization which advocated the restoration of the Horthy regime and was preparing to act as soon as the Soviet army of occupation was withdrawn according to the provisions of the peace treaty. Generals and high officials were involved in the organization, called the "Hungarian Community," and also deputies of the Smallholders Party who were close to Prime Minister Nagy. The organization existed without doubt, and its participants planned action to restore the old order. Rajk declared it a conspiracy against the republic and made large-scale arrests. The Prime Minister and his party acknowledged the existence of the plot and expelled those involved in it from the party, but they refused to lift immunity from arrest for one of the most important leaders of the party, General Secretary Bela Kovacs. In February, 1947, the Soviet army had him arrested, purportedly for espionage, and he was not heard from again until 1955, when he returned from prison in Russia.

On November 1, 1956, summoned by the insurgents, Kovacs came to Budapest from his home in the country. An eyewitness reported: "The man we had known in the old days was tall and erect, broadshouldered, with strong, firm features. The man standing before us was haggard and bent; he regarded us with sad, hurt eyes. He looked more like a retired scientist than the most popular leader of the Hungarian peasantry. . . ." Kovacs stated: "I believe that no one should even dream of a return to the old order. The world of bankers, counts, and capitalists is finished in Hungary."

CHAPTER SEVEN

Czecho-Slovakia

Those who revisited Prague in 1945 and remembered Bismarck's words that the master of Prague was
also the master of the European continent, had a shock
when they arrived by plane from London at the deserted
airport of the Czech capital. They noticed two Soviet
soldiers standing guard on the platform. Aloof, they
seemed to observe the sky, paying no attention to what
must have been the biggest event of the day—the arrival
of a converted British bomber and the passengers crawling
out of it.

Russian soldiers in the heart of Europe, as Prague, capital of old, historic Bohemia was rightly called, revealed
the changes that World War II had brought to Europe.

But outwardly Prague had hardly changed. The old
castle still loomed high above the city, which so happily
combined noble old styles with the glass and concrete of
modern architecture. The famous window of the castle
was in its old place, from which the imperial counselor
had been thrown by the Czechs in 1618 in retaliation against
the religious oppression of the Hapsburg emperor—marking
the start of the Thirty Years' War. Half the Czech people
had been wiped out during those bloody decades. It was
the same window where Hitler had stood looking down on
the city into which he had swept triumphantly in March,
1939, an act that was to boomerang in the form of World
War II. And behind that window, Dr. Edward Benes was
again working as President of the Republic—the man whose

destiny was twice to build up a state from the rubble of two world wars.

It is a rare grace of the gods, sometimes loaded with malice, which allows a man to face the same situation and problems he had once dealt with and failed to solve, to be able to try again, wiser this time by age and experience. At the same fork of the road he then has the opportunity of trying the other route. This happened to Dr. Benes, one of the three creators of the first Czechoslovak Republic which he had served as Minister for Foreign Affairs, Prime Minister and eventually President from its first moment to its last.

Dr. Benes had enrolled the new republic into the Western alliance system, modeled its institutions on those of the West, molded its cultural development by Western influence. When the test of fire came in 1938, however, the Prime Minister of Britain, Neville Chamberlain, appeared to be straining his memory to remember Czechoslovakia, a "far-away country of which one knows so little." Indeed, how could Britain risk war for the sake of such a country? Chamberlain, speaking in this way of the only democratic state in eastern Europe, also voiced the ardent wish in the trembling heart of the French Prime Minister, Edouard Daladier, not to honor the obligations issuing from the French-Czechoslovak military alliance. As a result of the diplomatic conspiracy of the West with Hitler at Munich in 1938, the Republic had been crushed, mutilated and submerged in the Nazi empire. Yet, the great President-liberator, Thomas G. Masaryk, had warned Dr. Benes, his disciple, that if the case of the Czechs were to triumph it had to be made a case for all Europe. Benes failed to make it so in 1938 when he chose to submit rather than to fight in the hours of agony and decision. The Soviets had intimated that they stood for their treaty of mutual assistance with Czechoslovakia, but Benes did not consider the Soviet offer, as this would have appeared to the West to justify Hitler's accusation that his country was an outpost of Soviet expansion. World War II came to pass nevertheless, after Hitler had acquired the up-to-date equipment of the Czech army and the immense war industry of Czechoslovakia. As a result, Soviet soldiers now stood guard at the airport of Prague.

No sooner had World War II ended than Benes began rebuilding the state, its constitutional and legal framework, and the alliances to guarantee its security. He took to heart the lessons of his failure in the past. Soviet Russia was bound to become the greatest military power on the European continent, and its new pan-Slavism, the alliance of Slav states, would block German expansion forever.

But this was a different Russia, rejuvenated and strong, eager to embrace the industrial civilization of the West and infuse into it the principles of the Communist revolution. Benes was enthusiastic about the Soviet concept of pan-Slavism. He resolved to transform multinational Czechoslovakia into a pure Slav country, ready to expel millions of Germans and Hungarians to realize this purpose; and he was anxious to have the Soviet Union as a neighbor of his future country to insure its security.

Benes reveals in his memoirs how early he had come to the radical conclusion that the Soviets should become neighbors not only of Czechoslovakia but also of Hungary, although this was possible only through the Russians' acquiring the easternmost province of former Czechoslovakia, inhabited mainly by Ruthenians, a people closely related to the Ukrainians. It was on September 19, 1939, during the honeymoon time of the Hitler-Stalin pact, that Benes entertained in his home the Soviet Ambassador to Britain, Ivan Maisky. Benes quotes himself:

But once I stressed to him the necessity for the Soviet Army reaching our frontier. "Indeed, I do not know in detail," I added, "how conditions will develop at home, but for the future it is necessary for the Soviet Union to remain the neighbor of ourselves and Hungary. After this new war we must be neighbors of the Soviet Union directly and permanently. For us this is one of the lessons of Munich! The question of Subcarpathian Ruthenia will be solved between us later and we surely will agree!"

Whereas Benes had put his main reliance on the West for the security of the first republic, he went to Moscow in December, 1943, to sign a military alliance with the Soviet Union as the cornerstone of the security system of the second republic.

Though his countrymen had great respect for Dr. Benes, they never loved him. "If Masaryk was the idea, Benes was the sword," an English diplomat said of him. His mind was cold and sharp, his logic like hammer blows; the premises might vary, but the conclusion remained the same. He fanatically believed in the final triumph of consistency, even though it arrived through loopholes and back doors if it failed in a frontal attack. He had won more battles at conference tables than any other leader had on the battlefield; indeed, he usually won more for his country than he had expected. This strongly built small man of peasant stock had only a public life, except for his unique love for his wife, a beautiful and wise lady who kept herself away from publicity. He never showed joy or sorrow in public, was bereft of jokes, and never smiled. One would look in vain for a metaphor in the voluminous collection of his speeches. He was all logic, yet always ready with formulas in which to wrap controversies that temporarily could not be resolved. His reputation as a compromiser was legendary at the League of Nations; yet he was unshakable in his stand and irrepressible in the execution of his plans. Aware, however, that he represented a small nation, Benes avoided frontal attacks. He was as formidable in his successes as in his failures.

It would have become him to enter the capital of the republic in a triumphal march hailed by the liberated and happy citizenry. But Benes would not take the risks involved in delay and hastened to join the first provisional government setup in eastern Slovakia behind the front of the Soviet army. He had no basic objections to the merit of the Communist-inspired government program, though it involved deepgoing changes in the constitutional and social structure of the state which could not be imposed on the country as long as democracy was to be preserved. Yet he was not a man to acknowledge a mistake while there was hope of putting it right. He believed that East and West would cooperate after the war, with Czechoslovakia to become the bridge between them—too important for the Soviets to destroy by Communist domination.

The liberation of Prague, in fact, showed how meticulously East and West could cooperate, although it disheartened the population and led to portentous events. General Patton's army was ordered to halt on the Czechoslovak frontier region of Karlovy-Vary–Plzen–Budejovice, since the decision of the Allies at the Teheran conference was that Czechoslovakia fell into the Soviet zone of military operations and the Russians insisted that they alone should liberate Czechoslovakia. However, the population of Prague rose before Malinowski's troops could reach the capital city and attacked the weak German garrison. The Germans wanted to break out of the town with the intention of reaching the Americans and surrendering, but they ran into an unexpected obstacle, General Vlasov's Ukrainian army. The Germans had allowed the anti-Communist and anti-Russian general to organize an army from prisoners of war, and it now blocked their way, attacked the Germans, and inflicted heavy losses. The Ukrainians grasped this last chance to redeem their treason to the Soviets by their bravery, since the Americans had not accepted their surrender. The Germans laid down their arms to the National Council in Prague.

The Soviet armies received a frantic welcome on May 5 from the people of the Czech capital. They were grateful for their liberation from German and Nazi tyranny and happy that it was the great Slav nation that had crushed their traditional enemy—the same great Slav nation which they believed had been ready to come to their aid when the West had flung them to the Nazi beast in 1938.

The Soviet troops remained in the country until December, when in agreement with the Americans both armies left the territory of Czechoslovakia.

Yet, the entire nation felt disillusioned with the Soviet people when it learned to know them by direct experience. The Czechs told outsiders about their disillusionment right after the Russians left their soil, throwing light on the future development of Soviet-East European relations in general.

The reaction of the Czech people to their first encounter with the great Slav brothers held special significance because they were prejudiced in favor of the Russians and because they could make themselves mutually understood through the affinity of their languages. They did not fear the Russians nor see them as conquerors. On the contrary they looked forward to putting the nation under their future protection against the recurrence of Germanic aggression.

Karel Capek, the outstanding Czech playwright, who died heartbroken at the Munich catastrophe, once made a trip following the track of the double-headed eagle, the emblem of the Hapsburgs, to all the lands the dynasty had once ruled. Whether he was in the former Austria-Hungary, Dalmatia, Northern Italy, the Low Countries, or Spain, he found that the routine and etiquette of daily life was the same. People had the same table manners, ate at the same time, set the tables in the same way; they understood the same hints, appreciated the correct measure of feelings, the seriousness of a polite phrase, the significance of a smile, a compliment, or an expression of sympathy. The intimate style of family life survived the common rulers and ruling classes who had set the tone, fashion, and manners for all their subjects to imitate. But the Russians were at odds with this intimacy. They were uneasy strangers from a land where words and gestures had unfamiliar meanings. Sometimes they were incalculable, indifferent, and mistrustful, as if they were of an altogether different species from the Westerners. Of a sudden, they would become effusive, kindly, warmhearted, eager to be loved. They stole things without the slightest idea of their use and soon gave them away. Their reactions were either non-existent or violent. The Czech intelligentsia held them to be primitive and attributed their extremist reactions to a lack of the balance that comes from the stabilizing effect of civilization. They considered the Russians childlike. It surprised the Czechs that the Soviet system appeared not to have changed the character of the people as it had been revealed in the writings of the great Russian classics.

The simple Czechs got over their first resentment over the misconduct and atrocities of some Russian troops as soon as they had left the country. It was unfair, they said, to expect a miracle of tenderness from warriors who had fought for years against a merciless enemy, who had seen their lands burned, their families killed and dispersed. Crossing the Czech frontier could scarcely change them suddenly into angels. The Czechs also condoned their looting, but with an argument that showed that they noticed the Russians had come from a poorer and less civilized country. It must have been maddening, they said, to the sons of a great and victorious nation to see that the peoples they saved were all richer than themselves.

Of the host of true stories told of the Russians in the Czech lands at that time, three may suffice to show Czech feelings and judgments about the great Slav people.

A Soviet officer in charge of the military court handling civilian complaints had an enlisted man shot for rape. People in the village heard of it and thronged into the antechamber of the officer the next morning. One of them was called in. The father of an eighteen-year-old girl, emboldened by the exemplary punishment, was encouraged to complain that his daughter also had been violated. The officer answered the man, "Get out of here, you old son of a bitch! You should have married her off long ago!" And that was the end of all rape complaints in the village.

Right after the Russians marched into another town they picked young men in the streets to help clear away the heaps of rubble from shellings and bombings. While digging in the debris and throwing it on a truck to be hauled away, the clearing crew found a machine gun outfit, completely new and of Russian make. They dutifully reported it to the guard who told them not to worry, just to throw it into the truck with the rest of the junk. The young men thought this procedure stupid and feared that it might result in dangerous reprisals against themselves, so they put the gun aside until an officer came by to whom they showed their find and described the guard's instructions. The officer listened to their story and without replying turned and went into a nearby building. A few minutes later he returned with a pick-axe. He dragged the machine gun into a clear spot, raised the axe and wielded it vigorously until the gun fell to pieces. Then he turned to the clearing crew. "Now you can throw it away—it's nothing but junk."

One of the Czech intelligentsia was reminded of a story Gorky told about a Russian soldier he met in World War I. The soldier had expressed concern over the many East Prussian people killed and the villages burned in the war. Gorky reminded him that many Russian villages had also been burned and that many Russians had also died on the battlefields. The soldier was not impressed. "Oh," he said, "it's nothing for us. There are so many Russians and so many Russian villages." This story by Gorky came to his mind when he witnessed this event:

A drunken Russian captain fell into the river from the pontoon bridge across the Danube. At his desperate cries for help two Russian soldiers ran to the scene and were preparing to leap in and rescue him, when a third arrived and held them back. "Forget about him," he said, "haven't we plenty of captains just now?"

When the Russians left in December this was the Czechs' farewell to them: "They are a great and good people, God bless them. But they can contribute nothing to our problems. Indeed, we can learn nothing from them."

Czechs in our days are considered opportunist, industrious, intelligent, and democratic, but unwilling to take arms to defend their way of life. But in the fifteenth and sixteenth centuries the world knew them as the great warriors of

Europe who carried a new faith as the standard of their
armies and defied the Holy Roman Emperor and his allies.

Speaking of Czechs, one has in mind the Slav people of
the historic provinces of Czecho-Slovakia in the western
part of that country, Bohemia, Moravia, and Silesia. But
the leadership belonged to Bohemia, whose fate the other
provinces mostly shared. Geographically, it is a natural
unit, surrounded as it is by wooded mountains with easy
access only from the South, from Moravia with its brother
Slavs. Goethe said admiringly of Bohemia's natural unity
that it was a continent within the continent. Bismarck
translated the statement into military terms by saying that
Bohemia was a fortress created by God. Unfortunately,
political geography jeopardized its natural security since
Bohemia intruded deep into the Germanic lands in the west.
Indeed, it looked as if it were in the wide-open mouth of a
Germany ready to swallow it.

The Slav tribes of which the Czechs were one had filtered
into the territories of the historic Czech lands in the fifth
century A.D., but a Slav state had emerged only in the ninth
century in Moravia and territories to the south—Slovakia
and Pannonia. Soon the Hungarians arrived from Asia and
destroyed this Slavic Moravian empire, but not before these
Slavs had turned Christian. Byzantium dispatched the mis-
sionary brothers Cyril and Methodius of Salonika to teach
the gospel in Slavic, but these western Slavs desired Rome's
spiritual leadership, and the Byzantine missionaries bowed
to their preference.

After the breakup of the Slav empire, Bohemia rapidly
developed into a principality and then, by grace of the
Holy Roman Emperor, into a kingdom. The tie to the empire was at times loose, and at others close, with Bohemia
flourishing whenever her king was Holy Roman Emperor
at the same time. The country also prospered when rich
gold and silver deposits were uncovered and exploited in
the fourteenth century.

The Luxemburg dynasty brought a French influence to
architecture and the arts along the shores of the Vltava

River, on which Prague, the capital of Bohemia, had been built. Charles IV established the independence of the kingdom as an appendix of the empire, embellished Prague with lasting monuments, and founded there the first university in central Europe. This university was dominated by German priests and students, as was the country at large. When Jan Hus became rector of the university, he protested against German preponderance in the institution and provoked a sharp dispute by his advocacy of reforms in the church. The King heeded Hus's protest and gave the Czechs at the university the decisive word. The German scholars refused to accept this ruling and left Prague to found a new university in Leipzig. Jan Hus continued to preach against the malpractices of the clergy and exhorted the faithful to cultivate their native language. But when he advocated lay participation in the sacrament in both bread and wine, the clergy accused him of heresy. Hus was summoned before the Council and was burned at the stake in Constance in 1415.

Hus died, but the nation followed his gospel. The main stream of Hussitism remained a great spiritual longing for a simple faith and a community of Christians equal before God. But inevitably the idea was absorbed by other sects who wished to spread equality on earth in a community of likeminded men who needed no compulsion from church or state.

The moral and religious revival combined with the ambitions of various classes to form a mighty national movement. The nobility eyed the estates of the high clergy who possessed a third of all the lands. Nobility and common people alike hated the commercialism of the townspeople and resented their wealth and influence. In addition, the high clergy and the townfolk were Germans, privileged strangers in Czech lands. But once the nobility became strong enough to dispossess the clergy, they turned against the equalitarian Hussite sects. It actually came to a battle between the conservative and radical Hussites which resulted in the defeat of the latter in 1436. Thereafter, the conservatives applied for readmittance to the Catholic church, and when the Estates elected a king from their midst, they deprived the peasants of their freedom and disenfranchised the towns.

Religious disturbances continued until the history of Bohemia arrived at another fatal turn. The young Jagiello King, who was also King of Hungary, perished in the battle of Mohacs in 1526 against the Ottoman Turks invading Hungary. Thereupon the Czech Estates elected a king who appeared to have enough force to stop the advance of the Turks toward the conquest of Christian Europe—a Hapsburg. This event initiated a long chapter in Czech history, ending only in 1918 when the Hapsburg empire collapsed and the Czechoslovak republic was born.

With the Hapsburgs a campaign began against Protestantism, against the power of the Czech nobility, and against all self-government in the kingdom. When it became obvious that the emperors would not be satisfied until they had destroyed them all, the Czechs rebelled. They appealed to foreign Protestant princes for help, but failed to receive sufficient aid to alter the outcome of the Battle of White Mountain on November 8, 1620. It was a short battle. The Czech nobles could not count upon the valor of the peasants whom they had forced into serfdom, and the imperial troops won the day—the last of the Kingdom of Bohemia.

"Thou shalt break them with a rod of iron; thou shalt dash them in pieces like a potter's vessel" was the slogan the court preacher rang out. Emperor Ferdinand had the leaders of the nobility executed, confiscated the estates of the Czech nobility—three-fourths of all the land—and expelled thirty thousand families who refused to give up their Protestant faith. He made the rest Catholic *en bloc* and distributed the confiscated land among Catholic Germans and other nationals. The Czech language was banned from church, school, and office. A foreign ruler, foreign clergy, foreign aristocracy, and foreign bureaucracy impressed their images on Czech life. The Thirty Years' War wrought ter-

rific havoc in the country. Less than a million remained
from its three million former inhabitants. Moreover, the
regime strewed rose petals on the road for deserters from
the Czech community. Those who coveted rank, title, adventure, and fortune left the Czech heritage to the common people.

But the peace gave impetus to an unprecedented prosperity all over Europe and specifically in Bohemia. The
country was rich in natural treasures and skilled German
workers in the mountains around the plain where Czech
peasants tilled the soil. At the end of the eighteenth century, the emperors promoted the industrialization of the
province to serve as a bastion against the Prussian-instigated
pan-Germanism that might have tempted the Germans of
the realm. The imperial policy softened toward Czech cultural initiative. At the same time, Czech apologists began
to discover that a supranational Hapsburg empire would
protect them from pan-Germanism. The imperial offices
were opened to Czechs on the lower levels. An armada of
Czech bureaucrats who spoke German with a foreign accent furnished the broad support for the higher symbol of
supranational unity, the imperial court.

The character of the Czechs underwent a deep transformation in the centuries of foreign rule. A people who
had been in the vanguard of the great campaigns of the
Reformation changed into cautious opportunists who remained nominally Catholic while keeping the Hussite protest
burning inside. They helped to administer the Hapsburg
empire, even while they hated it for imposing on them an
alien way of life and an alien language. They became real-
ists who saw the way to freedom through strengthening the
nation in culture and wealth, but rejected as phantoms pan-
Slavism or complete national independence. There was a
realistic hope, however, of living an independent national
life within the empire as its rulers were driven by the awak-
ening national consciousness of the Slav groups to shift
their weight from the Austrian Germans and Hungarians to
the Slavs.

But when the German Reich was formed in 1871, the direct danger to the Hapsburg empire from that side appeared to have vanished. The old Emperor then refrained from a radical reorganization of the realm and continued to rely mainly on the Germans in Austria and the Magyars in Hungary for its survival. The Germans in Bohemia, Moravia, and Silesia, the so-called Sudeten Germans, nevertheless began to distrust Vienna for flirting with the Czechs and endangering their favored status in the Czech lands. They threatened to join the German Reich rather than submit to the Czech majority in Bohemia.

However, the Crown Prince, Archduke Francis Ferdinand, approved of the imperial reorganization. The king was old, and national freedom without great risks seemed to be rising on the horizon. Moreover, the democratization of Austria progressed. The general and secret ballot returned in 1911 an imperial assembly that mirrored the actual composition of the country, with the Slav element predominant. The process of democratization appeared to be bringing forth recognition and prestige for the middle-class virtues of the Czechs, their well-to-do peasantry, skilled workers, technicians, industrious and learned intelligentsia, and homogeneous community. But a Serb fanatic shot and killed Francis Ferdinand in 1914, and hopes for national liberty within the empire vanished.

World War I confronted the Czechs with an awful dilemma. They were expected to fight on the side of the German giant whose victory would perpetuate their status as second-rate citizens in their own land. They would be opposing Russians and Serbs, Slav brothers who might turn the dream of a vast Slav empire into reality, and also the West which represented the triumph of middle-class ideologies over monarchist-feudalistic values. Huge forces were wrestling in a world-wide conflagration which would decide whether the aspirations of small nations would materialize or be buried. The Czechs thought they could do no more to influence the decision than to resist in an alert and disci-

plined way and sabotage the war efforts of the Central
Powers without furnishing them with a pretext for their
own repression.

But one great Czech would not stand for caution and
compromise when the time came for his people to rise to
the historic occasion. He was an educator of the nation as
Comenius, his predecessor, had once been. Thomas G.
Masaryk was a realist of heroic brand, who believed democracy to be a society of higher moral order than monarchies
and aristocracies, and trusted that progressively democracy
was bound to prevail over systems of oppression and privilege. He felt that history had chosen his people to become
a living example of the incorporation of high moral values
in a society by giving equal opportunity to all its members.

Masaryk, the son of a Slovak coachman and a German
mother, grew up to be a champion of unpopular causes at
home and abroad, and an inexorable searcher for the truth
in the conviction that it would prevail over obscurantism
and delusion. He reminded the Czechs how their ancestors
had raised high the torch of spiritual values so that the
whole of Europe could see the great longing in every human
for mutual respect in a community of good will. They had
led the first assault on the degenerate old order in favor of
reform in religion and society.

Masaryk chose a young, energetic professor, Eduard
Benes, as his right-hand man. While Masaryk stood for the
liberty of his nation because he believed that its cause was
the cause of democracy, Benes stood for the principle of
democracy because it involved the liberation of his nation.
A Slovak astronomer in Paris, Milan Stefanik, joined them to
publicize the fact that the projected new state was to comprise not only the people of the Czech lands but also the
Slovaks, who had parted ways with the Czechs when the
Magyars had broken up the ancient Moravian empire a
thousand years ago.

Masaryk also took up the heroic traditions of Hussitism.
He and his aides set themselves the immense task of ham-

mering into the brains of the statesmen of the West the
argument that Austria was hopelessly doomed. The French
were reluctant to give up the Hapsburg monarchy as a potential counterbalance to the German Reich; the British did
not like the idea of wiping out an ancient great monarchy,
and even the Americans were susceptible to arguments that
the empire offered a large market to all its nationalities for
economic cooperation.

The moment of decision arrived when the revolution
knocked Russia out of the anti-German front. Masaryk recognized that his group could now render an important and
spectacular service to the Allies by organizing the mass of
Czech and Slovak prisoners of war in Russia and transport-
ing them to the Western front to participate in the war that
was to bring about their national liberation.

The anabasis of the Czecho-Slovak legions through revo-
lution-torn Siberia made the unfamiliar hyphenated name
of the new nation known to the West. The accomplishment
made a lasting impression on the statesmen, particularly because they took note of the fact that the legions fought the
Red Army in Russia when it blocked the way of their exodus.

Meanwhile, the Czechs at home registered with satisfaction the activities of the émigrés, but they thought that their
task remained not to jeopardize the future of the nation
should the war end in a compromise as far as the fate of the
Hapsburg monarchy was concerned. They approved of
the fact that the Czech soldiers had surrendered to the
alleged enemy whenever they had the opportunity of doing
so safely; also that the legions had begun fighting on the
fronts of the West. But in Parliament the representatives of
the Czech parties publicly rejected Wilson's appeal for national self-determination and denied any connection with
the Masaryk-Benes team abroad. Only when the Allies one
after the other recognized the Czechoslovak Committee
abroad as the government of an "associated power" did the
Czech intellectuals raise their voices in a manifesto calling
upon the people to arise to the great moment. The state of

Czechoslovakia thus existed before it ruled over an inch of the land.

The agony of the old empire began. The young Emperor proclaimed himself ready to insure self-government for all peoples within the realm while saving the world from the chaos that inevitably would follow the dissolution of the broad political, historical, and economic unity of the empire.

Prague then hastened to set up a National Council as a kind of government. Involuntarily this gave the signal to the people for joyous mass demonstrations for national independence and the proclamation of the republic. The National Council did everything to prevent the outbreak of a revolution, aware of the presence of a large concentration of imperial troops able to frustrate such an eventuality. In this endeavor, the Council followed the warnings from the Committee in Paris to the effect that the Allies would see in disturbances and lawlessness the specter of Bolshevism which might nip in the bud all hope for complete liberation.

The Council had no difficulty in making people understand what was at stake and why they should refrain from violence while the empire went day by day further down the road to disintegration. It inquired of the imperial governor by the hour whether he had received advice from Vienna that the proclamation of a Czechoslovak state would no longer be opposed. Finally on October 28, 1918, the military commander of Prague told the National Council that no force would be used against such a proclamation, and it was issued the same day.

The news that they were going to break with the thousand-year-old tie with the Magyars and form a state with the Czechs found the Slovaks in old Hungary unprepared. The Slovaks were descended from Slav groups that had been integrated with other Slavs in the Moravian empire until the Magyars destroyed it. They may be a branch of the same family as the Czechs, as their language is closely related although not the same. They populated the mountainous northern part of Hungary where they lived for a thousand years while the Czechs in the west struggled to keep their identity in the Germanic world.

Contrary to the Czech lands, which had existed as political units through the long past, the Slovaks never had had their abode delineated by any kind of political or cultural self-government. They partook of the life of Hungary, the nobles becoming Hungarians, speaking Latin in public, and Slovak in the family; while the common people shared the fate of the Magyar serfs, free peasants, and craftsmen. They had come into contact with the Czechs in the fifteenth century when the Hussites had invaded Northern Hungary. The Hussite articles of faith had stirred lively echoes among the Slovaks. Under Czech influence about one-fifth of the Slovaks became Lutherans, and their scriptures in the Old Czech language remained a cultural tie between them and the Czechs. But politically their worlds split. The Czechs had a great antagonist, the Germans, to appease or oppose, while the Slovaks lived under Hungarian feudalism, beginning to have specifically Slovak grievances only at the beginning of the nineteenth century. The Hungarians then set out to Magyarize the whole country with its many nationalities, just at the time when the Slovaks also discovered that they were an ethnically and linguistically distinct part of the great Slav family of peoples and began to cultivate their dialect as the basis on which their nationality rested.

But the cult of Slovak nationality and language did not bring them nearer to the Czechs. In their efforts to establish a literary Slovak language the Slovak reformers took pains to stress that which distinguished it from other Slav idioms, and they came into controversy with the Lutherans who revered the Old Czech of their Bible. Not even the Lutherans dreamed, however, of a political tie with the Czechs as the way of developing their national character and language. They cherished much bigger dreams in their sleepy towns and villages in the valleys of the Carpathians, expecting the Russian Tsar to liberate all Slavs and unite them in a powerful empire.

The great majority of the Slovaks, deeply religious Catholics, had no sympathy with Czech Hussitism or Russian Orthodoxy. They strove for more freedom for their nationality inside Hungary, and when the Hungarians denied it to them they turned to the Hapsburgs in Vienna, expecting that the emperors, tired of Hungarian insistence on their own independence, would appreciate the loyalty of the Slavs and compel the Hungarians to grant them schools and freedom to cultivate their national traditions. In 1848–49, when the Hungarians rose in armed rebellion, the Slovaks favored the dynasty. But the Hapsburgs forgot their promises and made an agreement in 1867 giving the Hungarians a free hand with their alien nationals.

However, in the years that followed, the Hungarians accepted alien nationals who declared themselves Magyar. The Slovak intelligentsia grasped this opportunity for assimilation and careerism with an avidity that had no counterpart among the other alien nationalities in Hungary. The Hungarian civil service teemed with employees of Slovak origin. In half a century, all educated Slovak people broke with their national roots. Only a small minority remained immune to the attraction of becoming full-fledged Hungarians and returned to their people after their schooling, living in small towns as lawyers, doctors, and poets.

In the early twentieth century, a few Lutheran Slovaks came under the influence of Czech nationalists. They thought that the Hapsburg empire was bound to be reorganized on a broader, more democratic principle, and that this would encounter the stubborn resistance of the Hungarian lords. In that case, the dynasty would have to appeal to the non-Hungarian nationalities of Hungary to rally behind it to fight for their own freedom. These young Slovaks made contact with other nationalities in Hungary to prepare for this eventuality.

But they were few. The great majority felt that the Hungarians were very strong and saw nothing fantastic in the Magyars' determination to establish their rule for another millennium. Even when the Emperor made more and more concessions to the Slavs in Austria, the Slovaks surmised that he would only be the more driven to gain the support of the Hungarians.

World War I came and the pan-Slav intellectuals listened on lonely nights to the dull sound of the guns of the tsarist army from beyond the Carpathians. But the sounds faded and tsarism with them, while the broad Slovak population sent its children to the Austro-Hungarian army as a matter of course.

The Slovak intelligentsia knew little of what was happening in Paris in the name of a brand-new Czechoslovak nation. The foremost believer in the possibility of such a national combination, Vavro Shrobar, related that he had met a few like-minded Slovak people and exchanged information with them, but the reports seemed too fantastic to trust. On the other hand the intelligentsia followed with anxiety and hope what was going on in Budapest, where a radical and democratic movement made preparations to break with Germany and the Hapsburgs and to remake Hungary in harmony and understanding with all its nationalities. This signaled the end of old Hungary, an event so overwhelming for the Slovaks as to make the most unexpected developments possible.

Even when old Hungary actually collapsed in 1918, few Slovak people believed that a Slovak national state could rise from the chaos. Even though the reports were authentic, doubts persisted that the Allies had definitely resolved to create a Czechoslovak state. The Slovaks could not bring themselves to believe that the Hungarians would yield to the order of the Allies and give up northern Hungary which was so rich in raw materials, subsidized industry, and cheap labor. Still less did they think that a democracy in Hungary might last. And how could the peaceful Czechs enforce with arms what they had been granted by the Allies if the

Hungarians resisted? But for a couple dozen intellectuals, incredulity persisted among the Slovaks, even though some of them began to be friendly to the idea of a venture for community with the Czechs.

Vavro Shrobar was appointed Minister by the new Czechoslovak government to organize the administration of the future Slovakia. As soon as he had the commission in his pocket, he made an appointment with some nationalist Slovaks in the town of Zilina, a railway hub. Nobody waited for him at the railroad station. They met in a private home, the Minister and four professionals whom Shrobar intended to appoint as governors of four counties. The friends—doctors, lawyers, and teachers—politely listened to the plans of the Minister, but they would not take either his commission or their own appointments seriously. Shrobar implored them to wake up to realities—the hour of which they had dreamed had struck. Free Slovakia had issued from the triumph of the greatest powers on earth, and Shrobar's commission came from a government recognized by these powers. This they all very well believed, but they still doubted that he could give force to his orders. The country was in upheaval, with towns in the hands of Hungarians ready for armed resistance and villages split into robber bands which raided the towns for plunder. Workers deserted the factories and the fields. Nowhere was there a reliable police authority to insure safety and order. Shrobar's friends refused to risk their modest existence for the sake of an attractive but unrealistic offer. One of the Slovak leaders, Bishop Zoch of the Lutheran church, sadly remarked that power alone could convince the Slovaks that they were free.

If the gospel of freedom arrived in an unprepared Slovak land, how much more bewildered were the half million Ruthenians in the northeastern corner of old Hungary! Fugitives from the Mongolians, the ancestors of these people had climbed the Carpathians and found refuge on their western slopes. They called themselves Russians but were probably Ukrainians. The huge forest they had populated since the twelfth century belonged to the Hungarian crown to which the Ruthenians became direct subjects rather than through landlords. Most of them were illiterate in 1918, sharing one-room huts with their domestic animals. Their spiritual life had exhausted itself in religious antagonism since the seventeenth century, when the Hapsburgs had made the majority of them accept the Pope as head of their Byzantine church, while the rest remained true to the Orthodox faith whose head was the Tsar of all the Russias. The Ruthenians lived in a misery unknown in other parts of Europe, felling trees and pasturing goats and sheep. There was no middle class except for the priests and teachers. The educational policy of the Hungarian government forced the local dialect out of the schools. In 1918, only thirty-four Ruthenian elementary schools remained, and all the secondary schools were taught in Hungarian. But at the beginning of the twentieth century the Ruthenians discovered a way out of their misery by emigrating to America and Canada. From 1907 on, five thousand Ruthenians set out yearly for overseas, where they became outstanding workers in the forests, being at home in the vastness of nature and having no claims on a civilized life.

But the 800 square miles that the peace conference designated for the Ruthenians became a bone of contention between several states and a matter of serious consideration for the Great Powers.

Tsarist Russia had coveted the territory and people of the western slopes of the Carpathians, but all European powers opposed her setting foot on them. Once established there, a great power had no natural barrier to block its expansion to the Atlantic Ocean and the Adriatic Sea. Kerensky informed the peace conference, though unofficially, since he had been ousted by the Bolsheviks, that he upheld the claim of the tsars on Ruthenia. The territory could be left with Hungary, but several powers opposed Hungary's having common borders with Poland. Finally, the conference offered it to Czechoslovakia at least to keep the problem in abeyance until a democratic Ukraine could take over the land. The Czechs did not want to antagonize Russians of any shade, even though the narrow territory would make their country contiguous with Rumania and thus complete the encirclement of Hungary from which they expected trouble in the future. Therefore, they proposed that the Ruthenians be polled as to what country they desired to belong to. But the Ruthenians were completely bewildered and disoriented. At the first poll they preferred Eastern Galicia, believing that it would become a part of the Ukraine; eventually they decided for Czechoslovakia by a large majority. The peace conference thereupon conferred the province on Czechoslovakia with the understanding that it would enjoy autonomy within the state. The Ruthenians thus were given the rare privilege of determining their own fate.

This was how the Czechoslovak Republic became embodied—a 600-mile-long country extending from Central Europe to the Eastern Carpathians and covering a territory of 87,000 square miles, with a population of about fourteen million. It consisted of the historic Czech lands, Bohemia, Moravia, and Silesia, of the province of Slovakia, and of autonomous Ruthenia, also called Subcarpathian Russia.

Czechoslovakia's accomplishments in the twenty years of its existence reflected credit on the peace treaties of Paris which had created it. The fact that it showed signs of disintegration under the high pressure of aggressive German nationalism proved only that the pressure was too great for any small country, no matter how well governed. Indeed, the cooperation of its great Western Allies with Hitler was needed to make the process of disintegration effective. As a noteworthy exception from the rule in Eastern Europe, the Czechoslovak Republic preserved its democratic order during the economic depression of the 1930's and coped with the emergency situation with the help of an enlightened citizenry.

Its remarkable success notwithstanding, the republic failed in solving basic problems which contained the seeds of crisis. These problems were inherent in its composition as a multinational country and its position as a partly Central, partly Eastern European state.

Czechoslovak foreign policy was identical with Dr. Benes's who directed it for almost the entire duration of the republic. Benes could not erase from his memory the experiences of the war years and of the peacemaking that revealed to him to what a decisive extent the existence of the small states in Eastern Europe depended on the Great Powers. He remained fascinated with Great Power policies and diplomacy and was an active instrument in their formation rather than concentrating on the smaller but no less vital problems in the neighborhood of his own country. He had no policy toward Austria unless it was an aversion to the restoration of any large economic unit that smacked of the Hapsburg monarchy. He summed up this attitude by declaring that for Czechoslovakia the Anschluss of Austria with the German Reich was more bearable than a Hapsburg restoration. The compulsive identification of a Danubian combination of states with the Hapsburgs was a serious weakness in Benes's thinking, when in point of fact even Hungary, which had clung so intensely to the past, had repulsed the attempt of the former Emperor to recover the throne. Benes felt more at home in Geneva than in Prague and more at ease in helping clear Great Power controversies than in leading other Eastern countries to share in the political evolution toward democracy and higher economic and moral standards. Because of this weakness, the fate of Czechoslovakia was decided in London and Munich and not in Prague, Bucharest, Belgrade, Vienna, and Budapest.

Czechoslovakia as a national state had as its basis the fiction that the Czechs and the Slovaks were one and the same people. The synthetic unity was expressed in the Czechoslovakian nationality. Rationally, this should have held out a tremendous attraction to the much less developed Slovaks, to whom all positions were theoretically open as members of the dominant nationality. In practice, however, self-government exercised an increasing attraction for the Slovaks as they progressed in cultural and economic development, due in large measure to the assistance of their Czech brothers. But the regime could not part with the fiction of a Czechoslovak national state, and for a weighty reason. If Slovakia were given autonomy, it would hardly be possible to deny self-government to the Sudeten Germans, Hungarians, Ruthenians, and Poles, in which case a federation of nationalities would have replaced the national state. This alternative would have posed the question for Germans, Hungarians, and Poles as to why they should not join their kin across the borders rather than stay with the Czechs and Slovaks. In spite of its real success, Czechoslovakia's stability was tenuous.

When the republic began to function, there was no more important task for the Czechoslovaks than to possess the country in substance as well as in name—first of all the soil, of which a considerable part belonged to other than Czech or Slovak nationals. Nationals of foreign states owned 1¼ million acres, and 10 million acres were owned by two thousand Czechoslovak citizens who were mostly of German and Hungarian origin. Redistribution of the land had more than social significance, for it represented the conquest of the land by the Czechoslovak ethnic groups now risen to dominance. More than 2 million acres were distributed to the peasants, overwhelmingly of Czech or Slovak nationality. The national and social moving force behind the land reform was duly understood and approved by the majority, and they did not object when the government created new large estates—altogether about 500,000 acres—in recognition of the merits of about two thousand individuals.

Czechoslovakia also inherited approximately two-thirds of the industries of the Hapsburg monarchy, owned to a large extent by Germans and Jews. The conquest of the country would have implied the expropriation of alien-

owned industry, but here caution and patience were in order.
Such action would certainly have shocked the West, and
an outcry of "Bolshevism!" might have caused the Czechs
to lose what they had acquired with so much circumspec-
tion and intelligence. The statesmen were well aware how
much capital invested in industry depended for its income
on favorable tariff policies, government orders, and inside
information. They trusted that the foreign enterprises
would gladly have Czech bankers and individuals share in
their property to influence the government for favorable
treatment. The process could sometimes be speeded up by
direct interference, as when the world famous spa at Mar-
ienbad was expropriated on account of the land reform.
Another pretext was exploited when a grave catastrophe in
a coal mine killed several miners and the investigation
discovered as its cause the fact that the warning signs had
been printed in the German language alone, which the
Czech workers could not heed since they could not read
them.

Nationalistic viewpoints were also involved in a sudden
change in policy aimed at making the country self-sufficient
in food. Only one-third of the population was engaged in
agriculture; a tariff policy favoring the farmers to the detriment of export industry implied grave considerations at
work. The rise of German nationalism in the early thirties
gave the impetus, but it had not yet created an emergency
that would have justified the inevitable consequences. Such
countries as Hungary, which had exported grain to Czecho-
slovakia, retaliated by imposing prohibitive tariffs on industrial articles imported from the republic. Economic cooperation between the states that had belonged to the Hapsburg empire might have survived its political divisions but
for this rash step by Czechoslovakia, the only industrial succession state that might have alleviated the disastrous effect
of the world economic crisis on the agricultural countries
along the Danube and in the Balkans. The retaliative measures affected, however, mostly the textile, glass, and porcelain industries in which the Sudeten Germans had been

active. The Czechs in the plains thrived on high-grade agriculture and the food processing industry, and Czech banks strengthened their hold on heavy industry, busy exporting arms and military equipment.

The Czech agrarian representatives alone would not have been able to initiate and sustain this unnatural policy. They had to call for support by agrarian interests among the Sudeten Germans and Hungarians. This alliance transformed the character of Parliament into a forum for the representation of economic interests, instead of religious, ideological and national aspirations, and by so doing dulled the edge of national controversies. But the electoral system of party lists and proportional representation still preserved the national framework of the parties. Even the Catholics had separate parties for Czechs, Germans, Hungarians, and Slovaks. German and Czech Socialists had parties of their own. Only the Communists ran an all-national party, a fact that made them the second strongest group in Parliament, although they received only about 10 per cent of the votes.

Unemployment in industry was more extensive in the German-inhabited regions than in the Czech, a source of resentment in the years of the economic crisis. But Czechoslovakia overcame the crisis in a remarkably short time and, as an exception to the rule in Eastern Europe, without political upheaval. While nationalist Germany preceded its political and military conquest of the Danubian and Balkan states by economic penetration, becoming the only large-scale buyer of their agricultural produce, Czechoslovakia made itself increasingly independent from Germany with respect to commerce. It broadened the volume of its exports to Britain and the United States, who became the principal buyers of its industrial goods, including armaments as well as the famous glassware, porcelain, and textiles made in the Sudeten German area. In those years the government also made efforts to cooperate economically with the other succession states, allied originally by their common interest in preserving the situation created by the peace treaties.

But a Czechoslovakia largely self-sufficient in food was not in a position to counteract German economic penetration into the countries of its allies in the Little Entente and Balkan Entente.

Politically Czechoslovakia became rather well stabilized before Hitler's onslaught. German ministers in the cabinet became a permanent guarantee that the bureaucracy would not circumvent laws that assured to the more than three-million German minority the right of free use of their language in schools, offices, and courts.

But perhaps the constitutional provisions for the rights of the national minorities were not the most fortunate instrument for making the alien national groups feel at home in the state of the Czechs and Slovaks. They separated and isolated the aliens from the bulk of the citizenry and created a majority-minority complex, particularly since the exercise of those rights depended on a certain minimum proportion of aliens to the total population in a district. In many districts with a mixed population the critical number could be manipulated, or at least the fear and suspicion lingered that it might be manipulated. Special legislation of this sort instituted second-class citizenship which could have been avoided by a simple guarantee of human and civil rights to all, with the right to use their mother tongue implied. A satisfactory solution might have been arrived at by self-government of the territories in which the national groups constituted the majority. In such a case, the imponderable but irritating fact that an alien spirit was being interpreted through their own tongue in schools and laws could have been eliminated. Finally, minority rights are never complete without the proviso that the minority may secede. But Czechoslovakia went very far in granting freedom to her national groups and, without the intrusion from the outside of a formidable German nationalism, would have survived all internal crises.

There was another problem, however, which the Czechs had not taken as seriously as they should have until it blew up in their faces—that of the Czechoslovak nationality itself.

Shortly after a demarcation line had separated from Hungary the territories adjudged to Czechoslovakia, administrative personnel of Czech nationality filtered into Slovakia and began to reorganize government offices, communications, and economic life. It was at that time that it became evident how many Czechs had settled in the Austrian half of the Hapsburg empire down to Dalmatia in the south and Bukovina in the east. As the monarchy fell apart, the Czech civil-service personnel poured into their own new national state from all directions. In the Czech provinces change was needed only at the top; the subordinate bureaucrats stayed at their old desks as Czechs, the only difference being that they now greeted each other in Czech instead of German when entering their offices. The newcomers were assigned to Slovakia and Subcarpathian Russia, where the pro-Hungarian civil service had deserted or been chased away by the populace. Lawlessness reigned until the Czechs reorganized the provinces and guided them back to normal life.

But opposition to them among the Slovaks flared up early and violently. Their deeply religious Catholic majority became uneasy at the anti-Catholic character of the new regime. Masaryk and his pupils saw in the national liberation the rebirth of Hussitism. A Hussite spirit burned in the Czech public, and Hus had been the martyr of religious reform as well as of social justice and national consciousness. This gave rise to a mass movement to break with Roman Catholicism and establish a national church or join a Protestant denomination. It did not leave untouched even religious Catholics, who shared the general resentment of at least one aspect of the church—that its hierarchy had served the Hapsburg Germanization policy. The Czech Catholic party divested itself of clericalism and developed into a true democratic party which took a stand for the Loyalists at the time of the Spanish Civil War.

Not so the Catholics in Slovakia. For them Hus had been a heretic and nothing else. They had no animosity toward the Germans, since their oppressors had been the Hungarians with their Protestant liberal governments. As for the Hapsburgs, the Slovaks had appealed to them many times against the Hungarians, and when no assistance came they attributed it only to the fact that the Hapsburgs were not strong enough to stand up to the Magyars. Slovak liberty could in no way be connected to an anti-Catholic movement. But they feared that the Hussite spirit might infiltrate the schools and public life in Slovakia through Czech officials and teachers, the more so because the government, in its search for a Slovak intelligentsia, sought out Lutherans sympathetic to Hussitism. The Catholic Slovaks found themselves in greater danger when liberated than they had been under foreign domination. The Czech language flooded offices and schools and threatened to sweep away their tender native idiom.

A fearless Slovak priest, who had stood for Slovak rights and suffered prison in the Hungarian era, assumed leadership of their cause, demanding self-government for Slovakia with such violence and determination that he put the integrity of the new state in jeopardy. The government could not persecute him and his followers for fear of driving them into the camp of the alien nationalities, in which case the Czechs would have been reduced to a minority. Fortunately for the republic, the Slovak branch of the Agrarian Party captured a large part of the peasants by the overpowering asset of land reform. The party had a direct influence on the redistribution of the land and also represented agricultural interests in the government.

The violence of the Slovak claim for self-government abated, but the claim itself engulfed even the Lutherans as soon as enough of the Slovak-schooled youth were ready to take the place of the Czechs in the bureaucracy. The development of a home-grown intelligentsia went faster than expected because many people who had served the Hungarians came to recognize their Slovak origin beneath Magyar names and coloring. Hungary in its reduced state offered a poor livelihood, while the pulsing new republic held promising prospects for them.

However, the government paid increasing attention to the development of the Slovaks, particularly when the Sudeten Germans gave signs of being affected by the rise of nationalism in the Reich. The Czechs felt tenderness and admiration for the natural intelligence and charm of the Slovaks, as well as for their earthy life unspoiled by urbanism and German influence. The Czech contribution to Slovakia was immense in establishing a modern administration, school system, institutions of hygiene, advanced social security, agricultural cooperatives, and reorganization of agricultural production, in which 57 per cent of the Slovaks were still engaged in 1930.

Yet the average Slovak encountered Czechs as office holders, teachers, party chieftains, and not as peasants, workers, and craftsmen. Most of them lived in the new government-built housing developments, and to all appearances they were enlightened colonial administrators in Slovakia. The situation gradually improved, however, when young Slovaks, educated in the republic, gained access to positions in the administration and free professions, and armament industries were transferred or established in the center of Slovakia for strategic reasons.

The republic took long strides toward extending welfare, education, and democracy to its less developed regions as it confronted the revival of the German drive to the east. The Czechs sensed the danger in its full implications when Hitler, in 1936, marched into the Rhineland, breaking the Treaty of Versailles and meeting no resistance from the French whose security was directly imperiled. But the Czechs were not alone in their appraisal. Their Sudeten Germans hearkened to the clatter of German armor and to the silence of the French. The Germans in the Czech lands had been fascinated by the Reich even in the days of the

Hapsburg monarchy when the latter had begun to soften toward the Slavs. As Hitler progressed, undermining one position after another, the Sudeten Germans united in their clamor to join the Reich. The only exceptions were the Social Democrats and the Communists.

Czechoslovakia was well prepared for military aggression by the Germans. It had a well-equipped and trained army and an alliance with France. In 1935, it followed France in concluding a treaty of assistance against aggression with the Soviet Union, but the Soviet obligation to intervene issued from the treaty only if France lived up to her own obligation. The Czechs could not have been prepared for the situation that confronted them in the fall of 1938, when they had to resist not only German pressure but also the insistence of their allies that they should yield.

It became the task of Dr. Benes to convince the French and the British that no readjustment of the situation created by the Versailles treaty would stop Hitler, and that by helping him destroy Czechoslovakia they would but clear the way for further aggression. A stumbling block to persuading the Allies was the hope of influential circles behind their governments that Hitler's drive was directed exclusively toward the East, against the Soviet Union, and the understandable reluctance of the public in the West to go to war. Dr. Benes had to convince his friends before they destroyed the republic, and he failed to do so. Six months after Munich, Hitler rendered proof of the validity of Benes' argument when he entered Prague. However, if we are to understand the behavior of the Czech people in and after the war, it must be stressed that France and Britain bore the responsibility for the crushing of Czechoslovakia in 1938.

On the strength of the Munich decisions, the largely German-inhabited regions of Bohemia and Moravia were torn out of their geographic and economic unity with the plains populated by the Czechs. But the tribulations of the Czechs were not over with the loss of the industrial borderland. Poland followed with an ultimatum demanding the

Teschen region which had been awarded to the Czechs after World War I, and finally the Hungarians raised a claim to Hungarian-inhabited southern Slovakia. The Czechs yielded to the Poles, but the Hungarians' demand concerned the Slovaks, and they protested. Hitler and Mussolini convened to arbitrate the question and forced the Slovaks to give way.

In this time of crisis Slovakia put in her claim for autonomy. The mutilated country changed its name from Czechoslovakia to Czecho-Slovakia, the hyphen intended to demonstrate the end of the fiction of a common nationality. But the hyphen separated the two peoples rather than tied them, as the next few months were to prove. While the remainder of the Czech lands were left to Hitler's mercy, Dr. Benes resigned the presidency, and a pro-German government tried to fulfill Hitler's orders and preserve a semblance of independence. But the Slovaks were determined not to share their fate and to seize the initiative.

Abandoned by all friends, and having experienced the cruel and cold denial of solidarity by the Slovaks, the Czechs were filled with bitterness. They probably failed to reflect upon the fact that the Slovak intelligentsia alone among the oppressed nationalities of old Hungary had turned its back on its own people, turned Magyar, and participated in the Magyarization policy. They had also misjudged the merits of the Slovakian claim for autonomy, attributing it to the resistance of the old generation grown up in Hungary and unable to adjust to the changed environment and its social standards. The Czechs had trusted that the youth educated in the spirit of democracy and unity would turn out to conform with their own principles. But they also failed to notice their own contribution to separatism that consisted in their slowness to enlarge the scope of their thinking to encompass the cultural and political orientation and development of the Slovaks. The Czechs had lived in fascination with their three-centuries-old controversy with the Germans, whom they comprehended better than they did the Slovaks.

However, in 1938, the Czechs still could not realize the extent of the Machiavellism of which the Slovak intelligentsia was capable. They learned another lesson half a year later—and it was not to be the last. On March 14, 1939, the Slovak Parliament proclaimed its complete independence from the Czechs and appealed to Hitler for his protection. In a carefully synchronized move, Hitler summoned the new President of the Czech republic to Berchtesgaden and compelled the reluctant old man to sign an application to turn the republic into a German protectorate. The next day, Nazi troops occupied Prague.

The Slovaks wasted no time in chasing tens of thousands of Czechs from the government offices and housing projects. They also hastened to dispossess the Jews active in business and the free professions. The minuscule country offered itself to Hitler for window-dressing. Headed by a Catholic priest, Monsignor Joseph Tiso, it furnished a sanctimonious proof of Hitler's good will toward docile Catholicism. The Fuehrer rarely missed an opportunity to be photographed beside fat Monsignor Tiso when the latter was permitted to review the S.S. guards in Berchtesgaden. Slovakia was eager to become a model satellite. It fared quite well by furnishing the Germans with timber and industrial raw materials and turning itself into a vacation land for German officials and their families. The Slovaks believed that they had a foot in both camps. Should the Allies win, they would be on the winning side as part of Czechoslovakia, and if the Germans prevailed, Slovakia would also come in handy to the Germans as a pawn to be played against the Czechs or Hungarians.

When Czechoslovakia fell apart, the little easternmost province of Subcarpathian Russia ceased its artificial existence. The Czechs had done a great deal to lift the Ruthenians from the depths of ignorance and misery, but much more remained to be done, and time ran out too soon for significant results. When Hitler captured Prague, the Hungarian army marched into the province that the Magyars had ruled for a thousand years. The occupation improved

Hungary's strategic position by establishing a common frontier with Poland, but to no avail as the coming months manifested.

With the fortunes of the war reversed in 1945, the Soviet Union put an end to Subcarpathian Russia by attaching the territory to its republic of the Ukraine, thus forming a wedge between Slovakia, Hungary, and Rumania. But Slovakia, after having been the favorite of the Nazis, became the favorite of the Communists as well. The Slovakians were able almost to dictate the conditions under which they would be willing to re-enter the restored Czecho-Slovak republic. They had another alternative when Benes negotiated with them in Moscow and later in the Slovakian town of Kosice, temporary residence of the provisional government. The alternative was more of a threat, but it worked. They might apply to Stalin for the admittance of their country to the Soviet Union.

The Slovaks were riding high on account of an uprising in Slovakia in August, 1944, when the Soviet armies were advancing into Eastern Europe. It happened in middle Slovakia, along a secondary communications line through the country from west to east. The Germans had no troops in the region at the time, and a group of native Slovak officers, deserters from the Slovak army, Communists, Jews in hiding, and French refugees from Nazi labor camps captured the administration of the villages, setting up headquarters in a beautiful old town on the River Hron, Banska Bystrica. The rebels expected the Soviet army to join them, but it released only a Czecho-Slovak unit fighting with the Russian army and otherwise followed its course without concern for the uprising. The rebels requested supplies from the West, which was ready to send arms and food. But faithful to the Teheran agreement which had assigned Czechoslovakia to the Soviet zone of military operations, the West first asked for Soviet approval which was not forthcoming. The Germans, as soon as they had spare troops, pressed the rebels hard until they dispersed into the woods; and those who survived met the Soviet army in November.

At any rate, the Slovaks banked heavily on this asset, in comparison to which the Czech resistance to Nazi terror could show no spectacular achievements. When Benes met them, autonomy for Slovakia was a foregone conclusion.

After the Soviet army had swept the Nazis from Slovakia, Communists, Socialists, and Lutheran Slovaks assumed the high positions in the administration, while in the middle and low echelons the same people who had served the Nazis remained. Now part of the victorious Allies, the Slovaks set out to establish themselves completely. Bratislava, the capital, is the best example of how they did it.

The city was originally founded by German colonists who named it Pressburg and built it up into a quiet residential town on the left bank of the Danube. The Hapsburg emperors considered Buda too far from their Viennese residence and felt quite at home in this German-style town with its baroque church spires and neat mansions studding the land between the river and a hill topped by the famous Palffy castle. Here the Hapsburgs were crowned kings of Hungary, and here the assembly of the Magyar nobility fought bitterly to keep their ancient privileges. The Hungarians called the city Pozsony. Hungarian public officials and landlords also took up residence in the town, and peasants moved into the suburbs where industry offered a better means of living than their farms. This influx gave the city a Magyar touch. The old German settlers, however, persisted in their own customs and language. Then in 1918, it was annexed to Czechoslovakia, chosen as the capital of the Slovakian province, and renamed Bratislava, meaning, "Hail to the brethren," after the name of the oldest settlement on the site.

The noted Russian writer, Ilya Ehrenburg, visited the city before the war. There he saw the Germans in Pressburg, the old, established middle-class merchants, industrialists, and professionals; he saw the Pozsony of the Hungarian nobility and suburban peasants. But of Czechoslovakian Bratislava, he saw only the Czechs dwelling in the modern housing projects freshly erected on the periphery of the city. As to Slovaks, he could find none, strangely, in the capital of Slovakia.

Had he revisited the city in 1945 he would have recognized only the Danube and the buildings. In 1939, the Slovaks under Hitler's aegis expelled the Czech officials and families. Then they herded the Jews into labor camps, deported them, and moved into their places. Came the year 1945 and "liberation" from Hitler. This brought them the freedom to expatriate the German inhabitants who, not being pro-Nazi, had not followed the beaten Germans, and also to take their houses and businesses. Then, encouraged by the Russians to make the republic a simon-pure Slav country, they rounded up the Hungarians and moved them onto the opposite shore of the Danube. The Slovak intelligentsia and the peasants of the Slovakian villages took over. Only the stones now remind one of the languages of the past.

The Slovaks also made use of the new land reform laws to take land from the Hungarian peasants and Slovakian traitors and to distribute it among Slovak peasants whom they brought down from the mountains and settled in the plains of Southern Slovakia. They either expelled the Hungarians or moved them into the Sudetenland deserted by the Germans. Some of them were fortunate enough to stay until expulsion of the Magyars was stopped.

But Slovakia also benefited directly from the expulsion of Sudeten Germans from Czech lands. Nonsocialized light industries were left without workers and moved to Slovakia where manpower was ample and wages low. Moreover, the government set a huge budget for the industrialization of Slovakia. Many reasons were advanced for giving preference to Slovakia over the historic Czech lands. It was rich in untapped water power and industrial raw materials; and heavy industry could be built there in strategically well protected places and in the vicinity of mines and other sources. Indeed, Slovakia has developed into the most flourishing area in the Russian orbit.

While the Slovaks exploited a shrewdly calculated nationalism to despoil everybody else, Czech nationalism was furiously enthusiastic. The idea of an alliance of Slav states under the leadership of the Soviet Union (a non-Slav state) had originated with Stalin to end the threat of pan-Germanism. The new pan-Slavism had the basic weakness of never impressing the biggest Slav nation outside the Soviet—Poland. Czecho-Slovakia was to be turned into a Slav nation by expelling one-third of its population, which amounted to 12,300,000 in 1945. The Czechs thought that this would complete their liberation, and Dr. Benes subscribed to the program without reservation. But his predecessor, the great Masaryk, had infused into the political thinking of his nation a deep sense of morality, so that at least it strenuously endeavored to justify the use of Hitlerite methods against the Sudeten Germans. Indeed, the Czech press printed the word "moral" on any single page more often in 1945–46 than the press of any other country.

Yet America and Britain, as democracies, bear the brunt of responsibility for the barbarism of transferring an entire people from the homeland in which they had lived for more than seven centuries. At Potsdam, they accepted the principle of collective responsibility as far as the Germans were concerned. The Czechs stood emphatically for that principle by declaring that the proven anti-Fascist Germans must go as well, adding that they ought to teach democracy to their fellow Germans. The West's approval practically erased the blame they had put on the Nazis and on the Soviets for having transferred entire national groups against their will.

Indeed, those who had the opportunity of observing the zeal of Czech youth, their honest passion and misguided patriotism, shuddered at the thought that the flame of nationalism might engulf the billions of Asiatic peoples. Passionate nationalism was a consequence of the participation of the masses in the affairs of the state. Before that, kings and governments waged wars without being inspired by the ardor of their subjects and without inciting them to passionate approval. The people suffered or benefited from wars but remained calm. The war of 1870–71 drove the French into a national madness for revenge on the Germans. They had their revenge in World War I, when the Germans were defeated and humiliated. Out of this grew Hitlerite nationalism and its barbarous enslavement of other nations; and the victims, in turn, behaved barbarously when they prevailed in the end.

Serious rational arguments spoke against the West's assenting to the expulsion of Germans from Poland and Czecho-Slovakia. The millions transferred to Germany would make up for the entire loss in manpower the Reich had suffered in the war, leaving its strength intact. Moreover, these expelled Germans would harbor hatred and a passionate desire for revenge and would become a powerful force for restoring German militarism. The transfer of the Germans would keep the two countries permanently in the grip of the Soviet Union, the only protection against the forcible return of the expelled.

As to the Czechs, they became insensible to rational arguments. They replied that it was better to have an enemy outside than inside the country and that they were resolved anyway to entrust the security of the state to the Russians. They prepared to take in stride the loss of the biggest asset of a highly industrialized country, the skilled workers. They would lose entire industries, such as the glass and porcelain factories near Gablonz, which simply settled on the other side of the mountains in Germany, complete with the old management and workers who had learned the trade from their fathers. The coal mines would particularly feel the loss of skilled manpower which might cause immeasurable damage to the industrial development of the country. The Czechs knew all that, but it did not deter them from insisting that the Germans go—all of them.

National feeling was so overwhelming that even Jan Masaryk, son of the great President, whose flesh and blood was humanism, refrained from protesting publicly. If lesser men felt revulsion they did not show it. Only the press of the Czech Catholics warned them, obliquely castigating the policy of throwing criminal and innocent in the same bag.

It quoted the ill-famed declaration of Ferdinand II, Emperor of the Holy Roman Empire who, with an eye on the Czech lands in revolt against militant Catholicism allied with German domination, said in the seventeenth century: "I would rather have my land empty and devastated than populated by heretics."

The Czechs expatriated about 2,700,000 Germans and were able to settle only 1,700,000 in their stead. Whole towns were left to die; villages wasted away. About 200,000 German farms were taken over by Czechs, the rest left idle.

Meanwhile the country laid the foundations for a truly national state. General elections were held in May, 1946, completely free and secret. Only parties accepted in the National Front could put up candidates, but among these were conservative groups such as the Democratic Party in Slovakia, successor of the Agrarian Party, and even a Freedom Party for those in Slovakia nostalgic for Monsignor Tiso. The Communists polled 38 per cent of the votes (40 per cent in the historical lands), the Czech Socialists (Masaryk-Benes party) 18.2, the Social Democrats 12.8, and the Catholic Party 15.8 per cent. However, in Slovakia the Democrats received twice as many votes as the Communists.

The most important legislation had already been carried through by presidential decrees on the basis of the program of the Provisional Government. The main measures were the depriving of all Germans and Hungarians of citizenship, the confiscation of their properties, and the nationalization of heavy industry, banking, and insurance. Nationalization of that segment of the economy came about almost automatically as a consequence of the confiscation of German assets, since the Germans had acquired these industries and enterprises. Also, Jewish enterprises remained unclaimed since most of the Jews had perished. Light industries were left to corporations or individuals to run, and craft was free. But the turnover of management personnel and the mass expatriations caused chaotic conditions in production. The exceptionally generous help of UNRRA, with goods to the value of 260 million dollars in the two years after the war, made reorganization possible.

The Assembly elected Dr. Benes president. As Prime Minister he appointed Klement Gottwald, the old leader of Czechoslovak Communists who had spent the war years in Russia. Communists received the most important portfolios —those of the Interior, Finance, Internal Trade, Social Welfare, Agriculture, and Information; but this corresponded to their parliamentary hegemony.

The most substantial act of Parliament was to vote a Two-Year Plan for reconstruction, which laid stress on heavy industry, especially power stations in Slovakia. Agriculture received relatively less attention in terms of money.

The public had great confidence in the economic development of the country. A commercial treaty was signed with the Soviet Union in 1946, and people looked forward to Czecho-Slovakia's new role as supplier of finished goods for the huge Eastern market while keeping the old foreign trade association with the West. The feeling of safety from hostility in and outside the country, of freedom after the oppression and humiliation of the Nazi regime, and of approval of the Socialist democracy, generated an immense store of enthusiasm. A more united, more homogeneous and more vigorous republic than the first was building itself up into a clearing house of goods and ideas between East and West.

Part II

EASTERN EUROPE
IN THE COLD WAR

CHAPTER EIGHT

The Cold War Years

1.

In the spring of 1947 "the Government of the Soviet Union gave rein to a passion for imposing discipline and enforcing uniformity which had been the congenital strength and weakness of the Muscovite power whose traditions the Soviet Union inherited." Thus Arnold Toynbee described the immediate effect on the Soviet empire of the split between the Soviet Union and the Western world.

The "inherited passion" also included the claims of tsarist Russia for the Straits of the Black Sea. The century-long tsarist campaign to this end eventually liberated the peoples of the Balkan peninsula from Turkish yoke, but the huge shadow of the liberator made their freedom uneasy and problematic until the Revolution of 1917 undermined Russian power.

However, the Soviet government in 1940 claimed the inheritance. Molotov informed the German Ambassador in Moscow that the Russians needed the Black Sea Straits for the protection of the oil wells of Batum and Baku. In March, 1945, Moscow sent a note to Turkey demanding a military base at the Dardanelles. In support of its claims the Kremlin referred simply to "the changed situation" which implied that the Soviet Union remained the only real military power in that part of the world.

At the same time, only the presence of forty thousand British soldiers kept the government in power in Greece, opposed by leftists, supplied with arms from Jugoslavia,

233

Albania, and Bulgaria. The civil war threatened to develop into the pattern of the Spanish Civil War, in which the parties had fought over genuine political and social issues while great powers turned them into proxies in establishing politico-strategic positions.

Against the background of these events Winston Churchill, now out of office, came to the United States and made a speech in the presence of President Truman at Fulton, Missouri, painting the Russian devil as black as he saw him. He warned:

The dark ages might return, the stone age might return on the gleaming wing of science, and what might now shower immeasurable blessings on mankind might even bring about its total destruction. Beware, I say. Time may be short.

The speech stirred the public deeply. Some accused him of warmongering; many more advised caution toward the charm of his rhetoric lest America be saddled with the task of pulling the wrecked vehicle of British imperialism from the quagmire.

Almost a year passed after Churchill's Fulton speech. Meanwhile, the Turks held out, and the matter hung in suspense. And in Greece the civil war ran on.

In Moscow, a conference of foreign ministers opened on March 10, 1947. The Soviet claim for $10 billion reparation payment from Germany figured on the agenda. The amount was not exaggerated in view of the devastation the Nazis had wrought in Russia. But the West made its consideration dependent on the restoration of Germany as an economic unit, and the energetic stand taken by the United States at the last conference had made the Soviets, in dire need of reconstruction, more conciliatory than before. However, as Soviet ambitions were revealed, the West began to show less and less enthusiasm for letting the Soviets share in the control of the industrial complex of the Ruhr and Rhine and West Germany in general. In January the American and British zones of occupation merged, and the split in Germany deepened.

Two days after the Moscow conference opened President Truman made his historic declaration that the security of the United States would henceforth be involved wherever Soviet power or Communism committed direct or indirect aggression.

This Truman Doctrine was in fact the dramatization of a turning point in American history. It served to make the public aware of the responsibilities that accompanied her position as a world power. The declaration fell upon the American people from a seemingly clear blue sky, at a time when United States troops abroad were thinning out and the country was beginning cautiously to extricate herself from foreign entanglements. The shock treatment was administered through British-American cooperation. The British served notice on the State Department on February 24 that they would not be able to aid Greece after April 1, a move well calculated to leave no time for the United States to hesitate. President Truman drove home to the American public the belief that the alternative to taking over British foreign positions was the crumbling of the entire free world. The impending collapse of Greece threatened to dent Turkey's defenses and open a breach into the Middle East. But for the sake of replacing the faltering British in just one area, no matter how vitally important, it was difficult to persuade the public to accept a long-range involvement, financial and military, in all the four corners of the world where Britain and other European powers had been trying to stem revolutionary changes in the balance of power. President Truman warned the people of the chain reaction the collapse of Middle Eastern defenses would entail for the West everywhere. He said:

It would be an unspeakable calamity if these countries . . . should lose that victory for which they sacrificed so much. Collapse of free institutions would be disastrous not only for them, but for the world, and we shall surely endanger the welfare of our nation . . .

Indeed, immediate aid to Greece and Turkey and the dispatch of military missions and advisers were but the first steps on the road to the Marshall Plan and the establishment of military bases around the Soviet Union.

The Moscow conference broke down. On his return, the Secretary of State, General George Marshall, on June 5 unfolded the first phase of a significant program. He asked for $5.3 billion in twelve months for the recovery of Europe. Marshall said that "if action is followed by the enactment of a long-range European recovery program, this Congress will have written a noble page in the world's annals."

Congress acted and the noble page stands written. Some people thought that had the Marshall Plan been announced before the Truman Doctrine the Moscow conference might have turned out differently. Germany might have been restored, first under four-power control and later under its own government; and Russia and her pupils might have accepted Marshall aid. Yet, it was probably impossible to reverse the trend in public anxiety left over from America's vast war-time foreign entanglements except by rousing fear that threats to faraway countries insidiously imperiled domestic security and the American way of life. Fear remains the most effective inducement to make great sacrifices. It may have been such reasons of expediency that led Truman to announce his doctrine before Marshall made his plan public; in any case, this order of priorities inevitably fashioned the Marshall Plan into an instrument of the Cold War which the doctrine actually declared.

The Cold War policy aimed at containing the Soviets within their legitimate realm until their power disintegrated, since it was presumed to bear within it the seeds of its own decay. However, the heat of the clash of ideologies made the Cold War inflammable. Wars of ideologies know no limits but the total destruction or exhaustion of the enemy. Another danger of a shooting war issued from the polarization of powers in two giant countries with no independent third power left to prevent it by taking the side of one or the other.

As a consequence of the Truman Doctrine, Germany was split by the decision of the West to create a West German state, and the Iron Curtain descended to divide the country. But this event was preceded by a moment of hesitation in Russia. Her delegates appeared at the opening of the conference of European countries which was to determine the requirements of recovery, the extent of possible self-aid, and the help desired from the Marshall Plan. But the Truman Doctrine struck a discordant note. Acceptance of Marshall aid would have definitely involved economic and political dependence on America at a time when American foreign and military policy was geared to counter all expansion of Soviet influence. The situation may have reminded Moscow of the time of the Hitler-Stalin agreement when the world press had speculated whether the Soviets would eventually join the anti-Comintern pact.

The Kremlin decided to refuse Marshall aid. It branded the plan an instrument of American imperialism bent on making the European states its vassals and enrolling them in a war against the Soviet Union and its allies. Moscow compelled the satellite governments to follow suit and mobilized the powerful Communist parties in Italy and France in a campaign to prevent these countries from accepting the plan.

As a countermove, the Kremlin established its own mutual aid plan, which was intended to make the Eastern states economically independent of the West and eventually to integrate them into a huge, self-sufficient unit. The economic plans launched after late 1947 were meant to divide the world into two separate halves. The economic plans put the resources of the countries in the shadow of Russia into war production, distorting their economic development, wiping out their independence, and destroying basic liberties for their citizens. Eventually, these plans displaced the humanistic principles ingrained in socialism and Communism since all institutions allowed to function drew their inspiration from and justified their existence by promoting the fulfilment of the plans, which were instruments first of all for the preparation of a global war.

In a world shrunken by ever-faster planes and missiles loaded with atomic bombs, it was a miracle that an all-devastating war did not come to pass. In fact, both giants expected a *deus ex machina* to knock out the opponent. The Russians were confident of a coming grave economic crisis in America, and the Americans of the process of inner decay in the Soviet Union, accelerated by the Damocles sword of a nuclear war hanging over her.

Foreign policies based on these illusions may have prevented World War III from happening.

2.

Britain and France sent out invitations to a European conference on the Marshall Plan. This was to cause a grave political and moral crisis in Czechoslovakia, where the public believed that the country had preserved a limited independence in foreign policy. The success of its foreign trade with its traditional market in the West strengthened the feeling of independence. The severe drought of 1946 had imperiled the continuity of the powerful rhythm of economic growth, initiated, in the case of Czechoslovakia, by exceptionally lavish UNRRA aid. Help from overseas, America and Canada, was expected to make up for the failure of domestic crops, so that the invitation was unanimously accepted by the Czech cabinet. It is clear that Moscow did not then advise the Communists against accepting. The decision of the cabinet opened a broader perspective for the Marshall Plan, and a revision of the place of the East European countries in the European community seemed to be in the making.

Poland and Jugoslavia both pondered the invitation. Jugoslavia pioneered in rejecting it, and Poland, nearer the source of Soviet policies, eventually declined.

After accepting the invitation, a Czech government delegation left for Moscow for a previously arranged conference with the Soviets on a five-year commercial treaty. Stalin himself apprised the delegation, in which Prime Minister Gottwald and Foreign Minister Jan Masaryk took part, of the Soviet position with regard to the Marshall Plan. The plan was pursuing, he stressed, policies and interests directed against the Soviet Union and would inevitably lead to using Germany as a military and industrial basis against the Soviets. He concluded by stating that Czechoslovakia could not be both an ally of the Soviet Union and a receiver of Marshall aid.

The first postwar era of the Eastern countries had come to an end. These countries had been powerfully inspired by patriotism, which the Soviets had suddenly discovered to be a deep source of unity for a nation in hours of peril. The advisers moving ahead with the Soviet armies had carried patriotism as a torch to the peoples, conquered or liberated, to light the way to democratic unity. The Communist Party had led the flag waving and had opened its doors wide to receive new converts from all quarters, disregarding past records as irrelevant. Patriotism had proved to be a tremendous incentive for reconstruction. It had brought out creative forces and harnessed them to tasks that served the broader, deeper national community. The masses had become activated socially. Patriotism compensated even for the dislocations of families as a result of war. Indeed, solidarity and responsibility expanded beyond the family and friendship, creating an exalted emotion of self-respect. Work, when its social utility was visible, became gratifying, whether it was manual or intellectual. This was manifested in many ways: in organizing parties of doctors and nurses to serve the remote countryside, teaching illiterates, lecturing, rewriting the history books, printing the classics as popular literature, and so on.

Many estranged branches of the Slavic race fused into one nation in Jugoslavia, and nationalism made the Czechs relish a homeland no longer to be shared with aliens. The

nation took on a new meaning in Hungary when it finally
embraced the common people, and in the Balkans when it
seemed to begin directing its own destiny instead of being
ordered by foreign cliques. Outsiders were greatly impressed with the sincerity of the peoples' ambitions for a
better, more just national life.

As the next step, the governments resolved to marshal
patriotism to establish the basic requirements for restoring
the peacetime standard of living. The way they chose was
industrialization which, as its scope increased, would solve
such inveterate problems of the agricultural lands as overpopulation, ignorance, and backwardness. The process required capital investment which had come either from long-
term loans or from domestic sources, from savings or from
taxation on the income of the working people. In the last
instance, the population itself provided for the capital by
getting less money for more work. The speed-up of industrialization certainly increased their sufferings, but it
also increased their hope of being able some day to enjoy
the returns in terms of a better life.

The planners assigned the bulk of the investment to the
building or expanding of heavy industry. The plan was to
be completed in two years in Czechoslovakia and Bulgaria,
which had suffered the least war damage; three years in
Poland and Hungary to allow for the work of reconstruction. Rumania's economy was in such a chaotic state that
its short-term plan started only in 1948, a year later than
in the others and with but a single-year program.

The planners hoped that patriotism would inspire the
community with a single purpose. Each man should be
fired by the idea that, no matter how small or seemingly
unimportant his own post was, he had responsibility for
the whole project and an investment in it. Thus he would
not measure his contribution solely in terms of minutes and
pennies.

The plans in all countries, except Jugoslavia which took
a different path, budgeted 36–40 per cent of the total investment for heavy industry and mining; 22–28 per cent for

transportation and communication. Poland alone planned to invest more than 10 per cent in agriculture, while Bulgaria provided relatively more for electrification with irrigation in mind.

However, this was only the introduction to a series of long-range plans for economic development, the scope and rate of which were to transform the whole fabric of society. But instead of waiting for society to change as a natural result of economic development, the planners reversed the process. They tried to transform social and political life to insure that the growth of the economy would not be inhibited. The plan thus became the master of society instead of its servant. Exalted as an idol it controlled the whole political and social framework, philosophy, art, and literature.

Jugoslavia volunteered to be the model of the total planning concept by starting its five-year plan in 1947 in grand style. The Jugoslavs succeeded in capturing the heroic dynamism of the war years and making it the prime mover of their ambitions of growing into a great power. Only by enlisting these ambitions did the planners dare envisage a voluntary labor service powerful enough to substitute for the huge mass of unskilled labor that would otherwise be needed to carry the plan through. Compulsion would not do work which required devotion and sacrifice. Instead of compulsion, Tito and his friends thought that moral pressure would suffice to make the reluctant ones go along in the fear of being outcast. The general labor service included even children and the elderly. Adults, girls, and boys in every province built roads, bridges, railroads, and public buildings. They were carried by truck into regions they had never seen, inhabited by people they had known only from hearsay or from books, but who welcomed them as friends and brothers. The voluntary labor service became, indeed, an important element in the fusion of the many peoples of Jugoslavia.

Under the plan it was expected that production would grow by the end of the fifth year by 323 per cent in industry and 152 per cent in agriculture, as compared with the year 1939. With the increase of industrial production the electrical industry was to rise by 1,000 per cent; the chemical, 911 per cent; and the metal industry by 688 per cent.

Lack of skilled workers made the viability of the plan dubious. The government hired experts from abroad, enrolled German prisoners of war, called home Jugoslavs from foreign countries, and instituted technical courses in all schools and in the trade unions, which turned into training centers.

In the very first year of the plan, nationalization of the whole of industry was required. In the middle of 1948, foreign and internal commerce was also nationalized. The system of wages had to be adjusted. Piece work, extra pay, prizes for individual and unit accomplishments, competition between factories, publicity for shock workers—all the paraphernalia of exploitation had to be employed.

The first two years ended with remarkable success, particularly because unskilled work played a great part in the process. Factories, railroads, and buildings were finished and waiting for equipment and machines. Jugoslavia insured their delivery from abroad. The Soviet Union granted a long-term loan that financed the delivery of equipment for metal industries and raw materials for which Jugoslavia was to pay with copper, lead, zinc, pyrites, and food. Through commercial treaties with Czechoslovakia, Sweden, Hungary, and other countries, electric power stations and other capital goods were to be imported.

The government postponed a fundamental reform in agriculture since it did not want to disturb the food production needed for home consumption and for export. As an incentive for delivery, it paid for the foodstuffs partly in money and partly in coupons for which the peasants could buy badly needed farm and household implements in the state-run shops.

Other countries proceeded more cautiously than Jugoslavia. They first had to weaken and paralyze the political forces resisting the nationalization of industry, which in most cases were concentrated in the peasant parties. Imprisonment or exile of the leaders signaled the start of the process in 1947. The Russians arrested Bela Kovacs, the peasant leader in Hungary, in February; Prime Minister Ferenc Nagy of the Smallholders Party resigned in May and went to live in Switzerland; in Rumania, Julius Maniu, leader of the National Peasant Party, was arrested in July; Bulgaria, also in July, indicted Nikola Petkov, peasant leader; and Mikolajczyk fled from Poland in October.

But the Communists feared that the traditional spirit of other capitalist institutions might also disturb the course of planned development. The unions had served to defend the interests of workers against employers and management. But the employer now was the nation and management an organ of the state, so that the unions had to reverse themselves completely. Their task was now to promote the realization of the plan by raising production. A new spirit was to permeate them, but this was considered impossible as long as an obsolete spirit was entrenched in the old leadership. The Social Democrats had to be ousted from their positions in the unions. The pattern was to split that party into a right and left wing, dismiss or jail the former as traitors to the working class or agents of Western capitalists, and have the left wing merged into a workers' party, in practice identical with the Communists.

The Soviets strengthened their ties with those countries in their orbit which had belonged to the enemy front during the war. They extended to them the same military alliance that guaranteed mutual aid between the Soviet Union, Poland, and Czechoslovakia—"to take joint measures to eliminate any threat from Germany and from any other state which should join with Germany in an aggressive policy."

The Soviet Union also had an immediate answer to the Marshall Plan, a coordination of the countries in its orbit for mutual aid in production, trade, and commerce. Moscow previously had granted Poland a loan of $27 million in gold for the purchase of machinery, raw materials, and food; now she undertook to supply arms in exchange for Polish coal. A commercial treaty with Hungary provided for Russian deliveries of raw textiles in return for Hungarian oil, bauxite, and finished textile goods. Moscow contracted also to supply Rumania with industrial raw materials, trucks, and box cars against finished goods in exchange. All these and other treaties promoted the industrialization of the orbit countries, and now they were to be integrated into one block with the ambition—and perhaps the necessity—of becoming self-sufficient. On the whole, their economies did not complement each other, and their planned industrial expansion ran on parallel lines. Even Bulgaria set out to raise industrial production by 67 per cent over 1939. Meanwhile, the Soviet Union, and perhaps Czechoslovakia, were to replace the West as suppliers of capital goods and buyers of finished products and also to grant credits. Since the economic plans had to knit them more closely together than had been originally intended, the process was bound to have political implications. Local ambitions had to be reconciled and subordinated to a general principle.

Resistance could not be expected from countries where the Soviet army was the main support of the regime. But in the peripheries of the Soviet empire lay two countries which were free from direct Soviet interference, Czecho-Slovakia and Jugoslavia. In Czecho-Slovakia the middle-class parties strongly represented in Parliament, resisted encroachment on the country's economic and political independence, while in Jugoslavia the Communist regime itself insisted on respecting the country's national ambitions. Resistance from these two widely divergent sources culminated in events which caused immense repercussions within and beyond the Soviet orbit. They had a determining influence on the composition and spirit of the line-up of the Cold War fronts, and permanently affected its course.

Czecho-Slovakia planned to follow up its splendid record in production and foreign trade established during the first two years after the liberation. It restored commerce with the West while expanding trade with the East, showing a balance which mirrored the ambitions of its statesmen to become a bridge between them. The economic plan of 1947 entailed, however, the nationalization of industries that had been left in the hands of corporations and individuals by the laws of 1945. Enterprises employing over 400 workers had then been nationalized, but now the Communists in the government wanted to extend nationalization to industries with 50 or more employees—exactly those enterprises which were so successfully active in trade with the West. The parties of the middle class in the National Front government opposed the bill along with another one which proposed imposing a capital levy in order that the farmers be compensated for the catastrophic drought of 1946. The majority of the ministers in the Cabinet voted down the capital levy, but the Communists submitted the bill to Parliament which passed it, as it did the extension of the land reform by distribution of blocks of land over 125 acres. The Communists mustered a majority in Parliament with the help of the leadership of Zdenek Fierlinger of the Social Democratic Party. But in the Socialist ranks mistrust of the Communists grew as a consequence of Communist penetration into the factory councils and unions. The congress of the party refused to re-elect Fierlinger, now considered the arch-fellow traveler, and replaced him with a man known to be cautious in cooperating with the Communists.

The middle-class parties thus had reasonable hopes of counting on the support of the Social Democrats in opposing drastic Communist measures in the cabinet and Parliament. Together, they had a strong majority.

Elections were set for the spring of 1948, and the press—which was free, though only recognized parties were allowed to publish—became lively with support and criticism. The Communists made capital of the 200,000 tons of grain the Soviets had granted to Czechoslovakia to make up for

the poor crops, while the other parties frankly exposed
Communist abuses and government mistakes, including the
rejection of Marshall Plan aid. The mood in the country
showed a strengthening of the opposition to a shift to the
left. The elections might have resulted in a much larger
majority of non-Communist parties than they now possessed. Some people doubted that the Communists would
allow free elections under such circumstances; others did
not expect even a much stronger non-Communist majority
to coalesce against the Communists.

Meanwhile President Benes intended to renew the old
alliance with France and wrote Stalin an explanatory
note about its advantages for his own and Stalin's country.
But Stalin began to feel uneasy about the precarious hold of
the Communists on Czechoslovakia, which bordered on
the American occupation zone of Germany. Rumor had
it that the Kremlin was particularly worried about the huge
Skoda works, the greatest armament plant complex in eastern Europe. It lay only a few miles from the American
soldiers across the border, and it was said that the Russians
were pondering the transfer of the factory to central Slovakia with approximately fifty thousand workers and their
families. The Czech Communist leader, Klement Gottwald, opposed the plan which would have diminished his
support among the workers by adversely affecting many
more people in the region who benefited from the purchas-
ing power that the enterprise and its personnel represented.
He allegedly proposed to Moscow that he would assume
complete Communist control instead, protect the Skoda
works from the West, and cut the country off from Western
influence.

The non-Communist parties made a tactical mistake by
which they gave the Communists an opportunity legally to
assume sole power.

The parties received information that Vaclav Nosek, the
Communist Minister of the Interior, had transferred, retired, or dismissed non-Communist district commanders in

the police force around Prague and filled the ranks of the police with Communists in Slovakia. The majority in the Cabinet voted to advise the Minister to reinstate the commanders and report to the Cabinet. At the session of February 20, the Minister submitted no report, but the non-Communist members had information that he had failed to comply with the advice. They now made up their minds for a showdown. Twelve ministers sent their resignations to the President stating that they could not stay in a government with a member who refused to heed the decision of the cabinet. Unfortunately, the Social Democrats in the cabinet did not associate themselves with the resigning ministers. They argued that only a congress of the party could release them from following the previous party decision to cooperate with the Communists.

The Communists appealed to the people, alerting them against a reactionary attempt to subvert the Republic. They called on the Communist-dominated factory councils and peasant committees to prepare for action.

President Benes hesitated over accepting the resignations. He had suffered two strokes, and his hopes of combining socialism and democracy, friendship for the Soviet Union and good relations with the West, had waned as East and West had split over Germany—which threatened to rise again and ruin his second attempt to insure the peace and prosperity of the Republic. As the rift widened between East and West, the bridge Benes had meant to build was in danger of not materializing.

Gottwald knew the mentality of President Benes thoroughly. He had been Communist deputy in the first Republic and had fought against this serious little man with the devastating logic. All Gottwald had to do was to demonstrate to Benes that, if he chose to oppose the Communists or resign in protest, they would apply naked force in taking over, causing bloodshed and suffering and irreparably turning the state to the extreme left. Gottwald had the police occupy the radio and communications centers and other public buildings. He mobilized the workers for mass demonstrations and protest meetings all over the country with the slogan that the republic was in danger.

Valerian Zorin, former Russian Ambassador to Prague, arrived to take part in the celebration of the thirtieth anniversary of the founding of the Red Army and also to supervise the delivery of grain from the Soviet Union. Zorin now held the office of Deputy to the Foreign Minister. He diplomatically refrained from statements with respect to the situation in Prague, but the Moscow radio spoke for him, strongly approving of the stand Gottwald had taken and his alleged motives.

The Minister of the Interior reported to the public that the police had unmasked a plot to seize power with the help of a foreign government. Members of the Czech Socialist (Benes) Party were said to be involved in the plot. Arrests followed the Minister's announcement.

Pro- and anti-Communist columns marched on the Presidential castle to try to influence the President. But in the meantime, a split developed within the anti-Communist parties. Second-string leaders advocated dropping the ministers who had resigned and letting other members of the respective parties take their places. Thus a solution was offered to Benes that outwardly took care of his insistence on constitutionality and on having all legal parties represented in the Cabinet. Gottwald drew up the list of members for the future cabinet from the same parties as those of the resigned Ministers. Thus twice Benes had to legalize, under irresistible pressure, intrigues against a democratic republic by a despotism. He was now a dying man, tired of his fate.

On February 25, 1948, the Communists took over.

In a few days, the whole country realized the immensity of the change. The Communists had taken command of every cell of public life, from the ministries to the last outposts of the administration in the villages, from university to kindergarten. People were demoted, dismissed, jailed, and shifted until the trustees of the Communists held the key positions. The Party launched a drive for membership. It needed more and more people to come under its discipline in order to control all functions of the state and society. The dam had been broken, and totalitarianism had inundated the community.

Still President Benes held out—a sinking island of hope in the flood—together with his friend Jan Masaryk, who, not associated with any party, was Minister of Foreign Affairs from the time that a government-in-exile had been formed. Masaryk was, perhaps, an even more illustrative symbol of the presence of the West in the orientation of the new regime than Benes was. Son of the first President, Jan Masaryk had had an American mother and had spent most of his lifetime in America and England. For two decades he had represented the Republic as an envoy at the Court of St. James and as its Foreign Minister during World War II. Some of his very many friends abroad resented the fact that he had lent respectability to the new government by staying at his post after the February coup. They had expected him to flee, denounce the Communists, and take up the fight against totalitarianism. Masaryk had never shirked a good fight, but at the bottom of his noble heart he was not a fighter. A man of fundamental decency, goodness, and charm, he lived in the huge shadow of his great father, which kept spurring him to responsibility. On March 10, his body lay on the cobblestones beneath the window of his bathroom in the apartment he occupied in the palace of the Ministry of Foreign Affairs. Opinion was divided, at home as well as abroad, as to whether he had committed suicide or been murdered by the Communists. He had been in the delegation to Moscow that had listened to Stalin's warning that the cabinet ought to reverse its decision to accept the invitation to the conference on the Marshall Plan. Returning home, Masaryk had told friends that his country was no longer independent. He had remained, nevertheless, to stand by the ailing President Benes and try to save what still could be saved. He may have thought that a spectacular and meaningful suicide was the last service he could give his country.

At the time his presence in the cabinet was a great asset to the government. Undoubtedly, the Communists did not like the thought that Masaryk might escape and fight them from abroad; but if they had decided to get rid of him they would hardly have elected to throw his body from a window. Defenestration had a symbolic meaning for the Czechs, as every schoolboy was aware. It had signaled the Czech rebellion against the Hapsburgs and the greatest national catastrophe in their history. Masaryk was reminding the nation of the ominous significance of the February events, so his most intimate friends believe.

President Benes appeared at his funeral and returned to his country home near Prague. He said nothing. On June 7, he resigned the Presidency and died on September 3, 1948.

3.

Stalin's answer to the Marshall Plan involved integration of the Soviet orbit, economic and political. But the incorporation of the satellite states into the Soviet Union was not contemplated. They could always serve as objects of bargaining for a general settlement with America. Furthermore, the Western character of religion, traditions, and the social and economic stratification in these countries made them a hard bite for the Soviet Union to digest, at least until the total collectivization of their agriculture could be carried out and the middle-class mentality had died with that class itself. The Soviets were satisfied with the way they had controlled the huge but thinly populated state of Outer Mongolia by shutting it off from any contact with the world outside the Soviet Union.

Stalin had in mind another method of political integration. The Communist Party would become the medium of integrating the local governments with that of the Soviet Union by absorbing them. In this way state-to-state relations between Communist countries would no longer exist. There would be only Party relations, in which the supremacy of the Bolshevik Party of the Soviet Union was taken for granted by Stalin. He perhaps failed to consider the fact that this priority was due to the fact that the Soviet Union had been the only socialist country, but as other countries went socialist, Communist Russia's priority might come up for revision.

Stalin now held that the parties in the satellite countries ought to assume complete control over the state apparatus and become the agents of political integration. In the constituent republics of the Soviet Union, the Party had the same task. Why should this system not work in the satellite countries? All that was needed to complete political integration was that their Parties come under the total control of the Kremlin. The Kremlin decided to form an organization for this purpose and named it "Cominform," an innocent enough sounding title meaning "Communist Information Bureau." But it was meant to convey to the satellites the law as it was laid down by the Kremlin, to guide its application, and to survey its progress. In no sense would it be a reinstatement of the Comintern, a directorate of conspirators from the four corners of the world whom the Soviets might or might not use for their purposes. The new Cominform was to be an organization of Parties which held power in their states and were able to commit that power for the Soviet Union. As an exception, the parties of Italy and France would be included, since they had until recently been in the government, and it was highly desirable for Moscow that they return there.

Belgrade was chosen as headquarters for the Cominform, and it was decided to publish an official paper with the incredible title *For A Lasting Peace, For A People's Democracy!* At first, the organization appeared to be a forum where the member parties took the initiative. Tito, when the first session convened in September, 1947, with Andrei Zhdanov in the chair, censured the leadership of some parties in the satellite countries for tolerating enemies of Communism in their national fronts and for slowness and timidity in taking strides toward socialism. But very soon, with shocking bluntness, Tito was given to understand that the Cominform had been established for just the opposite reason; it was to put an end to initiative in the ranks.

Nobody then seemed to know that there was anything wrong in the relationship between Stalin and Tito; even less did it occur to anyone to suppose that it had been for the purpose of keeping Tito within bounds that the Cominform itself had come into being just at that time.

On second thought, however, several strange signs might have alerted observers to search more insistently for explanations. For example, Tito visited and was acclaimed in Prague in the late fall of 1947, and made Budapest his next stop. His reception there was somewhat perplexing. Matthias Rakosi, the Hungarian dictator, made but a single appearance to greet the Jugoslavian chief. For the populace Rakosi had Laszlo Rajk parade the visitor about town. Thousands of school children, workers, and citizens lined the streets in order to catch a glimpse of the legendary hero. Yet something always went wrong with the arrangements. At the very last minute plans were changed so that the parade took a different route from the one announced, and the people never got a chance to see Tito and Rajk except in the newspapers the following morning.

On one occasion, workers in a large factory which Tito and his staff visited were surprised at the speed with which the visit was concluded. The disappointed public could find no explanation except that Tito feared assassination. By whom? His Fascist enemies had long been destroyed. There were no groups in Hungary with any grudges against Jugoslavia and its leader. From what side did anyone fear an attempt on Tito's life? Of course, it was known to what length his bodyguard had gone in taking security measures.

But the complete mixup of the parades exceeded anything the gossips might have spread about his self-protection. The absence of Rakosi may have made Tito wonder. If anyone did, Rakosi knew the true state of Soviet-Jugoslav relations, and he might have thought it advisable to keep out of sight during Tito's visit and to give Rajk the dubious honor of playing host. He might himself have planted the rumor of an attempt on Tito's life to spoil the tour, but it was also possible that Tito suspected Rakosi of instigating an attempt and absenting himself so as not to fall victim of the scheme.

Naturally it was difficult to bring Tito and the Jugoslav Communists down to the same level as the other satellite bosses, who were saddled with or kept in saddle by the Soviet army in or near their respective countries. Only Tito's regime rested on broad popular support, and he alone was confident of keeping power by his own force. In the main he followed the Kremlin's recipe for the use of the people's democracies, but sometimes he varied the tempo, accelerating the socialization of industry and refraining from alienating the peasants by forcible collectivization. Tito and Jugoslavia were looked upon as the bastions of the new order and the prospective leaders of the satellites. Tito's radical foreign policy and aggressiveness had served Moscow well as a feeler that could be disavowed or followed up as circumstances warranted. But when the East-West split on the continent threatened a new war, the Kremlin fell back on strong discipline and central direction and saw no reason why the parties should not submit as of old, merely because they now ran a local government.

Tito saw the matter differently and acted accordingly. His bold dissent infected even such an old Comintern hand as Dimitrov of Bulgaria, although he had seen many men in Moscow whose greatness had gone to their heads and who had fallen with their heads. In August, 1947, Tito and Dimitrov met at Tito's favorite residence in Bled, and as a result they made public their intention of federating Jugoslavia and Bulgaria. Tito repaid the visit a few months later in Sofia and declared that cooperation between the two countries would become so close as to make federation a sheer formality. Dimitrov thereafter visited the Rumanian capital and discussed a customs union with Bulgaria. At a press conference he went so far as to forecast that the eastern countries might soon face the question of federation. Promptly, Markos Vafiades, Greek guerilla chief, announced the formation of a provisional democratic government in Greece. A Balkan federation under the leadership of Tito was in the offing.

Moscow, however, decided to cut short these runaway developments. *Pravda* publicly rebuked a Bolshevik as great as Dimitrov and stated that it disagreed with the idea of artificial federations, confederations, and customs unions. At a conference in February, 1948, Stalin took strong exception to Tito's making military agreements and moves with respect to Albania without informing him beforehand.

But he soon changed his mind concerning the federation of Jugoslavia and Bulgaria and advised Tito to go ahead. Tito himself lately had had too many controversies with Stalin and had seen how Stalin was irritated by his independent actions too often not to suspect something behind his change of heart. Stalin thought that he could always handle Bulgaria on account of that country's geographical situation and its people's traditional pro-Russian orientation. He could use it as an instrument to keep Tito's and Jugoslavia's ambitions in check. Tito reported Stalin's advice to his Politburo and recommended caution.

The world was shocked when the news was flashed that Stalin had broken with Tito.

On June 28, 1948, the Cominform made public its resolution stating unanimously, in the absence of the Jugoslav delegates, that the leaders of the Jugoslav Party had taken a position incompatible with Marxism-Leninism, placed themselves in opposition to the Communist parties, seceded from the united Socialist front against imperialism, betrayed the cause of international solidarity of the working people, and deviated into bourgeois nationalism. The resolution

called the heretics by name—Tito, Kardelj, Djilas and Rank-
ovich—and called upon them openly to recognize their
mistakes; otherwise the Jugoslav Party must replace them
with a truly internationalist leadership.

To the West the news sounded too good to be true.
People suspected a Soviet-Jugoslav maneuver the purpose
of which was sure to be sinister but was unfathomable. It
had a shattering effect on the public in the satellite countries. Not knowing exactly what had happened, the world
wondered what was going to happen and feared the worst.
But everyone was aware of the historic import of the event.
It was unprecedented. Nobody foresaw its consequences
as they actually unfolded, and all forecasts proved to be
wrong. Even after the facts had become known, people
failed to recognize the essence of the controversy which
had led to the break between Stalin and Tito, who was believed to be his most devoted pupil.

Predictions as to future developments took in all possibilities: Stalin and Tito would patch up their differences;
Tito and his associates would promptly be overthrown,
since Stalin would not have taken such a drastic step, particularly in public, without making sure that others in the
Jugoslav Politburo stood ready to take over; if the Politburo failed to act, the Party at large would overthrow Tito;
Tito would ally himself with the non-Communist parties of
Jugoslavia and resist Moscow; non-Communist parties
would get the upper hand and throw off Communist control; Titoism would spread over to the satellite countries
which would rise against Moscow; the Soviet army would
invade Jugoslavia; all satellite countries would be incorporated in the Soviet Union; the Jugoslavs would appeal to
the West, and there would be a new world conflagration—
these and many other guesses were heard, read, discussed,
and whispered. Neither Stalin who opened the incident,
nor Tito and his friends who provoked it, knew the next
step each would take in this unique case.

The essence of the controversy, hidden under its ideological cloak, was summed up in a statement by the Jugoslav

theoretician Edward Kardelj to the Central Committee of the Soviet Party: "No matter how each of us loves the land of Socialism, the U.S.S.R., he can, in no case, love his own country less, a socialist country."

This statement clashed with the principle publicly declared by the Cominform to the effect that the criterion of a Communist was that he adhere to proletarian internationalism, which meant serving the interests of the land of socialism, the U.S.S.R. In principle, there could be no clash of interests between the Soviet Union and a truly socialist state, the latter being by definition a state run by Communists. In case of a clash, the state running into controversy with the Soviet Union was not truly socialist.

Once the Kremlin had decided on this principle in its relations with the states in its orbit, Tito either had to submit or be lost to the Communist world. In vain he protested and tried to prove his unfailing allegiance to Marxism-Leninism while drawing a dividing line between interparty and interstate relations as far as his country and the Soviet Union were concerned.

Actually, the break came to pass on interstate relations. The Soviet Union refused to negotiate the 1948 phase of the Soviet-Jugoslav commercial treaty with $2 billion worth of Soviet deliveries at stake for the Jugoslav five-year plan; Marshal Bulganin also recalled all military advisers and instructors from Jugoslavia, and Soviet experts left the country as well. Tito asked Moscow for an explanation of the brisk action, stating how deeply it had hurt him. He received it in a long letter from which Tito gathered the gravity of the situation. Both interstate and interparty relations were involved. The letter reproached the Jugoslavs for having issued a decree forbidding the state organs to give economic information to anyone without the approval of the state security officers. This for the Soviets meant that the Jugoslav security organs controlled and supervised Soviet representatives. The Central Committee of the Soviet Party, whose signature the letter carried, also took exception to the fact that the Jugoslav Party was subject to the state security organs instead of the other way around.

The Jugoslavs inquired in their reply about the source of this information. If it had come from the Soviet Ambassador to Jugoslavia, they considered it improper

for an ambassador to ask anyone for information about the work of our party. That is not his business. Information can be obtained by the Soviet Central Committee from the Central Committee of the Jugoslav Party.

Tito was here insisting on a clear line between Party and state. On this distinction hinged the possibility of independence for a country in the Soviet orbit. But the Soviets stuck to their stand that the Party absorbed the government. It branded the Jugoslav statement

. . . incorrect and anti-Soviet. They identify the Soviet Ambassador, a responsible Communist who represents this communist government of the U.S.S.R., with an ordinary, bourgeois ambassador . . . It is difficult to understand how Tito and Kardelj could sink so low. Do these comrades understand that the Soviet Ambassador, a responsible Communist, who represents a friendly power which liberated Jugoslavia from German occupation, not only has the right but is obliged, from time to time, to discuss with the Communists of Jugoslavia all questions which interest them?

In the face of this attitude there could be no substance to such Jugoslav complaints as that "the agents of the Soviet Intelligence Service" recruited "in our country, which is moving toward Socialism, our citizens for their intelligence service. We cannot allow the Soviet Intelligence Service to spread its net in our country."

The rest of the Soviet accusations, ominously referring to the career of Trotsky and other principal victims of the Moscow purge, concerned the ideological deviations of Tito and his associates to the right and to the left, blaming them for policies imposed on the Jugoslavs by the Moscow-drawn party line and in many cases blatantly lying.

Tito professed a "comradely and brotherly feeling of loyalty" toward the Soviet Party, but he made two state-

ments, equally presumptuous in both spheres of Soviet-
Jugoslav relations. He said:

> . . . we study and take as an example the Soviet system, but are
> developing socialism in our country in a somewhat different form. In
> the given period under specific conditions which exist in our coun-
> try . . . we are attempting to apply the best forms of work in the
> realization of socialism. We do not do this in order to prove that
> our road is better than that taken by the Soviet Union, that we are
> creating something new, but because this is forced on us by our daily
> life.

This took care of the reproach for ideological deviations.
Another statement referred to Jugoslavia's usefulness as a
state and as an ally. It reminded the Soviets that they had
in Jugoslavia a most faithful ally against the capitalist
world; this alliance was in the interests not only of both
countries, but also of the other peoples' democracies.

Tito knew well what it meant to be lumped together with
Stalin's more prominent victims. But Tito was not in Stalin's grasp as long as the Party in his own country stood by
him. This must have made a difference to Stalin also. Tito
did not give up all hope that a final break could be prevented and tried hard to avert it without softening a stand
that would be supported by his own countrymen no matter
what happened. He assured the Soviet Committee that he
and the Jugoslavs would render proof of their loyalty to the
Soviets by their deeds in the future. But he wanted to
preserve in any case, in the interests of all concerned, the
alliance between the socialist countries and Jugoslavia.

Further developments now depended on Stalin's judgment, and his judgment proved to be wrong.

Meanwhile, Tito arrested the two members of the Politburo, Hebrang and Zhuiovich, who had taken the side of
the Soviets in the dispute, and who were suspected of having been selected by Stalin to overthrow Tito. The alert
Jugoslav frontier guards shot Arse Ioanovich, the army
chief of staff, when one night in August he tried to cross the
border to Rumania.

Tito laid the case before the Party congress. More than two thousand delegates heard the Soviet accusations, then Tito's defense and counteraccusations. They were distressed and bewildered.

When the world noted that Stalin's sentence had not broken Tito, and he had not been overthrown by rivals in the Politburo or by an army putsch, the outlook was seen as more serious. People thought that the Kremlin could not afford to lose its prestige before the satellite peoples, the Communist parties in the West, and the uncommitted countries. What was worse, its prestige would drop so catastrophically before the potential enemies of the Soviets as to compel the Kremlin to resort to armed intervention. Fearing a general war, many enemies of Communism prayed that Tito would surrender. But he refused to do so.

In August, Zhdanov died. Stalin chose the Hungarian boss, Matthias Rakosi, as the new chairman of the Cominform, which had moved its headquarters to Bucharest, the Rumanian capital. It was a faintly favorable sign that since the chairman of the organization that had excommunicated Tito was now a non-Russian, a face-saving retreat might be left open for Moscow.

But the Cominform now took up the great campaign against Tito and his "clique." It called upon the Jugoslav Party to change leadership. It organized groups of Jugoslavs in the satellite countries to send anti-Tito propaganda through the press, radio, and pamphlets. Each satellite began harassing the Jugoslav legations, insulting Jugoslavia by having it represented at congresses and festivities by dissident Communist groups from abroad. They stepped up the tone and the gravity of the indictments against Tito and his "gang," branding them hirelings of imperialists, traitors, spies, Fascists, and murderers.

The one satisfaction Tito still could have given the Great Inquisitor was to turn from Communism to Western socialism. This would justify the theory that deviation from the true faith must land the heretic in the enemy camp. Tito refused to do even this favor to Moscow. Slowly, and to the West suspiciously slowly, he began to discard Stalin from the gallery of Communist heroes. Tito knew Moscow and knew that its line might suddenly be reversed. The international situation was fraught with danger, and the success in China might warn Stalin that he ought to soften his course with regard to other socialist states. "The Soviets may find out that it is not so easy to give orders to a people's government which has come to power through the fighting of its own nation," as Dr. Alex Bebler, Jugoslav Deputy Foreign Minister, told the Czecho-Slovak envoy.

But Tito and his friends miscalculated. In January, 1949, Moscow established an organization for the economic coordination of the Soviet empire, called the Council for Mutual Economic Assistance. Its foremost task was to organize an economic boycott of Jugoslavia, but at the same time to eliminate the adverse effects of the boycott on the economic plans of the satellites. Jugoslavia's contribution of varied industrial raw materials was fundamental to the realization of their plans. Indeed, Stalin's early dissatisfaction with Tito had originated partly in Tito's refusal to be satisfied with the role assigned to his country by the planners in Moscow who wanted to concentrate on the exploitation of these resources and leave the processing of the raw materials to the more industrialized satellites. This would have put Jugoslavia in a colonial-type dependency on the Soviet Union and the industrialized countries. Tito wanted Jugoslavia, however, to grow as a military power, and that could be based only on domestic heavy industry. In this ambition he could count on the understanding and approval of the rank and file. Hamilton Fish Armstrong quoted a young Communist as telling him in the spring of 1949:

After the struggles of the old times against the Turks and Austrians and Magyars, after our own fights with the Nazis and Italians, we were to keep our muddy roads, walk in them in our peasant *opanke* and step aside when the Russian engineers rode past in their motor cars just as Serbs used to do when the Turks rode by on their mules.

The Russians stopped deliveries of oil and industrial equipment. The satellites refused to deliver machinery already paid for. The Hungarians stopped paying reparations in kind owed to Jugoslavia by the edict of the peace treaties, although they owed Jugoslavia over $20 million for goods delivered in advance. Czechoslovakia, whose industries would have been hard hit by a total loss of Jugoslav raw materials, at least stopped delivering the more essential goods to Jugoslavia. Albania, Jugoslavia's own satellite, was the first to renounce her economic treaties with Jugoslavia, charging Jugoslavia with having exploited the country, taken over the management of her economy, and depriving her of political independence. Jugoslavia was scandalized by the outrageous action. Albania owed her two and a half billion dinars for past deliveries.

While the economic strangulation of Jugoslavia was going on, the cold war began warming up. A complete break in East-West relations occurred over their most controversial subject, Germany. Both sides wanted the unification of Germany on their own terms or not at all. No compromise could be expected from the rigid positions of the two camps, engaged as they were in a determined struggle to improve their power ranges. The West made a final decision to set up a West German state, and the Russians also were inclined toward a split-up of the country since their prospects of imposing a pro-Communist orientation on all Germany had faded to the vanishing point. Russia was ready to fall back on her own zone in Germany as a country in its own right, a Soviet-type democracy. But this policy would have rough going since it was starting under an almost insurmountable handicap—the previous handling of the area. The Russians had treated the conquered country with ruthless spoliation and humiliation of the inhabitants, their only aim being the expropriation of as much as possible in the way of reparations payments to the Soviet Union and to Poland, while providing for the Germans only the subsistence necessary to enable them to work for them.

The East Germans had to be better fed and treated if their support was to be gained for integration into the Soviet orbit. The Slav accent of Soviet foreign policy that had

served to attract Poles, Czechs, and Jugoslavs had to yield
to international Communist solidarity which now included
collaboration with the suddenly discovered "good" Germans, the potential Communists. The Slav satellites now
had to swallow an unpalatable dish—friendship with the
East Germans. As Soviet efforts to court the East Germans
increased, the satellites feared that this might be only the
first step to the return of German workers expelled from
their countries after the war.

Party discipline had to be tightened in the satellite states
in the expectation of a possible radical change in the Moscow line. An event in Germany made this imperative. A
conflict developed between East and West over Berlin.
The Soviets held that when the West split Germany politically, it had broken the four-power agreement with respect to the four-power administration of the city; consequently, the Western military administration must leave
Berlin, which lay within the Soviet zone. To lend weight
to the Soviet demand, the Russians blocked road and rail
communications between Berlin and West Germany. The
Allies did not stop this time at protests, but resolved to stay,
regardless of the consequences. They agreed on an airlift
to and from Berlin to feed the population and to enable
them to make a small livelihood. It was a daring venture
and would not have worked without the cooperation of the
inhabitants. Both the airlift and the morale of Berlin turned
out to function better than had been expected. But the
long months during which the emergency lasted were
loaded with explosive possibilities. The Russians lifted the
ten-month blockade in May, 1949, without ado, passing
over defeat at one point and moving on to another one.
The result of Russian failure was the North Atlantic Treaty
in April, 1949, a sharpening of the polarization of powers,
and a tip of the balance in favor of the West. Any imbalance bore the danger of war, but the Soviets soon scored
gains in two directions. The State Department announced
in September, 1949, that an atomic explosion had been de-

tected in the Soviet Union. The American monopoly on the atom bomb had been broken. At the same time, the Communists terminated their conquest of China. After three centuries of decay, anarchy, and the pains of rebirth, the greatest power in Asia reappeared in the political and strategic field armed with the unrivaled prestige of an ancient culture, wisdom and political skill, and inexhaustible man-power. In unity with Russia, this power threatened to become invincible. But such unity was no foregone conclusion then, nor could one foresee the influence of such a vast country as an ally on the philosophy and methods of Russian empire building.

In this world situation, Moscow's fight against Tito became more than a struggle against deviation and defection in one small though important satellite country. It now entailed taking preventive measures against any potential factionalism in the Communist parties which might endanger the unity of the Soviet front in the face of cold and possibly even hot war.

The Kremlin resolved to weed out nationalism from the satellite parties before they proved to be unmanageable. Moscow proceeded with a refined technique but no less determination in the most important satellite in her immediate defense range, namely, Poland.

The General Secretary of the Polish Party, Wladyslaw Gomulka, was the archetype of a nationalist. He was courageous enough to display his heresy without disguise. The heresy consisted in taking at face value Soviet flattery of national feelings. Actually this was a means for Moscow to flush out nationalists. Gomulka's advance in the Party hierarchy was due to the fact that there had been no Communist Party in Poland at the outbreak of the war, since Stalin had wiped it out for its hopeless deviations. Some potential Communist leaders had fled to Russia when the Nazis had occupied Poland. Others, like Gomulka, had fought in the underground and created some respect for the Party itself as a possible Polish movement and not just a wing of

264 EASTERN EUROPE IN THE COLD WAR

the Soviet ideological front line. He cut a forceful figure
of great seriousness and struggled deeply within himself
to reconcile his sincere loyalty to Communism with Polish
national interests.

In June, 1948, Gomulka spoke in the Polish Politburo,
as he had done many times before, of the historic sources
of Communism in Poland. The significance of the speech
lay in its unmistakable reference to the happenings in Jugoslavia, three weeks before the official excommunication of
Tito and his friends by the Cominform. The old Polish
Social Democratic Party at the end of World War I had followed the line of Rosa Luxemburg, which advocated the
incorporation of a socialist Poland in the Soviet Union.
The other faction, the Polish Socialist Party, saw in socialism the means of transforming the institutions of the economy and society so as to serve the welfare and cultural
advance of the entire people of Poland. Gomulka held that
the true source of Communism in Poland was the heritage
of the Polish Socialist Party, which consisted of the effort
to develop a Polish way of Communism, the pattern of
which might differ from that of the Soviet Union. Such
opinions harmonized with the Moscow line in 1945–46, but
were out of tune in 1948. Gomulka's opponents in the Politburo were in practice the heirs of the Luxemburg line
though they would deny this since Moscow still considered
internationalism a left-wing deviation.

The General Secretary showed no liking for this extreme
loyalty to the Soviets. He was extremely popular, as much
so as a Communist could be in Poland, and was counted on
to defend Polish independence to the last ditch. The Muscovites had to cleanse the party leadership of the nationalism Gomulka and his followers represented, but they moved
cautiously. They needed Gomulka's confession, his acknowledgment that he had erred, and his promise to
reform. Without it, they dared not eliminate him on account of his popularity and the strength of his support in
the local Party apparatus. Aware of the new Party line,
Gomulka offered his resignation and expressed his readiness

to work for the Party in any small way, but he refused to recant.

The Muscovites were not satisfied. They replaced Gomulka as Secretary with Boleslaw Bierut, President of the Republic, who had also fought in the underground but had turned into a flawless trustee of Moscow. The pressure on Gomulka was increased. In September, the Russians succeeded in turning some of Gomulka's best men in the Politburo against him. Through three days of deliberations, Gomulka, in a torturous struggle to preserve the integrity of his beliefs while making every effort to avoid a Party split, gave more and more ground from his original stand, but stuck to certain reservations. It was meaningful for his countrymen as well as for Moscow that he and his friends who had been in contact with the Polish people had difficulty in recognizing the real connection between the Soviet and Polish parties, while others, who had lived in Moscow or joined Polish troops in the Soviet army, had not. But he confessed his error in delaying the collectivization of agriculture and advising caution against Tito. The Communists could not exact more from Gomulka, but they published his reluctant yielding to the new line. It was enough to convince the militant Muscovites that he could not be trusted, but it endeared him more than ever with the rank and file.

In December, 1948, the Party was thoroughly cleansed of "rightists." The Communist and the Polish Socialist parties merged into a new Polish Workers' Party after the Socialists had also undergone a merciless purge. Joseph Cyrankiewicz, a Socialist fellow traveler, became Secretary General of the new Party. Subsequently, Gomulka slid down the ladder of the Party hierarchy to lesser and lesser positions while his supporters were discarded and disgraced. The heresy of nationalism increased in seriousness from deviation and error to crime and treason. Gomulka landed in jail, but Stalin knew enough not to identify the strength that his faithful had been able to muster in the Politburo with their strength in the Party, not to speak of the country as a whole. Poland was strategically of prime importance, and, as a country of about 25 million people, its defection in case of emergency was too serious a threat. He appointed Marshal Rokossowski, a Soviet general whose closest connection to Poland was his alleged ethnic descent, to be the commander of the Polish army and Minister of War in Poland.

Under the impact of the international situation, Stalin came to the conclusion that spectacular trials must be mounted to impress on everyone's mind the right way of thinking and the consequences of deviation. The satellites had to get a taste of the Moscow trials in the 1930's if they were to realize that the Kremlin would eradicate any mental reservations about the Party line with the same cruelty and ruthlessness it had shown in the great purges. Stalin needed an important figure in one of the satellite countries who personified two of the criminal deviations, a man who was a nationalist and a cosmopolitan at the same time. All home-grown Communists became suspect of nationalism, and all Communists who had been in the West, especially those who had fought in the Spanish Civil War, were thought to be cosmopolitan—people who must be susceptible to Western influence and who necessarily had connections with the West.

Matthias Rakosi, the Hungarian dictator and head of the Cominform, had the man perfectly fitted for the part. It was the tough Communist, Laszlo Rajk, his rival in more lenient times, an inveterate revolutionary, as disciplined as a good warrior but poorly adjusted to the role of a Soviet bureaucrat. Rajk had made an impressive record as a young Communist student in the illegal movement in Horthy's Hungary; as a fighter in Spain where he was wounded three times; in jails and concentration camps in France, Germany, and Hungary; and finally in the resistance movement during the war. The black sheep of a right-wing family, he had rejected all it stood for, and had become and remained a Communist through all the zigzags of the Party line. He was a man dedicated to action rather than to echoing words. For this reason, his record was cleaner than that of his executioner, Rakosi, who wrote of Tito as late as October 19, 1947, in the official Party paper *Szabad Nep:*

The Jugoslavs enjoy of all peoples of the Danubian basin our strongest sympathy. The Hungarian democracy feels this sympathy not only because it admires and respects the heroic fight the Jugoslavs waged against the barbaric forces of Fascism, but also it expresses our gratitude toward liberated Jugoslavia and its chief, Marshal Tito, who were able to erase the memories of the atrocious massacre of the Bachka and the other abominable crimes the Horthy regime had committed against them and to offer first their hand of reconciliation and pardon.

Until Stalin began to look for an example, Rakosi had never accused Rajk of any fact or word indicating sympathy for Tito's nationalism, although Rajk had advised moderation in the Central Committee when the Stalin-Tito controversy had exploded. He had advocated this as a measure of prudence from the standpoint of the Hungarian Party and not from sympathy with Tito; and he did not oppose the strong line when adopted. But the public, even those who feared him much more than they did Rakosi, considered him a Magyar, albeit a Communist, because he had grown out of the Hungarian movement, fought the Nazis in Hungary, and had never lived in Moscow. Also, he was a Gentile among many Jews in the top leadership. Rajk had a blank record as far as deviations were concerned. Anything could be written into it.

The people of Hungary were kept busy with an orgy of public protests against Titoism, with the controversy over the nationalization of the schools, and with preparations for elections. In March, 1949, Rakosi stated that the People's Democracy was, in fact, a dictatorship of the proletariat except that its form differed somewhat from that of the Soviet Union. The statement threw light on the abrupt cessation of the playing of the Hungarian hymn that had usually opened radio broadcasts and the substitution of the "Internationale." Few people took note of a brief communiqué in the Party paper announcing that Rajk, Minister of the Interior, had left for Moscow. Nor was there much discussion when, upon his return, he was demoted to Minister of Foreign Affairs—an unimportant post for a Communist of the highest bracket such as he had been. But the report of Rajk's arrest in the spring of 1949 made people gasp. Rajk was charged with having conspired with Tito to overthrow the government, to subject the country to Tito, and in this way to deliver it over to capitalism and Western imperialism.

A shiver ran through the ranks of the Communists and their left-wing sympathizers in the West when Rajk stood trial in April, 1949, with his co-defendants, who held top jobs in the army and in the inner sanctum of the Party. The defendants were all either native Communists or had returned from exile in the West; some had been Trotskyites at one time. The case of the generals was assigned to a military court which convicted them and had them shot. Among the civilians, Rajk alone was prominent. It was really his trial.

He was deadly serious and showed an anxiety to confess to even the slightest details of his indictment, always stressing that the wrong he had done had issued not from principle or honest error, but from his lifelong profession as an informer, spy, and traitor. He had joined the illegal party to be a spy for the police, had been thrown out of the University to cover up his commission, was jailed for the same reason, and had even gone to Spain to continue his spying. But neither from Horthy's Hungary nor from the Nazis had he received any acknowledgment of his past services or appointment to some high post. He had gone underground instead, again to spy; had become leader of the resistance, then Number Two in the Party, Minister of the Interior. But all this, so his confession went, was only to seize the opportunity to conspire with Tito's Chief of Police to restore capitalism in Hungary and sell it out to the imperialists. There had not been a grain of honesty in him, even in the prime of his youth.

It was Rajk's trial, but not to the prosecutor or the court. The prosecutor insisted that it was the trial of Tito and his associates as well, and the court would convict not only

Rajk and his band, but, in the political and moral sense, also the Jugoslav traitors. In his last words to the court, Rajk said:

I share completely the opinion of the Prosecutor as to the facts he established. In this connection, I don't mean the details which have an almost negligible importance, but the essence. For this reason, I now declare that I, no matter what the decision of the Tribunal will be, hold the verdict just.

Rajk made his long and detailed confession in an unusual, colorless, impassive voice—like a student who, though tired to death, knows his lesson by heart. He was convicted, sentenced to be hanged, and hanged he was the next day.

The West was shocked. The dark methods of Soviet trial, the dread of which still haunted the nights of many intellectuals, now intruded again into their midst. Many people who in different phases of Rajk's life had met him, shared his experiences, troubles, fights, and prisons, spoke up and offered their testimony to the effect that his confession could not have been true. But of course no real effort had been made to make the indictment sound true, and no other proof than his confession had been produced. The public admission of sins never committed struck the West as a reversion to barbaric ages. They could not understand the use of such hollow confessions and trials that convinced no one in the West of the truth of the charges nor made any effort to do so. Yet, the obvious nonsense of one fact or another in the charge and confession did not make them incredible to the public behind the Iron Curtain. Considering the tight secrecy around the Communist bigwigs, anything might be possible. Rajk was considered a nationalist who might have associated with Tito to gain more independence for the satellite countries. Apart from that, the Communists knew that the trial served an important political purpose. It gave the impetus for wholesale arrests of Communists who had lived in the West, even in prisons or in exile, or for anyone who had the slightest connection with any of the convicted traitors.

The story of how Rakosi had made his rival confess a long string of untruths to incriminate himself was revealed after the revolution of 1956. Rakosi had sent the Minister of the Interior, who was none other than Janos Kadar, to visit Rajk in his cell. He was to tell Rajk that Communism needed his confession urgently, since this was the only way to unmask Tito. The Party did not demand from Rajk the supreme sacrifice—perhaps only a moral suicide. He would be convicted and his execution published; but he himself would be shipped to the Crimea to join his family. After a time, he would receive an important commission, under an assumed name, somewhere in Russia.

Rajk refused the offer. He was tortured for days and nights, but he had been tortured in the past and had never broken down. Kadar kept imploring him, but Rajk assured his comrade and good friend that the confession made no sense. No one would believe that he, who had belonged to the Party from his early youth, had been in the service of half a dozen foreign secret services including the Gestapo. But in the end, he came to the conclusion that he had no choice. Although he doubted Rakosi and his promise not to execute the sentence, there was a chance of survival for him, or at least for his young wife who had borne him a son shortly before his arrest. He had to trust Kadar, who was indebted to Rajk's wife. She had been tortured by the Gestapo in 1943 to disclose the names and hideouts of the resistance leaders, one of whom had been Kadar, but Julia Rajk had not given Kadar's name to the Gestapo. Eventually, Rajk asked for one favor only: that he be allowed not to besmirch the record of his youth. What is the use, he asked, for you to prove that I had always been scum? If you need a conspiracy, you should charge me with a plot against Rakosi. This would at least sound credible. But Kadar insisted that the confession was intended to convince the simple people with a black-and-white picture, and he again assured Rajk on his word of honor that he and his family would be left free in Russia after the trial. Kadar also conveyed Rakosi's message to the effect that the Party required such service only from its greatest members.

Rakosi and Kadar did not keep their word. Rajk was executed, his wife imprisoned, her son taken away from her. In all her years in prison she never found out where her child was until she was freed in 1955.

Bulgaria put on display a much clearer case than Rajk's, at least to the extent of making it obvious why Traicho Kostov had been selected to be the chief victim of the Titoist purge.

Kostov had been a prewar Communist leader, from 1935 on a member of the Politburo, from 1940 Secretary General of the Party, and a leader of the resistance during World War II. He led the Party after liberation until Georgi Dimitrov returned from Moscow. After that Kostov became Deputy Prime Minister and exercised control over the economic policies of Bulgaria. Kostov was the strong man of the Party who had jumped through the window of the Sofia police station when he had become afraid of revealing something while being tortured. He had suffered a fracture of the backbone and become a cripple for life. In contrast to the idol of the Party, Dimitrov, the hero of the Leipzig trial where he had been charged with setting the Reichstag afire, Kostov had opposed the union with Jugoslavia even when Moscow had approved of it.

There were weighty reasons why Moscow made this life-long, faithful Communist the victim of the hard Party line. In March, 1948, Vasil Kolarov, an old Bolshevik, honored with the presidency of the National Assembly, had suddenly taken exception to the all-powerful Kostov for having denied the Russian trade mission certain data on the Bulgarian economy. This may have been because the Russians bought rose oil and tobacco from Bulgaria at a painfully low price only to sell them immediately at a high profit. Kostov, like Tito, had designed overambitious plans for the economic development of his poor country, and their fulfillment was close to his heart. He may have resented Russian exploitation and sharp practices. His resentment en-

couraged Kostov's rivals to blame him for the economic
troubles of the country. These were due mostly to the ruthless collectivization of agriculture, in which Kostov pioneered in spite of the caution which Russia had advised in
the first postwar years when collaboration with the West
was still in practice. Kostov thus qualified for the show
case against Titoism in Bulgaria, but the ailing Dimitrov
had to be convinced of the need for sacrificing his most
reliable comrade. Dimitrov's brother-in-law, Vulko Chervenkov, volunteered to do it. He harbored high ambitions,
but his biggest asset was his brother-in-law. Chervenkov
visited Dimitrov in Russia where he had been taken to a
sanitarium, and he may have obtained his consent to the
purge. In June, Kostov was expelled from the Politburo
and the Party and demoted to librarian of the National
Library in Sofia. In July, Dimitrov died. Marshal Voroshilov himself accompanied the body to Sofia to be em-
balmed and displayed in a mausoleum. Old Kolarov took
his place as Prime Minister, and the ambitious Chervenkov
became his deputy in name, though it was actually he who
now ran the government and the Party. Kostov's friends
were thrown out of office at the same time and Kostov himself was arrested. On hearing the news of the arrest of his
toughest enemy in the Bulgarian Party, Tito dealt the final
blow:

[Kostov] was arrested during the war under the regime of King Boris
and was kept in prison together with a group of Communists. Though
known as one of the main leaders, he alone had his life spared while
the others were killed. Why? . . . We have today proof in our
hands that among the functionaries of certain Communist parties can
be found agents of certain capitalist states. Those people had been
recruited while in the hands of the Gestapo, like Hebrang and some
others in our country.

Chervenkov conveniently added Tito's charge to the rest
and ordered Kostov to be tried. Kolarov explained to the
press the danger that threatened Bulgaria as a consequence
of Kostov's deviation because it aroused distrust of the
Bulgarian leadership in the Soviet Party. But the charge

also reached back into Kostov's past: he had been a Trotsky-
ite; subsequently a spy for the Bulgarian police, as Tito had
suggested; then an agent of the British Intelligence Service;
and finally a tool of the Americans, who had encouraged
him to kill Georgi Dimitrov with the help of Tito.

The trial had a smooth beginning. Kostov pleaded
guilty. But then he raised his voice and declared to the
amazement of the court and the audience that he pleaded
guilty neither to having ever been an agent of the Bulgarian
police nor an agent of the British Intelligence, nor of conspiring with Tito and his clique. The judge ordered Kostov
out of the courtroom amidst the jeers of the audience. Then
he had the clerk read Kostov's pretrial confession. Kostov
was condemned to death and executed.

In little Albania, Premier Enver Hoxha, who made the
moves for Stalin and Russia there, volunteered for the campaign against Tito and Jugoslavia. Hoxha had a large se-
lection to choose from in purging Tito's collaborators.
However, the most compromised one, Koci Xoxe, Minister
of the Interior, quickly set about arresting Titoists himself.
Hoxha then took off for Moscow, where he had plenty to
talk about since the Russians had to take over plans, supplies, and finances from the expelled Jugoslavs. He obtained Stalin's consent to liquidate Xoxe and anyone else
whom he might brand Titoist and returned to bathe in the
warmth of popularity. The country hated the Jugoslavs
for keeping the Kossovo region and was little impressed
with them as officers or technicians. If they had to be subject to others, the proud Albanians preferred a powerful
nation like the Russians to a Balkan boss, poor like themselves. Moreover, the Russians had the advantage of not
living in their neighborhood. Albania was changing hands.

Not so Rumania. Since the Russians had overrun the
country, Soviet advisers controlled state, army, and Party.
The country was solidly anti-Russian and anti-Communist,
but a handful of devoted and proven leaders faithfully executed Moscow's orders and followed its directives. Even
before the Cominform had branded Tito a traitor, the Ru-

manian Party had got rid of Lucretiu Patrascanu, the Minister of Justice, an intellectual acquainted with Western
culture, an old-time Communist but no Muscovite, as a
"bourgeois nationalist." No anti-Titoist trial was needed
for education or intimidation. The oppressing presence of
the Russians did more than any campaign of fratricidal
arrests to warn the Rumanians to adjust to Soviet domination. Ana Pauker cracked the whip in the course of the
anti-Tito campaign. She shut off all communication between Rumania and Jugoslavia, including the postal service,
and broadcast threats and invective at the "hirelings of the
imperialists" across the border. Although Rumanian leadership was unfailingly dedicated to Moscow, furious inner
struggles raged as a consequence of economic disasters and
unsuccessful financial operations. It appears that Moscow
left its Rumanian henchmen generally alone to fight out
the issues among themselves, provided deliveries to Russia
went on. Eventually, the complete fiasco of repeated currency reforms cost Vasile Luca, Minister of Finance, his
position in the Party and cabinet. To everyone's stupefaction, Ana Pauker also lost out, first being demoted, then
gradually dropped from office, power, and sight. The fierce
Ana faded but was not jailed or tried. She was probably
the victim of Moscow's sudden anti-Israeli policies in its
displeasure over Israel's ever-closer ties with America. By
1952, Gheorghiu-Dej, an old but homegrown Communist,
had sole power.

In no satellite was it so urgent to weed out nationalism
and cosmopolitanism as in Czecho-Slovakia, but Moscow
hesitated for quite a time over whom to entrust as the sole
representative of the new, hard line. When the decision
finally came about, the process of liquidation destroyed both
the purged and the purgers. It eliminated all who stood in
the way of Stalin's choice of a domestic dictator.

Moscow's caution had nothing to do with the uproar in
the West when the Communists had taken over the government by force. That had to be expected. Czecho-Slovakia
had offered itself voluntarily to be under Stalin's protection,

and had set up a democratically elected pro-Russian and pro-Soviet government that had endeavored to prove by its own example that in such a case Moscow would keep its promise not to interfere with the internal affairs of the country. The coup of 1948 was a severe blow to the left in the West, particularly to those socialists who had hoped against hope that collaboration with the Communists was possible. Stalin himself had nothing but contempt for the left in the West, including the Communists, who had proved themselves unable to establish and keep socialism in power without the presence of the Soviet army. His caution issued rather from Czecho-Slovakia's bordering on Germany and the consequences an attempt at defection and its suppression might entail. He was satisfied with Klement Gottwald, the bulky prototype of a Czech worker, and the way he had engineered the coup without open Soviet intervention. But this solid pawn of Moscow was still parochial by roots and habit. Stalin might have more comfortably relied on Rudolf Slansky, Secretary General of the Party, one of those who would look at the world from the ramparts of the Kremlin even if delegated to the South Pole. But in the final analysis only one thing mattered, a man at the helm who kept the satellite fast within the Soviet empire as a single workshop for the Five-Year Plan, and for further plans already piling up in its wake.

While Gottwald and Slansky struggled for sole power, things took a bad turn because Moscow had forced Czecho-Slovakia to break with the West. The highly developed Czech industry had its traditional market in the West from which to draw supplies of industrial raw materials, and the Czechs had resumed this highly beneficial relationship shortly after the war with remarkable rapidity. Then, all of a sudden, the vast network of industry was reoriented toward the East, which had no requirements for a variety of consumer goods, but only for factory equipment, power stations, and heavy machinery. The plan called for an increase of production in engineering of over 90 per cent in five years from 1948. In addition, the boycott of Jugoslavia

had stopped the sources of some important raw materials
such as copper and lead. It had imposed a new orientation
while Russia had not entirely made up for the failure of the
crops of 1947. It appeared to the public that the economy
had taken a one-way street. All organs of the Party, the
state, and even the workers' own organizations urged more
and more production while the returns diminished. Slansky
was busy purging the Party, management, and office personnel of elements whose distaste for work under the existing
conditions served as foci of dissatisfaction. But the wholesale purge deprived the right places of the right men to the
detriment of production. Short of other incentives, the
workers had to be frightened into yielding to the whirlwind
of production by some spectacular warning such as the Rajk
or Kostov trials. Slansky had fixed his eye on a man long
before, a godsend who embodied the two-horned devil of
nationalist and cosmopolitan. He was Vladimir Clementis,
Minister of Foreign Affairs.

Clementis had been a lawyer in Slovakia and a Communist in the between-war years. He came from a Lutheran
Slovak family in which pan-Slavism and strong nationalism
were ingrained but not coupled with anti-Czech feelings.
When Czechoslovakia had collapsed, he had fled to Russia
but had not stayed there. Instead, he had proceeded to the
West and joined Benes and Jan Masaryk in London. After
liberation, Clementis had become the Communist watchdog
in the Foreign Ministry as deputy to Masaryk until he had
taken over the latter's place. Thus Clementis was a bourgeois by profession, a nationalist by tradition, and a cosmopolitan since he had learned in London to like the West
and had been charmed out of his morose distrust of outsiders. Moreover, he was guilty of the capital crime of
having doubted Stalin's infallibility at the time when Stalin
had tried to accommodate himself to Hitler. But Gottwald
was fond of Clementis and rightly suspected that Slansky's
campaign against Clementis was actually aimed at sapping
his own position.

In 1948, Clementis was in New York at the United Nations when the American press began to print rumors from Europe that he would soon be demoted. Vyshinsky ostentatiously walked arm in arm with him in the corridors of the U.N. to encourage him and to dispel the rumors. Clementis returned home, where he learned from the papers that he had resigned his office. Yet Gottwald still had enough power to protect him from the worst. Not until 1951 was Clementis arrested.

However, Stalin by then had instituted what was later branded the cult of personality, creating replicas of himself in the satellites, totalitarian dictators who ruled over Party and government, uniting in their persons both sources of power. Stalin held at the time that cosmopolitanism, that is, sympathy with the West, was a greater danger than nationalism. Typical cosmopolitans were the Jews, with their ties to Israel, a country which, in Stalin's view, had become a tool of American imperialism. His choice for Czecho-Slovakia thus fell on Gottwald rather than on the Jewish Slansky. But Gottwald had to pay the price of sacrificing his friend, Clementis. A truly peculiar trial was held in which both Clementis and Slansky, the latter having administered the former's downfall, were condemned to death. Other defendants had originally been arrested for having conspired to liquidate Slansky. Now that the tables were turned, they still had to stand trial for their lives; but they were accused of having conspired with Slansky to liquidate Gottwald.

The charge contained all the sins in the Communist book. But this time the fact was stressed that eleven of the fourteen defendants were Jewish, and Zionism was one of the sins held against them. The trial ended in death sentences for eleven defendants and long-term prison sentences for three. As usual, wholesale arrests followed the trial, this time mostly of Jews. The main "cosmopolitan" victims had been associated with the measures which had caused economic turmoil and as such were hated by the public. Latent anti-Semitism also contributed to public approval of the purge and made Gottwald somewhat more popular than he had been before.

4.

While the Kremlin was deciding whom to invest with the sole power in each satellite to carry out its policies, the local Communists prepared to break the political forces which could create obstacles to those policies. First on the list was opposition to the collectivization of the farms.

The peasant on the whole had only the parish priest to turn to for advice. The priest presided over the most significant moments of his life—deaths, births, and weddings—and gave solemnity to the peasant's rest from toil by reflecting for him on the meaning of life and suffering. It would have been preposterous for the Communists to believe that a party secretary could fill the role of a priest. Actually, they had no such illusions. They intended first to change the peasant to a worker educated on Party literature before expecting him to turn atheist. The peasant was now to be herded into collectives, and his probable resistance had to be deprived of the support of the clergy, which could harden it and enlarge its scope until he would oppose everything the Communists stood for. In order to prevent such a development, the Communists resolved to remove the priest from his flock once they were outside his church. He himself was to put his loyalty to the Communist state before his service to God.

Agricultural reform was one reason for the Communist campaign against the influence of the church on political thinking and action. The Cold War also made it imperative to compel the church to cut its ties with the West.

The anti-Soviet West was receiving inspiration from the Vatican for a crusade against a godless ideology. The Papacy rose again to a leading spiritual power after two centuries of decay. Of the Great Powers before World War I, it had guided only the government of Hapsburg Austria. Anti-church governments had ruled even over two important Catholic countries, France and Italy. Before World War II, the Pope had gladly accepted a Concordat from Mussolini and had hastened to be the first in recognizing Hitler's regime and making it respectable. By the end of the war, however, the Vatican appeared to be realizing its alleged plan, whispered to have Roosevelt's blessing, to unite the European continent under the aegis of the church. The enfranchisement of women gave a fresh impulse in that direction. Elections in France, Italy, and West Germany returned Catholic democratic parties to power. Indeed, not since the Middle Ages had Europe been so close to unity as at the time of this Catholic renaissance. Even Labourite England refrained from encouraging the German Social Democrats, while the United States openly supported the Catholic parties, participating so actively in the electoral campaign in Italy as to stop only at the ballot box.

This was the way the Catholic church and Communism became prime enemies. Their clash ignited a sinister spark in Hungary, rather a surprise to those who knew that political Catholicism had had little popular support in that country. For centuries Hungary had struggled under Calvinist leadership for national independence from the Catholic Hapsburgs. The fall of the Hapsburgs had ended the political significance of Calvinism, although, as the last flicker of a fading tradition, independent Hungary had still had Calvinist Horthy as its Regent and mostly Protestant prime ministers. But when it now came to opposing Communism, the Catholic church rose to leadership of all denominations in the nation.

The personality of the head of the Hungarian church, Cardinal Joseph Mindszenty, had much to do with the world-wide reverberations of the church-state controversy.

Freshly enthroned as Archbishop of Esztergom and Prince Primate of Hungary, he was fired by the zeal of a crusader and by the vision of martyrdom. Even directly after the war, when a genuine coalition government was working for the realization of a democratic program, he had filed a protest with the President of the Republic, taking exception to the proclamation of the republic by Parliament. He protested as Prince Primate of Hungary, whose predecessors had bestowed royal power on the kings at their coronations. He also protested against the ways in which the land reform had been carried through and the war criminals prosecuted.

The real battle started, however, when the government introduced a bill to nationalize all parochial schools. There were more than 5,000 of these, of which 2,800 were Catholic; they were run by churches but supported by the state. The church had, of course, always fought for the right to educate the youth. Mindszenty took up the fight with great fervor and bitterness, as if it were the first time a state had contested the right of the church to educate, although the bill provided for compulsory religious instruction in the nationalized schools. The bill further stipulated that the teachers would be taken over by the state at higher salaries. Cardinal Mindszenty insisted on a general settlement of the state-church issue, demanding the restitution of the church estates and freedom of Catholic associations and church publications.

When Parliament approved the bill, Mindszenty promptly excommunicated all Catholic members who had voted for it. He had pastoral letters attacking the government read in all churches. On December 26, 1948, he was arrested on a charge of treason, on the grounds that he was conspiring to overthrow the democratic order of the republic and to restore the monarchy.

During the months of investigation the public abroad worked itself into a state of excitement bordering on hysteria, expecting at any moment an uprising in Hungary. Some Hungarians expected America to declare war and liberate the Cardinal. Mindszenty may have expected both.

When neither came about and he had to stand trial before a Communist court, Mindszenty decided that the moment did not call for martyrdom but rather for a struggle to save the faithful.

The trial was an anticlimax, and it disappointed the public abroad which had expected the Cardinal at least to launch a shattering tirade against Communism. The press speculated that the Communists might have drugged the Cardinal or used other devious devices to break him. But Mindszenty was not a broken man. He preserved the dignity of a Prince Primate and confessed only to facts, denying that they constituted a conspiracy. He acknowledged his guilt, but with a significant reservation. He stated that if it was the law (which he would not admit since he had contested the legality of the regime) that what he had done constituted a crime, he could be considered guilty. The official organ of the Vatican, the *Osservatore Romano*, in contrast to the world press, accepted the Cardinal's defense as genuine and correct. He had never made a secret of his monarchist sentiments, nor that he would have liked the monarchy restored. He had written a letter to the American Ambassador to Hungary telling him that the present Hungarian regime could be overthrown with help from abroad and had talked with him about the prospects of a restoration. The same project was also the subject of his conversation with the pretender to the Hungarian throne. But he denied any part in a conspiracy, and no proof of a conspiracy was rendered in court. The Cardinal was condemned to imprisonment for life.

The struggle by the Communist governments against the church in the field of politics, particularly in trying to isolate it from the West, proved to be a protracted one. The method depended on the peculiar position of the church in each country, but the purpose was the same—to subject the church to the state. The non-Catholic churches had stood traditionally in a different relation to the state. They bent more easily under pressure, as long as the autonomy of their faith was not violated.

While the state-church controversy proceeded, an event took place which marked a turning point in the Cold War—the war in Korea. This came to pass inevitably after Russian troops had evacuated the north and the Americans the south, since the ruling political forces in both parts wanted unity exclusively on their own terms. Provocation from both sides preceded the aggression by the North Koreans, equipped with arms from the Russians.

America's prestige was such, and fear of Soviet aggression so great, that United States diplomacy succeeded in enlisting the United Nations on its side to contain the aggression. The Russians limited themselves to going as far as they could without letting the war develop into a general one. They therefore stopped supplying the North Koreans adequately before they had completed their initial victory over the South. But the Chinese Communists had no such concerns. A Chinese involvement would not necessarily entail a general conflict, nor would it provoke the use of atomic bombs for the second time against an Asiatic people. The Chinese had a vital interest in keeping Korea out of hostile hands, since Japan had formerly fanned out from Korea to occupy the cities of the Chinese continent. The Chinese warned America through India that they would intervene if the fight progressed beyond the 38th parallel, and when the line was crossed, they did so. Russia had to supply China's armies and cede Korea to Chinese influence. The war cost China little and organized it into a military power.

The Korean War had one result of inestimable value. It proved that war could be localized, which had been considered rather doubtful after the experience of two world wars. It also demonstrated a method of reducing such conflicts to a trial of strength between limited forces. A further result was the appearance of such powers as India and China as a third force, heralding the end of the polarization of powers with its imminent danger of a general war. It should not be left unnoticed that the ascendancy of such non-Christian powers as India and China induced the Vatican to extricate itself from the crusade against Communism, although it remained as hostile to it as before. But, while Russia, following a possible overthrow of its Communist regime, might revert to Christianity, India and China would be non-Christian no matter under what regime. The Vatican may have thought, like Toynbee, that Russia might someday become the last outpost of Western civilization.

Meanwhile, the Communists in Czecho-Slovakia aimed at transforming the Catholic church into a state church separate from Rome. Its nucleus had existed since 1920, when the revival of the Hussite spirit had created a mass movement away from Rome. The results had been a Czechoslovakian church, conversions to Protestantism, and a loosening of all formal religious bonds—results which had led the government to break off diplomatic relations with the Vatican. The Communists now found themselves up against a Prince of the Catholic church who could not be accused of being a reactionary nor of lukewarm resistance to Nazism. Joseph Beran, the Archbishop of Prague, had been in concentration camps under Nazism, and he was no less eager for martyrdom than Mindszenty. The battle was fought over the Communist demand that the clergy take an oath of loyalty to the regime. When Beran rejected it, the Communists launched a "Catholic Action" movement of priests and laymen ready to take the oath. The movement was led by a priest who remained in the cabinet in spite of a papal prohibition against priests being actively engaged in politics. Its members invited and received excommunication.

After Parliament passed a law enrolling the clergy in the civil service, the government appointed high church officials and authorized excommunicated priests to read the Mass.

The Czech Communists refrained from staging a trial, but they interned the Archbishop in a monastery and arrested recalcitrant priests, especially in Slovakia, where the opposition of the faithful was strongest. By 1951, four Czech bishops and most of the lower clergy had taken the loyalty oath; the rest were sent to labor camps together with the inmates of monasteries.

The state prevailed, but it could come to no agreement

with the authentic church, as it had in Hungary after Mind-szenty's condemnation and also in the biggest and most Catholic country, Poland. The church in Czecho-Slovakia bowed to force but remained adamant in the face of schism.

In Poland, where Catholicism had been historically a badge of identification for a Pole, the ascension of Cardinal Wyszynski in 1949 as Primate of Poland improved prospects for an agreement between state and church. The Arch-bishop issued a message stating that he was not interested in politics. In answer to it, the government declared it ex-pected no more from the church than that it refrain from hostility to the government. The Communists were fearful of running into a solid block of national resistance by mis-handling the church, and they entered into an agreement in 1950 that left intact the right of the church to religious administration, as well as its jurisdiction in internal church appointments. The church also retained its university at Lublin.

Nevertheless, the Cardinal forbade the clergy to join the Communist-sponsored peace movement and was promptly accused of vitiating the agreement. The Vatican also put difficulties in the way of reaching agreements by its decree of 1949 forbidding a Catholic to enlist in the Communist Party under pain of excommunication.

Jugoslavia had an old score to settle with the Catholic church as a consequence of the Croatian clergy's deep in-volvement in the mass murders and mass conversions of Orthodox Serbs. Strong public pressure from the Serbs compelled the government to try Archbishop Stepinac, who had endorsed the Ustasha regime and had failed to protest the crusade against Orthodox Christians and Jews. He was condemned to sixteen years' imprisonment.

After Tito broke with Moscow he became sensitive to American interest in the fate of the Archbishop, since it appeared that his confinement was making it difficult for the Truman administration to garner public support for aid to Jugoslavia. Tito finally released him in 1951, al-though he refused to reinstate him in the office of the Archbishop of Zagreb. Hostility flared up again when the Vatican granted the Cardinal's hat to Stepinac in 1952. The result was a break in diplomatic relations with the Vatican. Tito then set up an interfaith organization of all denominations, which the Vatican and the Croatian bishops condemned, so that relations remained strained. As in the satellite countries, the regime insisted on subjecting the Catholic church to the state in the same way that it had successfully imposed itself on the other churches.

In Rumania and in Czecho-Slovakia, the governments solved the problem of the Uniats summarily. The Hapsburgs in the eighteenth century had persuaded the Orthodox clergy in Transylvania and Ruthenia to accept the Pope as head of the church without changing the liturgy and the status of the clergy. The governments now compelled these so-called Uniats to return to the Orthodox church, which the Soviets had made a subsidiary of their political armory. The Roman Catholics in Rumania were all Hungarians and Germans. The government cut their ties with the Vatican, imprisoned the bishops and clergy who resisted, and finally brought the Uniats together with the other churches to sponsor the world peace movement.

The Serbian Orthodox church had been a national church. Resistance to the government issued only from its opposition to the multinational character of Yugoslavia and to Communist encroachment on the religious affiliations of the youth. Bulgaria, in its turn, called a national convention of the Orthodox church, which elected a Bulgarian patriarch, making the church a national one.

The Protestant churches complied with their governments' tutorship much more readily than did the Catholics. Their ties to the West were loose, and their political ambitions slight. But government interference with the appointments of bishops, and heavy pressure on them to take political stands, provoked resistance. This was quickly overcome by arrests in Hungary. In Czecho-Slovakia the government favored the Protestants, while in Rumania it moved cautiously, since the Protestants were Magyars, and it did not want a nationality problem on top of other much graver and more substantial difficulties. Bulgaria handled the tiny Protestant sects brutally for their past connections with the Anglo-Saxon world. English and American missionaries had once contributed to the cultural revival of the Bulgarians, and the Protestant sects, with 20,000 members, still preserved their heritage.

The Muslims in Jugoslavia had opposed no regime in the past, remaining true to their traditional opportunism. But in Albania, a Muslim state, the government wiped the slate clean to insure that the faithful would be under Communist leadership. It ruthlessly liquidated anti-Communist Muslim elements and put the rest to work propagandizing for Communism among the Muslim peoples.

The depleted Jewish communities presented no political problem for the governments in any Eastern country.

5.

In reply to British Prime Minister Attlee, who had charged the Soviet Union with increasing its armed strength rather than disarming, Stalin stated to the correspondent of *Pravda* on February 16, 1951:

. . . the USSR could not possibly have coupled its vast industrial and agricultural development schemes with the maintenance of a large army and the development of an armament industry.

And indeed, the satellite countries fell victim to the decision of the Kremlin not to engage their heavy industry in manufacturing arms to the detriment of large-scale construction programs. Stalin remembered how America had been able during the war to produce for war needs and still keep its population amply supplied with goods. He thought he could now do the same if he switched the great part of the burden of war production to the satellites. He went so far as to supply them with tractors rather than letting their heavy industry dedicate its efforts to manufacturing tractors instead of arms.

This stroke of genius, by which the Soviets developed peace-time industries while letting the satellite states take care of emergency armament needs, heaped misery on these countries, already bled white under the pressure of an industrialization race.

But in the end, the Kremlin paid a high price for its cleverness. As Communism became equivalent to the plans and the plans were eventually discovered to be serving the military might of a foreign power, indifference to work and disillusionment with Communism mounted even inside the Party.

The shift to armaments required an upward revision of the plans in 1951. In 1952, Poland spent 72 per cent more on defense than in the previous year. The production of the Czech Skoda works was raised by 38 per cent in relation to the year before. Hungary began to build small destroyers for the Soviet navy. Both Hungary and Rumania hastily built military installations and airfields.

Industrialization at the fast rate the plans had set meant immense suffering for the people, but the fact that their heavy industry was busy turning out arms and military equipment, instead of capital goods which would later produce goods for consumption, intensified their hardships.

Three-fourths of the investment provided for in the plans went into nonconsumer industries. Production of bauxite, a raw material for aluminum, had grown in Hungary by 1951 to twenty times the prewar output. By that time the satellites were producing 25 per cent more coal than in 1938 and doubling the production of steel and electric power. The most backward countries set the most ambitious goals. Bulgaria was slated to reach, in 1953, 682 per cent of the productivity of its heavy industry before the war. In Rumania, the last year of the Five-Year Plan was to produce 1 million tons of pig iron as against 50,000 before the war, 1,250,000 tons of steel as against 100,000, and 8 million tons of coal as against 2 million. The oil wells had suffered extensive damage so that their prewar output had first to be reached.

Forced industrialization required increasing manpower. Hungary needed 650 thousand additional workers, Czecho-Slovakia 482 thousand. Peasants had to be directed into towns, a process that went to the bottom of the problem of the agricultural surplus population. Czecho-Slovakia had no such problem, since it had been advanced in industrialization before the Communists took over, and consequently it had to look for other sources of manpower. The Czech government took office and store clerks from their desks and counters and sent them to the factories. But the influx to the towns created the problem of accommodating the newcomers. The plans had little or no money for building apartment houses, so that the governments resorted to the inhuman means of exchanging populations. The middle class, made idle by nationalization, was compelled to leave their houses and apartments for designated places in the countryside while the newcomers moved into their places.

Manpower shortages solved, the governments next had to create incentives to work. Since they paid for the importation of raw materials and equipment needed to fulfill the plans with food and other commodities, shortages of the goods that had been most abundant suddenly appeared in the countries concerned. Rumania lacked petroleum, Poland coal, and all countries food for home consumption. If the worker was unable to buy what he wanted and had the money to pay for, he could not be expected to show extra zeal at work. As a substitute for commodities, the Communists infused the spirit of socialist competition into the assembly lines. The Stakhanovites, the boys and girls who outdid the norm of per capita production, became the *élite* in society, but were hated and isolated by their co-workers. The output of shockworkers demonstrated that the working norms could be raised, and raised they were. This served a double purpose. Not only was production increased, but also salaries were cut, since the worker was now supposed to produce more for the same wages in order to reach the norm. As the rhythm of the work accelerated, the danger of inflation grew. More and more people earned salaries, but they could not spend their money on account of the shortage of commodities. To prevent inflation from running out of control, the governments repeatedly carried through currency reforms, exchanging new currency units for five, ten, and fifty of the old ones, according to the status of the bearer. To discourage the practice of saving, they set a high exchange rate on the saved amounts, while current wages received a sensibly low rate. By this measure, the governments simply robbed the people of that part of their past salaries which remained unspent because the government had nothing to offer in the way of goods.

Strain, overwork, and a stagnating standard of living went hand in hand with the development of the plans. An immense apparatus of propaganda was mobilized to overcome the steadily growing indifference, first to the quality, then to the quantity of work accomplished. The editorials of the Party, declared "must reading," daily hammered away at the barriers of distrust and indifference. They told the people that the plans were for the building of a socialist country and for the strengthening of the peace bloc against the forces of imperialism and warmongering. Seminars instructed key Party men in promoting the plan and infusing enthusiasm into each and every cog of the synthetic leviathan by giving them to understand that the tiniest contribution was as indispensable as the calculations of the grand planners. A totalitarian orchestra composed of all media of communication worked up a simultaneous presentation of victories in the Far East and dangers in the immediate neighborhood. They fed the working people dazzling statistics on the fulfilled plans, and then admonished them on the tasks that remained to be completed.

In addition to the usual compulsory meetings where Party officials announced that the standard of living was rising, sudden meetings interrupted the work for protests against this or that. Support for the North Koreans and the

Chinese during the Korean War put an additional burden on satellite economies, since Russia shifted onto them as much of it as was humanly possible. The war was also used as a whip for more and faster results. Moreover, collections took place among the workers in the form of pledges from their wages for North Korean orphans, which amounted to an additional taxation. It appeared that things were going rather well in faraway places and might go well for themselves in the distant future, but right then and there everything was miserable. Of course, the workers took the improved public services for granted, the paid vacations, the pleasant resting places, and the benefits for children and pregnant women. But pressure from above made the doctors into instruments of compulsion for keeping people at work. The lack of medicine and beds, overwork, fear, and shortages of goods invalidated the benefits and turned those services into mere auxiliaries of the compulsion to work more.

No matter where a worker turned with a complaint, he faced men whose sole duty was to watch that the section of the plan assigned to them was smoothly fulfilled and, if possible, overfulfilled. The representative of the union in the factory differed from the management only in that he checked directly on production, seeing to it that the workers fell into line, while the management was responsible for the use of materials and equipment, and for the accounting. In this environment, the worker had one weapon left, to report sick. Absenteeism began to take on such alarming proportions that the slacking worker was liable to be branded a saboteur. The fight against absenteeism remained unsuccessful in even the best-rewarded sector, mining, and the shortage in skilled miners made coercive measures unsuccessful. To send a miner to prison would deprive the mine of a worker who could not be replaced. High wages and extraordinary benefits proved to be no incentive to these men, who resented the slave-labor conditions. Recruiting was no more successful because the novices ran away. Soldiers were commandeered into the mines, and forced laborers were assigned to them; but they impeded rather than advanced production. Hungary evolved a new way to combat absenteeism. The sick worker was assigned to a clinic near the factory, and if he was able to do even reduced work he was shipped to the workshop or mine, accomplished any work the factory doctor allowed him to do, and was then returned to the hospital. Since the absentee was no longer allowed a rest-cure at home, he was not eager to remain sick. In Czecho-Slovakia, the Prime Minister in his rage against absenteeism obliquely accused those doctors who prescribed hospital care of a conspiracy with the absentees to sabotage production. He also reproached the doctors for being more concerned with the individual than with the interests of the community.

The great orchestra designed for generating enthusiasm proved unable to suppress the people's fatigue with work, slogans, high objectives, and the example set for them by that great mentor of the little nations, the Soviet Union. At this point, the Soviets provided further guidance. Slack working discipline became punishable by law. Corrective work, as a punishment, gave birth to the institution of labor camps, so convenient for sending forced workers to places in dire need of labor. The corrective camps were far from a perfect solution, since they were comprised of skilled workers who would have been of better use elsewhere. But forced labor appeared to be a perfect institution to get cheap, unskilled work performed by political prisoners, the number of which swelled as slackening interest became a punishable crime and as purges periodically weeded out hostile elements and those in the highest hierarchy blamed for the mistakes of yesterday. Ambitious public work projects, such as the Danube–Black Sea Canal in Rumania, awaited the forced laborers; also huge new steel plants around Kosice in Slovakia, Dunapentele in Hungary, Dimitrov in Bulgaria, and Nova-Huta in Poland. In each country the camps harbored between 100 and 200 thousand inmates (Bulgaria had about half these numbers). Poland and Czecho-Slovakia preferred large camps, the rest of the satellites found it more practical to have small ones in many places. Jachimov, in Czecho-Slovakia, was a place apart. Its uranium mines belonged exclusively to the Russians by an agreement made at the liberation of the country. The Russians had intended at that time to dismantle a huge, new synthetic gas plant at Most, built by the Nazis, as enemy property, but they accepted the uranium mines instead.

The plans openly coordinated the production of the satellites with that of the Soviet Union after January, 1949, when the Council for Mutual Economic Aid countered the Marshall Plan. Moscow took over the direction of satellite economies as part of a huge single economic unit of the Soviet bloc from Pilsen to Vladivostok. It appeared soon after, however, that the unit could not be made self-sufficient, and particularly that the Soviet Union was unable to supply some key industrial raw materials and equipment. As a consequence, they had to be bought in the West. But the Marshall Plan countries agreed not to export to the Soviet bloc a long list of goods labeled as strategic, so that subterfuge had to be resorted to by buying through Austria or Switzerland as "fronts," a process which raised the price considerably. Russia acted mostly as a clearing house for the Soviet orbit, disposing of goods grown or manufactured within the bloc.

The new economic orientation of the satellites was mirrored in their foreign trade. The Soviet share in it grew to 80 per cent in 1952. Soviet-Czech and Soviet-Hungarian trade increased about five times between 1947 and 1950; Soviet-Polish and Soviet-Bulgarian trade doubled. Interbloc commerce increased in the same period from 58 to 100 per cent.

However, while America brought pressure to bear on the Marshall Plan countries for an integration of the European economy, the "Molotov Plan" excluded the integration of satellite economies by working out blueprints for developing each satellite as an economic unit. No substantial deviation from this pattern was provided for in the individual plans, not even for such a compelling reason as the lack of

raw materials. Hungary, sh
immense steel production pr
confirmed the general rule.
Treaty of Economic Cooperati
tries in Silesia, which was split
It provided for a power plant
Slovakia supplied electric curren
in Hungarian Transdanubia, and
gary with Transylvanian natural
industrialization developed in th
rather than built up the economi
federation in the future.

The industrialization rapidly ch   composition
of the population in all these countries. The proportion of
the populace engaged in industries swelled, as did the urban
inhabitants. Agriculture became the stepchild of the plans,
receiving only a fraction of the total investment. Very many
former producers of food now turned into consumers. The
Soviet Union stepped in as a supplier of food, especially of
grain, even for countries which had themselves previously
based their foreign trade on the export of this commodity.

In contrast to industry, which had been completely so-
cialized, private property in agriculture remained predominant. This split in the economy was a serious failure for a
totalitarian Communist system since its aim had to be state
ownership of both. However, the Soviet Union itself had
failed to bring the socialization of agriculture into step with
industry. The satellites were at least supposed to advance
to the stage at which their great model had finally arrived,
but the drive met stubborn and bitter resistance by the
peasantry. Ruthless collectivization might have produced
serious famine as it had in Russia, and perhaps it would
have come to such a policy, regardless of the horrible results,
but for the presence of the threat of war. The Soviets could
at present afford to risk neither a famine nor a revolt among
their satellites.

But the struggle to eradicate the anomaly of private
farms in countries with total socialist ambitions went on,

er the food supply became endangered,
tion when the danger had passed or when
siderations demanded it. Failure to produce
ood led to purges against leftist deviationists for
collectivization; slowness in collectivization was
amed on rightist deviationists. Agriculture was a sore
spot for politicians and bureaucrats as well as for their victims, the peasants.

The easy way to gain the peasants' consent to cooperatives would have been to make them attractive. In some
countries, such as Bulgaria, cooperatives were an old tradition. But after a promising start, the peasants began to
resist collectivization when it appeared only to serve the
government in enlarging and collecting compulsory deliveries. Bulgarian collectivization charted a haphazard
course, going by leaps and bounds for a time, only to slow
down abruptly or stop altogether due to poor results or
resistance. But the ambition of the Bulgarian Communists
to conform entirely to the Soviets shortened the respite
periods, which were at times imposed on them by the Russians in order to make up for shortages. By 1952, 50 per
cent of the arable land belonged to collectives.

Instead of making the cooperatives attractive, the Communists chose to force them on the peasants by making private farming as unattractive as possible. They invented
seemingly inexhaustible means of harassing the individual
farmer, starting with carrying class warfare into the villages.
This was the campaign against the kulak, or "rich farmer,"
which, if the need for a scapegoat was urgent, ended in
sending him to jail and confiscating his property. To
smooth the transition to the collectives, different gradings
were established. In the mild initial grade, the members
did no more than coordinate their sowing plans and work
together with machines. In the extreme type, land and livestock all went into the common pool except for a strip of
land for gardening and some livestock, and each member
received his share in the profit according to the labor he had

contributed. In between were one or more transitional stages.

As in Russia, the state-owned machine stations operated tractors, combines, and cultivators, and performed a variety of missions, political and economic, in the collectives. They controlled the crops, set and collected the quota for deliveries, and played an important role in carrying out government-sponsored shifts from grain to industrial crops. In Rumania and Bulgaria steppe-lands were reclaimed by irrigation and protection by shelter-belts of trees. Oil seed planting was promoted by government grants and exemptions, cotton growing was favored in Rumania and Hungary, and rice between the rivers Danube and Theiss.

Collectivization progressed slowly in Rumania. In Czecho-Slovakia it advanced rapidly after a late start, but it spared regions where high-grade industrial farming had already been at work. By 1952, half the Czech land was in one or another type of collective, while in Hungary the figure was only 30 per cent; in Rumania, 16 per cent.

The state-owned farms in general did not live up to expectations. Their failure reflected adversely upon the final goal of collectivization, state ownership of all the land. But the unpopularity of the collectives does not mean that voluntary cooperatives will not grow up in the future. Nor does their economic failure prove that they will not produce more rationally and abundantly under free leadership and with efficient expert advice. Even though practically on a war footing with the government, agriculture still made great progress toward adjustment to the soil, improvement of fertility, shifts to more profitable crops, and more intensive cultivation. Such facts as that Poland had to import 100,000 tons of potatoes in 1952, or that Czecho-Slovakia imported a million tons of grain in the same year, had their causes in the way the industrialization and reform of agriculture were planned and executed. It may sound surprising, but it is true nevertheless, that the peasantry suffered far less than the industrial workers through all the zigzags of economic policy. The exploitation of industrial workers, although the dictatorship was exercised in their name, can be compared only with that of the years of early capitalism.

Jugoslavia resolved to break a different path after she had been excommunicated by the Soviet bloc. Years of agony, hesitation, and theorizing finally crystallized into a decision not to return to capitalism and a Western type of democracy, but to avoid the salient mistakes of Stalinism. Jugoslavia was to be a combination of socialism with democracy, actively neutral in foreign policy. Tito had his great moment as he started an experiment with a more far-reaching significance than any of his prior ambitions. New countries, especially in Asia, were groping to find ways of lifting their standards of living by industrialization while avoiding a new type of colonialization by foreign capitalism or Communism. Socialism combined with nationalism had a strong appeal to former colonies. Tito offered them leadership and guidance in both respects.

Fortunately for Tito's Jugoslavia, the West European countries quickly recognized the importance of the Jugoslav defection from the Soviet bond. It weakened the Soviets and also challenged the satellites to follow Tito's lead. The West European governments rushed to Tito's aid until the American government could act on its own recognition of the advantages of keeping Jugoslavia alive and away from Moscow, regardless of the regime. The anti-Communist coloring of the power conflict with the Soviet Union faded when America began to support Communist Jugoslavia with food, raw materials, machinery, and eventually arms.

But Jugoslavia was determined to follow its own brand of Communism. First, Tito carried through his program of decentralization of the state administration, with the intention of dissolving a bureaucracy which tended to identify the state with itself. Decentralization was also to bring the state and Party organizations back into closer touch with the masses of the people, and to reverse the direction from which inspiration to action came. In the past bureaucratic omniscience had decided what the people needed. The new Jugoslav constitution invested the constituent republics with much of the authority that had been concentrated in the federal government. This reform weakened the central bureaucracy and brought the administration into contact with local requirements.

The government also decentralized the management of industry, by establishing factory councils which elected their managements and controlled them, setting the wages and the price of goods produced. The workers were to share in the profits. Factories in one industry formed a higher unity, and regional councils, elected by the factory councils, had their own managerial board entrusted with a wider range of planning, advising and supervising. The general managers of these councils were to be appointed by the governments of the constituent republics.

Tito also changed the Soviet-model Parliament. He replaced the second chamber of nationalities with a chamber of "producers," the members of which were elected by those actively engaged in producing material goods. The voters participated in primaries, but opposition lists were not admitted. This gap still divided the Jugoslav Parliament from its Western counterparts. The one-party system was superior to the Western division of membership into governing and oppositional sections, said the late Moshe Piade who, in 1946, insisted in an interview with the author:

In the West, they think a government composed of the party or parties returned in the majority by a free election is the realization of the principle of a government of the people and by the people. It isn't. A true realization of democracy comes only when all parties returned by the elections participate in the government. Of course, parties which refute the fundamental issues and principles of the state must be excluded, not only from participating in the government but also from taking part in the elections. But for these elements, every member of Parliament must share responsibility for the administration. A sacrosanct opposition is ridiculous. The opposition should not be limited to barking principles or mouthing demagogy, because lack of responsibility makes it too easy a game. Instead, they should work vigorously to get principles through and to find in the coalition conferences partners who agree with them. The voters should not be frustrated by excluding critical members from responsibility. Criti-

cism must be made constructive by allowing it to contribute to molding government decisions. Only an all-party government is democratic because it is made up of all those elected by the people.

Tito and other Jugoslav friends of Piade in the leadership
of the Party probably held the same view. Tito did not
restrict decentralization to the state administration but extended it to the Party as well. Each constituent republic
had its own Party, independently applying general principles
to the given local situation. It was, of course, the national
Party that laid down the principles to follow. The Party
itself changed its role in the coalition front behind which
it had been governing. The Front was now to be the active
force in directing government policies, while the Party limited itself to inspiration and advice.

Tito took a step that was one of his most effective blows
against the satellite parties when he abolished the privileges
of Party members. These manifold privileges had developed a hierarchy in which the ordinary members simply
assumed the role of the lower nobility, while the bigwigs
became the aristocracy. They lived among themselves in
splendid isolation in confiscated villas. They had their own
schools and special stores which sold goods unavailable in
the same quality to a lesser mortal. This privileged status
of the Party hierarchy became one of the most resented
abuses, particularly because it threatened to become a
hereditary institution. The children of the high Party bureaucracy had first priority in the universities, which automatically made them candidates for high positions. However, the privileges were counterbalanced by purges that
toppled heads from one day to the other and turned the
victims' families into untouchables.

Since he was only trying to reform Soviet Communism,
Tito stuck to its basic principles. He proceeded with the
original plans for industrialization in the face of the dis-
ruptive effects of the Soviet bloc's boycott which set development back by years. Yet the achievements were remarkable, especially in the field of heavy industry and communications. His agricultural policy failed, however, and it did

so spectacularly. For when he tried to loosen his grip on the peasants and to stop coercion, the result was a mass flight from the collectives. But Tito still held the principle of collectivization to be indispensable to a socialist state, realizing that until the peasant becomes a salaried worker he remains a foreign body in totalitarian socialism. The alternative was to accept a democratic economy with most of the industry and communications run by the state, and private farming dominant in agriculture. This, Tito and Titoism rejected. He discarded some of the most unpopular features of Soviet Communism such as the machine stations and let the cooperatives acquire the machines, abolished compulsory deliveries, and introduced democracy into the cooperatives by giving them the right to elect their managements and set their own policies.

On the other hand, Tito made it as disadvantageous as he could for the peasants to leave the collectives, though he allowed it in theory. But nevertheless, the peasants fled the collectives and went back to individual farming. By 1954, of the almost 25 million acres of arable land only 1½ million remained in collectives.

6.

The course of life in the satellite lands took a radically new turn with the advent of the long-range economic plans, roughly in 1949. Belief in the ability of nations to gain in wealth and culture by means of industrialization through socialism had won wide support at a time when the short-range rehabilitation plans had visibly been realized. The long-range plans demanded, however, much more than enthusiasm and sacrifice. They demanded body and soul. They transformed even modest lives into a mis-

sion. The plans paid homage to an elusive god which remained as distant as ever even while the plans progressed.
The god was the Utopia promised in the future.

The plans enrolled in their service faith, ambition, knowledge, work, relaxation, sport, loneliness, family, friendship,
and society, day and night. People who visited the satellites reported that life there overshadowed the individual,
making work a calling and the slightest activity significant
since it was related to a great purpose. It was a time when
married couples came home late, tired from work and the
public duties of learning how to teach, teaching what they
learned, attending meetings, and checking on other people
to find out whether they had attended them—only to have
their children meet them at the door with the reproach that
they did not work hard enough.

What actually happened was industrialization at a wild
rate, designed to reform the country into a community of
cooperation for the common good and for the expression of
common aspirations. The objective was thus nationalization in the noblest sense of the word, and even those who
went along reluctantly identified the drive for industrialism
through socialism with the nation and its interests. During
the war Stalin had played upon national feelings. By doing
so he had found the key to the hearts of all backward peoples who now aspired to fast improvement in their way of
life through industrialization organized within the confines
of their nations.

By 1949, Moscow had given up having the Eastern peoples work on their own for their welfare and cultural advancement, cooperating with the Soviet Union and with each
other for their mutual benefit. Stalin had tightened the line.
He no longer wanted to take the chances involved in giving
any measure of freedom to a people to blaze its own trail,
even if its goal were the same as that of the Soviet's. The
local Communist chiefs spelled out the new law, which was
in Klement Gottwald's words: "There is no other road, there
can be no other law for us than the one Stalin decreed for
the Soviet people."

For many people in each satellite, that road led to forced labor camps, to the grave, or, at best, to debasement and misery. The peasants were expected to give up their land, join a collective, and become workers. For the middle class, final destruction was in store. The nation counted no more; its hymns and emblems were banished, its traditions condemned as bourgeois nationalism. The proletarian dictatorship was declared, with the principle of proletarian internationalism obliging all peoples to follow the example and directives of the Soviet Communist Party.

Industrial activity was to roll forward ever faster, but the dictators no longer cared whether it met the people's genuine aspirations. Assent was to be forced by elaborate propaganda to condition the mind—or by elimination through the police. The strength of their police showed that the regimes were aware of the magnitude of the problem. Of her military budget, Poland spent 60 per cent on the maintenance and equipment of the police force, which amounted to 200 thousand men. The strength of the police in the other countries was: 150 thousand in Czechoslovakia; 150 thousand in Rumania; 100 thousand in Bulgaria; and 20 thousand in Albania.

The children were indoctrinated to see the world as it was seen from Moscow. This started with the nursery, which was indispensable for families where both parents had to work. The Russian school system was adopted, and textbooks were exchanged for new ones translated from or modeled on the Russian. The Russian language became a required subject in the upper four grades of the eight-grade elementary schools and in the higher schools. But soon schools opened in which even the language of instruction was Russian. A Russian Institute poured out all the wisdom of the Soviets. More and more Soviet books were translated, beginning with the history of the Soviet Party. Stalin's biography, if not compulsory reading, was a compulsory purchase. Religious instruction was optional, but parents and children were discouraged therefrom. In the case of membership in the Party it was deemed unbecoming.

Children were given functions in the state plan at an early age: such assignments as collecting signatures for protests, getting out the vote, checking on the delivery of grain, assisting at meetings, and bringing class warfare into the home.

The tales the children read had as their background adults enthusiastically building huge projects, threshing the wheat energetically to produce more than expected, shock-worker parents bathing in glory—and all the while the little ones wove the same patterns into their games. And heroic tales introduced the child to the Soviet world where everything was bigger and better.

The curriculum was set in the framework of Marxism-Leninism, which rounded out a highly specialized education. The vocational schools provided skilled workers and technicians; the universities, applied scientists and professionals. Marxism-Leninism was a subject in its own right, cultivated in many branches of the national academy. There, anthropology, archeology, and a rewritten history confirmed the official philosophy through new or revised research material and arduous translations from the Russian. In basic research, stress was laid on teamwork. An astounding variety of scholarly magazines was published.

The regimes made great strides toward raising the number of students of working class origin engaged in higher learning. They encouraged adults to attend night courses and shortened the curriculum so that they might be admitted to technical colleges. This class made good, even outstanding specialists, but lacked well-rounded interests, a balanced culture, and a stimulating background upon which to draw. They stood apart from the sons and daughters of bureaucrats and the former middle class.

Scholars, writers, and artists lived at the top of the social hierarchy, like the aristocracy of the court of an absolute monarch in the old days. Only Stakhanovites equalled their prestige when they stood on the dais to accept the yearly prizes on the Soviet model. Lesser "creative" talents received precious incentives in the form of travel fellow-

ships within the Soviet orbit, or a year or two in a "home of
creation," located in former castles in magnificent surroundings. If the writer or artist was recognized by the committees on credentials, he received commissions in plenty.
The Party expected him to turn out manuscripts and art
works that lived up to their standards, and this became
increasingly difficult for an honest intellectual to do. Since
1949 socialist realism has been the rule, officially defined as
based on the observation of life, but in an optimistic vein
since art must be related to contemporary life in which
heroic efforts are at work to build a new society. In this
setting effective treatment of everyday life must aim at
general significance. Artistic form is the effective presentation of such a context. It can have national characteristics
provided that the context is socialist.

The young writers and artists put much zeal and enthusiasm into their efforts to live up to the requirements,
and they produced some remarkable works until the building of socialism transformed itself into a drive for more
work for less reward, and the plan into an idol devouring its
worshipers. But when the idol had taken the place of socialism itself and bent all institutions and functions of
society to its service, and especially when the plan showed
failures and flaws, haphazardness, and ineptitude in its execution, it became harder and harder for a writer or an
artist to recapture the initial zeal and yet remain realistic.
Thus, a great Hungarian novelist, Tibor Dery, was engaged
in writing a story, planned for three volumes, describing a
poor, alert, honest boy as he developed into a Communist
during the autocratic Horthy regime. After the second
volume was published, his critics were scandalized by the
length of time and the quantity of experience necessary for
the hero to see the light. Dery was taken to task, and an
acrimonious debate raged in which the cultural chieftain
of the Party had the last word. He made some illuminating
statements on the position of a writer in a totalitarian
society.

In the discussion which followed the publication of his novel, Dery declared that the writer endeavors to defend his right to write what he wants. But the writer has no such right in our community. He has even superior rights than that, for he is free to write the truth and nothing but the truth. We do not give safe-conduct to the writer, nor liberty to deface the truth in life. We do not admit . . . that the taste and judgment of the writer are the supreme criteria of what he has to write and the way of doing it. The taste and judgment of the writer may run counter to the judgment and interest of the people, of the state, and the Party. It is not for the state and the people to conform to his taste and judgment; it is the writer who must, by work and study, become identified with the interests of the building of Socialism.

The writers and artists kept producing lifeless and unconvincing works. Artists depicted on canvas throngs of youths bursting with vigor and anger, signing protests against bacteriological warfare. Even such subjects could have been treated artistically, but the Party held up to them the works of Soviet artists and authors, with their photographic realism which caused the artists to despair. For a change of pace, they painted portraits of the local dictators—depicting Gottwald, not with a prayerbook in hand entering St. Vitus Cathedral in 1948, but reading a book by Lenin in 1951; or showing Rakosi as a benign elderly gentleman who would not harm a fly. It was difficult to decide whom to envy or pity: the artists and authors whose works had been printed or exhibited and applauded unanimously, or the talented but uncompromising ones whom the regime subsidized but whose works never saw the light of day.

Yet, what a challenge it would have been to quench the thirst of a very fast growing public and make it capable of enjoying real art. In Poland, one in twenty had read a book before the war—after it, one in four; 10 per cent of the university students had been of working class origin before the war—now it was 60 per cent.

The regimes encouraged writers and artists to visit the factories and get acquainted with creative teamwork at first hand, but no great art issued from such contact with life. The workers distrusted these people who were pampered by the regime and who preferred not to see the truth lest it had to be told. They might have told the writers the truth had they not feared forced labor. They would then have told of the increasing working norms used as a means of cutting their real wage; the holidays and anniversaries of Soviet and domestic events which they "voluntarily" celebrated by working overtime; the comrades in Indo-China and Korea for whom they put in an hour of extra work without pay; the union representatives in the factory who kept index cards on everybody and spied on workers and management alike; the management that dared not report that the requirements were absurd, the raw materials inferior; the compulsory meetings where the speaker invited discussion but no one opened his mouth; the complaints which no one had jurisdiction to accept or forward, lest he become involved in a crime against the execution of the plan.

Because the workers kept silent, it was a surprise to the writers and artists when, during the short period of freedom in Hungary, the workers spelled out their deepest resentments. They did not refer to the misery, the exploitation, the waste, the incompetence, but to the dehumanization of their lives. A worker wrote in that brief interlude:

> People do not even notice that I exist; they hold me for a puppet. . . . How many times was I compelled to subscribe to opinions which I probably did not share at all. As those opinions changed, they expected mine to change as well. This hurts, however, more than if I were hit over the head. I also am a human being. I also have brains with which to think. I am no child. I am a grown man who gives my soul, my heart, my youth, my force to the construction of Socialism. I work more every day. Sweat is running down my body. . . . I work, but I want to be considered as an adult who has his own wishes and can think. I want to be able to tell my thoughts without fear and also want to be heard.

Or another voice out of many:

> The workers do not see things from above . . . and seeing things as they are they don't care to contribute, on top of their hard work, to discussions, with their advice, experiences, and ideas.

When the writers finally discovered how the workers in the workshops felt, they poured out such truths as these:

> Meeting these people taught me that they had, beyond their financial worries, a more painful grievance. After an hour spent with them I felt what it was, and when I left them, I knew. It was thirst. An avid thirst, overwhelming, sweeping away everything else. . . . I know what it was, I now know. It was thirst for human relationships. They had thirst to be greeted back when they greeted, that people cared for them, replied to their questions, . . . and not to treat human affairs with insensibility and dryness of the heart.

The reasons why Communism had ended up in inhumanity toward the workers were widely discussed by Polish writers. Jan Kott held that socialism had been mutilated by degrading it into a brutal and extremely costly way of industrializing backward countries. Another author, Leszek Kolakowski, thought that Communism had gone astray when it had substituted the myth of industrialization for the myth of socialism. He cited a grotesque example to illustrate his point:

> Several years ago, someone had called attention to the somber imbecility of a poster covering the walls of the Polish capital: "Tuberculosis retards reconstruction!" This poster demands the following train of thought: the struggle against tuberculosis needs to be justified as a means to accelerate construction. [In fact] anything good gained in daily life is an end itself, and needs no further justification.

Other Polish intellectuals pointed to the years 1948–49 as the turning point of Communism, when proletarian internationalism had made it obligatory in every satellite country to copy the institutions of the Soviet Union. Thereby Stalinism "did violence to the economy, to the thoughts and emotions, but also violence to the words as well." By the fiat of an autocrat, the Soviet Union demanded the first allegiance of the satellite peoples. In itself, this policy could constitute a primitive way of building and running an empire, but with the usual harmful effects. The nature of the allegiance made it insidious and unbearable. Proletarian internationalism was first of all a link between the parties in the Soviet Union and the satellite countries, and the parties in turn ran the governments. But the parties demanded total allegiance not only to Stalin, the Soviet Party, and the satellite branch office, but also to each and every action—expedient or criminal—which they performed. They asked for a total identification, with no distinction or gradation of values. A Polish writer expanded on the extent and intensity of this total identification and on the total responsibility it engendered. Wiktor Woroszylski wrote:

Let us remember what principles made us join the revolution. . . . No other ideology guaranteed so many things. As men, parts of a collectivity [the Party], we vouchsafed and took responsibility not only in our names but also in the name of the totality of people having the same convictions, the same moral principles, in the name of the collectivity of the Party. This maximum program of transforming life demanded a larger conscience than the individual conscience, a vaster concept of morality and responsibility, a sort of surpassing of our limits of action and conscience. One had to accept this burden. It sharpened the criteria, raised the expectations. . . . The revolution rejects half-hearted devotions. Therefore, when we gave ourselves to the cause of the Party with no mental reservations, we surrendered totally, as writers, accepting the name of the Party for our own. Anything we did in person was done, within the limits of our honesty and conscience, in the name of the Party, and all the Party did was done in our names. The errors, the injustices, the evil were also done in our names. In consequence even the slightest evil fell to our responsibility . . . because it was done in my name, in your name, in the name of the Party. . . .

Such values as these followed a foreign pattern, but they had ripened in the national context. When Stalin, with brutal unequivocality, superimposed on them his own alien values, he stretched to the breaking point this total identification with the principles, actions, accomplishments, crimes, and institutions of the Party. Small events revealed that even loyal Communists had been driven beyond the point of endurance.

Adolf Rudnicki, a Polish author, witnessed a soccer game at the Warsaw stadium in 1952 between a Soviet and a Polish team. In the grandstand, all seats were reserved for Polish government representatives and for people who had received tickets from the official organizations. About seventy thousand people attended the game, standing on the other side of the stadium. A Russian umpire, dressed in black, directed the game to its foregone conclusion with utter disregard for the presence of these seventy thousand people. The umpire was taking no chances. He was determined to demoralize the Polish team, to kill their courage and implant in them the conviction that their efforts had no purpose. Every minute he blew the whistle to stop the Poles, on pretexts that were transparently spurious. Rudnicki mused:

One had the impression that the injustice of his decisions incited the umpire and strengthened his will to manipulate the result against which the "truth" of the spectators appeared derisory. From his higher truth, the umpire drew his strength to affront the mass of the people. He felt on solid ground since he was sure of the support of the men seated in the grandstand—initiated people, taught by their everyday experiences of the inferiority of their lives, used to the omnipotent force that weighed on them heavily like a rock. If they wanted to live they had to look and not see. . . . In the grandstand, silence was complete and dead.

What strength the man in black had at his disposal to bear the pressure of seventy thousand people and not yield, to remain logical and inhuman in a role that requires a minimum of humanity! But his world was the product of the little umpires, reflections of the Great Umpire, who made the wheels of history turn. They live in a sort of surreality, in a hysteric daze of power. Life of any value ceases to exist beyond their circle.

Communism hurt and humiliated national and personal sentiment. Since it demanded total identification with all its tenets, it was totally rejected when the time came for a showdown. While it still maintained its hold, people were in varying degrees immune to any criticism of its doctrines and indoctrination. They could take an astounding number of contradictions, lies, and crimes as long as they believed that the Party was basically right. Once this rock loosened, people began to suspect the intentions behind even the most evident benefits. With the enthroning of proletarian internationalism came arrests, trials, executions, and the reshaping of all national values—policies which served alien purposes and were enforced only by the secret police. Eventually people came to the conclusion that what was taking place had nothing to do with their aspirations. Thereafter, they believed nothing of what the regime stated and suggested.

Communism had run its full course in the minds of the Communists and of the youth who had been educated with so much zeal to accept its teachings. The teachers themselves detected the bankruptcy of their indoctrination. They faced a wall of cold rejection in the icy eyes of mute students. In most cases, however, a tacit understanding developed between teacher and pupils, the former lecturing but apparently making no effort to sound convincing; the pupils learning their lesson as if it were a dead language. There was nothing new in this conspiracy in those areas where people had long lived under foreign domination. They had been taught in times past to hail heroes who, at best, meant little to them, and to abuse as villains those who in their hearts were venerated as great men. Indoctrination lost its effects even in the kindergarten, as a Polish writer was told by a scholar friend:

My wife and I make efforts not to counter the education of our children in the kindergarten. We don't want to disturb the happy image of the world offered to them. Anyway, what would be their image were they to know the virtues and sins of East and West? The elder one, however, more intelligent, hits on something that makes him stop and wonder. Once the child catches a lie the avalanche starts. I looked at him closely when he was singing "The Song of the Youth." He had his eyes lowered. I don't know my children: this is what you would hear in every family. Our youth is a sphinx.

The difficulties of total identification with all aspects of the regime concerned mainly the active members of the Party. The destruction of the image that the nation had woven of itself at first hurt only the intelligentsia, while the common people did not yet feel that their own uneasiness derived in final analysis from the same source. As in

1848, when liberty from foreign despotism and political
freedom were seen as the basic conditions for a decent existence, the intelligentsia and the youth unfurled the flag
of the nation, ready to hoist it at the barricades. But the
dehumanization of life that weighed so heavily on the common people was caused, as the people saw it, by something
less remote than the generalities of the learned. It was the
vicious bureaucracy that obstructed all functions and organs
which might conduct the wishes, suggestions, and aspirations of the public to the places where decisions were supposedly made. The most outlying village and factory council, or street block committee, had the sole function of
performing or checking on the correct execution of orders
from above. Modifications suggested from below would
upset the whole network of prearranged plans, in addition
to calling in question the authority and competence of the
highest places. The secret police, admitted everywhere
through the bureaucracy, took care that such attempts were
nipped in the bud. The system knew no mistakes that were
not crimes, and no complaints that were not attempts to
undermine the plan.

The system adjusted to actual situations through a series
of crises and breakdowns and jailings of scapegoats. In
Hungary, an insufficient investigation of the subsoil resulted
in the abandonment of the subway construction in Budapest
after millions had been sunk into the project. The steel
center of Stalinvaros underwent periodical crises because
the raw materials from abroad, on which it depended, could
not be perfectly coordinated to assure continuous production.

The bureaucracy, run by fear, had ears only for com-
mands from above, and none for listening to the people.
Apart from the fact that it was useless, the bureaucrats did
not dare to listen, and the people finally did not dare to open
their mouths. The isolation from each other became complete. Janos Darvas, the Minister of Culture in Hungary,
himself of peasant origin, discovered this dreadful isolation
when he visited his native district at the time of the "thaw."

A writer of distinction, he told of the shock of the experience:

> On Sunday, I made a speech on the main square of Nyiregyhaza to fifteen thousand peasants. This immense audience kept silent; one could hear neither applause nor protests. The silence was frightening and overwhelming. . . . Then I visited house after house in the village of Biri. I met the same obstinate silence. In one place, I found only the wife at home. She did not respond to my greeting. She was bent over the tub, washing her laundry. I put questions to her but she did not answer; she kept washing, washing as if she was to wash all the laundry of the world. . . . After many minutes she looked up and measured me with cold eyes. She walked to a closet, removed a piece of black bread and tossed it over to me. "Have it. They took everything from us. They emptied our barn and this is what we have in store for a whole week. How do you want me to feed my family?" Her voice was bitter and sad and accusing.

The isolation of the bureaucracy from the people was airtight in Hungary in the interests of the utmost secrecy. The top leadership kept from even the higher-ups in the hierarchy the facts and figures of their economic relations with the Soviet Union. In this respect, not all the satellites were in the same position. In Poland, the Party fought off Russian intentions to lay hands on the most important means of production as German assets. They reached an agreement under which such facts as the price of goods exchanged with the Soviets and the cost of the Soviet occupation of Poland were common knowledge. The Czecho-Slovak economy suffered because of the discrepancy between the prices the Russians charged for their supplies and those the Russians paid for articles sold to them. At one time the Russians raised their prices as a means of inflicting penalties on the Czechs for delays in deliveries. But this was an open secret, never aired publicly but disclosed to those who took part in the policy-making. Czecho-Slovakia's growing role as a supplier of capital goods to the huge Eastern market subsequently eliminated the abuses, and the expansion of heavy industry unquestionably served national interests in a land so rich in industrial raw materials. This became obvious when eventually more attention was paid to the consumers and to real wages.

Rumania lay prostrate under Russian exploitation. In Bulgaria, Russian interference was open but worked in favor of the national interest; after Jugoslavia fell into heresy, the Russians amply supplied the land with agricultural implements and power stations. Albania clearly had a colonial status, but politically this may have been the best arrangement for the moment as a defense against her covetous neighbors in Greece, Jugoslavia, and Italy.

There remained Hungary, where the Soviet-dominated plans and their misplaced focus were carefully camouflaged.

But even the plans do not tell the whole story of Soviet-Hungarian economic relations. For Hungary exported to Russia iron ore, steel, bauxite, oil, and other commodities that fell outside the scope of the plan. Both the fact and the extent of these deliveries were kept from the public as well as from those in control of the execution of the plans.

But the greatest state secret of all was probably the secret of Rakosi alone—that uranium deposits had been discovered in Hungary and that their exploitation had been reserved exclusively for the Russians. During the revolution the Vice-President of the Hungarian Atomic Energy Commission stated that he had had no official information on the existence of uranium deposits. Rumors, exaggerating the importance of the find, ran about the country, and bitterness grew that a treasure which might have lifted this poor country to wealth had been given away to the Russians through the complicity of Communist chieftains acting without power from even makeshift authorities.

If such important economic items were kept from even those next in charge by Rakosi, little of the broad lines of the plans could be disclosed to those further removed from the center. The bureaucracy worked as though blindfolded and kept its lips sealed.

As far as national feelings were concerned, the satellite regimes showed a liberal attitude toward minorities, endowing them with schools and institutions to cultivate their national languages. Scholarly efforts were directed to research into archeological and cultural data in the area rather than focusing attention on the internal development of national groups. Yet the ups and downs of the political line sometimes revived the old hatreds and prejudices. In the course of the anti-Tito campaign, both Rumania and Hungary harassed their Jugoslav minorities. Bulgaria quickly fell back into barbarism in its treatment of the Turkish minority as soon as foreign policy made it convenient. Nor did the Hungarians in Slovakia regain the full freedom to cultivate their traditions. Jugoslavia, on the other hand, became a modest center for publishing Hungarian books banished by the Stalinists. Rumania went furthest in solving the nationality question on the Soviet model. In 1952 it carved out a territory inside Transylvania in which the Szeklers could live as a compact majority and made it an autonomous region with Hungarian as the main official language. The government established Hungarian faculties at the University of Cluj.

Cultural democratization made the publishing of books and magazines a huge industry. Newspapers and magazines aped their Soviet counterparts in scholarly research, but in this instance to advantage. The range of scholarly publications was astounding. Attendance at theaters became as general as that at the movies. The publishing and staging of some of the great classics mitigated the dreary social realism of contemporary authors and playwrights. In the movies, attendance at films from the West was as much a demonstration of political or artistic preference as an escape outlet.

While the satellites vied with each other in working for the preparation of the war—trying spies allegedly parachuted in by the West or smuggled into these countries from Jugoslavia, sending tens of thousands to forced labor camps, and deporting the middle class, especially the Jews, from towns to remote villages and hamlets—the Korean War threatened to explode into an atomic war. The danger lessened toward the end of 1951 when the war stood in favor of the United Nations, but people of great influence in America still would not resign themselves to fighting local wars with limited means for inconclusive results; they advocated full-scale war and total victory over Communist China.

Subversion was openly added to the weapons of this not-so-Cold War. The Mutual Security Act empowered the President to spend up to $100 million in helping selected persons, residing in or escaping from the Soviet Union and its satellites, to form a military force in support of NATO. On the opposite front, the Moscow-inspired Peace Movement allegedly obtained 562 million signatures for a peace manifesto. Stalin stressed the vital importance of the movement in undermining hostile governments in an interview to *Pravda* in which he answered his own question, conveniently put into the mouth of a reporter. The latter inquired of Stalin whether the outcome of the struggle between warmongers and peoples would be war or peace. Stalin's reply was that the outcome would be peace if the people took the issue into their own hands, but that it would be war if the warmongers succeeded in entangling and deceiving the masses.

The United States had risen by 1951 to the height of her standing in the world as the unquestionable leader of the United Nations against Communist aggression. An American spokesman stated that there were practically no neutral governments left and that except for those held under Communist sway, the world stood firm behind the United States lead. When a second Soviet atomic blast was detected, the American press showed itself to be unimpressed by the Russian technical achievement in having manufactured atomic bombs years earlier than the experts held possible. Official sources reassured the public that a safe distance had been kept ahead of the Soviet menace, and it was hinted that America was working on an even more devastating weapon, the hydrogen bomb. But the world increasingly took cognizance of the fact that henceforth war would end in mutual destruction, and that, indeed, there would be no victor in such a war. To emphasize the stalemate, Stalin came forward again with a proposition for a five-power pact for the exclusion of war and also suggested resuming negotiations for the liquidation of Soviet Lend-Lease debts to America.

On November 16, 1951, it was announced that America had tested a hydrogen bomb. Yet, nobody was sure whether the Russians were not at the heels of the United States even in this development.

With the balance of power hinging on more and more destructive atomic and hydrogen bombs, and knowing that America was probably ahead in the race, Stalin appeared to be beset by war jitters. He launched an open appeal to the solidarity of international Communism. Stalin declared at the Congress of the Party that the Soviets needed the help of Communists abroad and that the Soviet Party would support them in turn. But he discovered a ray of hope on the dark horizon. It was in all probability a mere delusion of his decomposing brain. He saw another war in the offing, a British-Persian conflict, sparked by Persian determination to get rid of their long-term contract with the British for the exploitation of oil, and he believed that the American oil interests in the background were anxious to step in and take the place of the British. This old-fashioned rivalry between imperialist powers suggested to Stalin that a conflict for raw materials and markets might develop into war, and he predicted in the magazine *Bolshevik* that Germany, England, France, and Japan would break loose from the United States and take independent courses. He stated that the peace movement would delay but would not prevent war between the capitalist states.

The article, published in October, 1952, made many people wonder. Rumors persisted that there was tension between Stalin and his closest collaborators. An ominous broadcast by the Moscow radio, in January, 1953, confirmed the suspicion that Stalin had resolved to embark on an anti-Semitic course. It accused the Joint Distribution Committee, an American Jewish organization, of supporting espionage, terrorism, and subversive activities in a number of countries including the Soviet Union. Moscow also announced that Jewish doctors had been arrested and had confessed to causing the death of Zhdanov by false diagnosis and injurious treatment. *Pravda* reported that the authorities had unmasked rootless cosmopolitans and Jewish bourgeois nationalists in Lithuania and in the Ukraine, conspiring against the security of the state.

A few weeks later, on March 5, 1953, Moscow reported the death of Stalin.

CHAPTER NINE

The Ice Breaks

1.

> Stalin is dead. The Soviet people have suffered
> an irreparable loss. Stalin's name will be praised
> forever. He gave his life for liberating the workers
> and saving mankind from wars. His name stands
> alongside of Marx, Engels, and Lenin.

Thus Georgi Malenkov eulogized Stalin at
his funeral. As a Communist, Malenkov could pay no
higher respect to the deceased leader than to place him at
the side of the apostles of Communism. Yet his speech
sounded barren and cold to all those in whose ears still
rang the superlatives of adulation that had hallowed Stalin's
name. Malenkov, Beria, and Khrushchev appeared to be
in haste to sink the dead man in his grave and pass over
to the order of the day without a pause. The speakers were
anxious to warn the enemies within and without not to
entertain false hopes that Stalin's heritage would go to
waste in discord among his heirs.

Nevertheless, people could not help remembering that
the death of an autocrat in the past had usually set substantial changes in motion which had slowly developed another
commanding personality.

The chill of Stalin's funeral affected at least one of his
pro-consuls, Klement Gottwald of Czecho-Slovakia, who a
few days after returning home died of pneumonia.

Of the satellite dictators, Rakosi of Hungary alone ignored the hint by Stalin's heirs to get back to business and

proceeded with the mass mournings which he had ordered before he left for the funeral. Rakosi, the old Comintern hand, frowned on the program for the new era enunciated by Malenkov. According to this new program, the interests of the consumer were henceforth to have priority over heavy industry, the cult of personality would be replaced by collective leadership, and the inviolability of the rights of the individual would be established. But Rakosi did not take these statements at face value and was worried rather whether the three successors, even if they stuck together, would be equal to the task of replacing the granite figure of the short, rude despot.

In his grief and anxiety, Rakosi yielded to an irresistible impulse when he arrived back in Hungary. He admitted to his colleagues that he had somehow lost sight of the basic Communist principle that the most important value was man himself. He knew well what it meant when his deputy, Erno Gero, a staunch believer in terror as the highest incentive, appealed to the workers for a superhuman effort to fulfill the plan. It meant that human effort could not suffice to accomplish it. Shortages in resources and power were causing chaos in industry. In no satellite country had work quotas been raised as high as in Hungary, but production still lagged. Prices rose by 140 per cent from 1949 to 1952, but wages increased only 40 per cent over the same period. Not long before, even the Party bureaucracy had warned against bringing further pressure to bear on the workers and peasants, but Rakosi dismissed their concern. He knew that they could always face a resisting country more easily than a Kremlin dissatisfied with the deliveries from Hungary.

This time, however, Rakosi stood at odds with the Kremlin, who were demanding exactly what Hungary had been yearning for. Fortunately for him, he did not consider the situation in the Kremlin as stable and resolved to postpone the change to the new policy, which he detested, until the dust had settled over the fight for power between the new chiefs.

Meanwhile Czecho-Slovakia was forced to change the personnel of the high hierarchy in consequence of Gottwald's sudden death. Anton Zapotoczky, a trade union leader, became the President of the Republic and Viliam Siroky, Chairman of the Slovak Party, Prime Minister. Antonin Novotny, a faithful Moscow man, formerly secretary of the Prague district, took over the Party as its First Secretary. The Czechs thus pioneered the introduction of collective leadership in the satellites.

The Czechs had achieved staggering results in industrial development. In 1953 they produced as much steel per capita as Britain did. Industrial production increased 16 per cent from the previous year, of which 62 per cent was in capital goods. Capital goods constituted 50 per cent of all exports in 1952. At the same time, half of the farms were pressed into collectives.

Dizzy with success (to use Stalin's words concerning the Pyrrhic Communist victory over the peasant) the regime intended to turn the screws still tighter on the workers, who had put money aside because of the shortage in consumer goods. The government resorted to the drastic move of confiscating savings by introducing a new currency. Fifty units of savings were to be exchanged for one unit in the new currency.

This new addition to the workers' previous sufferings suddenly seemed intolerable. Until then they had endured their lot bitterly but without revolt. But now they sensed that a more lenient attitude was taken at the brain centers of Communism.

On June 1, 1953, the workers in the large Skoda plant, an armament factory in Pilsen near the German border, laid down their tools and rioted. The young men ran wild in the streets, stormed Party buildings, tore down red flags and posters with portraits of the Communist chiefs. The workers poured downtown and seized the city hall. The police were sent out in force and the army poised in readiness, but neither were willing to oppose the workers. Russian tanks lay not far away in East Germany, but the workers stood firm in their hold on the town and in their demand for new policies. The security police finally arrived, and a state of emergency was declared. But the government bowed to the workers' demands. It was a week before calm prevailed.

Here was a remarkable event, the first time a Communist regime had faced the open opposition of workers. For the first time also, the local police and army had proved to be unreliable if compelled to use force against the population. And finally, for the first time an uproarious protest by workers in a satellite country had turned against the Communist Party and the emblems of the Soviet Union.

But all this took place in a nation which, by merciless driving and exploitation of human energy, had accumulated enough capital to make a more lenient policy immediately effective. Czecho-Slovakia's economic expansion had a solid basis in a functioning industrial network and high-grade agriculture. The government met the crisis by reducing the price of commodities and delivery quotas in the farms and by investing more in consumer industries and agriculture instead of in heavy industry. Soon Czecho-Slovakia's stores began to fill up with goods, food became plentiful, and within a year the public was signing up on long waiting lists for refrigerators and other "luxuries."

The radio and press abroad had spread news of revolt in the satellite countries so often that the Pilsen revolt was left almost unnoticed. And truly, a more significant event soon overshadowed the Pilsen story. On June 17, East Berlin revolted.

Under the heel of Russian occupation armies and in the net of the East German security police, the workers had become restless in anticipation of some relaxation under the new Kremlin policy. The Soviet sector of Berlin offered a drab contrast to the free-flowing, colorful life only a few blocks away.

The Russians had demonstrated that a new era was coming. A new commander had replaced the man who had

executed the harshest policies, and he had reduced the role
of the troops to clear-cut military duties, withdrawing them
from interference in the lives of the population. The East
German government had heeded Moscow's advice and had
canceled their more drastic measures, which included taking away ration cards from unproductive persons and confiscating the land of farmers who had not delivered their
quotas. Strangely enough, the government thought that,
in view of these concessions, it could proceed with the old
line in at least one respect. It raised the basic quota in the
building industry. This sufficed to drive the workers of
East Berlin to riot.

The riot aroused the West Berliners and electrified the
world. The workers in East Berlin marched on Party headquarters, tearing posters into pieces. They set buildings
housing Communist institutions on fire. They hauled down
the Soviet flag from the Brandenburger Tor and burned it.
Unarmed crowds surrounded the tanks of the security police
and captured them. The Communist regime stood paralyzed in the face of hostility by the workers. Its police demonstrated that they had chosen the people's side when it
came to a clash. Temporarily the police refrained from
joining the rioters, but they did not raise a finger against
them.

However, Soviet tanks thundered into East Berlin and
other industrial towns where the rebellion had spread.
They opened fire, aiming above the heads of the rioters.
Some casualties made the reprisals bloody none the less.
The revolt was over.

Many people believed that East Berlin was a grand overture to the drama of the disintegration of the Soviet empire,
which might, as some thought, infect the Soviet Union in
turn. Moscow faced a grave decision. The new leadership
believed that the situation within the Soviet Union was ripe
for loosening the pressures on the population and enabling
them to enjoy the fruits of their labor, devotion, and sacrifice during three decades. The great change for the better

would thus unroll within the framework of the Communist regime, just as many changes for the worse had done during Stalin's reign.

And indeed, why should the abolition of arbitrary despotism, going hand in hand with improvements in public welfare and the lessening of war tensions, provoke outbursts of dissatisfaction? The Russian public had endured chaos and civil war, transformed a half-starved backward country into a great industrial power, fought the biggest war in history, and rebuilt the damage in record time. Though they had always worked under harsh conditions, they had never risen in revolt against the regime.

Other questions remained to be decided upon by Stalin's heirs. The new course might be a boon for the Soviet people, but Communist discipline had not had enough time to mold a generation into shape in the satellites. Could the Party afford elasticity in the satellite lands without endangering its hold on the country, and was that hold anything but a reflection of Soviet might? Finally, was the new policy to be upheld in the Soviet Union even at the risk of losing its European empire?

Moscow decided to proceed with the policy of relaxation. No mass retaliation followed the East German revolt, and Moscow declared it to have been the work of *agents provocateurs* and saboteurs in the service of America and West Germany.

The Soviet leaders were especially anxious to speed up the new course in Hungary, which lay exposed to the West by its frontier with Austria and was in a shaky condition as a consequence of overtaxing the resources of the population by ill-conceived planning. They summoned Rakosi and the Party chiefs to discuss a thoroughgoing reform. Rakosi heard harsh words from Mikoyan, who called the Hungarian plan adventurous and took particular exception to the grandiose development of the steel industry in a country which possessed neither iron nor coal. In 1952, the country had fallen short by 700 thousand tons of coal. He reproached Rakosi, saying that nobody seemed to care about the price of producing a ton of steel in Hungary under such circumstances.

Since the idea of collective leadership demanded a division of power between the Party and the government in Hungary, the Moscow leaders asked Rakosi whom he would propose to head the government. They took it for granted that Rakosi would keep the real power, which was vested in the Party. To their stupefaction, Rakosi could think of no suitable candidate. Since the Moscow chiefs feared an imminent economic crisis in Hungary, they overruled Rakosi's hedgings and nominations of inconsequential henchmen and chose as his partner the man whom he least wanted: Imre Nagy.

The Moscow leaders remembered Nagy from the time when he had come to Moscow from prison in Hungary, where he had spent three years for illegal Communist activities. He looked like a country doctor and was passionately dedicated to the cause of the poor peasants in Hungary. What had induced him to join the Communist movement was his experience in Russia, as a prisoner of war in 1917, when he saw the peasants take the distribution of land into their own hands. When he returned home he saw that in spite of the upheaval of war and revolution, the peasants still suffocated under the rule of the lords of big estates, who expanded in numbers while the living space contracted. This confirmed his conviction that only a revolution such as that in Russia could raise the peasants in Hungary to human standards.

Nagy survived the purges, studied agronomy at Moscow University, appealed to the peasants to revolt over the radio during the war, and came home with the Soviet armies. In 1944, the dream of his life came true. He was entrusted with the administration of land distribution by the provisional government. Nagy thus owed sole loyalty to the Hungarian people on the land, became convinced that the Communists alone could reverse their fate, and stuck to his conviction even when the Communist line curved away from the peasants' interests. But Imre Nagy

was a slow man among the quick-witted Hungarian Communists. At times, he inevitably turned heretic in the
thoughts which he disclosed, but he bowed to the Party's
decisions, considering them tactically desirable, while believing that the Party would come around to his ideas. In
1949, when Rakosi slaughtered and jailed the "national
Communists" in the Titoist purge, he confessed his "error"
which had consisted of warning the Party against hasty collectivization of the farms. He did this not out of cowardice
or opportunism but from knowledge of the Party rules. If
the international situation was such that the regime was
endangered, emergency measures would have to prevail.
He was a calm man, with an earthy wisdom and an air of
benevolence. But he was no leader.

Thus Nagy was elected to initiate a non-Rakosi course
under the watchful eyes of Rakosi, who was only waiting for
his opportunity to turn today's right into tomorrow's wrong.
Nagy believed it was his calling to take a firm stand against
a policy which had brought general misery to society while
maintaining that it served the general welfare. He had no
illusions about the share of power he had received, since
Rakosi was still entrenched in the Party, which in turn controlled government, bureaucracy, police, and army. All of
these knew very well on whom they depended for their
livelihood and even for their lives. But Nagy felt that this
time Moscow was supporting him, and he planned to bring
back to life the Independent Front, a coalition including
non-Communists, to appeal to the people over the heads of
the Party if Rakosi blocked his way.

Thus it was in Hungary that the new course first presented a positive program without a revolt to blur the fact
that the initiative had come from Moscow, the citadel of
Communism. On July 4, 1953, Nagy made a quiet but
great speech before a thunderstruck Parliament. Its language was bare of the jargon that had enveloped communication in a pretentious and misleading terminology.
With the simplicity of long established conviction, he spoke

to the people to remind them of the truth they already knew, rather than revealing it to them from on high.

It "has to be admitted," Nagy said, "frankly before the country that the objectives of the augmented Five-Year Plan are, in many respects, exceeding our resources, they are heavily taxing our capacity, hindering the growth of the material bases of well-being, and, what is more, they have of late involved the deterioration of the standard of living." Nagy promised to put an end to the "rude, forbidding, heartless attitude of the bureaucrats"; to liquidate cooperative farms where the majority of the membership wanted to, and to permit greater tolerance in religious matters:

. . . in developing our natural economy the government shall not fail to take into account the economic resources of the country; it shall not set itself tasks for the carrying out of which the necessary conditions are lacking, whether it be sources of raw material or investment . . . or other extravagant economic tasks which would be to the detriment of the living standard of the population. . . . There is no reason whatever for any excessive industrialization.

Nagy stated that he would slow down the development of heavy industry, put greater stress on light industries and the food industry, and increase investment in agriculture.

It is known that our agricultural production rests strictly on individual farms whose development is of national interest. Encouragement of production of individual farms is of the first importance . . . The only proper path of building Socialism which is acceptable and feasible in the eyes of the working people, is the raising of the living standard of the population and the constant improvement of their material, cultural, and social position. We must make this the central issue of our plans.

Rakosi interpreted Nagy's speech to the "activists" of the Party a week later by acknowledging that errors had been made but emphasizing that the program meant the slowing down of the plans, not their abandonment. Improvement could be expected only through fulfillment of the plans, Rakosi stated, not through their rejection. Obliquely alluding to Nagy's objections to the arbitrary rule of the regime and its persecutions, Rakosi warned that the enemy was not sleeping. Polemics broadly publicized broke the spell of totalitarianism. For the first time, the Party spoke in two antagonistic voices. It was not even discernible which one echoed its master's voice, since both spoke under the same Soviet authority. Such a baffling event could not pass without consequences.

The country was taken aback and kept silent. An underground battle was on between two sets of Communists. But Nagy's speech struck an echo among the intellectuals in the Party. Its ideological magazine printed these lines:

> We do not understand and apply the fundamental laws of Socialism properly if we permanently place the needs of society above the needs of the individual, if we look only at the final goal, and consider only the long range perspective, if individuals do not experience that Socialist construction directly serves the better fulfillment of their personal needs. . . . We must constantly keep in mind the fact that production is for man and what he needs.

The speech stirred the conscience of the poets to life. The poets had joined the Party because they wanted a better world for everybody and believed that Communism was the instrument for accomplishing this. They believed in what the Party enunciated as true and good and put it in songs to make others believe. At least one poet revealed that he now thought he had been misled and that he had misled others.

> I am wondering whether those people who opposed the poetic elaboration of daily political events were not right after all. As we see, the government has admitted that it was wrong to demand so many sacrifices from the people. I feel I am doubly to blame because I supported this demand for unnecessary sacrifice in the most convincing words, in the words of poetry.

The government decreed that craftsmen could again employ apprentices and encouraged them to leave factories and cooperatives since the country badly needed tailors, barbers, and shoemakers in the towns and villages. But less than nine thousand applications for licenses were filed by the end of the year. The craftsmen did not believe the new course would last and were reluctant to set up shop and invest money in ventures that might make them enemies of the working class overnight.

The tension in the Hungarian Party as a consequence of the divergent attitudes of the two groups cautioned the regimes in other satellite countries against showing any slackening of strength. They noted that Nagy's speech and his appeal to the people over the Party had a demoralizing effect on the militant element in the Party, but failed to increase confidence in the regime outside the Party. As a result of the Hungarian experience, the regimes elsewhere decided to switch to the new course without significant changes in the setup of party and government. The Politburo in Poland rejected the idea of rehabilitating and reinstating Wladyslaw Gomulka, the only popular Communist, who was still in prison. Instead, a former Socialist, Joseph Cyrankiewicz, was made Prime Minister while Boleslaw Bierut, the reliable Moscow-man, continued to run the Party. The Polish regime had many advantages over that in Hungary. They had refused to stage spectacular trials and indulge in wholesale executions, and they had not dared to use force against the peasants in order to herd them into collectives. At first they lagged behind Hungary in breaking the Catholic clergy. However, when the old tough policy had almost run its course, the Polish Communists confined the great diplomat, Cardinal Wyszynski, in a cloister, and put on a great show of trying a bishop for espionage. It accomplished its aim. Seventeen bishops and vicars made the pilgrimage to Warsaw to take the oath of loyalty to the regime.

But "victory" over the clergy only enhanced the church's prestige. The Poles, as in the past, gave expression to their protest against foreign rule by a massive demonstration of unity within the age-old church. Many church buildings had been destroyed in the war, but more than ever were built, and they were overflowing with faithful congregations. What most frustrated the regime was that young people comprised the majority of the attendance, in contrast with Russia where only old people congregated in the churches.

The regime ruled an almost totally hostile population. Four-fifths of the peasants successfully refused to join collectives. General poverty made a repulsive contrast to imposing accomplishments in industrialization. Production rose by 115 per cent in the four years to 1954, but heavy industry increased 135 per cent and agricultural output only 9 per cent. Real wages were miserably low. A month's wages bought a suit (only 60 per cent wool) and a week's wages a pair of low-grade shoes. The shortage of consumer goods led to scenes that explained more than the figures. An Englishman saw a long line in front of a little shop in a small Polish town. Inquiring what the shop was selling, people told him that news had spread that the shopkeeper had received buttons. The new course allowed the peasants to pay for deliveries partly in money, partly in goods, and shifted its investment program in favor of housing and agriculture.

The same development took place in Rumania, where the ambitious plan for the Black Sea–Danube Canal fell victim to the discovery of the consumer, by the Communists, after so much money had been sunk in it and so many forced laborers had perished. Rumania made progress in light industries, especially textiles which the country now was able to feed with cotton from its own crop, and also in chemical industries. She still advanced slowly in oil exploitation, due perhaps to the shortage of modern equipment, though it was possible that the wells had been drying up. The regime promised to reduce taxes, lower the price of electricity, and stop further collectivization.

Bulgaria, the favorite of the Soviets, completed its Five-Year Plan in four years in 1953. In its next Five-Year Plan agricultural development received priority. Much had been done in that field to bring the structure of farming into conformity with that of the Soviet Union. Sixty-eight per cent of the arable land was cultivated by the collectives and was amply supplied with machines. They delivered sufficient food to the government so that it was not much concerned with private farmers. Bulgaria needed no new course except for more respect for the rights of the individual and the law. Industry was run mostly by joint Bulgarian-Soviet companies. A railroad from Sofia to both harbors, Varna and Burgas, improved communications with Russia, for which purpose the harbors were enlarged and equipped with up-to-date machinery.

Albania's abundant and swift river streams began to be harnessed for producing electricity, twenty-four times more in 1952 than in 1938. Industrial production increased eight fold in the same period. The new course promised tax exemptions for the farmers, private and collective, and more attention for the consumer.

Following Stalin's death, Tito's Jugoslavia found itself in the enviable position of being courted by both blocs, West and East. She had well earned these favors by the impressive firmness of the people in supporting the regime when it stood for the independence of the nation, even if it was not overly popular in other respects. Tito also gained prestige in the United Nations where he succeeded in meticulously selecting certain issues on which he could stand apart from the power blocs. His first escape from isolation after the break with Moscow was the Balkan pact, which restored the old friendship between Jugoslavia and Greece and culminated, after many hesitations and delays, in a military alliance between the two countries with Turkey as a third party. The pact took great care to stipulate that Jugoslavia had no obligations should the two other partners be involved in war as a consequence of their membership in NATO. But the pact soon lost its significance when the old animosity between Greece and Turkey over Cyprus exploded, and the reconciliation between Tito and Moscow began.

Tito believed the successors of Stalin to be following his own course in many important respects. This development fed his pride, but he and his friends had long before resolved not to rejoin the Soviet bloc under any circumstances. As to reconciliation, Tito doubted the stability of the group who ruled in Moscow; and, as long as such inveterate Stalinists as Molotov and Kaganovich wielded power, he was wary of the sincerity and durability of the new course as well. Nevertheless, he had an interest in the new line of evolution in the Soviet Union and its satellites, because a serious deterioration would inevitably affect the Communist regime in his own country.

Nagy's speech concerned Tito because it had overstepped the limits of national Communism. Nagy's decision to allow the dissolution of collectives when the majority of its members so desired conformed with Tito's own decree, but with the significant difference that Tito reserved the right of proceeding with collectivization at the appropriate moment. Nagy's heresy over this tenet of Communism appeared to Tito all the more risky because he felt that the Hungarian people still had not divested themselves of reactionary inclinations. In this respect he concurred in Rakosi's opinion, even though he hated and despised the man. Rakosi's success with Moscow was mainly due to his ability to persuade the Kremlin of the alleged reactionary state of mind in Hungary, in spite of the fact that the economic and social foundations for such a mentality, the large landed estates and private property in industry, had been destroyed. Tito thus had a double concern over the new course. He feared equally that it might be turned back and that it might run out of Communist control.

But developments in the Soviet Union opened perspectives which dwarfed the significance of Tito and Jugoslavia. Both camps began new attempts to terminate the Cold War. General Eisenhower, now President of the United States, launched a positive policy for peace on the occasion of the new men taking possession of the Kremlin upon Stalin's death. Tito shared Moscow's favorable judgment of a Republican administration and Congress in Washington, at least to the extent that they would be freer in negotiating than the Democrats, who were paralyzed by the nation's suspicion that they had been soft toward Communism.

In an exchange of speeches concerning coexistence and peace, the President finally laid down the items which would give the Soviets an opportunity to demonstrate their sincerity of purpose with deeds, not words: an armistice in Korea, an end to the civil wars in Indo-China and Malaya, and peace with Austria. Few people believed that the Soviets could afford a peace treaty with Austria, since this involved the right of the Soviets to keep troops in Rumania and Hungary as guardians of their lines of communications. But the Warsaw pact equipped Russia with the instrument for insuring these same rights, and anyway much greater issues were at stake in ending the Cold War than legal pretexts for the Soviet military hold on her satellites.

In two years all the proofs Eisenhower required had been rendered. The Korean and Indo-Chinese wars ended in partitions on the model of Germany; the guerilla war in Malaya abated; and Moscow signed the peace treaty with Austria.

But in the meantime epoch-making events changed the world situation. In August, 1953, Russia detonated a hydrogen bomb. Both powers now possessed the weapon that could mutually annihilate them. Such a war might also destroy the rest of the world or contaminate humanity with unexplored perils to future generations. All mankind became directly concerned in preventing such an ultimate catastrophe.

India, with its ancient prestige, assumed the lead in organizing the peoples uncommitted in the power conflict between the two giants. A pact between India and China gave the movement high importance. Asian and African countries met at Bandung in 1955 to discuss mutual problems. For the first time, representatives of the majority of the inhabitants of the globe laid down general policies, with the West, and even the white races, not even present. Only ten years before, when the United Nations had been established, four Western countries (Russia being Western in

this sense) and only one Eastern nation had been vested
with permanent power to regulate the security of the world
in war and peace.

In a decade, the political shift was already reflected in
the structure and color of the General Assembly. More and
more former colonies had become members of the UN, and
the delegations of non-Western and non-white countries
grew in number and importance. At the same time, Western supremacy remained intact in the Security Council, reflecting the actual power situation. The Cold War did
much, however, to undermine the position of the Council.
Soviet vetoes and America's insistence on forcing issues
which Moscow was bound to veto, were instrumental in
this. Also, the quest for the support of noncommitted
peoples in the Cold War shifted emphasis from the Council
to the General Assembly. Possibly this development corresponded with the determination of the two world powers
to avoid major wars. Moral pressure took the place of possible sanctions against an aggressor.

During this period even some small, but intriguing problems such as Trieste found their solution. This problem was
solved because the conditions which had posed it no longer
existed. After World War II Trieste could have become a
great outlet to the Adriatic and Mediterranean seas for the
Soviet orbit, but the problem shrunk to the level of a Jugo-
slav-Italian quarrel when Moscow lost interest in Jugoslavia's
ambitions. At a time when Communist influence in Italy
had to be countered, the West had made a solemn promise
to the Italians that Trieste would be theirs. Relations between the West and Jugoslavia later turned from hostility
to friendship, but it was impossible for the West to go back
on its promise. A solution was delayed until the new men
took over the Kremlin and set about improving their relations with Tito. Against this background Jugoslavia and
Italy agreed on a compromise that gave the harbor and the
city to Italy, while some territory from the zone held by the
Allies was ceded to Jugoslavia in addition to the zone Jugoslavia had previously occupied.

Another much deeper and graver conflict began to dissolve. After years of harassment, insult, and injury on the part of the Cominform countries against Jugoslavia, during which time the old nationalistic and territorial issues had been ominously revitalized, Moscow gave the green light for reconciliation. But reconciliation needed two partners, and Jugoslavia was not in a hurry.

In December, 1953, peace was made at least on the River Danube. The Danube commission had a session at which the Cominform representatives gave their votes, as a matter of courtesy, to a Jugoslavian instead of a Russian for secretary of the commission. A Hungarian became president, and there was no controversy about making Budapest the headquarters of the commission. In the same year Moscow resumed normal diplomatic relations with Jugoslavia, and the satellites followed suit.

Moscow put great and sustained stress on improving relations with Tito. The new Soviet leadership acknowledged Tito's achievement in preserving a Communist-type state in spite of the murderous designs of the Moscow and Cominform governments to ruin all his accomplishments and plans, and in spite of his forced reliance on the aid of capitalistic countries. Moscow wanted to work out a new pattern for controlling the satellites in case the Cold War ended and some of them had to be released into neutrality. Jugoslavia had an interest in keeping its neighbors socialist, and at this point Soviet interests and Tito's ambitions might meet again.

But it was a long while before Tito would renounce his key position from which he was able to side with this or that power as the Jugoslavian regime's interests required. Beria disappeared from leadership and life, and the circumstances uncomfortably resembled the Stalin era. Moreover, in removing Beria and the dreaded secret police whom he commanded, Malenkov and Khrushchev needed the help of the army. Marshal Zhukov complied, and his contribution certainly was popular with the officers in the army. However, his action made the army a first-rate political factor and moved Zhukov up among the top leaders of the state. Malenkov's position rested on the state bureaucracy and the huge managerial personnel of the national enterprises. A showdown between him and Khrushchev, whose roots of power lay in the Party, might lead the army to seize supreme power or at least to intervene in behalf of one of the other contestants. Thus, the army threatened to become the actual power behind the victor in the political struggle.

The continuing instability of the Moscow regime made Tito cautious toward Khrushchev's attempts to win him back into the fold. Khrushchev felt the Soviets were strong and their prestige high enough to make humiliating apologies to heal the injury done to Tito's pride without too much self-consciousness. The presence of Molotov in the ruling set, the man Tito considered most responsible for his excommunication and for the campaign of character assassination against him, appeared to be hampering reconciliation with Tito. Khrushchev was ready to give Tito the supreme satisfaction of having Molotov, often second only to Stalin, publicly confess his error in slandering the Jugoslavian leader.

Rakosi, Stalin's leading henchman in the unsuccessful attempt to overthrow Tito, naturally had to eat a full dish of crow. Rakosi's cheap maneuver was to put the blame for the anti-Tito campaign on the chief of the security police, whom he had arrested. But at this lower level of the Communist hierarchy, Tito remained obdurate, declaring in reply to Rakosi's professions of friendship that the Hungarian dictator lacked the courage to acknowledge his mistakes.

Tito could not be charmed back into the old bond, but he demonstrated that he might do more for the Soviet empire by staying outside when it came to situations in which he and the Soviets had common interests. He maintained contact not only with India and Burma, more or less socialist in their political outlook, but also with Egypt, Ethiopia, and Indonesia. He helped organize the neutral bloc which compelled the two great powers to co-exist peacefully. The fear that one or the other might grow so powerful as to rule the world diminished as huge masses of peoples organized outside the two blocs.

President Eisenhower made a statement on February 6, 1955, in which he asserted that the Cold War had reached a stalemate. He also offered a definition for the word by characterizing the state of affairs as one in which neither side was getting what it desired in the global struggle, but in which both had at least enough sense to agree that they must not pursue success through force of arms. Molotov summed up the world situation at the same time in the same vein when he stated that a balance of power had now been established. The Geneva conference between the heads of states resulted essentially in an agreement that the possession of the hydrogen bomb by both sides had ended the Cold War.

Paradoxically, the Kremlin simultaneously ended its "new course." Georgi Malenkov publicly confessed that his lack of experience had held back Soviet economic development, asserting that he now recognized that the development of heavy industry must be the basis for increasing production, even in agriculture. Nikita Khrushchev consolidated his hold on the Party as well as on the government, since Marshal Nikolai A. Bulganin appeared to have been chosen by him as a figurehead. By holding on to his position as First Secretary, Khrushchev re-established the rule of the Party in the government. Malenkov did not vanish, and his "incompetence" did not prevent him from staying in the Politburo.

Molotov's reassuring declaration notwithstanding, the re-established priority of heavy industry suggested to some commentators in the West that a second Stalinist era was beginning. They attributed the change of heart in Moscow to the decision of the Allies to rearm Germany, but other considerations may have been involved in the reversal of the Malenkov course. China allegedly protested having its requirements for capital equipment shipments curtailed.

However, China may have induced the Soviet chiefs to participate in its grandiose undertaking to organize the undeveloped countries of Asia and Africa, committed only to peace between the two giant powers by isolating "warmongering" America.

Bulganin and Khrushchev took to the road, visited Jugoslavia, India, and Burma, making resounding declarations for co-existence and against atomic warfare.

The Soviets were successful in penetrating into the Middle East by persuading Nasser of Egypt to accept Soviet arms. This matched China's great diplomatic success at the Bandung conference in countering the American-inspired Manila pact. These events began peaceful competition with America in winning backward peoples through aiding their industrial development with supplies of capital goods and technical knowledge. Moscow had some initial success in impressing some Asiatic lands by its strict business arrangements and banked heavily on its ability to accept domestic raw materials for payment.

In fact, this new course compelled America to face a momentous problem. America had no use for the raw material the underdeveloped nations could pay with, and private industries were hardly in a position to compete successfully with the Soviets, who could manipulate prices for their purposes. Yet America had to meet the new challenge lest it surrender the greater part of the world to Soviet peaceful conquest. Japan volunteered a remarkable proposal involving a three-cornered enterprise. Under this plan America would finance industry in Japan to compete with Russia in the Asiatic and African countries. The low wages and need for raw materials in Japan would make them an ideal agent for the United States to meet Moscow on at least even terms. The other alternative was equally unattractive to America, a government-financed industrial expansion which might involve deep changes in the nation's economic and social structure.

The decision was postponed at this time, since disturbances in strategically important spots indicated that peaceful co-existence still had a long way to go. American and internal financial pressure forced Britain to evacuate the Suez Canal zone before an agreement could be reached with Nasser concerning the status of the canal after the concession of the Suez company ran out in 1968. Soviet arms and support emboldened Nasser's ambition to become leader of the Arab world, and he appeared to be preparing to carry matters to a showdown.

Domination of the Mediterranean by the Soviets working through Arab nationalism offered a nightmarish vision to the West, but the means of preventing it frustrated American diplomacy. France and Britain could not be expected to surrender their empires and influence, and thus their positions as great powers, without a fight. Should an armed conflict develop, America would have to face an awful choice. Either she would espouse anticolonialism in order to prevent Soviet political and economic conquest of a stronghold of decisive strategic importance, dropping her main allies; or she would side with them in order to prevent the Soviets from dominating the European continent.

But meanwhile volcanic forces were preparing to erupt under the soil of the Soviet orbit.

2.

The end of Malenkov's "new course" also ended the Hungarian regime that had shared in its reforms and its frustrations. Premier Nagy had penetrated to the bottom of the failure of Stalinism when he had exposed even its economic aspects in terms of violation of the humanistic foundations of socialism. "The previous economic policy," said Nagy, "reduced socialism to raising the production of steel and iron, to hyperindustrialization, disregarding man and society." He consistently advocated democratization as a remedy, with the Party membership taking part not only in the execution of policy but also in its very formation.

But Rakosi and his henchmen sat firmly in their positions and prevented the positive aspects of Nagy's program from realization while allowing its negative aspects to run free. Thus, production in heavy industry decreased and part of the peasantry left the collectives, but little progress was made in the production of consumer industries and state income from agriculture lagged. Thousands of inmates of prisons, labor camps, and concentration camps were released; but dazed and bewildered, their wrath only added fuel to the growing dissatisfaction. When the Party loosened its grip on the intellectuals, they ventured to publish true reports of the state of affairs and public opinion as they found them. But now the Party tightened the reins again and stopped printing articles in which writers had unburdened their consciences by facing and recording the truth.

Rakosi returned from Russia, where he had been marking time, waiting until the intra-Party wrangles had concluded in Malenkov's ouster. Thereupon he unleashed his wrath on Nagy, removing him from the government, from his position on the Politburo in the Central Committee of the Party, and eventually from the Party itself. Rakosi accused Nagy of rightist opportunism, for relinquishing the principle of socialist transformation of industry and agriculture and denying the leading role of the Party in it. Rakosi put a young figurehead into the front seat of the government while he himself pulled all the wires as First Secretary of the Party.

Rakosi's bark turned out to be worse than his bite, since he had inside information that increased consideration for the consumer would not be dropped in the post-Malenkov course. The principle would stay intact, although deviations from it would occur for reasons of expediency. Such a policy lay in the best traditions of Lenin and Stalin who had managed even to embark on counter-revolutionary courses, but always keeping ultimate ends in mind. Rakosi purged Nagy's supporters, but this time he was not allowed to go further than depriving them of their livelihood and shutting them off from the public in literature, journalism, and art.

But these writers, artists, and actors—sixty of them in all and all Communists—would not take his orders without protest. They filed a memorandum to the Central Committee of the Party in the fall of 1955, in which they referred to a decision of the Party in 1953 (when Nagy became Prime Minister) which had not been repealed and which condemned the "brutal and inconsiderate intervention of the administration in the field of literature—dictatorial and anti-democratic actions that had demoralized the militant Communists." They protested the confiscation of the *Literary Gazette* (*Irodalmi Ujsag*), the firing of two of its editors, the dismissal of many journalists on the staff of the official daily newspaper, and other abuses.

Rakosi promptly retorted through the Central Committee by branding the memorandum an anti-Party demonstration and stating that "dictatorship over the bourgeoisie, including bourgeois ideals, is essential for the regime and it can make no exception for literature."

Rakosi's triumph was short-lived. In February, 1956, less than a year after he had resumed full power, a bombshell shattered all his maneuverings. The Twentieth Congress of the Soviet Party listened dumbfounded to Khrushchev and Mikoyan explode Stalin's glory. Nothing was spared the dead despot. They started by revealing his real relation to Lenin and his wife. They continued with his ruthless trampling on "collective thought," that is, democracy within the Party, and his disposal of anyone who might have questioned his wisdom. They told of his wholesale purges of hundreds of thousands, his neglect of the country's defenses due to his limitless trust of Hitler, his bungling as a war leader, and his expropriating the credit of others for victory.

Rakosi witnessed this earthquake in the Communist world. To measure its effect on him, one should remember that only he and Molotov had shed tears at Stalin's bier. He returned to Hungary tight-lipped, ready to use all the skill and astuteness at his command to direct the de-Stalinization policy. Rakosi was determined to stay in power until a great reversal would re-establish Stalinism, for he was convinced that such a policy alone could preserve Communism. On June 28, 1956, an event shook the air which appeared to justify his expectations.

In Poznan, Poland, the workers of ZISPO engineering plant struck. A few days before, they had sent a delegation to the Ministry in Warsaw to ask for an investigation and correction of mismanagement in the plant. A complicated wage regulation had reduced their wages, as had the high tax on overtime pay. Irregular raw material deliveries also kept them idle from time to time, and this cut into their salaries. The delegation reported that the only result of their complaints was that the work quota would be raised.

The workers marched to the city hall, and people in the streets joined them. The town was in a festive mood owing to the presence of an international fair, with thirty-six countries exhibiting. The presence of foreigners, after many years of virtual isolation, exhilarated the people. Moreover, the condemnation of Stalin by his successors had leaked to the Polish public and instilled a confidence that things would soon improve. The workers shouted "We want bread," but as passions rose the demonstration took on a political character. People tore down a Soviet flag, stormed the headquarters of the security police, broke into the building of the Communist Party, unlocked the doors of the jail and freed the inmates. Militiamen made no move to restrain the crowd. Some of them gave their arms to the demonstrators. A shot was fired, and then the security police fired a salvo into the crowd. In the brawl that followed, forty-eight were killed and several hundred wounded. The army rushed to the scene with tanks, and it took them more than a day to restore order.

Just as three years earlier in Pilsen, Czecho-Slovakia, and in East Germany the death of Stalin had encouraged the workers to give vent to their accumulated bitterness, so now the disavowal of Stalin and Stalinism by the Russians resulted in an explosion of released tensions when a haughty bureaucracy refused to look into well-substantiated complaints. The need to fire repeatedly on industrial workers and the young people whom the Party themselves had trained was a terrific blow to the Communists. It caused an immediate crisis in Polish Party headquarters.

Premier Cyrankiewicz and his friends in the Politburo decided on a publicly acknowledged policy of leniency, excusing the workers since their demands had been legitimate. The so-called Natolin group, headed by Marshal Rokossowski, insisted that the blame should be placed on foreign agents who had chosen the opportunity to cause trouble while the town was being visited by foreigners. *Pravda* in Moscow energetically took up the Natolin line.

The name "Natolin" was that of a Warsaw suburb where the pro-Moscow group held confidential meetings. This group had its own program on how de-Stalinization was to be carried out without dissolving Party discipline and loosening the ties of the Party to Moscow. What it badly needed was popularity to counter the nationalistic element in the Party leadership. The Natolins were prepared to go to the limits of demagogy to acquire popular favor by promising to raise living standards by 50 per cent, counting on emergency supplies from Moscow to help keep their promise.

Although less than fifty thousand Jews in Poland out of three million had survived the Nazi terror, anti-Semitism had deep roots among the masses. The Natolin group resolved to revive anti-Semitism in order to create another bond between themselves and the people. Anti-Semitism was now finding a new focus in the fact that Jews held some

important positions. Since many Jews belonged to the Muscovite ruling group, the demagogic twist of the Natolin
clan was particularly Machiavellian.

Nevertheless, the disintegration of the Party took on
alarming proportions. Membership among the industrial
workers dropped from 54.9 to 38.4 per cent from 1950 to
1954. Among the youth, it dropped to 40 per cent, many
of that number consisting of peasant youth on the collectives
whose enrollment was more or less compulsory. The low
standard of living shocked even visitors from other satellite countries. Yet the Muscovites considered the intellectuals to be the cause of the dissolution of discipline and
of the undermining of Party authority.

This belief did have some basis in fact. The Communist
intellectuals, particularly the young ones, smarted under
the Khrushchev-Mikoyan debunking of Stalin which revealed that the crusades they had engaged in in good faith
had no foundation in fact. A prime example was the agitation against Tito, which was now admitted to have been
due to Stalin's autocratic demands and Tito's resistance
to surrendering his country's independence.

Shaken out of their delusions, these intellectuals searched
their consciences to find what their share of responsibility
for Stalin's crimes was. The Germans could plead ignorance
when they were reproached for the slaughter of millions
in Hitler's gas chambers. But the Polish intellectuals had
known that their countrymen in eastern Poland had been
deported to Russia. Furthermore, they could not really
have believed that all Polish Communist Party leaders had
been guilty of treason when Stalin had dissolved the Party
in 1938 and invited the leaders to Moscow to have them
executed. They also knew that members of the Home Army
who had fought valiantly against the Nazis had been imprisoned, deported, or discriminated against in getting jobs.

Some writers retraced the road back to where Communism had lost its impetus. They put their finger on
1948, when Poland had been forced to adopt the Soviet
pattern of building a socialist economy and society. The

economy had been militarized, and centralized planning based on distorted blueprints had led to waste and hidden unemployment which had made industrialization costly. The result had been a sinking standard of living, and the direction of the plan had been cut off from the people's aspirations. Stalinism had drained the Party of its revolutionary idealism by transforming the production process into an administrative function supervised by plain-clothes police.

The intellectuals publicly and sincerely examined past mistakes and loudly reflected on whether to blaze new paths to the old ideals or abandon them. Public attention was attracted by the sincerity of their approach and their fearless analysis of problems that everyone had felt but had formerly lacked the ability or courage to face. When this point was reached, the intellectuals and the public, particularly its youthful part, discovered each other. The intellectuals found that the cynicism and indifference of the youth was only a protective mask designed to counter the hypocrisy fed to them in broadcasts, press, and schools.

While the intellectuals and the youth were going through this moral catharsis, the anti-Stalinists prevailed over the Natolins in the Politburo. The minister who had so harshly rejected the demands of the Poznan workers was dismissed. The workers received compensation for the curtailment of their wages. Investigation showed that if they overfilled their quota by 25 per cent, their wages increased only 14.1 per cent, but even then the tax on this portion of their wages rose 40 per cent. Even more important, the anti-Stalinists refuted the Moscow version of the Poznan revolt as being incited by the West and officially judged it to have been justified in essence. In accordance with this position, the government prosecuted only those who had taken direct part in murder and agitation. They were tried publicly, with lawyers and journalists from the West in the audience. The sad truth of misery, exploitation, and indifference was exposed undisguised.

In the ferment of public opinion which the intellectuals and youth had engendered, patriotism and socialism united. Both these elements had formerly been present in the Polish Socialist Party, formed during the period when Poland had been partitioned and patriotism and socialism were reverse sides of the same coin. These elements had survived in the Communist Party until Stalin dissolved it in 1938 and had its leaders killed. But one of them, Wladyslaw Gomulka, had been in prison at the time and so could not follow his comrades to Moscow. Prison saved his life. He was again imprisoned in 1951, this time by the Communists, along with General Marian Spychalski. The general had since been released, but Gomulka remained in jail, for he was anathema to Moscow. But the faction in the Central Committee that stood for democratization in the Party and public life strengthened itself after Edward Ochab took Boleslaw Bierut's place, following his death in March, 1956.

Although democratization may have been in line with Khrushchev's general policy, it met mounting opposition among Soviet leaders in view of the dangers a defection of Poland would incur. The international situation was fluid again and threatened to run out of the control of America and Russia. The French became ever more deeply involved in a losing battle to preserve their North African empire. Nasser's Egypt was the main instigator of Arab nationalism, and his attempt to wrest the Suez Canal from British control created a unity of purpose between the two allies, usually at odds over their respective shares of influence in the Middle East.

Watching these developments, Moscow surmised that unprecedented combinations of powers might issue from the confusion and add fuel to the possibility of world conflict. At the same time, a Polish defection might inflame East Germany, with incalculable consequences to the painfully established balance of power on the European continent. The Great Powers might inadvertently find themselves in a war of annihilation.

And in a strategically less important satellite country, Hungary, portentous developments were taking place. Nationalist traditions there had found no place in the framework of socialism. The old Hungarian ruling classes had been the first to take advantage of nationalism, and the Socialists, in opposition, had attracted alien nationals as well as Hungarian industrial workers. It was no accident that the Socialist leaders were mostly of Schwabian or Jewish origin. The first genuinely Hungarian radical movement had begun in the 1930's, inspired by the "village explorer" intellectuals, but they had made a point of fighting only for the peasants, whom they regarded as the principal agents of national regeneration. The movement's organization, the National Peasant Party, had split over the question of joining the Communists, and those who joined had lost popularity with the people. Patriotic radicalism in Hungary had to reach back to pre-Socialist antecedents for a national background. The youth of March, 1848—with its poets and intellectuals who had supported freedom from tyranny, national independence, and the emancipation of the serfs—provided the only Hungarian tradition for a genuinely national program.

In no satellite country did democratization start as early as in Hungary or go as far as under Imre Nagy's direction. It now appears that the new leadership in the Kremlin used Hungary as a testing ground for a de-Stalinization policy. When they reversed the course, Khrushchev and his colleagues did so for reasons not concerned with the success or failure of the Nagy experiment. But Nagy's policy did not penetrate deeply enough to gain the confidence of the industrial workers, perhaps because Rakosi and the old Party retained a firm grip on them.

The course of revolutionary ferment ran almost simultaneously in Hungary and Poland in 1955 and 1956, but the revolt in Poznan and the way in which the Polish government gained control and eventually liquidated it demonstrated the important difference between the men in power in the two countries. Representatives of the Polish way of

Communism or socialism already held important posts in the Party and government. On the other hand, Rakosi was back in the saddle in Hungary, resolved to direct de-Stalinization in a manner that would preserve Moscow's hold on the Party and country no matter how many concessions he might be compelled to make.

The Polish revolution started with the riot of workers at Poznan, but Hungarian industrial workers were slow to react to its apparent success, or even to the dethronement of Stalin. Due to the traditional lack of communication between workers and intellectuals in Hungary, the former regarded the latter's current agitation as an internal affair within the Communist Party.

This is why democratic socialism was short of leadership when the time arrived for its establishment. Imre Nagy, if he was a leader at all, was concerned mainly for the peasantry and not for the industrial workers. The moment arrived, but Hungary failed to produce a leader who could use the mounting passions as an impulse for political transformation. In Poland, in contrast to Hungary, important Communists who had become national leaders survived the purges.

The Hungarian writers dated the start of their revolt from October, 1954, when it was disclosed that Rajk and his co-defendants had been condemned and executed on trumped-up charges. The *Literary Gazette* emphasized this point:

The Union of Writers arrived at a crisis when it learned that the Rajk trial had been fabricated and that the holy crusade against the Jugoslavs had been based on lies and calumnies. At that moment a moral change took place in our literary and political life. We realized that we were deceived but also that this did not alter our personal responsibility. A writer cannot excuse himself before posterity by saying that he was deceived because what counts is his work and his work testifies against him . . . Excitement, bitterness, impotent anger, took hold of the writers. Some suffered nervous breakdowns, others could not be appeased by tears and fits of anger and debated in anguish and indignation. Then the moral union of the writers was born, sealed by this profession of faith: never again to be a party to lies and inhuman crimes . . . [But] the Twentieth Congress was needed to unveil illegality and injustice. Misinterpreted concern for the interests of the revolution and—why deny it?— fear restrained them from telling the truth . . . [However] the writer cannot indulge in an equivocal attitude towards the moral values of society . . . The writer has no right to make concessions in the realm of truth and justice.

Moscow decided to tolerate but not encourage a turn to national Communism in a meeting with Hungarian Communists held in Russia in July, 1956. Rakosi had in mind a step-by-step liberalization of the regime in a manner that would not get out of control. But he had to go to greater lengths than was safe for him or his policy. Following the Moscow line of appeasing Tito, Rakosi publicly had to "rehabilitate" Rajk and release the Communists whom he had arrested as "Titoists." As victims and witnesses to his crimes, with Mrs. Rajk as their most formidable mouthpiece, they became a force Rakosi eventually could not cope with.

The writers found a clever way to outmaneuver Rakosi. The resolutions of the Twentieth Congress had directed the Communist parties everywhere to explain the important events that had taken place there. When Rakosi tried to stop the public discussion which was undermining his authority, the writers appealed to these resolutions, which came from the highest Communist authority of all.

The Communist Youth movement had organized a debating circle, the Petofi Club, with the intention of drawing young non-Communists into discussions engineered by Party men so as to attract them to the Party. The magic name of Petofi, a great poet and fighter for freedom in the revolution of 1848–49, in which he died a hero's death, was expected to attract their interest. It was in this club that the writers finally faced the youth, students, and workers. The news of unrestricted debates spread until thousands tried to get in and loudspeakers had to be mounted to convey the speeches to the masses in the streets. Similar clubs began to mushroom in country towns. Soon the whole country was caught by the fever of free speech.

From May 30 on, economists, scholars, teachers, lawyers, judges, artists, and musicians succeeded one another as speakers before the club, baring the violence that the regime had done to all facets of the nation's life. But it was the appearance of Rajk's widow and the flaming passion of her speech before an audience of two thousand that stirred the whole country with excitement. She told of her five years in prison, denied news of her baby who was only five months old when she was jailed. She challenged the Party chiefs to punish the murderers, who had not only destroyed innocent men but also, morally, the Party and the country.

If Mrs. Rajk had inflamed already excited emotions, an atomic scientist, Lajos Janosi, fired the imagination of the public with a more startling disclosure. Uranium deposits had been discovered in the country, said Janosi, but although he was Vice-President of the Atomic Energy Commission, not even he had any information concerning the extent of the find or the pact with Russia under which uranium had been transported to the Soviet Union. Uranium had a magic sound, for it meant a story-book change from poverty to boundless riches for a poor country like Hungary. The disclosure touched on a sore point that was on everybody's mind but nobody's lips, namely the presence of the Russians in the country. The Warsaw treaty allowed them to have garrisons stationed in Hungary. It appeared that Rakosi by himself had sold the Russians the right to exploit the uranium ore without informing even other top Communists. The presence of Soviet authority in the country came under public attention. At a momentous meeting of the Petofi Club on June 27 before a packed audience, speakers openly demanded the resignation of Rakosi and the return of Imre Nagy to power. The meeting lasted from 7 P.M. to 3:30 A.M.

The next day, the news of this political bombshell coincided with the bigger news of the riot in Poznan. The public had the feeling that the result of the Poznan revolt might indicate the course of events to come in Hungary. When the national Communists gained the upper hand in the Polish Communist Party, Rakosi could delay his resignation no longer. But he sacrificed his person only, not his policy. Rakosi did a last disservice to the country by imposing on the Central Committee a successor who personified what the people hated most—inhumanity.

The man was Erno Gero. He had become a Communist in 1919, had been jailed in 1922 for Communist activities, exchanged by Moscow for a Hungarian in a Soviet prison in 1925, and after that had lived in Moscow until 1944, with the exception of a brief interval fighting in the Spanish Civil War in 1936. He had returned with the Soviet armies and become head of economic planning. He was known as a fierce worker, intimate only with charts and figures, the archetype of the bureaucrat, and as staunch a Stalinist as Rakosi himself. Tito later disclosed that Moscow had agreed to let Rakosi go only on condition that Gero replace him. "This was wrong," Tito said, "because there was no difference between Gero and Rakosi. Gero followed the same policy and was as guilty as Rakosi." The change meant no change in fact, and caused grave disappointment throughout the country.

From later statements of Tito it appears that Soviet-satellite relations occupied the spotlight in the prolonged discussions between Khrushchev and Tito at this time. Mikoyan had participated in the Hungarian Committee meeting in July, in which Rakosi had proposed drastic action against the Petofi Club in order to restore Party authority. Mikoyan had opposed this, and the majority of the Committee had voted Rakosi down. But Mikoyan still shared Rakosi's stubborn view that any relaxation of Party authority would lead to the shifting of power into the hands of political groups hostile to the Soviets and socialism. Rakosi pointed to the results of the premiership of Imre Nagy when power had moved further and further toward elements outside the Party. Rakosi did not of course mention that this had happened because he gave Nagy no support from the Party. Nevertheless, Rakosi's argument carried weight with Mikoyan, and so Gero was appointed rather than Nagy, or even Janos Kadar, a man Moscow was grooming for the future.

The Khrushchev-Tito discussions shed light on the great role the Soviet leader intended to assign to Tito in keeping the satellite countries from falling out of orbit in case the Soviet Union loosened her control. According to Tito, when Khrushchev visited Belgrade in September, 1956, the Russian leader considered weakening the ties with the satellites, but thought that "unfortunate consequences might result if the Soviet Union completely abandoned these countries, or if, for instance, they were given the status of Jugoslavia." The Russians feared "that in those countries reactionary forces might then prevail."

A few weeks later Tito returned the visit and went to the Crimea. There Khrushchev insisted he meet Erno Gero who was "accidentally" present. Tito agreed to receive Gero at the head of a Hungarian Communist delegation to improve relations between the two countries. He understood that he was strengthening Gero's position by meeting him, but Tito has given a reason why he accepted the proposition although he disapproved of the Hungarian leadership. He said: "We wanted to establish relations with the Hungarian Workers Party because we thought that by not isolating it, we could *more easily influence their proper internal development.*"

Tito's part in consolidating Gero's position lowered his prestige in Hungary to an extent significant for later developments in that country. Concessions to public opinion were being made tumultuously. Executed or condemned Communists, Socialists, Catholic and Lutheran clergymen, all were rehabilitated. In practice, freedom of speech and of the press was complete. The morally awakened Communist intellectuals visited local centers in the country where they inspired the students to reappraise the past politically and morally, and to debate plans for the future.

Finally, the regime made its greatest concession, because they feared the event could not be forestalled and might otherwise turn into a powerful demonstration against the Party and government. When the intellectuals around the Petofi Club decided on a solemn rehabilitation of Laszlo Rajk and others executed for Titoism, the Party assumed official sponsorship of the event. The intellectuals chose October 6 for the date, the traditional memorial day for the martyrs of the revolution of 1848–49. On that day thirteen generals of the Hungarian army had been hanged by the Hapsburg emperor in connivance with the Russians, whose military help had doomed the insurrection to defeat.

No one anticipated that people from all walks of life, especially the industrial workers, would inundate the cemetery and the streets around it. Two hundred thousand people gathered there and joined the intellectuals and students for the first time. In his eulogy of Rajk, a writer friend of his named Tibor Meray said at the reinterment:

> Your fate was terrible: they put you to death in the name of the very cause to which you had dedicated your life. It was not we who forged the charge or passed judgment. But we believed the ghastly calumny, echoed it and howled with the wolves . . . Help us speak and confess, dear dead one . . . because only you can help us to have faith. The knowledge of your fate killed our blind faith. It revealed to us our sins—the whip, the prisons, the guns of the tyrants. Your tragic fate has inspired us to never again uttering either under the threat of torture nor for misunderstood love of the cause, a word more than is true. Your fate imposes on us love for humanity and for our nation, love of truth and freedom . . . I will not use the worn phrase they use over the graves of martyrs, that you did not die in vain, since there was no need for you to die.

Meanwhile, Nagy asked the Central Committee of the Party for readmission. He maintained that his expulsion had been engineered in violation of democracy within the Party. At the same time, he professed his acceptance of the principles of the Twentieth Congress of the Soviet Party and the resolutions of the Hungarian Central Committee that ensued, and promised to fight for their realization even though he held different views on certain points. The Central Committee decided to annul Nagy's expulsion, stating that, though he had committed mistakes, they did not justify his expulsion.

On October 12, it was announced that Mihaly Farkas had been arrested. Farkas, former Minister of Defense, had wrenched forced confessions from "Titoists" by torture. Two days later a delegation headed by Gero, in which Janos Kadar and others took part, left for Belgrade.

3.

Meanwhile, the official newspaper of the Polish youth grew in mass circulation and penetrated into the factories. But the youth did not restrict themselves to the printed word. Young intellectuals traveled around the country, collecting facts for blunt critiques of Communist ideology and practice. Their bankruptcy was laid bare in the figures which showed productivity in collectives lagging behind private lands, and that in state farms below collectives. Flaws were revealed even in that spectacular achievement of the Stalinist era, the Nova-Huta steel center. The regime had hidden unemployment there by keeping masses of unskilled workers on the payroll although there was no work for them, because they could not find them work elsewhere, or even send them back to the farms from where they came. The intellectuals visited farms and factories, breaking through the isolation in which Stalinism had segregated the future aristocracy from the people. A national unity appeared in opposition to the foreign pattern of ideology and practice forced on their country. If dissatisfaction had not been channeled into a program of action, one that distinguished between what was possible for Poland and what was not, a chain reaction of revolts might have led to a national catastrophe.

Edward Ochab, the new First Secretary of the Party, visited China in September, 1956, and discussed the situation in Poland with Mao Tse-tung. The Twentieth Congress of the Soviet Party left the way open, in principle, for other kinds of socialism than the Soviet Communist variety. But Poland lay inside the strategic belt of the Soviet Union, due to its bordering on Germany with no natural barriers in between. Furthermore, the Russians had strong garrisons in the country under the Warsaw treaty, and the Poles occupied a position too delicate to experiment with a reversal of existing relations between the two countries.

In addition, the Soviets had direct representation on the Polish Politburo, especially in the person of the Defense Minister, Marshal Rokossowski, who commanded the Polish army. Russian officers were planted in key positions. On the other hand, the situation and mood in the country demanded initiative from above lest it deteriorate into anarchy. Mao assured Ochab of his support for a national course in Poland, and his support took on substance when he made his stand public.

Returning home, Ochab proposed the election of Gomulka to the Politburo at the next session of the Plenum of the Central Committee. Gomulka and his friend, General Spychalski, were out of jail now and making no secret of their determination to change Soviet-Polish relations.

The Kremlin invited the Poles to hold their meeting in Moscow so that Soviet representatives could be present. But Ochab set the meeting for October 19 and refused to move it to Moscow or postpone it. When the day had already arrived and the meeting started, a plane landed at Warsaw Airport bearing Khrushchev, Molotov, Mikoyan, and Kaganovich. They had Marshal Rokossowski surround Warsaw with the army.

News of the Russian intervention spread rapidly to the factories and the police—the old security police had already been dissolved. In no time, the workers and youth procured arms from the arsenals and occupied strategic positions in town. The presence of the Stalinist group of Molotov and

Kaganovich in the Soviet delegation was ominous. It showed that Khrushchev and Mikoyan were not prepared to approve the policy of disentanglement in the case of Poland.

Gomulka was called in and he bluntly gave his view that reforms had to be made immediately, and publicly, in order to prevent a revolt from engulfing the whole country. He proposed to put state relations between Poland and the Soviet Union on the same footing as any two sovereign nations allied for reasons of state. He promised to uphold the Warsaw treaty, since it defended Soviet and Polish interests from a re-armed Germany, and promised to sustain the right of the Soviets to keep garrisons in Polish territory. Gomulka insisted, however, that the Soviet garrison in Poland should be controlled by the Polish government to the extent that it be informed beforehand on any movement. He wanted no repetition in the future of the present surrounding of Warsaw by a Soviet-commanded army, capable of bringing pressure to bear on vital Polish decisions.

Gomulka also rejected Communist universalism and proposed that the Polish Party be put on equal terms with its Soviet counterpart. He espoused the Polish way of building socialism in a mixed economy, reviving free enterprise but preventing the resurgence of capitalist exploitation. Regarding agriculture, Gomulka claimed that forced collectivization had been a complete fiasco, and collectivization of farms appeared to be a mistake even in principle. He still stood for Communism and the mutual interests of socialist states, in common defense and close cooperation in the face of capitalism. But they would have to co-exist with capitalism for a time.

The Soviet delegation departed. Gomulka was elected First Secretary of the Party, while Rokossowski was not re-elected to the Politburo.

A fever of triumph took hold of Warsaw and Poland when the Soviet leaders had departed. On October 24, Gomulka spoke at a mass meeting to a crowd of 350 thousand people. He declared that a new system of elections would be introduced giving the public the right to choose candidates. Amidst immense enthusiasm, Gomulka reiterated that Poland would organize her economic and political life according to her own needs and potentialities. The craft industries would be free as well as private commerce. Cooperatives formed under compulsion would be liquidated; socialism in the villages could not be built on misery. The peasant would be free to buy and sell land. Socialists and members of the Peasant Party would be rehabilitated as well as the fighters in the Home Army. But the audience cooled when Gomulka warned them to take a look at the map and see that a military alliance with Russia was vital for Poland.

Each day brought forth a new decree liberalizing the regime and establishing more freedom and independence. A week after the Soviet delegation had left undecided, Khrushchev called Gomulka over the phone and assured him that the Kremlin approved of his program. Khrushchev and Mikoyan had prevailed over the Stalinist old guard in the Soviet Politburo. A general election was fixed for January 20, 1957, and the Parliament was to be sovereign. A revision of charges against the Poznan rioters was ordered, and special stores for privileged Party members were closed. Marshal Rokossowski was removed from his post as Minister of Defense, and General Spychalski replaced him. All Soviet officers in the Polish army were returned.

In November, Gomulka paid a visit to Moscow to seal a Soviet-Polish agreement on his terms. It laid down a new pattern of relations between a state in the Soviet orbit and the Soviet Union, and also between Communist Parties. A joint declaration announced that the basis of Party relations would be the Leninist principle of equality of rights. As to state policies, a special agreement would regulate the situation of the Soviet garrisons in Poland; they would stay, but under the supervision of the Polish government. Polish debts to the Soviet Union were to be canceled. Moscow would grant long-term credit and undertake the supply of grain to Poland. Poles from eastern Poland, which had become western Ukraine under the Yalta agreement, would be repatriated to Poland if they had settled elsewhere in the Soviet Union.

The Polish October revolution accomplished its aims without bloodshed.

But Gomulka had to take a step which was looked upon with grave concern not only by old-line Communists, but by the Jugoslavian Party as well. He made an agreement with Cardinal Wyszynski, who had been released from confinement shortly after Gomulka assumed power. This gave the church the same freedom and power it had enjoyed in the state before World War II. In exchange, the Cardinal promised the support of the church for Gomulka and his policy as the only one Poland could afford under the circumstances. The church regained the right of religious instruction in the schools which, though optional, became compulsory in practice through the pressure of public opinion. It also regained the autonomy of its administration, the unhampered development of its institutions, and its organizational universality through its ties with the Vatican.

Gomulka needed wide popular support for his program. Enormously popular though he was for his undaunted courage in the face of the greatest Soviet political and military pressure, his popularity did not extend to his program. Gomulka thus invited the church to help him influence the public into accepting even the Communist-inspired items of his policy. Yet the church was a symbol of the nation's opposition to Communism. How long could Gomulka depend on the support of such a paradoxical expedient, and at the same time marshal public opinion behind his program in its own right? This remained a problem for the future.

Undoubtedly, the large-scale concessions made by Moscow signified that the Kremlin stood behind the principles of the Twentieth Congress concerning the interrelations of socialist states and Communist Parties. Poland was a test case which also indicated the limits of these principles.

But events in Hungary provoked a new showdown in the Kremlin concerning Soviet policy towards the satellites.

These new developments occurred simultaneously with the Anglo-French conflict with Egypt, which in turn telescoped into an Israeli thrust. In the rush of these events, traditional positions in international politics shifted with lightning speed, fraught with present danger but pregnant with highly favorable prospects for the Soviet Union in the future.

In Hungary, the intellectuals and students excitedly followed the Polish developments. When the Soviet leaders bowed to Polish determination voiced by Gomulka, Hungarians interpreted this as a green light to follow the Polish example. As has already been described, political activity became feverish. The clubs at the Budapest universities resolved on a peaceful and orderly demonstration of solidarity with the Poles. In 1848, many Polish youths had joined the Hungarian armies. One of their best generals, a man by the name of Joseph Bem, had led the Hungarian revolutionaries to many victorious battles. His statue stood on the right bank of the Danube. The students planned to demonstrate around his monument and that of the great friend of the Polish general, Alexander Petofi, who had fought in his army and perished in battle.

The government first prohibited the mass meeting, but later lifted its ban. It was a huge orderly march, joined by soldiers, civilians, workers, the youth, and the aged. They sang the national hymn, the song of Kossuth and the 1848 revolution, and an actor recited Petofi's poem: "Arise, Hungarians!," which had ignited that revolt. Part of the demonstration proceeded to the Bem statue. Trucks drove up and distributed national flags.

In the meantime, workers left the factories to come join the marchers. A writer of peasant origin read the demands of the nation, as formulated by the Writers' Association in ten points. This document demanded new relations with the Soviet Union on the basis of equality, free trade unions, freedom for the peasants to decide whether or not to join a cooperative, removal of the Rakosi clique with a place for Imre Nagy in the government, and free and secret balloting at the elections of the people's representatives. The crowd swelled to 200 thousand people, and the procession continued from the Bem statue to Parliament Square, the marchers singing and shouting: "Send the Russians home," "We want free elections," "We want Imre Nagy."

One group of marchers branched off to the broadcasting station building, with the intention of making public a list of claims adopted by the university students. The front door of the building was locked. The students decided to send a delegation to the management with their request. When the delegation had not reappeared after a time, suspicion arose that they had been detained by the security police, who also had headquarters inside. It was getting late. The crowd lost patience and moved toward the front door, which was now guarded by security policemen with bayoneted rifles. Other policemen shot tear gas to disperse the crowd, and when this was without effect, fired into the mob. Some of the people procured hunting rifles from a nearby military sports organization and returned the fire. Then army trucks arrived, probably at the call of the radio police. Due to their hatred of the AVO security police, the soldiers stayed in their trucks and let the people take their submachine guns. The crowd laid siege to the radio building, and next day the people captured it.

Meanwhile hundreds of thousands waited at Parliament Square for long hours, expecting the announcement of changes in the government. Gero had just returned from Belgrade and was about to report on his trip over the radio. Some friends of Nagy drove to his home to carry him to government headquarters. He had no inkling that all of Budapest had been transformed suddenly into one singing, revolutionary mass, seized by unity of purpose in the greatness of the moment. For Gero, a spontaneous demonstration was nonsense. If not organized by the Party, it could only be set in motion by clandestine counter-revolutionary groups. Gero took the microphone and called the demonstrators counter-revolutionary hoodlums. The insult drove the masses gathered on Parliament Square into a fury, since they were out to demand for Hungary what the supreme Soviet leadership had already conceded to the Poles.

However, a portentous fact should be considered. Stalinist circles in Hungary had held since the time of the ferment among the writers that the anti-Party spirit had to be lured into the open to be crushed before it spread throughout the country. Gero may have welcomed the opportunity of a bloody repression.

Meanwhile Nagy heeded the call of the huge crowd and went out on the balcony to address it. But when he began his speech with the usual "Dear comrades," his words were drowned by roars of "We are no comrades." In a flash, the shocked Nagy realized that their accumulated bitterness had hardened into a wholesale rejection of Communist ideology and aspirations as well as of the deeds of the regime. But Nagy, as an old Party hand, respected the bureaucratic legalism of the Party even though he was at present only a newly readmitted member with no office. He made only vague promises and disappointed the majority that were insisting on immediate action.

Then young men came with the news that the AVO was shooting people in front of the radio station. Fury gripped the huge assembly. In a moment trucks were seized and groups were formed to get arms from barracks and police stations. Thousands surrounded the Stalin monument, toppled it, tore off the Soviet star, cut the Soviet emblem out of the flags, threw up barricades in the streets, stormed Party centers, and went in search of AVO men.

That night Gero and his gang were informed that they could not depend on the regular police or the army. They conceived the idea of publicly appointing Imre Nagy Premier and calling for Soviet military intervention in his name. By this means they frustrated any beneficial effects of Nagy's premiership, since it took days for the fraud to be discovered and for the public to be convinced that Nagy was not responsible for the intervention. In the early morning of October 24, Soviet tanks droned into the city, and the revolt seemed to be over.

On the 25th, a terrible massacre occurred in Parliament Square due to either a mistake or provocation. A peaceful demonstration, composed mostly of women and children, took place with Soviet tanks guarding the Parliament but fraternizing with the population. Either some AVO sniper fired into the crowd, sending a Soviet tank into action, or a tank manned by the AVO may have opened fire and panicked other tanks into shooting. Soon the square was covered with dead and wounded, amounting to about two hundred. This massacre began the skirmishes between civilians and the Soviet tanks, the one fighting with small arms and Molotov cocktails, the other with cannons and machine guns.

On the next day, Suslov and Mikoyan landed in Budapest. According to insiders, they berated Gero for involving the Soviets in a painful venture when there was no substantial need. They removed him from his post as First Secretary of the Party and put Janos Kadar in his place. Nagy made a speech over the radio in a conciliatory tone. In particular his statement, to the effect that he had initiated negotiations with the Soviet Union to withdraw all Soviet forces from Hungary, appeared to have a good chance of persuading people to stop the revolt. But it was too late. Workers' councils took over the factories and established political rule over industrial centers of the country, independent of the government. These councils demanded the immediate removal of the Soviet forces. They declared a general strike until their demands had been met.

An unusual feature of the Hungarian situation was its full coverage by the Western press. During the prerevolutionary period of ferment Hungary had already flung its frontiers wide open to newspapermen from the West. The population overwhelmed them with testimony of their sympathy and attachment to the West, eager to convey to them every bit of information concerning the inside story behind events. They acquainted them with the truth, hoping the testimony of the journalists might bring about the intervention of the West, from whom alone they might expect effective help.

But the Hungarians, including even responsible statesmen, did not appreciate the true value of the words of
sympathy uttered by the makers of foreign policy in the
West. They had learned how to interpret Soviet-fabricated
communiqués but had forgotten, in ten years of isolation
from the West, how to read between the lines of authoritative releases from the other side of the Iron Curtain. Thus
the Hungarians did not pay the attention it merited to a,
report from the State Department printed on October 27 in
the *New York Times*. It read:

> The view of the State Department is that there is little doubt that
> the troops have a right to be there [in Hungary]. But a question
> may be raised about the legitimacy of their use to put down an in-
> ternal rebellion. Even this raises a problem, however. The Soviet
> troops are being used at the request of the Hungarian government.
> There is little effort in Washington to deny that U.S. forces abroad
> could be used in the same way if there were a Communist-led revo-
> lution in, say, Italy. In 1944 and 1954, for example, British troops,
> at the request of the Athens Government, fought Communist rebels
> in Greece. Furthermore, any possible United Nations approach is
> at the moment clouded by French threats to use force in Morocco
> and Tunisia to protect Europeans there.

A careful reading of this statement would have informed
the Hungarian public what it could expect from America,
from the West, and from the United Nations. Indeed, much
more was later done than informed people had expected.
This was due to the wealth of information in the newspapers
and the sympathy it evoked in the world. The pressure of
outraged public opinion compelled statesmen in America,
in Europe, and also in Asia, to go much further in interfering
with Soviet orbit affairs than they had believed it safe to do.

Once Gero and his gang had bungled the Russians into
military intervention, Moscow was forced to justify the step.
It viewed the situation in this light:

> Events in Hungary made it evident that a reactionary, counter-
> revolutionary, underground, well-armed, and thoroughly prepared
> movement had been organized with outside help, and was prepared
> for action against the people's government.

But by adopting such an entirely false stand the Kremlin was falling back on the debased moral standards of Stalinism that had so deeply hurt the peoples in satellite countries. It again did "violence not only to the truth but violence to the words" when it called black white, and a lie the truth. "The lie, like the truth, is indivisible," wrote a Polish author.

On October 28, the revolution appeared to have ended with victory for the insurgents. Premier Nagy announced that he was negotiating for the immediate withdrawal of the Russian forces. Fighting stopped. In the last center of fighting, the Maria Theresa barracks, hostilities ceased on October 30. The Soviet troops moved out of the country.

However, in the meantime the tense Middle East situation exploded. An ideal situation for a military attack had been created by a convergence of purposes at a single, critical point.

The Israelis, alarmed over Soviet shipments of jets and other modern war equipment to Egypt, were ready to attack to forestall Egyptian superiority in arms. France held Nasser to be the chief obstacle to her coming to terms with the Algerian rebels. The British were determined to force Nasser into some kind of internationalization of the Suez Canal, the lifeline of her empire. All three had already made military preparations for an attack, when the Hungarian revolution broke out, appearing to paralyze the Soviets in the international field.

Israel thrust first, invading Egypt on October 29. The next day Anthony Eden, the British Prime Minister, sent an ultimatum to both the Israelis and Egyptians, demanding that they stop fighting within twelve hours. When Nasser rejected it, the Franco-British coalition launched an attack to seize the Suez Canal.

For Moscow the aggression was a godsend. It deflected attention from their embarrassing intervention in Hungary, and offered them an opportunity to enter the Middle East in the capacity of a defender of underdeveloped countries against colonial imperialism.

For the United States, unnotified of the Franco-British plan, a moment of "agonizing reappraisal" of their traditional alliance with France and Britain arrived. Was the preservation of the alliance worth giving up another traditional and highly effective line, that of anticolonialism? The decision was epoch-making. It caused the British attempt to end in a fiasco which convinced the world and the British themselves that Britain had ceased to be a great power capable of independent action. The American decision was greatly influenced by the Soviet radio, which promised to come to the assistance of Egypt, hinting that its intervention might take the form of volunteers joining the Egyptian army. Whatever the dominant motive, the decision resulted in the first instance of American-Russian cooperation to avoid a general war.

The second Soviet intervention in Hungary probably was decided under the impact of the tension in the Middle East. It was a military rather than a political decision. The Hungarian revolution had to be crushed by overwhelming force to demonstrate Soviet strength, to frighten other satellite peoples from following the Hungarian example, and to make the hinterland secure in case of Soviet military action in the Middle East.

Before the second intervention took place, *Pravda* reviewed the Hungarian situation on November 2 and stated that the further presence of the Soviet troops in Hungary might aggravate the work of the government. This was why the Kremlin had decided to withdraw the troops from Budapest as soon as the Hungarian government had considered this necessary. Moscow was also ready to enter into negotiations with the Warsaw pact countries with regard to evacuation of the Soviet troops in Hungary.

On October 31 Nagy re-formed his government by composing it of the same coalition of parties which had governed after the free elections in 1945. But reports reached the government from several points on the eastern frontier to the effect that new Soviet forces were entering Hungary.

Nagy, who was engaged in negotiations with the Soviet envoy on the question of troops in Hungary, now came under increasingly extreme nationalistic influences. The government decided to appeal to the United Nations with the request that the Soviet armies withdraw immediately from Hungary. It also informed the U.N. that it had declared the neutrality of the country, asking that the defense of its neutrality be put on the agenda of the General Assembly. The government communicated the step it had taken to the Soviet envoy.

One of the reasons why Khrushchev deviated from his conciliatory policy in Poland in the first phase of the Hungarian revolution was that the Communist Party had lost control in the political turmoil. This development, inadmissible as it was to the Kremlin, distinguished revolutionary Hungary from Poland, where Gomulka had managed to keep the Communist Party in power, or even from Jugoslavia, where Tito, in spite of his heretical course, had not relinquished an inch of power to groups organized outside the Party.

Imre Nagy could not stop at the point beyond which the Kremlin would make no concessions, as Gomulka had done in Poland. Nagy was not cut of the cloth that makes a leader. But another personality also failed where a man in the same position in Poland had risen above parochialism and commonplace patriotism. Cardinal Mindszenty, like Cardinal Wyszynski, was freed in the midst of the upheaval. But Mindszenty at first refused to give a thought to the political situation. Later, when a government delegation came on November 3 to pay its respects to him, Mindszenty told them that he wanted a Christian Democratic Party in the cabinet and could not support the regime unless this was accomplished. The damage his words caused to the stability of the government, and the impulse it gave to a Rightist turn, could not be undone.

But the Social Democratic Party also played its share in pushing Nagy over the brink. It agreed in principle to take part in the government, but delayed actual participation until Nagy adopted its conditions—namely, Hungary's release from the Warsaw Pact and the declaration of the neutrality of Hungary. Nagy badly needed Socialist support, but instead of statesmanship the Hungarian Socialists only brought harmful pressure to bear on Nagy.

An impressive feature of the revolution was the emergence of the workers' councils in areas of political and economic life, as stated earlier. On the other hand, the peasants kept clear of the revolt. They may have been sympathetic, and some peasants delivered food free to the workers in Budapest, but on the whole they feared that the turmoil might bring back the lords of the big estates. Now that forced collectivization had ended, they hoped to own their own land undisturbed.

By October 22 the Hungarian Communist Party had officially adopted the reform program that the intellectuals and youth had formulated in numerous resolutions. When the AVO fired into the crowd the next day, and the Party chieftains called upon the Russian army to defend the AVO from the people, the Party disintegrated. Nobody was more qualified to point this out than George Lukacs, the famed Communist philosopher who had consistently supported the nationalist line of Communism. Lukacs told a Polish writer the following December that Communism in Hungary had collapsed in disgrace. He thought that the workers would join the Social Democratic Party, but that a small group of intellectuals, writers, and young people would stick to the Party and save the idea as an intellectual center.

Janos Kadar, as the new First Secretary of the Party, announced over the radio on November 1 the foundation of a Socialist Workers' Party which on the whole adopted the nationalist line as it was formulated in the long discussions before the revolution. He was later seen talking with Suslov and Mikoyan, who dropped in again and persuaded Kadar and his group to break with the Nagy government and stay at their disposal. The Soviet Politburo emissaries were busy selecting people for the government that the Soviet army was to put in office. Kadar and his friends disappeared from sight for a few days. Meanwhile Soviet forces sealed Hungary off from the West, encircling the towns and all airfields. In the early morning of November 4, they launched a general attack. Hungarian army units and civilian groups took up the fight, but the battle was hopeless. Kadar announced over a radio station that he had formed a revolutionary worker-peasant government. Nagy and several ministers in his cabinet asked the Jugoslav embassy for asylum. Cardinal Mindszenty found asylum in the United States legation.

On the same day, an incredible exodus of the population began. An irremediable insult to their sense of justice drove the young and the brave from their home country in hopeless desperation. The same deep-felt protest kept the industrial workers idle for months in the strangest general strike in history. No promises, no threats, no arrests could break it—only hunger did.

The Hungarian tragedy taught many lessons. It may have promoted the idea of demilitarization of the satellite countries in exchange for the demilitarization of West Germany, since the Kremlin discovered that it could not depend on the satellite armies. This recognition may resign them to releasing the satellite states politically, though close economic ties may survive political independence. Moreover, the Soviets may discover that the satellites are as much a millstone around their necks as the English Liberals once believed their empire to be. These countries cannot be integrated even economically without force, as the decollectivization of agriculture in Poland and Hungary has demonstrated.

Perhaps such thoughts led Hungarian statesmen to believe that the Kremlin would let a small and strategically unimportant country like Hungary leave their orbit. Their mistake was in thinking the Kremlin would make such a concession without receiving some concession in return.

In the field of international affairs the Hungarian revolution revealed a danger to peace in the future. The hydrogen bomb may restrain the two great powers from war and even bring them to cooperate permanently in isolating wars between other countries. However, they will inevitably face situations again where revolts against established governments will endanger the security of a much vaster region than the country involved. Such revolts may present the two powers with a moral problem as to which revolts are justified and to what lengths the established governments are entitled to go to master them. Probably each case will have to be dealt with on its own merits or demerits, even if a general rule is worked out. But more often than not public opinion will grow so strong that it will be difficult if not impossible for one or the other of the great powers to cooperate in either removing the government or subduing the revolt. In either case, the people or the government concerned—and perhaps other peoples and governments as well—may feel such interference to be worse than war. General peace upheld by the great powers might degenerate into enslavement of the rest of the world. Interference would be more tolerable if the two great powers exercised their police function as a part of collective security, but this would still not eliminate the problem.

The Hungarian revolution at least showed a way to lessen the burden which peoples may have to bear for the sake of general peace. The exodus of those who choose exile rather than life under a regime they hate, together with the sympathy and aid these people will receive from the other great power, may act as a safety valve.

4.

The Polish and Hungarian events intertwined in their effect on the other East European countries. After the example of Poland, the intelligentsia was be-

wildered by the destruction of all elements in the Hungarian
government that did not owe sole loyalty to Moscow. They
were repelled by foreign-imposed spiritual and material patterns, though not with the same intensity in all countries.
De-Stalinization had lessened fear and increased individual
freedom and security, while the new concern for the consumer had stirred a mood ready to enjoy life.

But the events deeply disturbed the Party leaderships
and governments.

Tito reacted in an independent, morally dialectical way
to the outburst of civil war in Hungary. He commented on
November 16:

> When the Hungarian delegation headed by Gero returned to their
> country, Gero found himself in a difficult position and he fell back
> on his old code. He called those hundreds of thousands of demon-
> strators . . . a gang—insulting almost the whole nation. Imagine how
> blind he was! At such a critical moment, when everything boils and
> the whole nation is dissatisfied, he dares to call that nation a gang
> whose great majority may have been Communists and young people.
> This was enough to blow up the powder keg. . . . Gero called the
> army. It was a fatal mistake to call Soviet troops when demonstra-
> tions were still going on. To call upon foreign troops is a great mis-
> take even if shooting takes place. It infuriated people even more
> and this is how a spontaneous uprising came about.

Thus, Tito condemned the first intervention of Soviet
troops, but not the second one. Consistent with this view,
the Jugoslav representative at the United Nations opposed
putting the Hungarian case on the agenda of the General
Assembly.

Tito followed Gomulka's concessions and Nagy's turn to
the Right with anxiety and misgivings, for he feared the
countries would veer toward a so-called bourgeois democracy. Such developments could have had repercussions in
his own country where the Party still controlled democratization. However, Tito was equally concerned over the
effect of these events on the power situation in the Kremlin.
Pravda reflected on the hardening Kremlin mood when it
commented on the occasion of the meeting of satellite
leaders with Khrushchev and Suslov in Budapest by saying:

"the false slogan of so-called national Communism is being used for the purposes of splitting the Communist Parties."

In Poland, sympathy with the Hungarians had been traditional but rather abstract, except for the Hungarian revolution in 1848, and Hungarian hospitality and complicity in helping Polish refugees construct an underground railway to the West after Poland's collapse in 1939. The public was awed by the unity and bravery of the Hungarians, but it could not help feeling relieved that this time Poland had kept her senses. What happened in Hungary undoubtedly enhanced Gomulka's prestige and justified Cardinal Wyszynski's unorthodox stand. In the electoral campaign, Gomulka appealed to the people not to erase the names of the top candidates on the voting list, as a mark of confidence in him. In the churches all over Poland, the priests instructed the faithful to comply with Gomulka's request. On January 20, 1957, in a completely free election, 94.14 per cent of the voters went to the polls and 98.4 per cent of them voted for the government's united front. All top candidates were elected.

In Czecho-Slovakia, the ferment in neighboring countries stirred echoes among the intelligentsia. But the public became nervous when the revolution in Hungary increased in nationalistic fever, for this might have again threatened the territorial integrity of their country. The most democratic country in the Soviet orbit disappointed the West by remaining quiet during the upheavals in its back yard.

There were several reasons why the Czech intelligentsia and workers failed to act violently against tyranny. Except for a few months in 1945, Czecho-Slovakia had suffered no Soviet occupation. Experience shows that foreign rule welds a people into resistance, but domestic tyranny demoralizes them. Furthermore, the standard of living kept improving steadily after the Pilsen revolt in 1953. And the Czech public still had an ambivalent feeling toward the West, which had delivered the nation to Hitler in 1938. The West was suspected of favoring Germany over Czecho-Slovakia. It was feared that they would repatriate the

Sudeten Germans to Bohemia in order to please the Germans, a consideration which made the Czechs reluctant to desert the Soviet orbit. Finally, Gottwald had executed and imprisoned the Stalinists, not the national Communists as in Hungary and Poland. (Clementis' "crime" had been Slovak separatism, not national Communism.) In fact, Gottwald was the first to establish national Communism, by the grace of Moscow.

Rumania was unable to make a move without Russian encouragement, while Bulgaria had no reason to revolt although its intellectuals grumbled and the people would have been happier with less attention paid to them by the Russians. Albania has never been more faithful to Moscow than in times when Soviet-Jugoslav understanding threatened to turn them back under Jugoslav domination.

In spite of such shocks as the Polish showdown and the Hungarian revolution, Khrushchev's course has prevailed over momentary setbacks, panics, and hesitations. It was China, not Russia, which became thoroughly frightened at the break in Communist discipline. Whereas China had encouraged Gomulka in 1956 to stand fast on national Communism, Chou En-lai came to Warsaw during the electoral campaign in January, 1957, and warned Gomulka not to stray too far away from the Moscow line. The "let every flower bloom, every bird sing" principle had been left to hibernate until a new spring arrived.

Khrushchev at this point still maintained that his policy of decentralizing the economy, restoring legality in public life, paying more attention to the consumer, and granting enough leeway to institute specific national policies, helped to keep the satellites in the Soviet orbit. He still seemed to believe that more independence for these nations and their Communist parties will ultimately create a massive solidarity of Socialist states in place of the conspiratorial internationalism of the Party bureaucracy. This voluntary solidarity for the common defense of socialism then would eradicate the moral alienation of foreign Socialists from Moscow.

In August, 1957, Khrushchev and Tito met in Bucharest. Both were anxious to erase their differences over the Hungarian revolt and its handling by Moscow. But Tito had a fresh complaint. Soviet security police had kidnapped Nagy and ten other people, one of them being Julia Rajk, after they had left the Jugoslav Embassy, which had granted them asylum. This had happened on November 23.

Khrushchev had just thrown the conservatives off the Politburo—Molotov, Kaganovich, Malenkov, and Shepilov —and now felt free to travel further on the line of democratization. Tito and Khrushchev's joint communiqué emphasized the need for unity and cooperation between the Communist parties and the peoples of all Socialist states. This was an important step taken by Tito toward restoring good relations with the satellite parties. And an elastic application of this communiqué could even make Jugoslavia the link between the satellite parties and left-wing parties in the West and in Asia.

Actually, decollectivization, and support for the individual farmer, was beginning to create a mixed economy in the satellites, although its direct purpose had been to raise the standard of living. Curtailment of bureaucracy through decentralization of the government's economic administration brought the pattern close to that which Jugoslavia had set. There was a difference, however, between Tito and Gomulka. Tito frowned on the liberalization of political and public life in Poland, and the relative freedom of opinion and of the press. Gomulka, on the other hand, disliked the broad jurisdiction of the Jugoslav Workers' Councils, which transformed Jugoslavia's industries into corporations under government guidance. Gomulka did not think local groups should appropriate for their own benefit what the whole community had built.

Because of lavish American loans, commerce with the West, and compensation paid by the satellite countries for their anti-Tito campaign acts, Jugoslavia became fairly prosperous. The factories produced consumer goods, and the peasants provided food in sufficient quantity. In the long run, however, free craft and individual farming were hardly compatible with a politically monolithic Socialist state. Poland was proceeding down a similar road. Its most urgent need was to raise the standard of living of its workers, who now suffered from dismal poverty. Moscow reimbursed the damage it had done to Poland by economic exploitation, and American loans were slowly coming in. Small craft and commerce were thriving and appeared likely soon to create an old-fashioned middle class along with individual farmers. It did not seem to be beyond the bounds of possibility that the Eastern countries might develop into welfare states not too far removed from the West European model.

These were the conclusions which could be drawn in the aftermath of the Polish revolt and the Hungarian revolution. Subsequent events in 1957 and 1958 showed, however, that an opposite reasoning appeared to prevail in the Kremlin. On May 24, 1958, the heads of twelve Communist-run governments gathered in Moscow for a Communist summit conference. They represented roughly a billion people. As a result, it was disclosed that the economies of these countries, comprising China, Outer Mongolia, North Korea, and North Vietnam as well as Eastern Europe, were to be integrated into a single unit, called the Socialist camp. This act was to remove the East European nations from their historic background and tie them instead to the countries of the Far East. Russia was to bridge the vast gap between the European and Far Eastern groups in their approach to all the factors that mold individuals, peoples, and communities. But this pact embodied only part of the total program for the integration of the Communist camp. Previously, in November, 1957, the so-called state-ruling parties had accepted political principles for the Communist camp which reinstated the international discipline of these parties. Moscow's leadership was to coordinate the state policies of the Socialist countries.

Those who could only with difficulty envisage Poland, Czecho-Slovakia, and Hungary in the same community with

North Vietnam, deemed it enlightening that Jugoslavia had refused to join the camp. This came as a bitter disappointment to Khrushchev, who had been willing to condone Tito's public condemnation of the first Soviet intervention in the Hungarian revolution. Tito's acceptance of a single set of principles for all Socialist governments would have vindicated Khrushchev's policy of reconciliation with Jugoslavia. But Tito remained adamant in shying away from any "camp," even though the pact left each country free to apply the common principles in its own way.

Yet it was not Russia that launched the new attack on recalcitrant Jugoslavia, but Communist China, the same China which, in 1956, had encouraged the Poles to fight with Moscow for their right to take their own way to Communism. However, Mao swung around full circle under the impact of the Hungarian revolution and the unexpectedly bold criticism which had sprouted from his liberalizations in China. He now stood for reasserting old ties and bolstering stark discipline. The presence of the United States Navy along the shores of China, with American bases in Formosa, South Korea, and South Vietnam, made it impossible in his view to co-exist peacefully. Neither did Mao hold that agreement was feasible with respect to the control of atomic weapons. In the absence of China, such an agreement would leave Russia free to manufacture and pile up atomic bombs in China, and China would not be a party to any agreement until its government had been recognized and had taken its due place in the Security Council. Hungary's breaking loose from the Warsaw pact warned Mao of the danger Tito represented to the solidarity of the Socialist countries as upheld by the international discipline of the Party. His independence remained a possible rallying point for anti-Communist movements in case of emergency.

In June, 1958, the Chinese started a venomous attack on Jugoslavia, going as far as to state that the denunciation of Jugoslavia by the Cominform in 1948 was basically right. Khrushchev repeated the statement and broadened the attack against "revisionism," by which he meant any break with the organizational internationalism of the Communist parties. He gave, however, an important clue to the conclusions intended to be drawn from Jugoslavia's second excommunication. Khrushchev said that the nations of the Communist camp would try to achieve understanding with Jugoslavia *on a government level*. This qualification made a sharp distinction between Party and state and insured that the 1948 blockade against Jugoslavia by Russia and her satellites would not be repeated. This was in spite of a brutal slap in Tito's face in June, 1958, when the Hungarian revolutionary leaders, Imre Nagy and General Pal Maleter, were executed, though the Jugoslav embassy in Budapest had released them from asylum against a guarantee from the Kadar government that they would not be prosecuted.

Khrushchev's declaration that the Soviets had suspended credits for $285 million to Jugoslavia does not contradict the assumption that no boycott is contemplated. The suspension hit Jugoslavia hard, since the credits, granted in 1956, were to be used to build an aluminum plant and other important projects. But East Germany, Czecho-Slovakia, and Albania hastened to conclude agreements with Jugoslavia right after the new excommunication, on the grounds that increased trade between them was mutually advantageous. This means that the Communist camp will trade with the heretic state, as with any other government outside the camp, on a purely business basis. Brotherly mutual aid remains reserved to the countries in the camp.

Khrushchev stressed again in a speech on November 10, 1958, that he, in contrast to Stalin, distinguished between inter-Party and inter-state relations with respect to the socialist countries. He said of Jugoslavia:

Unfortunately, Jugoslavia's leaders are sliding down from the positions of the working class, to the positions of its enemies. For this reason no one can count on mutual understanding on the party level in our relations with the Jugoslav Communist League. . . . on the state level, we shall strive to develop friendly relations with Jugoslavia, to expand trade and cultural relations.

But any progress from Stalin's handling of the satellites was more apparent than real. The crucial point was that the camp declaration re-established the priority of the parties over the governments. Gomulka could not afford to reject it, though he was allowed a slight reservation as to the autonomy of each Party in the application of the common principles.

Was Stalinism coming back? In Soviet Russia, Khrushchev subsequently eliminated collective leadership. He banned Molotov and Kaganovich, the supposed Stalinists, as well as Malenkov who would have subjected the Party to the government. Zhukov, who had assisted Khrushchev in the purge with the prestige of the army, was purged in his turn so that the Party alone would wield all power. Khrushchev was already First Secretary of the Party, and on March 27, 1958, the Supreme Soviet elected him Prime Minister as well. His power became totalitarian.

Meanwhile, Khrushchev has not relented in following Tito-like policies in Soviet Russia. He has decentralized the state administration and industrial management, and instituted reforms in agriculture which give independence in business administration to the kolkhozes. The state machine stations have been dissolved and the collectives empowered to buy their own machines. Khrushchev has also abolished deliveries in kind and introduced normal buying by the state for cash. The satisfaction of the consumer has remained the directing aim of planning, in spite of the renewed stress on heavy industry. Soviet production capacity can now afford to produce both capital and consumer goods, to assist the satellites and to export industrial equipment to backward countries on credit.

The economic relations of the Soviets with the satellites have thus changed basically to the advantage of the satellites who are now receiving loans under privileged conditions to help their industrial programs to actual requirements and free capital for investment in agriculture. Poland has made no attempt to bring pressure to bear on the peasants to form collectives. One of the results of the revolts appears to be the prosperity of the individual farmer in all satellite states. In Hungary, in spite of political persecution of those active in the revolution by a government composed of the most despicable stooges of Moscow, the individual farms are booming and industry has recovered due to the large-scale assistance of the Soviets and the other satellites. Freedom in all fields except the political is much greater than before the revolt.

East Germany and Czecho-Slovakia have remained the last strongholds of die-hardism. The Czechs insist on complete collectivization of the farms. With 11,350 collectives, 65 per cent of the total acreage had already been collectivized by March, 1958, according to Prime Minister Viliam Siroky. But he stated in the same breath that agricultural production had not been substantially raised above the prewar level, although, of course, he attributed the failure to the remnants of small-scale production. The Czechs refuse to follow the Soviet example of selling the machine stations to the collectives. Instead, they extend agriculture to the "virgin" lands abandoned by the expelled Sudeten Germans, a Soviet method of making up for stagnant agricultural production. The Czech Party keeps clear of revisionism, and it does not ease discipline or political pressure. But since industry is becoming more balanced by the promotion of light industry, general welfare there is the highest in the seven states.

The launching of the Sputniks and Lunik was a deviation from Stalin's policy of keeping the strength of Soviet industrial capacity secret. Stalin's policy had resulted in the West's handling Russia as a negligible quantity prior to the outbreak of World War II. The Sputnik demonstration achieved the opposite effect. The West, particularly America, is now inclined to overestimate the total power of Russian production. But Khrushchev has rolled up the Iron Curtain and compelled the West to discard its own. Exchange of experts, students, actors, and tourists, and free conferences between professionals of East and West have become the order of the day. Indeed, public admiration for the Russians, admiration for success, can hardly be dampened by the warnings of the more politically minded. The two peoples, Russian and American, who have so much in common, appear to like each other, even though the danger of war between them has only lessened, not vanished.

Meanwhile the Asian and African peoples are fast redressing the imbalance which allowed the West for two centuries to rule the rest of the world. The conspicuous role Communist China played in condemning revisionism and reading Tito's Jugoslavia out of any ties with the Communist camp, demonstrates how the East has regained its vitality. Even though China now has an important word to say in the policies of the satellite states, all the clashes and tensions of the last two decades, as we have tried to retrace them, reaffirm their historical links with Europe as connections between East, Center, and West. This is true of Russia as well. China's rising power will most probably impel Russia to rely more forcefully on her European domain, and in general to ease her relations with the West. Should this happen, the Eastern countries may serve as her direct links to the West. After all, Marxism was a product of the West. A return to its more humanistic inspirations may wipe out the artificial dividing line between West and East in Europe.

A Note on Sources

Of standard works in the English language the author will mention here only his main sources:

ARMSTRONG, HAMILTON FISH. *Tito and Goliath*. New York: Macmillan Co., 1951.

BETTS, REGINALD ROBERT. *Central and South East Europe, 1945–1948*. London and New York: Royal Institute of International Affairs, 1950.

HALECKI, OSKAR. *The History of Poland*. London: J. M. Dent & Sons, Ltd., 1942.

MACARTNEY, CARLILE AYLMER. *History of Hungary, 1929–1945*. New York: F. A. Praeger, Inc., 1957.

ROBERTS, HENRY L. *Rumania*. New Haven: Yale University Press, 1951.

SCHMIDT, DANA ADAMS. *Anatomy of a Satellite*. Boston: Little, Brown & Co., 1956.

SETON-WATSON, HUGH. *The East-European Revolution*. London: Methuen & Co., Ltd., 1956.

SETON-WATSON, ROBERT WILLIAM. *A History of the Rumanians*. New York: Macmillan Co., 1934.

SHEPHERD, GORDON. *Russia's Danubian Empire*. London: William Heinemann, Ltd., 1954.

WARRINER, DOREEN. *Revolution in Eastern Europe*. London: Turnstile Press, 1950.

WISKEMAN, ELIZABETH. *Germany's Eastern Neighbors*. London and New York: Oxford University Press, 1956.

WOLFF, ROBERT LEE. *The Balkans In Our Time*. Cambridge: Harvard University Press, 1956.

The author also made use of close-up surveys by the following:

BARKER, ELISABETH. *Macedonia*. London and New York: Royal Institute of International Affairs, 1950.

FEJTÖ, FERENC. *La Révolte de la Hongrie*. Paris: Les Temps Modernes, 1957.

HALASZ, NICHOLAS. *Czechoslovakia*. Budapest: Szazadunk, 1938.

LASKY, MELVIN J. (ed.). *The Hungarian Revolution*. New York: F. A. Praeger, Inc., 1957.

OSTOVIC, PAVLE D. *The Truth About Yugoslavia*. New York: Roy Publishers, 1952.

Articles in periodicals are too numerous to be listed. However, the *Slavonic and East European Review, Les Temps Modernes,* and *Der Monat* deserve particular mention as sources for our period.

Index